MW01230777

FOREIGN AFFAIRS

AMERICA AND THE WORLD 1981

Pergamon Titles of Related Interest

Foreign Affairs, AMERICA AND THE WORLD 1980
Foreign Affairs, AMERICA AND THE WORLD 1979
Foreign Affairs, AMERICA AND THE WORLD 1978
De Volpi et al BORN SECRET: The H-Bomb, the *Progressive* Case and
National Security
Douglass SOVIET MILITARY STRATEGY IN EUROPE
Duncan SOVIET POLICY IN THE THIRD WORLD
Edmonds INTERNATIONAL ARMS PROCUREMENT
Feld WESTERN EUROPE'S GLOBAL REACH
Hoffmann/Laird THE SCIENTIFIC-TECHNOLOGICAL REVOLUTION
AND SOVIET FOREIGN POLICY
Nogee/Donaldson SOVIET FOREIGN POLICY SINCE
WORLD WAR II
Mroz BEYOND SECURITY: Private Perceptions
Among Arabs and Israelis
Pettman BIOPOLITICS AND INTERNATIONAL VALUES
Rice REPORTING U.S.-EUROPEAN RELATIONS:
Four Nations, Four Newspapers
Spanier/Nogee CONGRESS, THE PRESIDENCY AND AMERICAN
FOREIGN POLICY
Yost NATO'S STRATEGIC OPTIONS

PERGAMON
POLICY
STUDIES

FOREIGN AFFAIRS

AMERICA AND THE WORLD 1981

William P. Bundy, Editor

PERGAMON PRESS

New York • Oxford • Toronto • Sydney • Frankfurt • Paris

Pergamon Press Offices:

U.S.A.   Pergamon Press Inc., Maxwell House, Fairview Park,
                     Elmsford, New York 10523, U.S.A.

U.K.   Pergamon Press Ltd., Headington Hill Hall,
                     Oxford OX3 0BW, England

CANADA   Pergamon Press Canada Ltd., Suite 104, 150 Consumers Road,
                     Willowdale, Ontario M2J 1P9, Canada

AUSTRALIA   Pergamon Press (Aust.) Pty. Ltd., P.O. Box 544,
                     Potts Point, NSW 2011, Australia

FRANCE   Pergamon Press SARL, 24 rue des Ecoles,
                     75240 Paris, Cedex 05, France

FEDERAL REPUBLIC Pergamon Press GmbH, Hammerweg 6
OF GERMANY   6242 Kronberg/Taunus, Federal Republic of Germany

L.C. Card No. 24-9921
ISBN 0 08 028827 8 (pbk.)
ISBN 0 08 028834 0

This is a simultaneous and unabridged printing of
FOREIGN AFFAIRS, Vol. 60, No. 3, exclusive of
advertising.

Printed in the United States of America

FOREIGN AFFAIRS

AMERICA AND THE WORLD 1981

THE CONDUCT OF AMERICAN FOREIGN POLICY
  The Revitalization of Containment .... *Robert E. Osgood* 465
  Ideology in Search of a Policy .... *Raymond Aron* 503
U.S.-Soviet Relations: The Long Road Back .. *William G. Hyland* 525
Alarm Bells in the West .... *Flora Lewis* 551
"The Elephant in the Boat?": The United States and the
  World Economy .... *Robert Solomon* 573
The Middle East: A House of Containment Built on
  Shifting Sands .... *John C. Campbell* 593
Latin America: Change or Continuity? .... *Paul E. Sigmund* 629
America in Africa, 1981 .... *David Anderson* 658
East Asia and the Great Power Coalitions ....*Richard H. Solomon* 686
Chronology 1981 .... *Elaine P. Adam* 719

EDITOR'S NOTE

The past year has been on the whole an inconclusive one. It saw a great many events at least at the "medium crisis" level, and several trends that may turn out to have had enormous portent for the future. But until December there had not been any single event as salient as the Soviet invasion of Afghanistan in late 1979 or the Iranian Revolution that began in late 1978. As of mid-January 1982 it remained to be seen whether the imposition of martial law in Poland in December will turn out to have been a decisive turn in that clearly central ongoing crisis, or whether the crisis may still have much wider and more immediate international implications than it has yet had.

And it was a shakedown year for a new American Administration that entered office with a particularly strong set of preconceptions and in response to a national mood well described by Daniel Yankelovich in our last year-end issue. Some of its initial resolves were carried forward; others were modified in response to events and the changed perceptions of actual responsibility. While it may be fair to describe the year, in Churchill's phrase, as "the end of the beginning," it remained far from clear what approach the President and his advisers would take to many of the issues that will probably confront them in 1982 and beyond.

Thus it is not surprising that almost all the individual articles in this interpretive survey convey themes of uncertainty. As in our previous three efforts, their authors have attempted to put the events of the year into historical focus and also to suggest what the future may hold, often with policy advice. Inevitably those authors represent different vantage points and viewpoints. But the balance, we believe most readers will agree, is heavily on the side of objective (or at least middle-of-the-road) analysis, criticism and prescription. Blunter defense and attack will be found in ample measure in our regular issues.

This is an annual publication. AMERICA AND THE WORLD 1982 will be available February 1983.

Robert E. Osgood

THE REVITALIZATION OF CONTAINMENT

T he Reagan Administration is repeating the first beat of a familiar rhythm of America's international and political life. Each newly elected Administration of the alternative political party launches its foreign relations with themes that were developed during the national campaign in opposition to the policies of its predecessor. But then comes the down beat: unexpected domestic and international conditions contradict (or appear to contradict) the underlying premises of the "new" foreign policy. Then either the Administration abandons or modifies its themes (in substance, if not in rhetoric) or it takes uncontested credit for the transformation. This phenomenon began with the Eisenhower Administration. It has deep roots in the American political system and the American approach to the outside world.

Beneath this familiar rhythm the continuities of American foreign policy are always greater than the political claims to innovation would have one believe. The greatest discontinuities spring from responses to unanticipated events, not from changes of Administration. Moreover, the rhythm is itself one of the most notable continuities. It corresponds to the oft-noted oscillations in America's world role between assertion and retrenchment, between the affirmation and restraint of national power. And in the postwar period it has responded to the onset and aftermath of crises and wars. As the nation revises its estimate of the Soviet threat to its foreign security interests upward and downward there is an alternation between repeated efforts to close the chronic gap between ever-expanding interests and the available power to support them, and efforts to seek relief from the ardors of containment.

The Reagan Administration has assumed the task of once again augmenting and reaffirming American power, under the impetus of heightened fears of the Soviet threat. The Carter Administra-

Robert E. Osgood is currently the Christian A. Herter Professor of American Foreign Policy at the School of Advanced International Studies of Johns Hopkins University. He was formerly Dean of SAIS and served as a member of the Senior Staff of the National Security Council in 1969-70. He is the author of *Ideals and Self-Interest in America's Foreign Relations, Limited War, Limited War Revisited* and other works.

tion had already substantially reversed its initial policy of re-trenchment and self-restraint, but the themes of the new Admin-istration's efforts reflect a vigorous reaction to those that its predecessor brought into office in 1977. It launches this new effort, however, in the face of a set of troublesome domestic and inter-national conditions which have emerged largely in the last decade and which impose unprecedented constraints on the effective exercise of American power in its economic, diplomatic, and military dimensions. Most of the policy expedients to which previous administrations resorted in order to close the gap between interests and power—whether by enhancing U.S. power, accom-modating the Soviet threat, or blunting its impact—are, in prac-tice, either no longer available or seriously limited.

How well the Reagan Administration performs in bringing American power into a safe balance with American security interests and commitments under these novel constraints will not only determine the reputation of President Reagan's Administra-tion; it will establish an historic landmark in the nation's capacity to adjust the principal continuities of postwar foreign policy—most notably, the overriding objective of containment—to porten-tous developments that have deprived the United States of its primacy while extending its involvement in world politics.

II

A brief review of the previous oscillations of U.S. foreign policy since World War II indicates the magnitude and significance of the task of national revival that President Reagan has undertaken.

At the outset of the cold war, Soviet moves in Iran (Azerbaijan), Poland, Berlin, Greece and Czechoslovakia refuted hopeful expec-tations of a new international order based on U.S. collaboration with the U.S.S.R. and Great Britain; in 1947 Britain's abandon-ment of its strategic role in Greece began the still-expanding process, unforeseen at the time, of America's global role of con-tainment. Nevertheless, it took the shock of the Korean War to drive the United States to close the widening gap between its expanding commitments and the military power available to support them. The latter had been restricted by a rigid ceiling of about $13 billion on the defense budget and by a military strategy adapted only to the defense of Western Europe and a chain of Pacific islands running southward from Japan (thereby excluding the Korean peninsula from the U.S. "defensive perimeter").

In the aftermath of the frustrations and exertions of the Korean War and the accompanying four-fold defense build-up and expanded commitments to the defense of Europe, the Eisenhower Administration came into office with a dual mandate: economic retrenchment and avoidance of future Korean Wars, on the one hand; deterring Soviet aggression-by-proxy more effectively, on the other. Its formula of substituting nuclear deterrence and a network of alliances—a "political warning system," in Secretary of State John Foster Dulles's words—for conventional forces and local intervention worked well enough for a while. The 1955 summit meeting with the Russians seemingly confirmed the success of this formula in a widely perceived "thaw" in the cold war and the "spirit of Geneva." But then the Soviet orbiting of Sputnik, the fear of an imminent "missile gap," Khrushchev's instigation of a second Berlin crisis and his harsh antics in May 1960 following the shooting down over Russia of America's acknowledged U-2 spy plane, coupled with growing troubles with Castro, political turmoil in the Congo, and Nasser's turn toward Moscow for arms, put an end to the incipient détente.

President Kennedy came into office dedicated to campaign themes of restoring American power and prestige on the basis of a revived American economy. He translated these themes into policies intended to strengthen and diversify the nation's military power, counter the new threat of wars of national liberation, identify America with the forces of non-communist nationalism in Africa and elsewhere, and overcome the vulnerability of the less-developed countries to Communist penetration through economic development keyed to social and economic reform. By the mid-1960s the resulting military build-up, a surge of domestic economic growth, the successful surmounting of crises in Berlin, Cuba and the Congo, and new evidence of Soviet troubles in Eastern Europe and with China produced perhaps the greatest sense of security and well-being that Americans have enjoyed in the entire postwar period.

Kennedy's successor, Lyndon Johnson, took office determined to concentrate his and the nation's attention on domestic social and economic improvements. But fate and the inertia of settled axioms of containment, given new impetus by the heightened confidence in American power born in the Kennedy years, determined that Johnson's Administration would be preoccupied with a war in Vietnam which could not be won—perhaps not even at the price of a protracted and expanded war, which neither Johnson nor the nation was willing to pay.

Given the national trauma inflicted by the war in Vietnam, any succeeding Administration was bound to oscillate again toward retrenchment. The Nixon-Ford-Kissinger regime conceived its first task, after honorable extrication from the war, as bringing American power into balance with vital interests at a reduced level of national effort and a lessened risk of armed intervention. It sought to shore up containment at a level of involvement that would be acceptable to the American public and consistent with constraints on unilateral American power that had emerged during the last two decades. But to reconcile containment with retrenchment it could not resort to the expedients available to the Eisenhower Administration. Instead, it turned to a more selective projection of U.S. force in Third World crises; a greater reliance on less-developed countries to help themselves in countering internal threats; the orchestration of a global modus vivendi, or détente, with the Soviet Union (with SALT as the centerpiece); instrumental to détente, a rapprochement with the People's Republic of China; and reliance on Iran as a security-keeping surrogate in the Middle East.

On the whole, this strategy worked well, but over the years some of its underlying premises about the international environment began to run into conflict with intractable realities. The atmosphere of détente helped to reinforce post-Vietnam restrictions on U.S. defense expenditures (which declined in real dollars), although the U.S.S.R. continued an annual four to six percent increase in its defense outlays—beyond the requirements of parity, as Americans saw them. The underlying assumption of the Nixon-Kissinger strategy, that the turbulence of the Third World—contrary to Kennedy's dramatization of its significance as the decisive arena of the cold war—need not impinge on vital American security interests was refuted by the Yom Kippur War of 1973, with an ominous, though muted, threat of Soviet intervention to compel a cease-fire, and with the emergence of an Arab embargo on oil to the increasingly oil-dependent United States. Then the unanticipated collapse of the Portuguese empire in Africa in 1974 led directly to Soviet intervention, in collaboration with Cuban troops, in the Angolan civil war; the withdrawal of America's indirect and covert participation in that war under pressure from Congress portended, in Kissinger's view, a repetition in resource-rich southern Africa of the fateful 1930s scenario of unopposed piecemeal aggression, which underlay America's whole postwar effort to vindicate the interwar lessons through vigilant containment.

Even these developments, however, did not overcome the post-Vietnam mood of retrenchment. The apparent success of Kissinger

in blending containment with détente blunted the force of retrenchment, but it also postponed a revival of containment. This
enabled the Carter Administration to focus its criticism on the
containment side of the Nixon-Ford-Kissinger strategy, in what
became a less constrained, delayed accommodation to the psychological wounds of the Vietnam War. President Carter came into
office with an avowed mandate to reverse what he and his aides
portrayed as Kissinger's Machiavellian and anachronistic preoccupation with the containment of the Soviet Union through clever
personal diplomacy and Realpolitik. Without really abandoning
the overriding objective of containment, the new Administration
set out to implement it in a manner congenial to American
geopolitical retrenchment and moral resurgence—by downplay-
ing the "inordinate fear of communism" that had led the country
"to embrace any dictator who joined us in our fear" (as the
President put it in his famous Notre Dame speech on May 22,
1977); aligning the United States with the forces of black majority
rule in southern Africa; and concentrating on the transcendent
"global questions" of justice, equity, and human rights through
revising the international economic order to accommodate the
needs of the "South," preventing nuclear proliferation, curbing
the arms trade, and promoting the rights of the individual against
cruelty and oppression.

In the face of a steady Soviet military build-up and of mounting
turbulence and new opportunities for the expansion of Soviet
influence in the Third World, the Carter Administration's emphasis on "world-order politics" and the "global agenda," in the
fashionable academic phrases of the time, was bound to enlarge
the interests-power gap that was already emerging under the cover
of Kissinger's Realpolitik. Reacting against this trend on pragmatic and domestic political grounds, the Administration began
after only a year to modify, abandon or reverse major components
of its original grand design. As in previous oscillations of American
policy, the driving factor was a shift in the prevailing estimate of
the Soviet threat.

After Moscow's 1977 intervention (with East German and Cuban assistance) in behalf of Mengistu's self-styled Marxist-Leninist
regime in Ethiopia, Zbigniew Brzezinski, the President's National
Security Assistant, emerged as a militant critic of Soviet violations
of "what was once called the code of conduct." By the spring of
1978 he was depicting an "arc of crisis" that came to include the
Soviet alliance with Vietnam, the 1978 installation of a puppet
regime in Afghanistan, the establishment of military dependencies

in South Yemen and in Ethiopia (in the latter case with Soviet military personnel and proxy forces), and the invasion of the Katanga (Shaba) province in Zaïre from Angola. President Carter reversed the decade-long decline in the real defense budget (notably in his address at Wake Forest University in March 1978) and declared that détente must be based on reciprocal restraint, whereas the Soviet Union, he charged (at the U.S. Naval Academy in June), had exploited détente to cover "a continuing aggressive struggle for political advantage and increased influence in a variety of ways."

This rhetorical reaffirmation of containment was matched, not only by a reversal of the decline in real defense expenditures, but also by increased arms sales (especially to Middle Eastern countries), U.S. leadership in establishing a Long Term Defense Program under which the NATO allies pledged to increase annual defense expenditures by three percent in real terms, and support of a long-range theater nuclear force modernization program (first publicly advocated by Chancellor Schmidt) culminating in the NATO decision of December 1979 to install 572 Pershing II and cruise missiles on European soil.

Capping this shift, President Carter, in urgent response to the dual shock of the overthrow of the Shah of Iran (followed by the imprisonment of American hostages) and the Soviet invasion of Afghanistan, proclaimed the most far-reaching extension of American commitments since the redefinition of America's Pacific defensive perimeter after the Korean War. In his January 1980 State of the Union address, he declared, in what immediately became known as the Carter Doctrine: "An attempt by any outside force to gain control of the Persian Gulf region will be regarded as an assault on the vital interests of the United States of America, and such an assault will be repelled by any means necessary, including military force." Giving substance to this new sense of urgency, he promised to increase defense expenditures by five percent a year, ordered the creation of a Rapid Deployment Force (RDF), deployed naval forces and sent heavy arms to protect North Yemen from the Soviet client in South Yemen, imposed a partial grain embargo and other sanctions on the U.S.S.R., and removed some restrictions on militarily significant sales of technology to China. With the ratification of SALT II already doomed by Afghanistan, it was formally withdrawn from the Senate in Carter's last days in office.

This reassertion of American power in support of containment, however, did not save the Carter Administration. Beginning in the middle of the 1970s (according to the opinion polls), the tide of opinion which President Carter had ridden into office had been reversed; by 1980 it was flowing strongly in the opposite direction. Indeed, Carter's switch only reinforced the politically fatal image of an indecisive, somewhat schizoid President presiding over an erratic, incoherent policy.

In the 1980 presidential campaign Governor Ronald Reagan emerged as the rallying point for, and articulator of, the pent-up reaction to the "Vietnam syndrome." Like President Kennedy, he interpreted his political mandate as, above all, the restoration of the nation's power and prestige in response to a heightened and neglected Soviet threat. But he did so in the face of domestic and international constraints that Kennedy never imagined. Unlike Kennedy, Reagan approached this task with a clear priority in favor of economic restoration. Lacking Kennedy's familiarity or concern with foreign affairs, his pretensions to innovative policies, or the ebullience and missionary impetus that Kennedy had imparted to his program of American resurgence, the simplicity of Reagan's foreign policy themes stood in even sharper contrast to the complexity of his task.

III

President Reagan avowed that in foreign policy, as in other matters of public policy, simplicity has its virtues and should not be equated with simple-mindedness. He had a point. It would have been difficult, even in the luxury of one's analytical imagination, to invent a single strategic concept to embrace the full complexity of the international conditions of 1981. And the failure of previous concepts—really stratagems more than strategies—to fulfill the expectations they raised (for example, Eisenhower's massive retaliation, Kennedy's promotion of self-sustaining economic growth and nation-building among the LDCs, the Nixon Doctrine, and Carter's vision of world-order politics) suggest that the absence of a grand strategy may be prudent as well as pardonable.

Journalists and academics complained that the vaunted simplicity of Reagan's foreign policy was an excuse for incoherence. By normal standards, however, it was not the incoherence of the new Administration's policies that stood out—in fact, they were comparatively coherent in action as well as rhetoric—but rather their incompleteness, both in scope and detail, when measured against the realities of the international environment. One reason for this was the President's decision, as a choice of political strategy as well as substantive priority, to concentrate on domestic economic goals at the beginning of his Administration. But there were other reasons: the failure to organize an effective system for the conduct of policy that would enable the President to make reasoned choices of strategic implementation (a failure due, in large part, to the downgrading of the National Security Council staff); the President's unfamiliarity with foreign policy and his lack of interest in taking an active role in the implementation of policies; the resulting lack of a dominant locus of policymaking, whether in the State Department, the Defense Department, or the White House; and the associated lack in any of these quarters of articulate intellectuals with the role of rationalizing policy for domestic and foreign audiences.

Nevertheless, despite the slowness of the Administration to formulate and articulate the components of a national strategy, the outlines and much of the substance of a set of foreign policies, linked to the central goals of policy and fairly well integrated with each other, were emerging by the end of 1981. As in the case of previous new Administrations, the process of elaborating the outlines and filling in the substance would be the result of themes and positions developed in the victorious campaign for office rubbing up against the stubborn continuities of the past. At the end of its first year the Administration was altering the tone and content of its original policies in response to intractable domestic and international constraints at a faster pace than most of its predecessors. Perhaps this was partly because the elementary nature of its strategic design enabled it to adapt more readily to elusive realities; but it was also because some of its own priorities—particularly rejuvenating the economy and refurbishing alliances—were, at the outset, in conflict with other themes and programs developed in the campaign. Some of the President's own simple objectives, in practice, also conflicted with each other.

The dominant theme of President Reagan's foreign policy, to which all major policies were subordinated, was revitalizing the containment of Soviet expansion. Of course, declarations about the urgency of strengthening containment were accompanied by familiar affirmations of containment's twin: the achievement of a world hospitable to free societies, where the Soviet Union would observe the international code of decent conduct, and peaceful change would become the norm. But the attainment of this world-order goal was declared to depend centrally on containing the enemy—not, as in the Carter Administration's initial formulations, on addressing the transcendent problems of the global agenda or, as in the Kissinger era, on achieving a global modus vivendi with the competing superpower.

The centrality of containment, moreover, followed from a new emphasis on the danger of the Soviet global threat. In the incoming Administration's view, while Americans had been paralyzed by illusions of détente and the trauma of Vietnam, the Soviet Union had achieved an epochal reversal of global power. Transforming itself from a continental to an ascendant imperial power, it had pursued global preponderance through a steady build-up of military capabilities ever since the Cuban missile crisis. It made no practical difference whether one attributed Soviet ascendancy to ideologically driven expansionism or to the defensive paranoia of a geopolitically encircled power center—both interpretations were to be found in the new Administration. The result was the same: a cautiously but relentlessly expansionist state opportunistically capitalizing upon its two great assets, military ascendancy and the political turmoil and vulnerability of the Third World.

To counter this Soviet threat, the priority task for the United States was to reverse the trend toward Soviet ascendancy and regain a safe military balance. Military revival would require liberation of the American spirit from the paralyzing effects of an era of national self-doubt and timidity. It would require overcoming the "strategic passivity" that had subordinated urgent security concerns to unrealistic scruples about the moral and political purity of friendly countries. And the revival of American power and spirit, the President and his spokesmen repeatedly stressed, would depend, above all, on the rejuvenation of the American economy by liberating the creative impulses of free enterprise from the dead hand of government control.

In proclaiming this central theme, there was no pretension of an all-embracing grand design or even intimations of a Reagan Doctrine. The important point was to establish a central purpose and priority and to develop coherent policies consistent with each other.

The closest the Administration came to elaborating or refining this common-sense view in its first year were the oft-repeated but little noted "four pillars" set forth by Secretary of State Alexander Haig, who called them the President's "coherent strategic approach."[1] But the "pillars" were really goals: the restoration of American and Western economic and military strength, the rein-

---

[1] At the end of the year, these were succinctly presented in an article by the Secretary, "A Strategic American Foreign Policy," *NATO Review*, December 1981. The summary of the "four pillars" is taken directly from that article.

vigoration of alliances and bilateral relationships with friendly states, the promotion of progress, in an environment of peaceful change, among less industrialized countries, and the achievement of a relationship with the U.S.S.R. based on greater Soviet restraint and reciprocity. They fell far short of delineating a strategy, if strategy means a comprehensive plan for applying the instruments and resources of national power most effectively to support a hierarchy of interests in a range of specific contingencies and circumstances.

But their very generality made it easier to adjust campaign themes to the complexities of domestic and international realities. Furthermore, despite the fact that the Administration's organization for conducting foreign policy was woefully deficient in analyzing policy options at the NSC level and did not regularly engage the President in strategic choices, and despite an extraordinary amount of "turf-fighting" in the foreign policy structure, the existence of unusual ideological affinity among the key policymakers made for relative coherence in the major substantive areas as policies evolved. The greatest substantive differences were between unilateralists and multilateralists (to use oversimplifications current within the Administration). By the end of the year the latter clearly prevailed, but the balance was unstable.

IV

The overriding goal of the Administration's foreign policy was to make American and Western power commensurate to the support of greatly extended global security interests and commitments. There was no disposition to define interests more selectively and no expectation of anything but an intensified Soviet threat to these interests. Hence, the emphasis in closing the gap between interests and power would be placed on augmenting countervailing military strength—first of all unilaterally, but also collectively with allies and bilaterally with countries willing and able to defend themselves against Communist incursions and revolution.

In pursuit of this goal the Administration's determination to increase the U.S. defense budget was clearer than its strategy for applying military resources to foreign policy requirements. After initially projecting more than double the percentage increase of the Carter budgets for FY 1981 and FY 1982, the program leveled off to a seven percent annual increase instead of Carter's five percent for the next four years, and added up to $1,280.6 billion by the end of 1986, which was about a $200 billion increase beyond the projected Carter program. In terms of constant dollars, these amounts would be by far the largest peacetime military outlay in American history.

This ambitious target, however, was arrived at without the benefit of any comprehensive strategic review, and it depended on equally ambitious targets of growth in domestic economic production. The scattershot approach to defense spending, along with Secretary of Defense Caspar Weinberger's decentralization of the management of programs and resources into the hands of the separate armed services, meant that defense expenditures would be undisciplined by strategic guidance until budgetary and other constraints compelled choices among priorities.

Initial strategic pronouncements indicated little more than that the new Administration intended to restore American military power to meet an extraordinarily wide range of contingencies. First of all, it would close the "window of vulnerability" resulting from the presumed Soviet capacity to destroy most of American land-based missiles in a first strike and regain a "margin of safety" in the U.S. strategic nuclear posture. (Significantly, even before taking office the Administration had dropped the 1980 Republican platform's less credible pledge to "superiority," which implied the rejection of parity.) In Europe it would move ahead with the development of 108 Pershing II and 464 ground-launched cruise missiles (GLCMs), in accordance with the long-range theater nuclear weapons program (LRTNF). But it also stressed the necessity of strengthening conventional capabilities and reaffirmed that the NATO commitment to three percent annual real increases in the long-term defense program (LTDP) must be fulfilled.

Outside the NATO theater, too, the Adminstration's objectives were comprehensive. It would build up general purpose forces, not only to support the previously planned Rapid Deployment Force in the Gulf with a full-time regional presence and reinforcement capabilities, but also to prepare the United States to fight protracted conventional wars in more than one theater simultaneously. In this connection Secretary Weinberger explicitly rejected the artificial constraints implied by previous commitments to a 1½- or 2½-war strategy. If one took his repeated statements about the need to meet Soviet aggression in one location by responding at points of vulnerability elsewhere—a concept soon dubbed "horizontal escalation"—as a strategy with operational significance, this would put an even higher premium on a multi-theater capability. For no one could reasonably assume in the

1980s that the threat to respond at "places of our choosing" would—as John Foster Dulles seemed to hope when he used the same phrase in the 1950s—so enhance deterrence as to obviate the necessity of fighting local wars at all.

One indication of how the Administration's goals might be translated into strategy and forces was Secretary of the Navy John Lehman's exposition of a posture of "unquestioned naval superiority," based on a 600-ship fleet with 15 battleships clustered around large aircraft carriers, surface ships with cruise missiles, and enhanced amphibious forces. This formidable force would do far more than control the sea lanes and establish a presence in crises. It would be capable of coping singly or simultaneously with local conflicts in every theater, at least in terms of maintaining access to land against Soviet or Soviet-proxy forces and thus, if necessary, removing the need to depend on U.S. or other land-based forces. But it would also be able to fight a global war between U.S. and Soviet forces at sea and perform traditional naval tasks in general war, such as protecting the sea lanes.

If nothing else, these intimations of all-purpose strategic goals indicated the Administration's firm intention to change what a number of its officials had criticized as America's "Euro-centered" strategy and to prepare the armed forces, for once, to support the nation's global commitments with truly flexible, global capabilities. The far-reaching scope of this intention was confirmed by the demanding objective, as put forth by the Under Secretary of Defense for Policy, Fred Iklé, to expand the capacity of the industrial base of American defense production so that it could support not only rapid mobilization for a crisis but also a prolonged large-scale war.

But the extent to which the Administration would actually implement its expansive strategic goals, or maintain the goals if they could not be implemented, was another matter. The major factor likely to move the Reagan Administration toward a revision and refinement of its strategy over the long run was the state of the American economy. Ronald Reagan came to office pledged to balance the budget, lower taxes, and reduce inflation and unemployment, yet at the same time greatly increase defense spending. Only with at least an annual four percent growth in the economy, by the Administration's own accounting, might these goals be reconciled. But, as of the end of 1981, the prospect of tax reductions had failed to stimulate growth. Despite extensive reductions in other government expenditures, increased defense budgets ensured an expanded federal deficit. Higher interest rates and continuing inflation discouraged productive investment, while unemployment rose. The President, although acknowledging a recession and the prospect of bigger deficits, found it politically difficult to raise taxes by much.

This left reductions in the defense budget as the most obvious economic adjustment. Reagan's strong commitment to defense kept him from approving more than a $13 billion cut over fiscal years 1982–1984, but the economic trends were bound sooner or later to have a restricting effect on defense appropriations requests and grants. For FY 1982 the Administration had already cut several billion dollars from its projected budget. Congress would be extremely reluctant to permit further cuts in social programs without exacting comparable cuts in defense. Equally restrictive, and one of the most costly deficiencies to correct, was the shortage of trained military personnel to operate sophisticated weapons, flesh out the Rapid Deployment Force, and man the increased number of naval ships envisaged. To meet these manpower needs would be difficult even with a draft, which the Administration continued to oppose.

The caution of the Reagan Administration in confronting the dilemmas that afflicted its first "pillar" was demonstrated in the surprising decision, announced on October 2, not to go through with the "race-track" deployment of the projected MX missile in Utah and Nevada. Instead, the plan is to emplace a limited number of MX missiles in existing silos while continuing to explore other possibilities to reduce the vulnerability of land-based strategic missiles. This decision may have been motivated more by domestic political objections and technical military factors than by economic considerations. Nevertheless, in so conspicuously subordinating the highly advertised urgency of closing the window of vulnerability to other considerations, it showed how readily initial defense projections might yield to unanticipated constraints.

Moreover, the organization, program support and funding of the Rapid Deployment Force continued to proceed at a sluggish pace that belied its declared urgency—and the strategy for using it remained unresolved. The Administration's discovery of the political obstacles in the Middle East to local stockpiling of military supplies and equipment, let alone stationing military brigades, strengthened advocates of sea-based projection forces; but the utility of naval and Marine forces in implementing a trip-wire strategy against a hypothetical Soviet drive toward the Gulf was highly questionable.

Nevertheless, as its decisive vote to approve a defense budget of almost $200 billion in December showed, Congress remained prepared to support an unprecedented peacetime increase in defense appropriations. Whatever the details of actual programs, authorizations, and outlays in FY 1982 might turn out to be, the President could correctly declare that the U.S. government had definitely reversed the military decline of the 1970s. This tangible expression of national will might be the most important achievement of Reagan's defense policy, but in the long run it would be an empty achievement if increased expenditures were not translated into increased capabilities related to a coherent strategy.

V

Domestic economic difficulties, strategic incoherence, and a range of bureaucratic and external political obstacles to defense programs were not the only factors modifying and shaping foreign policies. Equally important were critical tensions abroad that impinged on vital interests of established priority. This was especially the case in Western Europe, where differences between the United States and several of its allies had created a more deep-seated challenge to the cohesion and security of the Atlantic Alliance than any of the half-dozen previous crises. What made this crisis more serious was that it turned upon fundamentally divergent approaches to East-West relations and that it occurred when the United States had lost the economic and military primacy—and therefore much of the confidence of its allies and its influence with them—that it had enjoyed before the 1970s.

At the root of the trans-Atlantic crisis was an insoluble but manageable predicament. On the one hand, there was the dependence of West European security upon American nuclear protection—more specifically on the efficacy of a nuclear first-use strategy as a deterrent to Soviet conventional aggression. On the other hand, there was the unavoidable reality that if the deterrent had to be used, it would lead to a nuclear war that included European soil. This geostrategic fact, plus the contrast between the global scope of American security interests and containment concerns and the more restricted national or regional concerns of the European allies, had from the beginning of the Alliance been the source of European anxieties about American policy. Depending on the occasion, Europeans were almost bound to fear that the United States might—or that it might not—counter Soviet aggression with nuclear weapons, that it might destroy an accommodation with the Soviets—or reach one unilaterally.

When Reagan took office this predicament was once again the

source of tension between the United States and its European allies—most importantly, with the Federal Republic of Germany. The demise by 1980 of the U.S.-Soviet détente threatened to jeopardize the European-Soviet détente, which to Germany especially had become a primary national interest during the 1970s. In addition, the suspension of SALT, coupled with the American rearmament effort, portended a new arms race that might undermine the general bargain that European governments had struck with domestic political constituencies dedicated to expanded social welfare programs: that European defense increases would be sustained at a politically tolerable level while arms control negotiations were conducted in parallel.

This bargain took on new importance when the allies' agreement in 1979 to deploy 572 intermediate-range missiles on European soil was followed by the resurgence of a European anti-nuclear movement with anti-American overtones. This deployment was now attacked not only as a provocation to an arms race, but also as the implementation of an American limited war-fighting strategy that would confine a nuclear war to Europe. From the American standpoint the military program had been intended, in response to Chancellor Schmidt's 1977 proposal, to reassure the European allies that the defense of Europe would remain coupled to an American strategic response and that the rapid Soviet deployment of the SS-20 missile against European targets would be countered by visible European-based weapons that could reach Soviet targets. Thus the rising opposition seemed a frustrating demonstration of allied irresolution and irresponsibility.

If, in addition to this opposition, and following Europe's faint support for sanctions to punish and warn the Soviet Union with respect to its behavior in Southwest Asia and Poland, European governments began to renege on their long-term defense commitments, the American congressional reaction might go beyond frustration to the threat of withdrawal. Surely, if allied governments felt compelled to accept Soviet arms-control proposals that clearly upset the military balance, let alone to accede to suggestions of a European nuclear-free zone, America would have to reappraise the viability of a Continental strategy. Meanwhile, the interaction of European "pacifism" and American "unilateralism" might lead to real European neutralism.

Thus the Reagan Administration faced a serious prospect of the paralysis and unraveling of the North Atlantic Alliance. In the face of a heightened Soviet threat, the foremost European response was to urge renewed arms control negotiations, which President Reagan had condemned during the campaign and suspended upon taking office. The popular stereotype in Europe of Reagan as a bellicose cold warrior, some militant statements by his Cabinet and staff, and some artless remarks about neutron weapons and limited nuclear options added to the tension. Yet the Administration's general response to the existing and potential crisis was not to scold or threaten the allies or to retreat to unilateral globalism in reaction to European "appeasement" and "neutralism." Rather, it went out of its way to avoid the aggravation of U.S.-European divergences on defense policies, arms control, and East-West relations and set out to revive a trans-Atlantic consensus.

Secretary of State Haig and his Assistant Secretary, Lawrence Eagleburger, both familiar with the European political scene for over a decade, reassured allied governments with their comprehension of the European perspective. Administration spokesmen were firm in their support of the LTDP and the LRTNF and continued to argue for a more equitable sharing of defense burdens, particularly to support and replace the diversion of American resources to Southwest Asia, where European security was even more directly imperiled than American security. But they refrained in public from the exasperated tough-talk that was attributed to some other American officials in private conversations. In fact, there was less behind-the-scenes arm-twisting and more intensive consultation than in the Carter Administration and no rigid insistence on a percentage increase in defense expenditures.

The most dramatic evidence of the Reagan Administration's effort to restore the trans-Atlantic consensus was its eventual position on arms control negotiations. One of the President's first acts had been to suspend the SALT process indefinitely, pending reappraisal, although significantly he refrained from terminating U.S. adherence to the unratified terms of SALT II. A number of Reagan's supporters who had taken positions in the Departments of State and Defense were convinced that the utility of arms control had been oversold; that arms control had become an excuse for the West's "strategic passivity," pursued at the expense of defense programs essential to Western security. The Administration's first pronouncements on arms control reflected these skeptical reservations, restating the original 1960s rationale of arms control as a complement to defense policy, as only one element of national security policy, not the centerpiece of U.S.-Soviet relations. Without specifying any particular quid pro quo, Secretary Haig and others had reiterated the moderate concept of "linkage" which held, as "a fact of political life," that Soviet violations of the civilized code of international conduct would jeopardize arms control. Having maintained that the world had become less secure in the 1970s despite—indeed, because of—continued arms control efforts, President Reagan and his Cabinet logically emphasized that the precondition for successful negotiations was the restoration of the military balance as well as Soviet reciprocity in self-restraint.

But however warily the Administration approached arms control, it was also convinced that the priority of "revitalizing alliances" required adhering to NATO's "two-track" agreement of 1979—that discussions to limit intermediate-range missiles by treaty must be conducted in parallel with the program of deploying TNF. It insisted that the latter should be the condition of the former, but it knew that the compelling political reality was the reverse. The rise of the anti-nuclear movement and the resulting pressure on Chancellor Helmut Schmidt and other European leaders made acting on this judgment an urgent imperative. So even while it was publicly discounting the impact of the anti-nuclear movement, the Administration agreed with the Soviets to begin discussions on TNF limitation in November 1981 "within the context" of strategic arms negotiations.

On November 18, as the negotiations approached, the President announced in a public address that the United States was prepared to cancel its deployment of Pershing IIs and GLCMs if the Soviets would dismantle their SS-20s, SS-4s and SS-5s. This was the "zero option" urged by Schmidt and other anxious European leaders. It signified not only a concession to European views but, more fundamentally, to the arms control process. Coming after the discovery of economic constraints on the defense budget and before either a military build-up or any improvement in Soviet behavior, it was a particularly significant sign of the Reagan Administration's priorities and its flexibility in adjusting policies to the "four pillars" when some of the pillars clashed.

Not that this solved any of the formidable technical and political problems of improving military security through arms control. The unprecedented complexity of assessing, verifying, and equalizing the military balance by mutual agreement, and the difficulty of inducing the Soviets to accept what the United States could consider an equitable balance when that would require offsetting a perceived Soviet advantage, guaranteed prolonged negotiations full of political and technical obstacles and the risk of thwarted popular expectations. But for better or worse the process had begun. Unlike the mutual and balanced force negotiations (MBFR), these negotiations could not go on fruitlessly forever without evoking concern by anxious publics and governments. The zero-option initiative signalized the revival of a temporarily blocked strand in U.S.-Soviet relations, which, if past experience were a guide, would have a life of its own, affecting defense and foreign policy in sometimes unexpected ways.

That arms control might exceed the restrained subsidiary role that Reagan's experts originally preferred was suggested by the President's adoption of the acronym START (strategic arms *reduction* talks), put forth by the forceful new Director of the Arms Control and Disarmament Agency, Eugene Rostow. Appealing to both the Left and Right and promising a bilateral solution to the economic burden of defense, START might turn out to be an object of enthusiasm no less beguiling than SALT. Or, considering the difficulty of achieving agreement on arms reductions that would scrap programs and change the ratio of power, as compared to agreement on ceilings to existing programs that would ratify an existing balance, START might dash unrealistic expectations once again.

VI

The revitalization of containment through a unilateral defense build-up and through the strengthening of allied cohesion and defense was squarely within the core of the American consensus on U.S. foreign policy. The way the Reagan Administration handled alliance relations, moreover, promised to keep U.S. policy in the mainstream of the trans-Atlantic consensus.

Similarly, the Administration's management of relations with the other two major counterpoises to Soviet power, Japan and China, was consistent with established continuities of containment, although in both cases it faced great potential trouble. The relatively discreet urging that Japan increase its contribution to defense, in terms of roles and missions within the ambiguous limits of "self-defense" permitted by Article IX of the Japanese Constitution, avoided public acrimony. By the end of the year it seemed likely to lead to a marginally more satisfactory division of regional security efforts with American naval forces. But the record $15 billion surplus in trade with the United States, combined with Japan's reluctance to assume a larger share of the burden for its defense, was provoking a congressional reaction that could spell serious trouble for U.S.-Japan relations if Japan did not continue to increase its defense expenditures.

The lifting of restrictions on arms sales to China was an important extension of the policy of selling "dual-purpose" technology, in line with a trend established by the previous Administration. Despite general references to further strategic collaboration against the Soviet Union on such issues as Cambodia and Afghanistan, this action did not portend any basic change in the U.S. relationship with "a friendly non-aligned country." The limited convergence of interests and the economic constraints on China's military modernization inhibited such a change. But the geopolitical logic of the entente with China that began with the Nixon-Kissinger rapprochement might nevertheless be overridden by the legacy of Reagan's commitment to the Republic of China on Taiwan, if the Administration met Taiwan's request to sell it the FX advanced fighter aircraft or even military spare parts. Calling such military sales a "litmus test" of the whole Washington-Peking relationship, Peking, at the end of December, charged that they constituted "hegemonic" interference in China's sovereign affairs and warned that they would compel a downgrading of diplomatic relations to the level of chargé d'affaires.

From the problems incurred in relations with Japan, China and the European allies it was evident that revitalizing relations with major allies and friends would be more difficult than anticipated. Revitalizing containment in the Third World was likely to be even more difficult and also considerably more controversial both at home and abroad—especially if campaign themes were literal standards of policy. The extension and implementation of containment among the less-industrialized countries had always raised the most agitated issues at home and the greatest opposition abroad. In the politically turbulent and largely non-democratic Third World, the application of the interwar lessons about the necessity of stopping piecemeal totalitarian aggression, although compelling in security terms, repeatedly confronted the American conscience with the awkward expedient of supporting authoritarian and inhumane regimes. In this vast post-colonial area, America's implementation of containment inevitably carried the opprobrium of imperial intervention, and the opprobrium was sharpened by foreign acceptance of America's own claim of unique righteousness as a standard of judgment. At the same time, in this area lay the greatest opportunities for the expansion of Soviet influence, whether directly or by proxy.

The Reagan Administration entered office committed to a major campaign theme that condemned the Carter Administration for neglecting too long the expansion of Soviet influence, subversion, and presence in the "arc of crisis" and for failing to respond to the threat of Marxist revolutions and Cuban subversion in America's own "backyard": Central America and the Caribbean. According to this theme the Carter Administration's misguided moralism and conscience-bound timidity had not only obscured the threat and paralyzed countervailing action; by applying unrealistic standards of moral censorship, particularly liberal Western standards of human rights, against friendly authoritarian governments, it had precipitated their replacement by unfriendly totalitarians. The latter claim was directed particularly, though with doubtful historical accuracy, to the fate of the Shah in Iran and of Somoza in Nicaragua.

In contrast, the Administration proclaimed, President Reagan would restore cooperative relations with countries primarily on the basis of their sharing America's concern to halt Soviet and Soviet-proxy expansionism. As an instrument of this expansionism, international terrorism was said to be the greatest threat to human rights, while Soviet-inspired revolutions and interventions were the greatest threat to world peace and security.

In the aftermath of the Carter Administration this forceful message was bracing to many Americans, but it was unnerving to many governments in the Third World and also to West European governments responding to the growing interest of social democrats in supporting "progressive" forces in the developing countries (especially in Latin America and Africa). Furthermore, insofar as the risk of American armed involvement in local revolutions was implied, a broad cross-section of the American public, still in thrall to the bitter memory of Vietnam, would oppose bold reaffirmations of containment. In the forefront of this opposition would be traditional liberals whose special concern for getting on the right (which, in practice, meant the "left-center") side of social and political change was reactivated by official talk of supplanting concern for human rights and reform with opposition to terrorism.

VII

The worst apprehensions that Reaganism meant a militaristic revival of the cold war in the Third World, with the intention of destabilizing leftist regimes and defeating incipient wars of national liberation, were seemingly confirmed by the new Administration's first major foreign initiative. In February, Secretary Haig charged that the shipment of arms to the guerrillas opposing the Duarte regime in El Salvador was a "textbook case" of Sovietinduced, Cuban-executed subversion. He issued warnings that the United States might "go to the source" if outside involvement did not cease. In an action reminiscent of the Cuban missile crisis, he dispatched emissaries to allied governments in Europe with a White Paper documenting Cuban arms shipments to explain the seriousness of the threat. More tangibly, the U.S. government lifted restrictions on lethal arms aid and sent 56 military advisers to help the junta.

The alarmed reaction in Latin America and Europe and the revival of the Vietnam analogy in the United States evidently convinced the Administration that it had made a tactical error. A campaign that the press widely interpreted as an effort to draw the line against Communist aggression quickly subsided. Haig emphasized that far more economic than arms aid was being sent to El Salvador. Without dropping the charges of Cuban complicity, he acknowledged the internal sources of political turbulence in Central America, as elsewhere in the Third World. He announced a multilateral program of economic aid for the Caribbean Basin, which in the nature of its members' political orientation could not be overtly directed against Cuba, and launched an effort to engage Mexico and Venezuela diplomatically as well as economically in some sort of regional security relationship.

Actually, the Administration had substantially followed its predecessor's policy—indeed, the preferred American policy in all revolutionary situations—of supporting a supposedly centrist regime and hoping that it would be sufficiently reformist to broaden its political base and prevail. It acted about as the Carter Administration would probably have acted, although with neither apology nor self-righteousness. But its analysis of Central American developments remained pessimistic and might well be confirmed by events.

The Duarte regime seemed to be losing control. Whether either an election or a negotiated settlement could restore order under a not-unfriendly coalition of factions was doubtful. Meanwhile, Nicaragua continued to build up with Cuban help one of the largest armies in Latin America, to an extent that could hardly be explained solely as a defensive reaction to the Reagan Administration's rhetoric. In the background there were signs that Moscow was looking covetously toward Central America as the next disturbed area in which the support of "national liberation" movements (that is, pro-Soviet regimes) might remove U.S. influence, establish Soviet proxies, and tie down U.S. forces.

Faced with this situation, the Reagan Administration was understandably disposed to back diplomacy with private and public contemplations of the use of force. The trouble was that wielding a big stick in the 1980s might so arouse the domestic and international apprehensions of friends as to undermine the impact of tough words on enemies. All the worse if the stick were weak or not suited to the task. Administration officials hinted darkly of naval blockades to stop the flow of arms, and they kept up verbal attacks against Cuban global interventionism. But against either Nicaragua or Cuba there were probably no effective small-scale military options, and a serious blockade would entail a significant naval draw-down elsewhere, not to mention an explosive reaction among European allies and Latin American friends.

Consequently, although Secretary Haig would not explicitly renounce the use of force, President Reagan said in November: "We have no plans for putting combat troops anywhere in the world." The Administration prudently resorted to making the most of active bilateral and regional diplomatic representations in order to isolate revolutionary forces and limit their damage to other countries, while standing ready to reward diplomatic cooperation with increased military and economic aid. As in Europe, the prior condition for revitalizing containment had become the enhancement of America's credibility as a promoter of multinational diplomatic solutions to regional security threats. Only on this basis could a revival of military strength effectively support diplomacy.

VIII

The area of the Third World in which diplomacy seemed most promising was southern Africa, where American policy was conducted with little or no reference to U.S. military power, arms aid or covert action. Again, it was the rhetoric, tone, and tactics rather than the substance of diplomacy that most distinguished the Reagan Administration from its predecessor. Its keynote was basing relations in the area more on common security concerns against Soviet or Cuban penetration and relatively less on the national and racial concerns of black Africa, including the condemnation of South Africa.

The major immediate objectives were the same: to strengthen pro-Western regimes, to get the Soviets and Cubans out of Angola, and to get the South Africans out of Namibia—and, integrally related to this objective, out of Angola, which was a haven for the revolutionary group SWAPO's attacks into Namibia—under conditions that might stabilize the area against revolutionary and anti-Western forces. The first objective was most importantly implemented by economic aid to the pragmatic Marxist Robert

Mugabe's constitutional regime in Zimbabwe. The other two objectives had been effectively blocked by South Africa's refusal to go through with the agreed plan for Namibian independence. The Carter Administration's strategy for removing this obstacle, including the threat of sanctions against South Africa, was demonstrably impotent. The Reagan Administration's strategy, largely developed and executed by Assistant Secretary of State Chester Crocker, charted a different course.

The strategy was to cease public censorship and pressure against South Africa and convince the government that cooperation with the conservatively oriented Reagan Administration offered the last best opportunity to secure its northern border with a stable independent buffer in Namibia and an Angolan regime (based perhaps on a coalition between the Soviet-backed government and Jonas Savimbi's principal insurgent group, UNITA) free of Cubans and no longer a base for SWAPO attacks. To back this strategy the Administration secured the diplomatic support and cooperation of the other members of the so-called "contact group": Britain, France, West Germany and Canada.

To put all these logically related pieces together to solve such a complicated diplomatic puzzle, in an international environment of conflicting interests in which the United States had only limited leverage, would be difficult. But there was no good alternative to achieve the same objectives, and all the key parties seemed to recognize this. SWAPO's acceptance in mid-November of Western proposals, backed by the contact group, for guaranteeing the rights of the white minority in an independent Namibia was an auspicious sign.

IX

Of all the critical areas of the Third World the problem of strengthening containment was most important and most difficult in Southwest Asia: most important because of its strategic position, the dependence of the United States and its major allies on Middle Eastern oil, and the proximity of the Soviet Union, with a great concentration of Soviet forces athwart the border from Afghanistan to Turkey; most difficult because of the many clashes of national, ethnic, ideological, and religious interests in the area; the absence of reliable military counterpoises; the destabilizing effects of modernization on traditional regimes; and the special American commitment to Israel in an area in which few governments or movements were prepared to accept its legitimacy. Moreover, this was the area most responsible, in the aftermath of the collapse of Iran and the invasion of Afghanistan, for accentuating the chronic gap between American security interests and commitments, on the one hand, and effective power to support them against the Soviet threat, on the other.

Ever since the withdrawal of the British from this area in the 1950s (completed in the early 1970s), the United States, in its role of global container, had been faced with a "power vacuum." The problem was that each successive effort to fill the vacuum seemed either to upset the intraregional balance of power, as the 1955 Baghdad Pact had led Egypt to become a Soviet military dependent, or upset the internal equilibrium of the local base of American power, as the unrestrained U.S. assistance to the Shah had contributed to his demise. In either case, the effect was to facilitate Soviet penetration and influence.

Moreover, the problem of finding a reliable political base for American military power in the area was compounded by the deep-seated conflict between Israel and the Arab states, which became more acute after the 1967 War. Israel was by far the strongest and most reliable counterpoise to Soviet expansion in the Middle East, but its hostile relationship with the Arab states made it unsuitable as a base or surrogate. This was particularly the case after the political activation of OPEC in the course of the 1973 Yom Kippur War, for this development gave the United States a new degree of interest in maintaining harmonious relations with the major oil suppliers. And this interest merged with containment because of the presumed threat that the Soviets might directly or indirectly deprive the West of access to the oil fields. It also put the United States in the awkward position of trying to reconcile a cooperative relationship with Arab states with the security of Israel.

Confronted with these obstacles to containment, the American strategy was, first, to promote a stable peace between Israel and its Arab neighbors. After the Carter Administration's abandonment of a comprehensive settlement and Sadat's astonishing transformation from Soviet dependent to peacemaker, this objective had come to focus on an Egyptian-Israeli settlement through the process envisioned in the 1978 Camp David Accords, which by the time of Reagan's victory had either entered their final stages or an impasse, with Israel's scheduled withdrawal from the Sinai and the question of Palestinian autonomy remaining to be resolved. At the same time, the American logic of containment called for development among the "moderate" (that is, anti-Soviet and not anti-American) states a sufficiently cooperative arrangement to facilitate the operation of the RDF in the Gulf. Toward this end, the key states would have to be Egypt and Saudi Arabia, which, especially after Sadat's assassination, would regard movement toward a Palestinian settlement as an essential condition for their cooperation.

The Reagan Administration's approach to the regional problem—contrary to campaign rhetoric that strongly favored Israel's position—was essentially an extension of the prevailing strategy. It continued to play the role of broker and lever toward the consummation of the Camp David agreements, with a combination of sticks and carrots intended to enhance Israel's receptivity to a minimal formula for Palestinian autonomy. At the same time, it concentrated on building the political and physical foundation for military collaboration in Egypt and Saudi Arabia as well as in the older outposts of the Northern Tier, Pakistan and Turkey.

Consistent with the Reagan Administration's emphasis on the revitalization of containment, Secretary Haig gave this latter policy the name of "strategic consensus." He did not suppose that a common concern for containing Soviet influence and preventing Soviet aggression in the area would overcome all regional conflicts, least of all the conflict over Palestine. Nor was he insensitive to the political obstacles to stationing American troops in the area. But he did hope that this common concern might sufficiently mute the Saudi-Israeli antipathy and consolidate the Saudi-Egyptian convergence of interests to permit arrangements for the use of pre-positioned supplies, technical facilities, and bases in collaboration with local forces strengthened by American arms sales and assistance.

In 1981 the badly bungled sale of AWACS aircraft to the Saudis again showed the difficulty of strengthening Saudi collaboration without undermining Israel's sense of security. The Administration's concession to Israel's security was sign a pact for military cooperation, but this concession fell far short of the collaboration Israel sought and did nothing to reconcile the Begin government to a Palestine solution that the moderate Arabs might accept. Some European allies thought that Saudi Arabia's implicit recognition of Israel in its eight-point peace plan might break the impasse over Palestine, but the Arab states' rejection of this démarche was almost as adamant as Israel's. Meanwhile, the steady extension of Israeli settlements in the West Bank and Gaza convinced many observers that Begin's intention was annexation, which would foreclose any Palestinian settlement. Israel's annexation of Syria's Golan Heights in December and Begin's bitter retort to U.S. criticism and suspension of the pact for military cooperation seemed to move the dream of an Arab-Israeli accommodation even further from reality.

Added to these obstacles was an underlying uncertainty about the long-run stability of the Saudi regime. President Reagan's apparent extension (in a news conference on October 1) of the Carter Doctrine—initially characterized by Secretary Weinberger as "clumsy and ill-advised"—to cover any internal upheaval in Saudi Arabia that might shut off vital oil supplies to the West was an effort to reduce this uncertainty, but clearly it entailed some added risk of extending American commitments beyond American power. Furthermore, since stationing even small numbers of specialized American forces on Saudi or Egyptian soil was unwelcome by the hosts and politically disturbing in any case, the utility of the RDF even in contingencies involving Soviet forces seemed highly questionable. Against local military or internal revolutionary conflicts that threatened Western access to oil supplies, the utility of American forces had always been viewed as limited.

X

In the Third World the tone and rhetoric of diplomacy, the tactics and emphasis of policy, most differentiated the Reagan Administration's policies from those of its predecessor. In most respects, the content, as opposed to the style, of policy was marked by continuity; but in some cases the change of style amounted to a change of substance. This was markedly true in the case of policies concerning the trans-national issues on the global agenda that so engaged Third World representatives and liberal Western spokesmen in the arena of world opinion.

The style of the Carter Administration in addressing these issues was initially to elevate them to the status of critical elements in an emerging new international order, in which North-South relations would impinge upon American vital interests at least as significantly as would East-West relations. The Reagan style, in contrast, was to approach the "so-called" Third World as a huge heterogeneous aggregation of countries with a variety of political and economic problems deserving of American sympathy and help on grounds of enlightened self-interest, but to do so on a practical case-by-case, issue-by-issue basis, not as a class of states demanding a massive transfer of wealth to redress the economic inequalities of an unjust international system. Rejecting what it considered the false dichotomy of North-South and East-West relations, the Administration also rejected the view that one set of relationships turned upon social and economic, the other on security concerns. Rather, these relationships and concerns were fused and interdependent.

One aspect of this fusion to which the Administration gave extraordinary emphasis, implemented by a variety of countermeasures as well as words, was the threat to the security—and, therefore, the development—of less industrialized countries arising from the aggressive interventionism of two Third World states sponsored by the Soviet Union: Cuba and Libya. Indeed, against these two disturbers of the peace the Administration directed such a vigorous verbal onslaught as to convey the impression that it welcomed the chance to discipline them as more vulnerable extensions of the Soviet Union. And yet its actions were, in fact, cautious—even in response to what it publicly charged was an effort by Libya's Qaddafi to assassinate leading members of the Administration.

Notwithstanding its emphasis on Communist threats, the Reagan Administration did not ignore the Third World's preoccupation with economic development. Even though it did not speak with the compassion of the two preceding Democratic Administrations, in substance its approach was about the same as that of the Carter Administration. Both accepted the generalities about the West's commercial and humanitarian interests in economic progress and stability among the less industrialized countries, but Western governments had long ceased to regard development aid as an effective means of achieving this end except under congenial internal conditions which were usually beyond their control. Nor was the response of the two Administrations to Third World demands for an internationally organized transfer of wealth essentially different: rejection of most of the items put forth by the Group of 77 for structural reform of the international system, coupled with a willingness to bargain about a few of the more practical demands for economic concessions within the framework of the existing system.

The principal difference was that the Reagan Administration was less susceptible to egalitarian appeals and was unapologetically committed to capitalist self-help. That the candid but not unresponsive Reagan style of neither "confrontation" nor "condescension" in dealing with the less industrialized countries might enjoy some diplomatic success was suggested by the President's performance at the meeting of developed and developing countries at Cancún, Mexico, in October.

This meeting followed Reagan's effective opposition at the July

Ottawa summit to Canadian Prime Minister Pierre Trudeau's proposal for "global negotiations" on increased aid to the Third World, and his warm endorsement in September of the International Monetary Fund (IMF) and the World Bank (IBRD) as instruments for stimulating development through the private sector. At Cancún he gracefully agreed to the dominant concern of the less-developed countries for continuing global negotiations, but deftly defined these negotiations as a dialogue in the United Nations (not subject to votes) and within U.N. and multilateral bodies such as the IMF and IBRD (where weighted voting would prevent futile haggling)—while emphasizing the superior benefits of private investment and free enterprise demonstrated in the striking economic progress of some newly industrialized countries.

In its approach to two other issues on the global agenda, the Reagan style expressed the Administration's more candid emphasis on the objective of security and cooperative relations with friends: the transfer of conventional arms and nuclear proliferation.

The Carter Administration entered office with a strong disposition to regard arms transfers as wasteful and provocative distractions from economic development which must therefore be restrained. In practice, it found that arms sales, for a variety of political and military purposes, were one of the most effective instruments of policy that the superpowers have. It proceeded to develop a set of restraints that more or less came to terms with U.S. diplomatic and military interests. The only substantial planned reduction of arms sales was to Latin America—always in domestic political terms the most appealing and, in terms of U.S. security, the least costly arena for applying sanctions of various kinds—but the result was simply to substitute foreign for American sales.

The Reagan Administration entered office with a bias in favor of arms sales as a means of narrowing the gap between security interests and unilateral power—by strengthening friendly countries, revitalizing mutual security relationships, and fostering regional and internal stability. It developed a set of guidelines designed to restrain arms sales, but for purposes of cost-effectiveness rather than political virtue. It avowed an interest in multilateral restraints on arms transfers; but, seeing little or no foreign (including Soviet) interest in such restraints, it was opposed to jeopardizing U.S. security interests through unilateral restraints. Putting its money where its policies were, the Administration greatly increased military assistance to Southwest Asian countries and relaxed the Carter restraints on co-production of arms, on the production of weapons specifically for export, and on assistance by American embassies to arms exporters.

This shift of emphasis compounded the usual difficulty of restraining energetic arms salesmen in the Pentagon—especially the salesmen of advanced aircraft—but Administration spokesmen insisted that the new emphasis was not a disguise for uncontrolled sales. They pointed to the new program adopted for Pakistan— $3.2 billion over six years in military and economic aid, divided about 4-to-1 in favor of loans for military purchases and including the sale of F-16 aircraft—as an effective use of military transfers for overriding security interests, in contrast to the Carter Administration's suspension of military assistance as a sanction against Pakistan's nuclear program (and Pakistan's rejection, on grounds of inadequacy, of Carter's post-Afghanistan effort to resume aid). The explicit purpose of the program was to strengthen Pakistan against a "serious threat" from Soviet troops in Afghanistan; but, as often, arms transfers also seemed to be intended for purposes served best by public silence: bolstering the Zia government against neutralism and Soviet inducements; preserving a base for the harassment of Soviet occupation forces in Afghanistan; and gaining bases and access rights for the RDF. As in other cases in Southwest Asia, arms aid to enhance the security of one country tended to threaten the security of its rival—in this case, India. But the Administration evidently calculated that it could manage this dilemma without upsetting the balance in the subcontinent. In any case, India's quasi-alignment with the Soviet Union inclined the Administration to discount the cost of displeasing India.

The Reagan Administration, partly moved by Israel's air raid against Iraq's nuclear facilities, endorsed the well-established American goal of curbing the spread of independent nuclear capabilities. But, as with arms transfers, it integrated nonproliferation policy more explicitly with U.S. security policy. It put new emphasis on the position that, in the final analysis, discouraging a nation's acquisition of nuclear weapons depends on helping to meet its security interests by other means, and it added the argument that reestablishing the United States as a reliable partner for peaceful nuclear cooperation under adequate safeguards was essential to gain the support of recipients for nonproliferation goals. At the end of 1981 it was too early to say precisely what this emphasis would mean in operational terms, beyond the general relaxation of restrictions on nuclear reactor fuel sales and on civil reprocessing and breeder reactor development abroad, which had often been political irritants but seldom effective nonproliferation devices. It was clear, however, that nonproliferation policy would have to come to terms with the revitalization of containment and that, where the two conflicted (as was widely considered to be the case in Pakistan), the burden of proof would now rest on those favoring restrictions. Again, arms aid to Pakistan provided some indication of how the new emphasis might work out in practice. While giving precedence to mutual security interests, the Administration made it clear, informally, that the aid would be terminated if Pakistan were to explode a nuclear device; and Congress added provisions to the appropriation bill to make this explicit.

On human rights policies the divergence between the Reagan and Carter Administrations was, as both saw it, the sharpest of all the divergences on global-agenda issues. Representatives of the Carter Administration, with some reason, considered these policies the most distinctive and enduring expression of their moral enhancement of America's global posture. Representatives of the Reagan Administration considered them the most quixotic, biased and counterproductive. The controversy excited during the campaign by the New Conservatives' charge that human rights policies had undermined friendly right-wing authoritarian countries while turning a blind eye to left-wing totalitarians reached a crescendo in the Senate Foreign Relations Committee's opposition that led Ernest W. Lefever, a long-time critic of misguided moralism, to withdraw his nomination as head of the Bureau of Human Rights and Humanitarian Affairs in the State Department.

Yet the new Administration did not renounce the application of human rights standards to the conduct of foreign relations. In November it reaffirmed them as "a principal goal" "at the core" of U.S. policy. It did not dismantle the often intrusive machinery in the State Department for implementing human rights standards nor, for the moment, challenge the legislation that required such implementation, including the extraordinarily undiplomatic reports on foreign countries' state of moral health.

The State Department memorandum on human rights policy, published on November 4, amounted to a forceful restatement of the Carter Administration's policy, but there was an underlying difference of emphasis and philosophy. President Carter and his spokesmen often gave the impression, though seldom confirmed in practice, that they regarded this policy as an ideal to be pursued altruistically, in contrast to the policy of supporting right-wing dictators for the sake of containment. The State Department's memorandum, on the other hand, frankly stated the instrumental justification for such official idealism. Human rights, it affirmed, must be an integral, not just rhetorical, part of American foreign policy in order to maintain public and congressional support of foreign policy initiatives, to stave off neutralism, and to mobilize ideological opposition to the Soviets. This justification of official morality on grounds of enlightened expediency might offend moral purists, but the end result could nevertheless be to exalt moral values to the greatest practical extent, if the Administration adhered to the memorandum's view that to be credible and effective human rights standards must be applied evenhandedly, even if they adversely affect relations with friends as well as enemies.

The eventual continuity of human rights policies was apparently confirmed by the rapid and overwhelming congressional approval of the Administration's nominee to replace Dr. Lefever, Elliott Abrams, who advocated the reinvigoration of the human rights bureau. But, of course, the actual content of human rights policies would depend, as before, on the kinds of judgments the U.S. government would make in reconciling (and often subordinating) human rights standards to equally compelling diplomatic and security interests and means-ends calculations in particular cases. Here one could be sure that the Reagan Administration would apply human rights policies less publicly, be more discreet with friendly countries and tougher with enemies, give greater emphasis to "civil" and "political" (as distinguished from "individual") rights, apply all three components of human rights with more deference to favorable trends, seek amendments to legislation singling out particular countries as targets for restrictions on military and economic assistance, and give greater weight to security considerations and the necessities of combatting terrorism.

XI

To assess the general course of foreign policy in the Reagan Administration it may help to speculate how it might look in retrospect five or ten years from now. It is always too early to conduct this kind of exercise of the imagination for the purpose of prediction, but a year is time enough for a contingent evaluation.

It will be argued that the contingencies implicit in the following evaluation are skewed toward unwarranted optimism. I would say they are skewed toward *plausible* optimism, which may be refuted by the Administration's deficiencies and by events beyond its control. I assume, for example, that the preponderant influence in U.S. foreign policy of the judicious and informed pragmatic multilateralism which is now concentrated in the State Department will prevail; that President Reagan's best qualities of leadership will become actively engaged in the making of foreign policy; that the Administration will avoid the hazards of talking toughly with a weak stick it does not even wield; and that it will eschew the inclinations of some of its members toward the kind of unilateralism that could lead to disastrous national self-isolation. The reason for such conditional optimism is partly to present an appropriate model for emulation and partly to provide an antidote to widespread derogatory stereotypes of the Administration (especially abroad) that are even less warranted than absolute confidence that performance will coincide with the model. As for the multiplicity of adverse events and developments in trouble-prone parts of the world that may occur no matter how wise or foolish the U.S. government may be, I can only concede that some of them will almost surely occur, yet hopefully assume that the worst possibilities will remain only sobering hypotheses.

Whatever the future holds, it is safe to say that in retrospect the continuities in the broad outlines of American foreign policy will seem more striking than in November 1980. Both the Administration's claims and its opponents' fears of innovation will seem less important; and so will the inept remarks, bureaucratic collisions and tactical pratfalls that the media magnify. But, of course, continuity of the outlines does not preclude significant changes in the substance of policy. The momentous changes in American postwar policy have resulted from the process of translating the enduring premises and purposes of containment into policies and actions, in response to unpredictable events and basic changes in the international and domestic environment.

Amid the predictable continuities and unpredictable changes, the success or failure of the Reagan Administration, in retrospect, should be judged by the extent to which it has achieved its central goal, the revitalization of containment. The achievement of this goal requires bringing American power, in all its dimensions, into safe balance with America's expanded security interests and commitments—at a level of effort and by means that engage the moral and material support of the nation. The principal obstacles to achieving this balance lie precisely in the areas of policy concern— the four pillars—that the Reagan Administration has identified as most critical to the achievement of its central goal.

The obstacles are particularly formidable with respect to the two most immediately pressing objectives: the rejuvenation of the American economy and the restoration of the military balance. Inextricably related to restoring the military balance are two other objectives to which the Administration has properly assigned top priority: the revitalization of the North Atlantic Alliance and the achievement of a stable military and political equilibrium in Southwest Asia. Tying all these objectives to the revitalization of containment is the Administration's goal of achieving a relationship of restraint and reciprocity with the Soviet Union.

This constellation of related objectives deserves the highest priority simply because it has the greatest impact, for better or worse, on American security and well-being as Americans broadly define their vital interests. To be sure, the record of the past shows that developments in the Third World, even outside Southwest Asia, can become as critical to American interests as what happens in these major areas of policy concern if the mistakes and excesses of American policy make them so, but intrinsically they do not impinge on U.S. security nor strain U.S. power to the same extent.

In 1981 the Reagan Administration's most serious weakness lay in the foundation of its first pillar: the restoration of the nation's economy and, closely related to this objective, its defense posture. In 1982 one should be able to tell whether the Administration will be able to overcome its economic problems; it may take longer to judge the real efficacy of its defense efforts. Let us assume, not unreasonably but without any pretense of prediction, that in the course of the next few years the resilience of the American economy and society; the abundance of American resources, technological prowess, and ingenuity; the national consensus for a defense buildup; and the President's mobilization of the country behind the reaffirmation of national power and prestige will succeed in establishing this first pillar. Then, in retrospect, one could say that this achievement had given the United States the opportunity to cope with the closely related security problems in Western Europe and Southwest Asia.

It is unlikely that this Administration or any other will come very close to *solving* the complex of problems in these two areas, because these problems are, at their roots, insoluble dilemmas under any conditions that one can reasonably foresee. It is not unlikely, however, that the United States, as in the past, will at least *cope* with the dilemmas of the Atlantic Alliance by once again providing the key to preserving the essential security and cohesion of the Alliance, based on a solid core of common interests. The Reagan Administration has auspiciously entered the rocky two-track road to validate this judgment—but in the shadows of the Polish crisis, which could invalidate it.

It is less likely but not impossible that the Administration will be able to cope with the dilemmas of the Middle East. Whatever it does, there will be a lively danger of local wars and revolutions. The Arab-Israeli impasse over Palestine seems likely to continue, and it is not inconceivable that some kind of Israeli fait accompli may totally preempt movement toward a settlement. In either case, the situation will almost surely strain Arab as well as Arab-Israeli relations to an extent that will preclude a reliable regional "strategic consensus" for the projection of American military power. And even if the Palestinian question were settled, there is not likely to emerge among the Arab countries the kind of internal and inter-state stability that will provide a congenial environment for an RDF capable of containing a Soviet military incursion locally and short of the Gulf. Consequently, it will be a considerable tribute to the Reagan Administration if one can say in retrospect that it avoided the most serious hazards of excessive commitment to any of its several conflicting objectives in the area at the expense of the others, but retained a sufficiently credible political and material base for the projection of its power to reinforce Soviet caution against the military exploitation of regional turbulence.

If these minimal, yet challenging, objectives were achieved, would the Reagan Administration have succeeded in closing the chronic gap between American security interests and American power? Would it, thereby, finally have established the basis for sustaining containment over the long run without the disturbing oscillations between the assertion and retrenchment of American power? Not necessarily.

At the end of 1981 there were no signs, and no reason to think, that the extent and scope of American security interests and of American involvements in their behalf would cease to expand. Quite the contrary. At the same time, the disparity between security interests and the means of supporting them against internal, regional, and global threats seemed greater than at any time since the Korean War, partly because a military conflict in Southwest Asia would be more likely to spread than previous local wars in East Asia. Hypothetically, there were several ways to narrow the gap between interests and power to a safe margin; but in reality only a few of them were likely to be tried or to have much effect on the interests-power gap if they were.

In the abstract, the simplest way to narrow the gap would be simply to define security interests—especially those that might require the use of force to support them—more selectively. In practice, however, there seems to be no safe formula for doing this that would be consistent with containment. To plan to exclude some interests from the ambit of containment while trying to revitalize containment would be particularly disadvantageous and hardly something that the Reagan Administration would contemplate.

There is a beguiling geopolitical logic to the possibility that the Western European allies and Japan might fill in the expanded interests-power gap by contributing more to defense in their region and in the Middle East, where, after all, their security is more directly imperiled than American security. Some redistribution of security roles and contributions is, indeed, politically essential and feasible; but the political constraints against the scale of devolution that would be necessary to compensate for the shortfall in U.S. capabilities are too obvious to make it a practical target in the 1980s.

As for arms control, we must know by now that it cannot end the arms race, nor substitute for maintaining the military balance. At best, it is a complement to defense programs. It can make a military balance less volatile and provocative, more predictable and safer. It may also save money if it does not become an excuse for letting the military balance deteriorate. But it cannot, by itself, do much to close the gap between interests and power.

There remains one crucial key to narrowing the gap to a safe margin—one essential complement to redressing the military balance. This is diminishing the threat to American security interests by diplomatic accommodation. In the Third World this means putting the full weight of American power and prestige behind the resolution of regional conflicts and tensions through patient and discreet diplomatic intervention.

Even more important, in East-West relations this means maintaining a restraining balance of will and strength against Soviet expansion, while establishing over a number of years a set of formal and informal reciprocal restraints. If the Administration's other three pillars were firmly erected, it would have a good opportunity to construct and sustain such an equilibrium. Intractable internal and external problems could be important incentives to the Soviets, providing that they know that they cannot exploit U.S.-European divergences. The volatility of the Middle East, the persistence of the interests-power gap, and the imperatives of allied cohesion provide compelling incentives to the United States.

Needless to say, the opportunity for a new East-West equilibrium would be destroyed for a long time by Soviet military suppression of Poland. It would be enhanced if the Poles are able to settle their own affairs through peaceful compromise and the Soviets abstain from military intervention. General Jaruzelski's repression of the independent Polish labor movement in December cast an ominous cloud over East-West relations, and tested the Reagan Administration's ability to reconcile the management of

East-West tension with the cohesion of the Atlantic Alliance. The Administration's cautious and measured actions manifested its determination to preserve two of its pillars of policy under difficult circumstances.

Against the Polish government the Administration applied economic sanctions of graduated severity, while trying to distinguish between sanctions against the state and humanitarian concern—especially in the form of privately distributed food aid—for the people. Against the Soviet Union, which the Administration publicly held responsible for Jaruzelski's crackdown, it also applied phased sanctions, contingent upon the continuation of repressions; and it repeated previous warnings of unspecified reprisals in the event of overt Soviet military intervention. The President also pledged that if the Polish government reached an accommodation consistent with basic human rights, the United States would do its part to restore the Polish economy, as it had helped the countries of Europe after World War II.

These measures fell far short of the full-scale political and economic sanctions advocated by some labor leaders and Congressmen, but even these were not matched by the European allies. Failing to secure parallel sanctions by its allies, the Administration nevertheless felt compelled to impose them unilaterally; but it refrained from publicly pressuring the allies to follow suit. Indeed, on the diplomatic level the Administration conspicuously eschewed a tougher stance and continued normal relations, not only with allies but with Moscow as well. Thus, it explicitly de-linked the Geneva negotiations on TNF from the Polish situation on the grounds of their "unique character and significance," and it guardedly looked forward to a summit meeting between Presidents Reagan and Brezhnev.

To some critical observers, these actions merely confirmed a pattern of talking loudly while carrying an inadequate stick. But underlying the Administration's actions were substantial considerations of Realpolitik. The threat of military intervention to deter Soviet intervention was, of course, excluded. Massive multilateral economic aid, with political strings, to prevent repression by the Polish government was of doubtful economic or political efficacy and was politically unfeasible to organize with the Allies anyway. That left rhetoric and sanctions as a protest and deterrent, and the promise of economic aid as an incentive toward a peaceful accommodation and a rescue operation if accommodation were achieved.

The Administration had not yet devised a comprehensive strategy for East-West trade, but it was skeptical of the utility of economic sanctions as an instrument to affect Soviet actions or weaken Soviet power to carry out its actions—a view amply supported by the whole history of sanctions. (In April President Reagan's lifting of the partial grain embargo that President Carter had imposed on the Soviets in response to the invasion of Afghanistan reflected this skepticism as well as the payment of a political promise to American farmers.) On the other hand, no Administration, and least of all one as vehemently anti-communist as President Reagan's, could fail to express its condemnation of Polish repression by the most widely accepted tangible means available to major trading countries in modern international politics: punitive or demonstrative economic sanctions.

In imposing such sanctions, however, the Administration was mindful that, for sanctions to be effective economically or symbolically, the European allies and especially Germany would have to take parallel action or at least not rush in to supplant American exports. Partly because they were major trading partners with the Soviet bloc they were reluctant to curb exports, either for the purpose of putting pressure on the Polish government or to hold Moscow responsible for repression. Therefore, the Administration was anxious that sanctions at least not divide the United States from its allies, as they had tended to do after the Soviet invasion of Afghanistan. It was also anxious that sanctions not foreclose the opportunity for East-West accommodations—especially in arms negotiations, where suspension of the TNF talks would be far more damaging to the United States in its relations with the allies than to the Soviet Union, which would seize upon the suspension to exploit U.S.-allied differences. In the end, sanctions could hardly improve conditions in Poland, but they could easily worsen relations with the allies and the Soviet Union. More constructive might be multinational implementation of the President's proposal of a program for economic restoration if the Poles were to achieve a stable and liberal resolution of their internal affairs.

Whether the Reagan Administration would succeed in translating these several considerations and objectives into successful policies would depend, in the final analysis, on developments in Poland that are fundamentally beyond American influence. But if it were to emerge from the Polish crisis with a realistic prospect of more constructive relations with its allies and with Moscow, it would not only have earned valuable credit for statesmanship. It would also have demonstrated a familiar fact of American political life: it is easier for a conservative Republican than for a liberal

Democratic administration to exercise restraint and secure reciprocity in dealing with recalcitrant allies and with the principal adversary.

If the Reagan Administration could capitalize on this political advantage, it might eventually be known best for an achievement it seemed least to seek when it came into office. Having put the Vietnam syndrome to rest and consolidated the restoration of the American economy and defense, it might be known best for constructing a safer and more secure relationship with the Soviet Union. Such a relationship could be more substantial than the atmospheric détente of the late 1950s or the ephemeral détente of the 1970s precisely because it was neither a superficial escape valve for public anxieties nor the core of a grand design for a global modus vivendi, but the consequence of an integrated set of policies that brought American power into balance with vital interests on an enduring basis.

Raymond Aron

IDEOLOGY IN SEARCH OF A POLICY

Three signal events marked the year 1981 (at least, from the point of view of a Frenchman): the arrival of Ronald Reagan at the White House in January; the election of François Mitterrand to the presidency of the French Republic followed by the election of an absolute majority of the Socialists to the National Assembly in the spring; and, of course, the assassination of President Anwar Sadat in October. At the same time, no crises were settled during the past year (not even the Polish one), no wars begun, and none ended. The official calendar did not coincide with a historic period in any part of the world.

In the Middle East, Iran and Iraq continue their military operations without any decisive breakthrough on either side. In Iran, the Islamic Republic has held on in spite of attempts against the lives of the highest officials of the regime. In the Middle East the Camp David accords continue to be implemented; both the new Egyptian President Hosni Mubarak and Israeli Prime Minister Menachem Begin solemnly swear that the evacuation of the Sinai will take place, as scheduled, in the spring of 1982. On the other hand, the negotiations on the autonomy of the West Bank are leading nowhere. While a precarious cease-fire has been concluded in Lebanon between the forces of Israel and the Palestine Liberation Organization (PLO) by the American intermediary, Philip Habib, the most serious question, involving the Syrian missiles in Lebanon, has yet to be settled.

In Eastern Europe, the Polish crisis continues: General Wojciech Jaruzelski, chief of the armed forces and of the Communist Party, proclaimed martial law, eliminated all civilian authority, and installed a military regime. The workers' organization, Solidarity, was crushed, but the people's will to resist endured. In Western Europe, the modernization of Euromissiles through the proposed deployment of intermediate-range U.S. Pershing II and cruise missiles on European soil resulted in protests both from sincere

Raymond Aron, the French political philosopher, is a Member of the Académie des Sciences morales et politiques. He is the author of *The Century of Total War, The Opium of Intellectuals, Peace and War Among Nations,* among many other works.

pacifists and from movements manipulated by Moscow. Arms negotiations between the United States and the Soviet Union had only just begun by the end of the year.

In Africa, the destiny of Namibia remains unsettled, and the contact group (the United States, Great Britain, Canada, France and West Germany) has not reached an agreement with the South African government on the conditions for the elections in Namibia.

In Asia, the Soviet troops have not left Afghanistan. The same man, Babrak Karmal, is officially in power. Popular resistance has not been crushed, but neither has it made any great progress.

Within such a context, it seems advisable to take the new American Administration as a starting point. Not that it has achieved any successes or suffered any defeats in its first year, nor even that it has surmounted any obstacles; on the contrary, neither success nor failure nor ordeals seem particularly striking to me. Ronald Reagan concentrated his attention on economic problems and reduced negotiations with the Soviet Union to a minimum. It is therefore better to discuss those ideas which the Administration in Washington openly espouses rather than its policies, which are still far from concrete definition. Ideology in search of a policy—such seems to me to characterize the state of Ronald Reagan's Administration at the end of 1981.

II

Perhaps the most noticeable feature of the Reagan approach to foreign policy is its use of rhetoric from the cold war; the President and his advisers denounce Soviet expansionism and perceive a Soviet presence underlying all the turmoil which disturbs mankind around the world. But anti-Soviet rhetoric does not help in sorting out the different schools of thought in the United States. In fact, in the political realm, commentators on international relations remain profoundly divided over the nature of the politics and plans of the Kremlin.

To begin with the facts and debates that they give rise to: Is the Soviet Union assured of military superiority over the United States? No simple and categorical response can be given to a question of this sort since in advance we possess only quantitative and not qualitative knowledge; the true value of weapons and armies can only be tested in combat. That said, quantitative knowledge, which can be measured, and qualitative estimates, which can be gained over time, provide us with at least some means of judging the nature of the Soviet military buildup.

On such a basis, it seems undeniable that the Soviet Union possesses a stock of weapons far superior to that of the United States and an industrial weapons production capacity equally superior. For example, according to *The Military Balance* published by the London-based International Institute for Strategic Studies, the Americans have 11,400 tanks as compared to 45,000 for the Soviets, and a comparable divergence is evident in most of the other ground-based weapons. It is a simple truth that the size of the Soviet military industry surpasses that of the American military industry as it now stands. (It goes without saying that the United States could compete industrially if it chose to, but this decision would probably demand a war economy.) In the year 1980, for example, the Soviet Union produced 3,000 tanks, 5,500 armored vehicles, 1,300 towed field artillery, 150 self-propelled field artillery, 1,300 fighter bombers, 200 intercontinental ballistic missiles (ICBMs), 100 intermediate-range ballistic missiles (IRBMs), 300 short-range ballistic missiles (SRBMs), 700 submarine-launched cruise missiles (SLCMs), 175 submarine-launched ballistic missiles (SLBMs), 11 submarines, et cetera.

Should one attach that much importance to 50,000 tanks, 20,000 artillery pieces, or 5,000 helicopters? Some will object that these global figures demonstrate nothing very significant, that logistics will not permit the deployment of all these weapons on a battlefield, that the Soviet armed forces are spread out along several fronts, and that large battles comparable to those of the Second World War are inconceivable from now on, at least between great powers armed with nuclear weapons.

Let us put these global figures aside, then, and look at the central strategic balance. The SALT II strategic arms accord, although not ratified by the U.S. Senate, is in fact being respected by the two parties (assuming that verification by satellites is essentially viable). According to the treaty, the United States possesses 1,054 ICBMs, of which 550 are mounted with multiple independently targeted reentry vehicles (MIRVs), 656 SLBMs, of which 496 have MIRVs, and 573 heavy bombers, some equipped with cruise missiles. On its side, the Soviet Union possesses 1,398 ICBMs, of which 608 have MIRVs, 950 SLBMs, of which 144 are equipped with MIRVs, and 156 heavy bombers.

Does an equilibrium then exist? The American triad of strategic weapons comprises a relatively reduced portion of ICBMs, probably because American leaders assume that they will never strike first and because they rely more on submarine-launched missiles, which are less vulnerable to a first strike. If it is clear that each of the two superpowers has the capacity to inflict on the other "unacceptable destruction" in response to a first strike, equilibrium is established. But, the pessimists reply, to respond to a preemptive counterforce first strike against U.S. land-based missiles by bombing Soviet cities is to risk a similar response against American cities.

The Soviet Union produces large missiles whose payload capacity is considerably greater than that of American missiles; in particular, the SS-18, which SALT II limited to 308, can carry eight nuclear warheads, each with an explosive force of two megatons. Thus, at least on paper, the more than 2,000 nuclear warheads of the SS-18s could put 1,000 American Minuteman ICBMs out of action. In recent years, Americans have been debating the degree of rearmament necessary to counter the 308 SS-18s in order to reduce the vulnerability of their ground-based missiles. The Reagan program of October 1981 calls for the construction of 100 B-1 bombers, and 100 land-based MX missiles in better protected silos. In comparison with the Carter program, this means, on the one hand, an addition and, on the other, a reduction. The B-1 had been scrapped by the Democratic President and the Republican President has reestablished it. The MX program, however, has been scaled back; instead of Carter's plan for 200 MX missiles, moving among 1,000 shelters, 100 MX missiles are to be placed in reinforced silos.

At any rate, the fundamental U.S. nuclear triad of land-, air- and sea-based forces will continue to exist, and each of its components will be reinforced: the ground component will receive the MX; the air leg will be strengthened by the B-1, and it, along with the old B-52 bombers, will be equipped with cruise missiles; and for the naval component, one Trident submarine per year is expected to be produced between 1983 and 1987. A larger and more precise ballistic missile (Trident 2 or D-5) will be placed on the Trident submarine sometime after 1989. At the same time, the means of control and communication will be improved in order to assure the maintenance of a reliable and secure command structure.

So far the Congress has only accepted the first year's increases in the Reagan long-term program. Nonetheless, some evaluation can be made at this stage of the American program of rearmament. Strictly speaking, it does not constitute a response to the alleged vulnerability of the most precise American land-based missiles, the only ones suitable for a counterforce strike. At a time when the Americans are deploying the Trident, tests of a Soviet

25,000-ton submarine are taking place; the Soviet submarine will be armed by the SS-N-8 with a range of 6,500 to 8,000 kilometers, probably with an improved missile. Even now, the Delta III submarine missiles fired from Soviet waters would be able to reach nearly any target in the United States.

These brief remarks do not pretend to measure the American effort or anticipate its results. If anything, they tend to refute simultaneously the claims of both the new Administration and its critics. The rearmament program, insofar as it concerns the central strategic balance, does not restore the superiority of the United States; it updates the U.S. arsenal at a time when the Minutemen as well as the submarines, which are armed with Polaris or Poseidon missiles, date back about twenty years; the B-52 also dates back about twenty years. On the Soviet side, the missiles, the submarines and the bombers were put in service during the 1970s. The President is thus trying to catch up from behind, while the opposition reproaches him for setting an arms race in motion. Yet between 1965 and 1980, the Soviet Union alone was in the running.

Ronald Reagan declares from time to time that in the event of an arms race, the United States will surely win it. This is a gratuitous and ambiguous declaration. The gross domestic product of the United States amounts to perhaps double that of the Soviet Union, but in this case such a comparison is of very little significance. The Soviet Union maintains a war industry which is always in production; the United States could also provide itself with a powerful war industry, but arms orders go to private enterprises which produce for the private market as well. If naval orders increase, shipyards will enlarge their means of production. But it takes time. As long as the United States is not run on a war economy, it hasn't much of a chance to equal the potential and the capacity of Soviet military production.

Has the vulnerability of U.S. ground missiles then created a "window of opportunity" during which time the Soviets could be tempted by a counterforce first strike? I have never taken such a scenario seriously. The Soviets have always been prudent, or more precisely, they have never been "adventurist"; missiles do not always follow a fixed course; their accuracy as observed in tests will not necessarily be the same in a real shooting match. The leaders in the Kremlin—whoever they may be, the old men of today or another generation tomorrow—will surely hesitate before engaging in a poker game in which they would risk millions and millions of lives including their own.

The balance of strategic nuclear forces thus exerts a broad influence, which is very difficult to measure, on statesmen in Washington, in Moscow, and, indeed, in all world capitals. At a time of crisis those in positions of responsibility will surely examine the risks of escalation and each other's resources in the event that, despite everything, escalation should take place. Former Secretary of State Henry Kissinger exclaimed one evening: "For God's sake, what is the meaning of superiority when it comes to strategic nuclear forces?" Yet ever since then he has taken the opposite view. Personally, I would take an intermediate position: the possible scenarios for an exchange of missiles haunt men's minds rather than determine their decisions.

What results from the current state of the nuclear forces of the two superpowers seems to be the following: the threat of escalation no longer belongs to the United States alone, the counterthreat of Soviet escalation is at least as plausible as the American threat. Whether it is a question of short-range missiles, the SS-21 and SS-22, intermediate-range missiles, the SS-20, or the intercontinental missiles, the Soviets are, at every level, at least equal and perhaps superior.

If they are reasonable, Europeans ought to draw a lesson from this analysis: in an age of nuclear parity, the balance of conventional forces acquires greater weight. Instead of wondering if and to what extent the nuclear umbrella of the United States continues to protect them, why should Europeans not ask themselves if and how they could contribute to deterring the aggressor and to defending their own territory? In an article such as this there is no room to analyze the relationship between conventional and nuclear forces on the central front and to specify the possible contribution of the Europeans themselves. But, at the root of the present German-American malaise, I perceive moral repercussions due to the relative military decline of the United States. Moreover, these are repercussions which are often emotional, since the Europeans wish, above all, to preserve détente and, in turn, dread both weakness and a provocative rearmament on the part of the United States.

III

By its very nature, Western Europe's dependence on the United States for its own defense is unhealthy. It is the Americans who elaborate the defense doctrine and who command the forces of the Atlantic Alliance. At the same time, they control the international monetary system and profit from the status of the dollar.

Transnational or international in nature, American currency throughout the entire world allows the United States to accept deficits in its current accounts. Americans settle their foreign commercial transactions in their own currency—a privilege reserved for the only country whose currency functions as a standard of value and a means of exchange for the entire world market.

Europe's military helplessness thus results from circumstances, some permanent, others accidental, that do not wholly curb Europe's aspirations. West Germany includes only two-thirds of the German people; adjoining the Soviet zone, it refuses to lose hope for reunification and is wary of doing anything the Kremlin would judge as provocative. Germany, moreover, does not possess nuclear arms. France, on the other hand, withdrew from NATO's integrated command without leaving the Atlantic Alliance or even NATO itself, and built her own strategic nuclear forces. The French government assures the people that the national territory is sheltered from aggression and has been transformed into a sanctuary, since, if France is attacked, she would make the aggressor pay a price far out of proportion to the value of France herself. This is a doctrine more easily accepted by the French because it relies exclusively on the notion of deterrence and seems to exclude the possibility of war. Under these circumstances, a European defense, which should take as its nucleus Franco-German cooperation, becomes impossible. Great Britain, out of a firm belief in the Atlantic Alliance, and the other European countries, out of resignation, continue to rely on American protection.

For two decades now, Western Europe has found itself vulnerable to Soviet medium-range (340 SS-4) and intermediate-range (40 SS-5) missiles. Since 1977, however, the Soviets have been deploying intermediate-range SS-20s, each of which is armed with three nuclear warheads. The SS-20 is mobile, therefore practically invulnerable, and very accurate (with an estimated average targeting error of less than 500 feet). Indeed, it was West German Chancellor Helmut Schmidt who first alerted the Americans to the danger that was threatening Europe with the arrival of the SS-20 in the Soviet arsenal. The political battle over Euromissiles is now in his hands.

Militarily, what is at stake? The Americans proposed, and the European governments agreed, to place 108 Pershing II and 464 cruise missiles (both of which are capable of attacking the western provinces of the Soviet Union) on European territory. According to current strategic thinking, the function of these Euromissiles is to avoid "decoupling" the European theater from the U.S.-Soviet central strategic balance. If the Soviets were to take a military initiative, whatever it might be, they ought to strike at these missiles and simultaneously strike at U.S. missiles on American soil. Alternatively, according to another line of thinking, the Euromissiles, in the event of a flexible response, create the risk of nuclear escalation. Any missiles reaching Soviet territory, wherever their starting point, would be considered by the Soviets as aggression by the United States itself. In other words, the Pershing II and cruise missiles were supposed to reassure the Europeans by reducing the risk of a war limited to Europe. Now the Europeans, or at least those who have protested against the modernization of Euromissiles, have reversed the argument: they now see a threat of nuclear war actually limited to Europe itself, with the latter serving as a nuclear battlefield while the territories of the two superpowers are spared.

The decision which was taken by NATO—deployment of the Pershing II and cruise missiles in 1983 and negotiations with Moscow with the possibility of renouncing this gradual deployment in exchange for Soviet concessions—has been maintained, although neither the Netherlands nor Belgium is considered entirely firm on this matter. Chancellor Schmidt, moreover, insists that other countries in the Alliance as well as his own must agree to accept the Euromissiles on their territory; his acceptance is therefore conditional, subject to the acceptance of at least one other member of the Alliance.

What has happened in this regard in 1981? In April, the Socialist International, following its conference in Amsterdam, urged the two superpowers to start negotiations as rapidly as possible on the limitation of theater nuclear weapons in Europe. Soviet President Leonid Brezhnev invited West German Socialist leader Willy Brandt to the Kremlin on June 29–30 in order to apprise him of his moratorium plan.[1] On July 15 and 16, the Presidium of the Socialist International made an appeal to the superpowers to reopen the SALT negotiations and start up negotiations on Euromissiles. On the other hand, François Mitterrand, after his election to the presidency of the Republic, supported the American argument, which urges the necessity of reestablishing the equilibrium broken by the SS-20.

The popular demonstrations, which have brought together up to hundreds of thousands of people, are multiplying in West

---

[1] The Soviet Union halts the deployment of the SS-20, but the Europeans rescind their decision to deploy any theater nuclear missiles.

Germany. According to the polls, the majority of the Germans remain favorable to the Atlantic Alliance and the military presence of the United States in Europe but are worried about nuclear weapons. Thus, by an irony of history, a plan conceived in order to strengthen ties between the Old Continent and the United States in order to demonstrate unity between the two parts of the Alliance risks creating a kind of moral divorce between the European governments and their public opinion, and between the European governments and Washington.[2]

The Reagan team may well have inadvertently contributed to the progress of the pacifist movement through its language, its refusal to resume SALT negotiations, and the martial tone of its speeches. It led the Europeans to believe that the United States was claiming a military superiority that had already vanished and was, at the same time, triggering an acceleration in the arms race. The figures demonstrate that this is not so. The Reagan program, even if executed, would not give America superiority either on the ground or in the air. Yet the edginess of European public opinion manifests itself in every encounter. In a conversation with a journalist in November, President Reagan, responding to a specific question, said that the utilization of nuclear weapons in Europe did not necessarily imply total nuclear war unleashed by strategic nuclear weapons, although it was unlikely such a war could be limited. From this, European newspapers and commentators concluded that the American President was suggesting limited nuclear war as a plausible scenario, if not the expression of a doctrine.

In order to back up Chancellor Schmidt on the eve of Leonid Brezhnev's visit to Bonn, Reagan proposed the "zero option" formula. Since President Brezhnev was speaking constantly of peace and disarmament, the American President determined to beat him at his own game. Reagan was not content to propose reducing the number of missiles to a provisional limit or to defer the decision on the deployment of the Pershing IIs; he was eliminating in one stroke all the intermediate-range missiles on both sides. A poker game? By no means. A propaganda coup?

---

[2] Judging from the polls, German opinion remains favorable to the American alliance, i.e., to security by deterrence. Fifty-three percent of the people interviewed last July approved the policy of the government, with 22 percent against. At the same time, 56 percent have good feelings toward Americans, compared to 18 percent against. (The question asked was: *Mögen Sie eigentlich die Amerikaner oder mögen Sie besonders nicht?*)

A majority of Germans continue to doubt Brezhnev's peace initiatives, but this majority varies according to circumstances. However, a majority of the Germans believe in the military superiority of the U.S.S.R. over the United States. A majority of Germans is also hostile to the neutron bomb. It seems to me, then, that the mass demonstrations and the press reports do not accurately reflect German opinion.

Certainly. But what is to follow?

Let us distinguish between two interconnected problems: the defense of Europe and the unity of the Atlantic Alliance, both of which are threatened by popular reactions to military initiatives.

The zero option is obviously unacceptable to the Soviets. Ronald Reagan is asking the Soviets to renounce the SS-20, already deployed, as against weapons which will perhaps be available in 1983. The exchange would not be an equal one. The SALT accords, like many interstate agreements, recorded in large measure the state of the military balance of the two powers. No one around a green table obtained any advantages which had not already been acquired on the ground. The 1973 Paris accords did not oblige the North Vietnamese troops to retreat from the South; SALT II has not appreciably reduced the dangers posed to the American Minuteman force by the Soviet heavy missiles and, in particular, by the SS-18. The Soviets will only renounce this trump card on the day when the United States has the ability to imperil Soviet ground missiles.

The negotiations which began at the end of 1981 have no chance of reaching an accord in a few weeks or even months. From the outset, the Soviets and Americans do not even agree on the actual balance of forces. If the SS-20 replaces the SS-4 and the SS-5, is or is not the equilibrium tipped in favor of the Soviet Union?

How can we evaluate the forward-based systems, the advanced bases, the F-111, and the F-4? Is it necessary to include in any count the nuclear forces of Great Britain and France? The question of the SS-20 cannot be separated from the whole panoply of strategic forces which should be the subject of SALT III. In the meantime, the new Administration, without denouncing SALT II, does not conceal its hostility to a treaty which was not ratified by the Senate. In fact, Eugene Rostow, now director of the Arms Control and Disarmament Agency, played an important role in the hard-line Committee on the Present Danger.

At the time of this writing, the new Administration has not made known its doctrine, and has perhaps not even established one, for future negotiations. What we do know is that "reduction" will replace "limitation" in the title of the treaty and in the minds of American negotiators. We also know that verification obtained exclusively by satellites seems inadequate to the Reagan team. In addition, the Administration, though it may not require any direct linkage between negotiations on arms and other aspects of Soviet-American relations, persists, it seems to me, in thinking that the negotiations make no sense unless the two superpowers operate within a positive climate of mutual restraint.

IV

The troubles in the Soviet zone go beyond those of Western Europe. I am thinking, above all, about the events in Poland. And I use the word event purposely (this was also the word applied to France in the weeks of May 1968) because it wavers between the words revolt, revolution and liberation. The Polish people in the wake of the shipyard workers' strike liberated themselves from the yoke of the single party system, won at least partial freedom of speech, and organized a non-Party union to which peasants, workers and intellectuals adhered. In the course of 1981 the Soviets continued to denounce Solidarity as counterrevolutionary, but they refused to risk the same type of military operation that they did not hesitate to unleash against Hungary and Czechoslovakia.

In Hungary, the revolution was violent. The army joined with the insurgents against the secret police. The pluralism of the parties rose up of its own accord even though the premier of the revolutionary government was an old and loyal communist. The Kremlin risked loosening the cohesion of the Soviet imperium in Europe if it tolerated the victory of the revolutionaries. Only ten years had passed since the end of the war, and three years since the death of Stalin: the loss of one piece risked the whole.

In Czechoslovakia, a change in the majority in the Politburo of the Party's Central Committee brought some reformists into power. Then Secretary-General Alexander Dubček and his companions were not considering breaking with either the Soviet Union or even with democratic centralism: the explosion of liberty was not willed but only tolerated by the new leaders of the Party. What exasperated the Soviets the most in Czechoslovakia, it seems to me, was to see the end of the empty language of Marxism and the return of the ordinary, true sense of words. The men in the Kremlin calculated that an invasion would not run into any resistance. Their allies—including the East Germans—participated in the action. In a few days the Dubček team was liquidated, and in a few weeks order was reestablished in Czechoslovakia.

In Poland, the Soviet army or armies of the Warsaw Pact would not have run into a combat army fighting against the police, as in Hungary. The Polish revolt was general but nonviolent. The Kremlin could also not count on the nonresistance of the army. Moreover, it would not be easy to reconstruct a Communist Party, as the Soviets had successfully done in 1956 in Hungary as well as in 1968 in Czechoslovakia. The Polish phenomenon is *sui generis*, without precedent. The workers, in alliance with the intellectuals, demanded their rights to a free union and, simultaneously, the official union fell apart; the Party itself had been losing authority all along.

The situation was totally new in Eastern Europe; the decision taken by General Wojciech Jaruzelski, chief of the armed forces and First Secretary of the Party, was equally new. He declared martial law, created a Military Council of National Salvation, "suspended" all civilian authority, all personal liberties, closed the country to foreign observers, and cut all contact by phone or air with the outside world. On Sunday, December 13, the security forces and the army rounded up thousands of people (5,000, according to the official statistics, 15,000 to 20,000 more probably), among them all the leaders and advisers of Solidarity. Poland was occupied by its own army.

The General and his spokesmen suggest that, by doing the dirty work, they seized the last chance to avoid an invasion by the armies of the Warsaw Pact, which the extremists of the Party were demanding from Moscow. There is no way, at the present time, to choose between the different interpretations. What remains beyond any doubt, however, is the role of the Kremlin in the Polish drama. Leonid Brezhnev knew and approved of the military coup, which was perhaps made inevitable by his threats. The Russian troops, permanently stationed in Poland, provided, at the very least, logistical aid to the Polish forces.

Shocked by the brutal repression, deprived of its leaders, the Polish people, after two weeks, were reduced to only passive resistance. The last pockets of resistance, in the Silesian coal mines, finally had to give in. Order and silence now reign in a country subjected to a military regime similar to the worst forms of foreign occupation. Even to travel from one town to another requires authorization. Is the crisis therefore solved? Certainly not. General Jaruzelski accused Solidarity of paralyzing production efforts. But why should the workers produce more under the army, which does not offer them anything and strips from them even the freedoms which they had won for themselves?

The military coup of December 13 was as much a surprise for the Western governments as for the Polish people. They had agreed on the measures they would take together if Soviet troops or members of the Warsaw Pact should intervene in Poland. But they had not envisaged a military regime by the Polish army. To what extent was the Kremlin responsible for the event? Did Leonid Brezhnev suggest or impose this "normalization?" Should sanctions be directed at the Soviet or the Polish government or at both? The Europeans did not agree among themselves on the answers to those questions; neither did they agree with President Reagan.

After a few days of hesitation, the American President chose the hard line and announced economic and diplomatic sanctions. The Bonn government took the opposite view. After all, it was a Polish affair, even if the Soviet Union had exercised a major influence on the Polish actors. In France, the government and the Socialist Party were outspoken in their moral condemnation of this violation of human rights. But it is difficult to know how far President Mitterrand is ready to go in deeds rather than just words. In any case, the first crunch for the Reagan Administration (Israel annexed the Golan Heights while the whole world was fixed on Poland) did make clear the profound disagreement between Bonn and Washington: the West German Chancellor first and foremost wanted to safeguard détente and good relations with Eastern Europe; President Reagan's first priority was to demonstrate visible opposition to Moscow.

The military coup is not by itself the solution of the Polish crisis. Tanks and guns can crush a rebellion, they do not suppress a movement like Solidarity. Without the Church, General Jaruzelski will not be able to govern Poland. And without Lech Walesa, the Church will not cooperate with the army. Nothing has been settled. The army has replaced the Party, revealing the essence of the Russian empire, a military empire whose ideology is dying. The absence of the Party on December 13 was a clear symbol of this.

v

In the Middle East, the Reagan team is pursuing a policy determined by the Camp David accords. It is, in fact, trying to do better by associating the moderate Arab countries with Egypt and Israel, with a view toward a military coalition that would form a barrier to any eventual thrust from the Soviet Union. The assassination of Egypt's President Sadat did not move American leaders to revise their plan. In November, a short time after the death of the Egyptian President who had chosen peace and the American camp, Egyptian-American joint maneuvers took place.

Superficially, nothing appears to have changed. The new President, Hosni Mubarak, can hardly say otherwise for two reasons:

he worked in close cooperation with Sadat and he has to respect the Camp David accords in order to obtain the planned evacuation of the last part of the Sinai in April 1982. But the new President does not belong to the generation of free officers who overturned the monarchy and have governed the country ever since. He doesn't enjoy the same prestige as his predecessor and probably will strive to pull his country out of the isolation to which the peace treaty with Israel had condemned it.

None of the events of the last year encourage hope for a comprehensive settlement. On June 7, the Israeli air force destroyed the nuclear installations constructed by the French in Iraq. Prime Minister Begin declared that the reactor would soon have become operational, that Iraq had not signed the nonproliferation treaty, and that it did not conceal its intention to destroy the state of Israel. Under these circumstances, he could not accept the risk that the Iraqis would construct an atomic bomb. The Israeli raid, a technical feat, was condemned by all the countries of the world, even the United States; after going along with everyone else in a symbolic censure of Israel, the French government immediately suggested that it would be disposed to rebuilding the Iraqi reactor.

The Europeans continue to support their plan for a general settlement, namely the formation of a Palestinian state on the West Bank following conversations between Israel and the Palestine Liberation Organization (PLO) on mutual recognition. The American leaders also seem to discreetly favor this solution, but it still remains little more than a long-range goal. In the meantime, the Israelis remain single-minded. They continue to establish settlements on the West Bank—which the Americans deplore but are incapable of preventing. Finally, Reagan won his battle with Congress and was authorized to sell five Airborne Warning and Control Systems (AWACS) surveillance planes to the Saudis despite Israeli protestations. What took place in 1981 did not alter the deadlock. It made it worse.

No Israeli government will accept a Palestinian government in the West Bank which would inevitably be taken over by the PLO. Menachem Begin, reelected in 1981 to a four-year term, will not make any concessions regarding the Jewish settlements on the West Bank. His rival, Shimon Peres, could have been and might still be less rigid on this point, but he also believes that the Palestinian state exists in Jordan. On the other hand, the Fahd Plan, put forth by the Saudis—which seems to imply the recognition of Israel and which was refused by Israel—has not been approved by the Arab countries as a whole. The simple truth is that at the moment there is no chance that a general settlement will be reached.

Whether conscious or not of this impossibility, U.S. Secretary of State Alexander Haig visited the region and then sent roving Ambassador Philip Habib there in order to dismantle bombs (for example, the Syrian missiles in Lebanon that Prime Minister Begin threatened to destroy if they were not removed). It stands to reason that American diplomacy suffers from the contradiction between its alliance with Israel and its friendship with the Saudis. The United States is unable to sacrifice either the alliance or the friendship, and it is also unable to reconcile the inherent contradiction between them. The immediate goal remains the same: to avoid a new round of fighting between Syria and Israel.

Some people in the United States argue for a return to Geneva, that is to say, invite the Soviet Union to take part in the negotiations. But it is hard to see how Soviet participation would contribute to a general settlement, unless it compels Israel to evacuate the territories that it has occupied since 1967 and to tolerate the creation of a Palestinian state.

Finally, in December, during the Polish crisis, Prime Minister Begin proclaimed the annexation of the Golan Heights through a vote by the Knesset. He then replied to an American sanction by denouncing the U.S. suspension of the strategic agreement between Israel and the United States. At the end of 1981, the conflict between the Arabs and Israel seemed more intractable than ever.

Meanwhile, the war between Iraq and Iran prevents one of the rejectionist states from intervening actively against Israel. Moreover, Khomeini's Iran, unlike the Shah's, has demonstrated greater hostility toward Israel. Iraq was hoping to bring off a quick victory and perhaps overthrow the regime of the Imam. Yet, despite the purging of its military, Iran's army, aided by the guardians of the Revolution, demonstrated that it was still relatively efficient; the Iraqis dared not attack the cities. Thus, the troops of the two countries maintained a small war of position; in 1981, in fact, it was the Iranians who pulled off a few successes.

But more than this war, it is the domestic evolution of Iran (largely forgotten by the press) that will influence the world situation. The Iranian revolution has already reached its extreme violent phase of state terrorism. Now it is the object of counterterrorism, that of the Mujahedeen, and simultaneously it must combat the Kurdish rebellion. The question that observers and statesmen ask themselves bears on the future of Iran: What will happen after the death of the Imam and the probable crisis of the Iranian Republic? For the moment the Tudeh Party, obeying the dictates of the Soviet Union, supports the Islamic Republic and the party of the Imam, while awaiting its hour. Who will win the contest for power, the Tudeh Party, the army, or the Mujahedeen, when the people no longer support the regime of the mullahs and when the voice of the Imam is silent and no longer mesmerizes the masses?

One final word: the United States can almost certainly do nothing to influence in one way or another the evolution of the Iranian revolution.

VI

In Africa and Central America several crises constituted a challenge to the new Administration: Chad and Namibia on the one hand, Nicaragua and El Salvador on the other.

Libya's intervention in Chad was just one more irritant to upset Americans over the impetuous Colonel Muammar el-Qaddafi who rules in Tripoli. Then, in the month of November, Qaddafi suddenly decided to withdraw his troops from Chad following the demand formulated by the head of the government, Goukouni Oueddei. The French government in the meantime had become reconciled with Goukouni and had promised him some light arms. Moreover, the French were acting in accord with African governments in order to make up a military force designed to symbolize and guarantee the national unity of the country. The withdrawal of the Libyan troops constitutes a success for a French policy that was supported by the Americans. On the other hand, the future of Chad remains uncertain: the Muslim north and the animist south do not have much in common. The forces of former Defense Minister Hissen Habré are making progress. Neither the reestablishment of peace nor the reconstruction of the regime is as yet guaranteed.

The case of Namibia, formerly a German colony (South West Africa), then under the mandate of the League of Nations entrusted to South Africa, indirectly affects the major interests of the great powers. The authority which is installed in Angola with the aid of Cuban troops claims itself to be Marxist-Leninist but has resumed relations with the West. The national liberation movement in Namibia (the South West African People's Organization or SWAPO) has its outside bases in southern Angola. American policy can waver between two tactics: either it can support

Angolan insurgents of UNITA (National Union for the Total Independence of Angola) in order to destabilize the regime in Luanda; or else it can abandon UNITA to its fate and exert pressure on South Africa so that it consents to elections in Namibia in the hope that once the buffer state is free and at peace, the Angolan government will request the withdrawal of Cuban troops. It does not appear that as yet Reagan has definitively chosen between these two tactics.

Namibia in itself is of little importance but it touches on a stake of incalculable importance in the international system, namely the destiny of South Africa. As it happens, the territory of South Africa contains raw materials indispensable to war industries— magnesium, chrome, titanium, lithium, gold, diamonds, etc. For certain raw materials, such as chrome, which is of primary importance, the West does not now have substitute sources at its disposal. If South Africa were to fall under the control of a foreign power, the American arms industry would be, at least for a time, paralyzed. Understanding this, we can also understand the ambiguity that the Americans and the Europeans (the latter, more hypocritically) display toward South Africa. On the one hand, they have to condemn apartheid and the yawning gulf between the privileged whites and the black masses. On the other hand, they don't want to see the disintegration of a modern and effective economy which by itself constitutes some 50 percent of the gross national product of all sub-Saharan Africa.

Finally, above all else, they know that they cannot do without chrome, magnesium and titanium from this country. Yet neither the Europeans nor the American leaders have a plan for a solution in the near future. They invite the leaders of Pretoria to proceed with reforms but they don't know themselves which reforms will contribute to an orderly evolution and not to civil war.

The only reform which conforms to the current ideology of the West is one man-one vote, in other words, universal suffrage. But this reform would precipitate the breakdown of the entire system. Westerners thus recommend the reform without believing in it. In the Security Council of the United Nations, the United States opposes through its veto sanctions against Pretoria. As for Namibia, however, the contact group tirelessly conducts a mediation process between South Africa and the United Nations.

The Carter team seemed careful not to alienate itself from the African countries, while avoiding a confrontation with the leaders of South Africa. The Reagan team, in its first phase, has leaned in the other direction. On March 20, 1981, U.S. Ambassador to the United Nations Jeane J. Kirkpatrick declared that the United States would take its national interests into consideration in its relations with South Africa. In addition, she had conversations with five ranking officers of the South African Intelligence Service. On the other hand, the Secretary of State reaffirmed several times his desire to see Namibian independence come to pass.

Yet a settlement has still not been found. South Africa's Prime Minister P.W. Botha has repeated several times that he will not deliver Namibia over to SWAPO, which he considers tied to the Soviet Union. On the other hand, the U.S. Assistant Secretary of State for African Affairs, Chester Crocker, has affirmed that SWAPO, which has received weapons from the Soviet Union, is not totally subject to Moscow's wishes. Once again, the Reagan team is being pulled in different directions. It still strives to arrange elections which will lead to the independence of Namibia and the departure of the Cuban troops from Angola. Alone among the Western nations it does not recognize the authority of the Luanda regime and maintains relations with Jonas Savimbi and UNITA.

South Africa pursues its military actions against SWAPO in Angola just as Israel does against the PLO in Lebanon. Different as the two states are—in many respects both are pariahs banned from the international community—they have tightened their bonds. Taiwan appears in the same category: like South Africa it is undergoing exceptional expansion and prosperity.

In Central America the Sandinistas, victors in a ruthless civil war in Nicaragua, are turning themselves into a Castroite regime. During the fighting they maintained a broad coalition in which the liberal bourgeoisie and several economic leaders participated. Since then, they have organized an army greater in numbers and better equipped than Somoza's ever was; members of the Sandinista party are already being sent out to control the *quartiers* of the cities and villages. Although the Sandinista spokesmen continue to declare that they will respect pluralism and freedom of the press, it has become more and more difficult to take their word for it. The arrest of four leaders of private enterprises, the repeated suspension of the major liberal journal, *La Prensa*, the positions taken in foreign policy leave little doubt about the nature of the regime and its ideological affinities. Furthermore, the economic situation, despite considerable foreign aid, has forced the government to take some extreme measures (for example, declaring a state of economic emergency and prohibiting strikes for a year, etc.)

In the weeks that followed the inauguration, the Reagan Administration highlighted the case of El Salvador, where a civil war rages that has been marked by particularly gruesome episodes (for example, in 1980, the assassination of three American nuns). Early on, the State Department transmitted to the Europeans dossiers which demonstrated the part taken by Nicaragua and Cuba, even more than by other communist countries, in arming the Democratic Revolutionary Front (FDR), the group which has organized the guerrillas after having failed to seize power in 1980. Initially, the new Administration seemed to want to make El Salvador a test of Alliance solidarity and of the resolution of the new President. But the seemingly limited value of the stakes at hand prompted the President's spokesman to return to a more moderate tone.

The new Administration continues the essential policies of its predecessor. It supports President José Napoleón Duarte who is striving to resist the armed struggle of the FDR which is led by Castroites or communists. At the same time, Duarte has had to fend off the conservatives who are hostile to the reforms that he had announced and which he is having great difficulty trying to impose. The commandos of the extreme Right and the extreme Left are multiplying their assaults, each more cruel than the last. Meanwhile, the United States has dispatched a few dozen military advisers and a few million dollars in economic aid and arms. In this respect, Ronald Reagan has not done much more than the previous Administration would have done, except in his words and threats. A conflagration threatens to overtake all of the countries of Central America, including Costa Rica which is the most democratic country in the region and whose army is the smallest and plays no real role. But as yet the Reagan team has not conceived a more general plan for the Caribbean/Central American region as a whole.

Yet El Salvador has produced the first direct collision between the French Socialist government and the Reagan Administration: in agreement with Mexico, the French government proposed negotiations between President Duarte and the Democratic Revolutionary Front in order to put an end to the civil war. This took place while the United States was supporting the current government, which had announced that elections would be held in 1982. Seeing that a number of Latin American states protested against the Franco-Mexican declaration, which was, however, applauded by Nicaragua, the incident had scarcely any repercussions.

VII

In order not to take up too much space, I have omitted the problems of Asia. A few remarks will have to suffice. Japan resisted

Reagan, as it did Carter, in his request for a greater defense effort. Japan keeps its defense spending fixed at about one percent of its gross national product. Perhaps it will some day decide to build up its own arms industry which it will then seek to develop for exports like its other leading industries.

Reagan's interest in Taiwan and his plan to sell Taipei advanced aircraft clearly upset the Chinese leaders in Beijing. The visits to Beijing of the Vice President and the Secretary of State diminished but did not eliminate the uneasiness in that quarter, even though the Secretary of State let it be known that the United States would welcome armaments orders from mainland China. By now the Chinese press is denouncing once again the two superpowers, just as it did during the time of Mao.

In Southeast Asia, Vietnamese troops control most of the Cambodian territory. The Pol Pot government, according to the United States, remains the legal government. Moreover, the Chinese are aiding the opponents of the regime, which was created and supported by the Vietnamese; however, the opposition has not yet succeeded in forming a common front.

The chief omission of this review of the year concerns the economy, which is not perhaps directly relevant to this study. However, it is important to note that the exchange rate of the dollar and the very high interest rates in the United States—two interconnected phenomena—have upset the Europeans far more than U.S. declarations about El Salvador. The world economy has not recovered its stability after the second oil shock. The recession in the United States during the second half of 1981 affected the industrialized world far more than the controversies over Euromissiles.

All that said, the conclusion of this article must deal with the diplomacy of the Reagan Administration. The debates in the United States, it seems to me, center on the intentions of the Soviet Union. Those who claim to be reasonable do not attribute to the Kremlin a plan to dominate the world: the old men in the Politburo want the Soviet Union recognized as a superpower without which no conflict can be settled. The moderates also recognize that the Kremlin seizes every opportunity to expand its zone of domination. A communist party exists in nearly all the countries of the world; some communists participate in national liberation movements and try to direct them as far as possible toward the Soviet model and the Soviet camp. From this it follows that the Soviet Union behaves not as a satiated state but as an expansionist state. This interpretation excludes any master plan, that is, a plan fixed in advance to dominate the entire world. It also excludes any plan to trigger a great war. But it does not exclude the dangers of what the Chinese call hegemonism.

The other school of thought, which Richard Pipes, a member of the Reagan team, represents, agrees that the Soviet leaders do not act according to a master plan; but it stresses that expansion is the major and permanent objective of those who govern the Soviet Union. The Soviet rulers continue to believe in a universal mission of communism, *their* communism. That the Soviets reduce as much as possible the risks inherent in the advancement of their aims no one will deny. But the risks, in their view, diminish progressively as they acquire more and more arms. The occupation of Afghanistan constituted a challenge to the international community and to the United States but was not a dangerous one. The United States was not disposed to employ any military means of resistance or, indeed, any effective retaliatory measures. The embargo on grain sales to the Soviet Union, maintained over several years, would perhaps have affected the care and feeding of the Soviet population—but the American farmers protested. The refusal of the Europeans to provide financial credits and to sell their technology to the U.S.S.R. would at least have embarrassed the Soviets, but the Europeans cling to détente and to East-West trade.

Clearly, most of the conflicts and the problems which face the United States will not be solved through the use of military force. But, among other things, what differentiates the 1980s from the 1970s—and still more from the 1960s—is the shifting balance of nuclear and conventional forces between the Soviet Union and the United States at the expense of the latter. Public opinion is almost unanimous in Europe as in America on the need for a certain degree of rearmament. What is still in question are the means, the manner and the style of rearmament.

The first MX missiles installed in reinforced silos will themselves also be vulnerable, although studies continue on techniques which would assure a quasi-invulnerability. In the absence of a draft, the U.S. Army finds it difficult to recruit manpower capable of making the best use of sophisticated weapons. The organization of a Rapid Deployment Force able to intervene in the Persian Gulf zone is being pursued, although this force will not be able to face Soviet divisions on the battlefield for several years. Logistics and geography work in favor of the Soviet Union.

What the Reagan Administration can be reproached for is having given the impression that it relies too much on military force and that it is proceeding with a massive rearmament while, in fact, its actions do not correspond to its professed aims. Outside the Near East, the United States, after the Iranian Revolution, finds itself in a position of inferiority. Moreover, difficulties there more often than not derive from domestic problems rather than from overt aggression. Today, Saudi Arabia fears an internal revolt far more than it does an invasion. Resistance to a revolt would require perhaps the military assistance of the United States. But to prevent a revolt, which would surely be preferable, requires on the part of the United States both discretion and savoir faire.

At the end of the year, then, the Reagan Administration still retains credit with its allies as well as with its adversaries. European governments are pleased with the American rearmament decision but are not about to take it as a model for themselves. A portion of European opinion reproaches Reagan for having put off conversations with Moscow, conveniently forgetting that the SALT accords have never led to anything other than a ratification of the existing military balance. Observers of Eastern Europe assure us that the economic crisis there affects the communist bloc and even, directly, the Soviet Union. But, despite all this, a totalitarian state with a deprived population remains the leading military power in the world: the West cannot avoid asking itself why.

William G. Hyland

U.S.-SOVIET RELATIONS: THE LONG ROAD BACK

A merican presidents have usually inherited poor relations with the Soviet Union. President Eisenhower, of course, was confronted by the tensions of Korea and President Kennedy by the Berlin crisis. Lyndon Johnson was a temporary exception, but Richard Nixon inherited Vietnam and the Czech crisis. Gerald Ford had to deal with a faltering détente, and Jimmy Carter was embroiled in early disputes. In January 1981, Ronald Reagan found himself in much the same position as his predecessors, except that relations were worse than usual. Indeed, relations were frozen. Even the outgoing Administration was pessimistic. The departing American Ambassador to the U.S.S.R., Thomas J. Watson, Jr., summed up the prevailing gloom: "I don't think the West has any conception of how dismal the future looks for East-West relations."

The incoming Administration, of course, was not likely to contest this appraisal, though its members analyzed the causes quite differently. They believed that Carter's reaction to the "most brazen imperial drive in history" by the Soviet Union had been too little and too late. The new President immediately set a new tone when he asserted that the Soviets reserved the "right to commit any crime, to lie, to cheat." Other pronouncements from the new Cabinet secretaries and their minions echoed the President, though not as crisply or dramatically.

The basic Reagan attitude toward the Soviet Union was no surprise: the President himself had enunciated it over many years; he had challenged the Ford presidency over détente, and had campaigned vigorously in 1980 on a strong anti-Soviet platform. Moreover, there was a large body of scholarly and political literature that buttressed and elaborated his general concept of the nature of the Soviet threat, its future direction, and the proper American response.

The Union of Soviet Socialist Republics was seen by the Reagan

William G. Hyland is currently a Senior Associate at the Carnegie Endowment for International Peace. He served in the Department of State in 1974–75 and as Deputy Director of the National Security Council Staff from 1975 to 1977.

Administration primarily as a military menace and only second-arily as an ideological and political adversary. This was because the appeal of the Soviet state as a model for development had long since declined. Most of Moscow's new clients claimed little ideological affinity with the theories of Marx or Engels and rejected the Stalinist economic monolith. They might appreciate Lenin's revolutionary tenacity or his organizational genius, but Leninism and Stalinism (or Brezhnevism) were remote from the conflicts in Angola or the Horn of Africa. In terms of economic performance, Moscow's influence would scarcely be spread on the basis of its superior agricultural achievements, and the forced industrialization model of the 1930s was irrelevant to the complexities of economic development in the 1970s and 1980s. The Soviet Union, of course, did have political weight. That was undeniable. And its patronage was valuable, whether measured in terms of potential protection in a regional crisis, votes at the United Nations, or material assistance.

Had this been the extent of the Soviet global threat, however, it would have been quite manageable with the traditional instruments of the 1970s and 1960s. But in the Reagan view, Soviet policy had gone well beyond geopolitical maneuvering. The U.S.S.R. had become a military giant. It was able and determined to project its power to distant areas, to intervene in regional military conflicts, to extend its position through a complex of foreign bases and a corps of proxy troops, and to seek and encourage new treaty relationships and regional alliances.

All of this, it was strenuously argued by the Reaganites, was a direct consequence of a significant shift in the balance of military power at every level. While America had allegedly put its confidence in the agreements and negotiations that comprised détente, the U.S.S.R. had not only failed to reciprocate, but had invested massive resources in its military establishment.

This accumulation of military power was not a product of the momentum of a massive bureaucracy. Rather, the Reaganites believed, it was a systematic and purposeful effort to meet the requirements laid down by Soviet doctrines which prescribed: (a) overall strategic superiority, (b) the necessity to prepare forces for both deterrence and actual warfighting, (c) the possibility of achieving victory in a general nuclear war, and (d) the decisiveness of striking first.

This analysis, despite the critical situation it suggested, did not cause the Administration to despair. For, on close examination, it could be seen that the fundamental underpinnings of the Soviet system were weakening—and this weakening was manifested in the accumulating internal and external crises. The Soviet state and Russian Communism had entered a historical decline.

Yet, it was argued that for the next few years this very trend was cause for even further apprehension. For if a Great Power saw that it had passed its zenith or soon would, and if that power was inherently aggressive and expansionist, it followed that it would desperately try to retrieve its historical fortunes through a series of forays and adventures. The Soviets, of course, were true believers in the "correlation of forces." History was predetermined in a broad Marxist sense, but the world position of the Soviet Union could be altered by skillful strategies and tactics, so long as the bedrock of massive military power remained unaffected. Thus, a unique and bizarre combination of strength and weakness made for a period of particular danger.

This was the challenge as seen by the Reagan Administration. As it was relatively simple and straightforward, so the American response had to be similarly simple and straightforward:

— to restore the military balance, achieving or preserving at least a true equality and preferably superiority in key equations (e.g., naval power). The Soviets were developing a nuclear war-fighting capability, the new Deputy Secretary of Defense testified, and "we are going to have to develop the same."

— to contain Soviet expansion and reverse it; Secretary of State Alexander M. Haig warned that Moscow was the "greatest source of international insecurity."

— to negotiate only from a position of genuine strength; refurbishing America's nuclear arsenal was "a necessary prerequisite" for negotiation, the new Secretary of Defense concluded.

— and, above all, to dispel the psychological lethargy of America and its allies in dealing with the Soviet Union; hence the new rhetoric: "It is not going to be business as usual," the new White House Chief of Staff, James A. Baker, explained in early February 1981.

The Soviets' response to the "new direction" in American policy was hardly a surprise. They have been dealing with successive American administrations from a well-developed post-Stalin strategy. First, the new Administration would be greeted with a generous offer to talk, to meet, and to settle "outstanding differences." Then, there would be a display of pique over a hesitant or negative American response. Then would come a Soviet decision point: either to launch more aggressive testing or to shift to a posture of more genuine accommodation. This process was usually not a matter of weeks or months, but often of one or two years.

The Reagan-Brezhnev encounter has passed through the first stage and is well into the second. During the election campaign there had been no great sympathy for Ronald Reagan. At a Central Committee plenum in mid-1980, the Soviets had concluded that no matter who occupied the White House, certain adverse trends were developing in American policy: strategic rearmament (the new mobile MX missile), rapprochement with China (including arms sales) and refurbishing NATO strategy and forces with new Pershing and cruise missile deployments. Nevertheless, the Soviets seemed puzzled by the prospect of a Reagan presidency. Would it be reminiscent of the Nixon presidency, in that a conservative would move toward the Soviet Union? Or would it be closer to the avowed objectives of the Republican platform?

In any case, underlying Soviet apprehension had to be subordinated to the obligatory gesture which just might be reciprocated, and, if not, serve as the start of an accusatory record. Thus, Soviet Foreign Minister Andrei Gromyko, in a letter of January 28, 1981, answering charges against Soviet policy contained in a letter from his new counterpart, Alexander Haig, expressed an interest in an exchange of views on a wide range of issues. Soviet President Leonid Brezhnev, from the rostrum of the Soviet Party Congress in late February, offered another peace program and a summit meeting. After a confusing flicker of interest in the summit, the offer was dutifully turned down by Secretary Haig on the grounds that an unprepared summit would be "self-defeating in the extreme."

On the surface this was the end of the initial minuet. But, it was later revealed, the dialogue of the two Presidents continued in an exchange of initially secret letters. In early April, President Reagan, from his hospital bed, sent a hand-written letter to Brezhnev in which he asked, "Is it possible that we have permitted ideology, political and economic philosophies and governmental policies to keep us from considering the very real, everyday problems of our peoples?"[1] This was a far cry from liars, cheats, etc.; it suggested at least a greater pragmatism than the Administration's public rhetoric. Brezhnev's reply on May 25 was properly cantankerous, but he reverted to his summit proposal:

[1] Quoted by President Reagan in his speech before the National Press Club in Washington, D.C., November 18, 1981.

"An exchange of correspondence has its limitations, and in this sense a private conversation is better." But either Brezhnev's expectations or his interest was waning. Brezhnev now also favored a "well-prepared" meeting at a "moment acceptable to both of us."

There was a four-month lapse, until a Reagan letter of September 22 (released only in paraphrase). The tone was sterner, the accusations crisper, the rhetoric more reminiscent of the campaign. Yet, another shift was evident. With his initial defense budget battles behind him, the complexities of various strategic decisions (the MX missile and the B-1 bomber) pressing in on him, the pressure from Europe growing, and Haig about to meet Gromyko, the President emphasized that the United States was interested in a "stable and constructive relationship" with the U.S.S.R. The letter set forth what was, in effect, a rough agenda for Soviet-American relations: arms control and security, geopolitical conflicts, economic relations, and the situation in Poland. This was not a radically new framework. Except for Poland, the issues had been on the agenda for at least a decade.

On the first issue, arms control, the Reagan Administration has moved from preconceived positions on the Right toward the mainstream of postwar American foreign policy. The President's speech and proposals of November 18 may well represent a turning point; he not only emphasized his commitment to major reductions in strategic weapons, but he also proposed that the United States and the Soviet Union agree on "zero" intermediate range missiles, which could mean canceling the intended American deployment in Europe. On the second issue—regional conflicts—the clash of interests between the two powers has remained severe and threatens to worsen. The third issue, economic relations, was becoming less relevant as other forces have overtaken American policy. And on the fourth issue, the Polish revolution, broad uncertainties cast an ominous shadow over the future.

Soviet-American relations thus remain surrounded by a strong sense of foreboding. Despite the prospects of a summit meeting in 1982, only a small start has been made on the long road back to something resembling a more normal relationship.

II

Every Administration since Truman's has felt obliged to express an interest in achieving greater security through arms control. Each Administration has been skeptical of the prospects for any durable arrangement to restrict, let alone reduce, the level of weapons. Yet, American Presidents and those who seek the office cannot afford to denounce the humane objective of controlling nuclear weapons. The most they can do is to oppose a specific agreement, or insist that much better, safer solutions are possible. As a candidate, Reagan took this course by opposing the second Strategic Arms Limitation Treaty (SALT II), while insisting that substantial reductions could be achieved provided America began to rearm to impress on Moscow that the alternative to agreement was a severe competition.

Given this approach, the Reagan Administration had to give priority to the resolution of certain strategic issues, primarily how to deal with the much advertised "window of strategic vulnerability." This theory held that U.S. land-based intercontinental ballistic missiles (ICBMS) were or would be highly vulnerable to a Soviet surgical strike; Soviet ICBMS, however, were almost immune because of the limitations on U.S. ICBM capabilities. The United States, therefore, had to deploy a new, larger ICBM capable of threatening the Soviet force, but deceptively based in multiple "shelters" so as to exhaust any potential Soviet attack. By 1986–89, the infamous window would not only be closed, but the Soviets would also feel the harsh draft of their own vulnerability. Confronted by such a prospect, Moscow supposedly would negotiate an accommodation in SALT III.

This scenario was initially embraced by Reagan, especially the catch phrase of the "window." But the timing of the MX program, its technical and political complexity, and its SALT origins made it suspect. Many Reaganites argued that a "quick fix" was needed. But quick fixes are by definition elusive (otherwise, preceding administrations would have grabbed them). Negotiation from strength was a theory looking for an operational plan. This was one dimension of the strategic problem confronting Reagan.

The other dimension involved Europe. The Administration inherited the dual-track NATO decision of December 1979: the first track was to deploy 572 new American intermediate-range missiles in Europe starting in 1983; the second track was to negotiate with the Soviet Union for an arms control agreement covering intermediate-range missiles on both sides. With Washington now strongly emphasizing the military character of U.S.-Soviet relations, a backlash sprang up in Europe, where for a variety of reasons the Soviet threat was viewed less urgently. The NATO allies were suffering under diverse but severe political pressures applied by a bewildering coalition of anti-nuclear, pacifist, environmentalist and other activists. The Europeans argued that they would not and could not sacrifice détente to justify Reagan's campaign predilections. In their view, détente in Europe had, after all, brought about a significant reduction of tensions over Berlin and Germany, expanded economic relations, and even contributed to the beginnings of the Polish revolution. The way out of the growing transatlantic conflict was to resume negotiations with the Soviet Union over theater nuclear forces in Europe. Otherwise, it seemed likely that the worst outcome would be realized: NATO would unilaterally abandon or scale down its TNF deployment plans, while the rapidly growing Soviet force of SS-20 intermediate-range missiles would be unaffected by the clamoring crowds in Bonn, Amsterdam or Aldermaston.

The nature of these European anxieties was badly misperceived by some elements of the Reagan Administration, whose initial response was to cry appeasement. But there was also in the Administration an underlying suspicion of the Carter TNF plan because it was believed to be militarily flawed. Land-based missiles in Europe would be vulnerable to a Soviet preemptive attack. They were cumbersome and lacked real mobility, and in times of crisis their rapid movement into firing position would be subject to European political vetoes. Deploying 572 new missiles in any case was not an effective counter to the longer range and highly mobile Soviet SS-20s, which in early 1981 were already at a level of 600–700 warheads. Countering them would require a much larger force with longer range than the Pershing missiles, which was politically infeasible in Central Europe. For the Reagan Administration, an attractive alternative was to fill the strategic gap with sea-based cruise missiles—truly mobile, under American command, and consistent with a new strategic emphasis on naval power. But such a shift risked "decoupling," i.e., creating the impression that the United States was eager to avoid a firm link between the territorial defense of Europe and the use of America's central, strategic weapons. This risk was enhanced by the impression in Europe that the Reagan Defense Department was looking for ways to disengage from the Continent in favor of an off-shore strategy, supposedly based on the British nineteenth-century model (incidentally, a bad misreading of history).

The Soviets, of course, exploited the European climate, as well as the growing divergency between Washington and its NATO allies. Brezhnev threw out a number of approaches. Basically, what he proposed in 1980–81 was a simple bargain: NATO should suspend its program, and Moscow would negotiate a "substantial" reduction in its intermediate-range missile force. This would be reasonable because—the Soviets contended—a balance of "intermediate" forces already existed of around 900 to 1000 on each side if one counted the British and French strategic forces and U.S. aircraft on carriers and in Europe (the so-called forward-based systems). It followed from this view that the new American missiles would radically alter the balance and, of course, force the Soviets to adopt a counter program. A bargain need not even await the resumption of SALT, even though the Soviets acknowledge that theater and strategic military forces were related.

For much of 1981, Brezhnev had the field to himself because of the Administration's resistance to premature negotiations. The Reagan Administration saw an early commitment to negotiate as a threat to the timetable for implementing the TNF program. Even if the Administration decided to enter talks with the Soviet Union, their preferred purpose would be to legitimize further NATO deployments, or to justify the shift to sea-based forces.

Inside the Administration there were strong counter-arguments to this tactical approach. The pro-negotiating group, largely in the State Department, argued that the NATO alliance was dangerously strained, and weak governments were under strong political pressure. Reagan's election was being used in Europe by critics who claimed that war was suddenly more likely, and his refusal to negotiate over SALT or theater weapons was cited as proof. Moreover, a stubborn refusal to explore a European accommodation on nuclear weapons, a solemn American commitment since December 1979, could only aggravate European relations. In a second-level NATO meeting on March 31, the Administration tentatively agreed to resume the talks on theater nuclear weapons but to hold back on SALT.

But there was a prolonged rear-guard action against this decision, conducted by the Defense Department. While Secretary Haig was publicly resuming his contacts with the Soviet Ambassador after the Soviet Party Congress, the Secretary of Defense, Caspar Weinberger, was lecturing Europeans, "if the movement from cold war to détente is progress, then let me say we cannot afford much more progress." Weinberger also introduced a new issue by linking negotiations on European missiles to prior Soviet restraint on Poland. The State Department countered by issuing repeated assurances that the United States was committed to negotiations; restraint in Poland was not a precondition, although Soviet action there would make any talks "impossible."

This skirmishing was simply a preliminary to the real decision by the President, made just before the NATO ministerial meeting in Rome in early May. At a National Security Council meeting, Haig was instructed to confirm the willingness of the United States to negotiate and to begin the talks by the "end of the year." Ironically, this new commitment had no great effect: the peace activists in Europe were not interested in diplomatic timetables; they wanted *all* American nuclear weapons out. Some of the NATO governments were still skeptical about U.S. policy. Moscow was contemptuous but did slightly improve its bargaining offer during a visit by two key Europeans, West German Socialist Willy Brandt and British Labour Party leader Michael Foot. Brezhnev offered a more substantial missile reduction as a reward for suspending the NATO missile program for the duration of negotiations.

The procedural fight having been settled, the United States and allied governments moved to the substance of the negotiations. Out of the second round of this arms control debate emerged the "zero option," proposed by the President on November 18: the United States would cancel its missile deployments if the U.S.S.R. would entirely "dismantle" its intermediate-range missiles.

During this debate, a quiet revolution in approaches occurred within the Administration. The skeptics in the Reagan Administration embraced the zero option as a simple but effective device to expose Soviet intransigence. The proponents of negotiation, who saw the talks as a means to bridge transatlantic differences, saw serious pitfalls in the zero option: could the United States negotiate for, say, 18 months, and then repudiate its own proposal by beginning actual preparations for deployments? Would NATO remain united in the face of tempting Soviet counter-offers? Nevertheless, the final Reagan decision contained in the speech of November 18 was both plausible and a shrewd tactical maneuver, meeting several problems and providing an effective counter to the Soviets. Yet, differences within the Administration and within NATO made it vulnerable to a Soviet counterattack.

The nature of the eventual dilemma was illustrated by Brezhnev's response. Contrary to the clever arguments for the zero option as a means of placing the Soviets in the dock, the Soviet rejection was coupled with a further offer. Brezhnev took another small step by offering to reduce "hundreds" of weapons if the United States and NATO canceled the deployment. Of course this was brushed off by Washington, though less so by Bonn. But it pointed to an eventual decision point after the preliminary posturing was completed in the Geneva negotiations that began on November 30. Would NATO give up its weapons for a low ceiling on Soviet SS-20s? This could result in a missile threat of less magnitude than Europe had faced for two decades from older Soviet missiles. But it would nonetheless be a substantial retreat from the position of December 1979. Or would a token NATO deployment be sufficient psychological compensation?

Whatever the outcome, the process of arms control in Europe has been revived, if only temporarily, and this simple fact illustrates a significant new dimension in superpower relations. Arms control and other security issues have ceased to be the domain of the statesmen in Washington and Moscow. New weapons are involved, and new actors; new strategic debates have begun under new popular pressures. The politics of protest has reared its head, and both Moscow and Washington are now involved in a new triangular relationship with Europe. As one observer put it, the struggle for the hearts and minds of Europe has begun—a sad commentary on the policies on both sides of the Atlantic.

The collision between theory and reality was also evident in the Administration's handling of strategic arms limitation talks. It entered office not only opposed to the SALT II treaty, but to the very idea of a SALT "process." The approved tactic seemed to be to allow the treaty to lie in limbo and let the SALT dialogue atrophy. This fitted the program of rearming and deferring negotiation until the American position was clearly strengthened. Initially it suggested that the SALT agreements might be allowed to lapse or even be repudiated in order to focus priority on bringing weapons systems into operation. This view was publicly expressed by a junior official early in the year, only to be severely and publicly repudiated by the Secretary of State.

Presumably the Secretary recognized the American dilemma. There was no immediate gain from explicitly freeing the Soviets from the SALT II constraints, which were being observed on both sides. With Reagan in the White House, the Administration did not need the psychological booster shot of officially denouncing SALT. Its defense budget would pass easily. And the Administration had no clear strategic program of its own; it could not even decide on the mix of new strategic programs (MX, B-1, etc.). Thus retaining SALT as a tactical hedge seemed to make sense, especially in light of the growing nervousness in Europe over the Reagan Administration. But having accepted the strange position of abiding by a treaty it had no intention of ratifying, the Administration for many months offered no substitute for SALT, other than the hackneyed insistence that substantial reductions were necessary.

The approach that finally began to evolve flowed from the three principal objections to SALT I and II made by SALT critics, including some prominent members of the Administration. First, there was the problem of developing a new unit of measure or new "common currency" for strategic weapons negotiations. Hitherto the unit had been numbers of launchers (e.g., missile silos, bombers). This was misleading and dangerous because it equated quite different elements of power. What was needed was a more comprehensive measure of what Administration officials loosely termed "destructive power." But the slogan was difficult to translate into a technical formula that might have operational significance and still prove negotiable.

Second, there was the question of reductions. Some reductions were obviously more effective than others. Some might even be dangerous. The United States would not want to reduce its own forces to a point where it might lose its second-strike capability and a first strike might prove tempting to the Soviets. Fewer fixed ICBMs with multiple warheads would not necessarily create greater stability. Fewer strategic submarines were in fact more vulnerable, and fewer bombers confronting an unconstrained air defense might be downright dangerous. But token reductions (already achieved in SALT II) were certainly illusory. So it appeared, more and more, that what would eventually be involved was in fact an old and unsuccessful demand, namely, that the Soviets reduce their heaviest ICBMs—scarcely a "new direction."

Third, there was a recasting of the problem of verification. The new structure of arms control would require more than national technical means, a euphemism for relying on intelligence monitoring, principally by satellites. The old approach was perhaps adequate for simple numerical limits on fixed weapons, but complex reductions would make residual forces highly sensitive to cheating, to circumvention, and to breaking out of an agreement. It followed that broader cooperative measures were necessary.

The Administration had not even embarked on a leisurely review of the fundamentals of strategic arms control when Brezhnev rather unexpectedly relieved some of the political pressures. At the 26th Party Congress in February he engaged in the obligatory attacks on the United States for failing to ratify SALT II, but then he created an escape from confrontations. Rather than insisting on ratification, he called for the preservation of the "positive elements" of SALT II. His main target was the theater nuclear forces rather than the strategic ones.

The Soviets' calculation was to prove a shrewd one. For it was the theater force negotiations that came to take precedence in the new Administration's hierarchy, though not necessarily by design.

Pressure from Europe was also in part responsible for a gradual acceptance of the inevitability of the resumption of strategic force negotiations, which were finally confirmed by a presidential offer to begin talks "as soon as possible" in 1982. This intent was confirmed in the President's speech of November 18, which at the same time rechristened the new talks START (Strategic Arms Reduction Talks).

Thus an arms control negotiating schedule took shape in 1981, but without linkage or preconditions. The Reagan Administration had initially insisted that a broad improvement in Soviet conduct was mandatory, lest another agreement suffer the fate of its SALT II predecessor. Yet, the program outlined in the President's speech of November 18, putting forward a new four-point arms control plan, ignored any political conditions. It was only accompanied by some informal statements by Administration officials that seemed to suggest that Soviet "restraint" for the first nine months had met some minimum criteria and that movement toward both the TNF negotiations and SALT was thus justified. The Administration avoided confronting the implications of its own policy pronouncements: namely, that arms control agreements were not viable without political restraint; and that arms control for its own sake was bound to fail because of the realities of "linkage."

The substantive outlook was thus hazy. The Administration constantly emphasized that arms control could not be a "centerpiece" in a relationship with the U.S.S.R. But it was vague as to the role arms control could play. Some parts of the Administration still saw arms control as a threat to a sound military rearmament program, rather than a complementary effort. And they continued to believe that arms control served as a test of Soviet good faith: negotiations would demonstrate whether the Soviets would settle for a true balance of strategic forces and genuine stability, or would simply use any negotiations as a means of ratifying or concealing their own buildup.

The Soviet response was equally tactical in its inspiration, i.e., slight variants on the general theme that new agreements had to address America's forward-based systems. But an intriguing question was whether Soviet military policies were undergoing a reconsideration, perhaps stimulated by the increases over Carter's defense budget for fiscal 1982 and Reagan's commitment to continued increases over the next four years. As the European nuclear debate quickened in 1980–81, the Soviets appeared eager to dispel any suspicion that they sought strategic "superiority," that they would strike first, or that they believed in "victory" in nuclear war. Brezhnev took this line, and one widely quoted Soviet pamphlet even resurrected the old Malenkov heresy: that nuclear war would "probably" mean the end of civilization.[2] While there were sound tactical reasons for introducing these nuances, nonetheless a serious question remained: were the Soviets grudgingly accepting the implausibility of continuing to justify large expenditures of scarce resources, in pursuing strategic goals that would inevitably prove elusive if they provoked American counterarmament?

Even if Soviet theory was, in fact, evolving, a different aspect of Soviet declaratory policy was disconcerting. In attempting to exploit Reagan's remarks in October about the possibility of limited war in Europe, Brezhnev insisted that if a nuclear weapon were to be used, then "unavoidably" the war would assume a "global character." These remarks, too, could be explained as tactical expedients, but it was possible that the U.S.S.R. was foreshadowing a new deterrent theory for Europe. After fifteen years of emphasizing the roughly equal likelihood of war beginning with a conventional or a tactical nuclear phase, well short of all-out escalation, it was possible that Moscow envisaged using the threat of its new and more accurate SS-20s to neutralize the accepted NATO strategy of threatening the first use of nuclear weapons. It was perhaps a significant confirmation of Soviet strategy that a number of observers, including some members of the Reagan Administration, believed the credibility of the traditional doctrine of flexible response and first use of nuclear weapons was deteriorating. In part, this explained the Defense Department's interest in new "long-war" strategies that might be fought entirely with non-nuclear weapons.[3]

In any case, the outlook for the Reagan arms control program is not very bright. What is being proposed, in essence, is a massive restructuring of Soviet nuclear forces, including the abandonment of several thousand missile warheads. Even in the best circumstances, when détente was flourishing, the Soviets showed great resistance to such a concessionary course. Moreover, U.S. strategic plans remain vague and tentative. The MX decision of October 2 to proceed with a limited deployment in hardened Titan missile silos was clearly a holding action, a weak alternative with strong opposition, and abandoned in 90 days. (Now the first 40 MX missiles will be installed in Minuteman missile silos.) The "zero

[2] *The Threat to Europe*, Moscow: Progress Publishers, 1981.
[3] Richard Halloran, "U.S. Said to Revise Strategy..." *The New York Times*, April 19, 1981.

option" in Europe obscured the Administration's new commitment to a substantial force of sea-based cruise missiles. Counterforce strategies aimed at attacking hardened military targets were still under serious consideration in both Moscow and Washington. There was a general uncertainty in NATO over the validity of a strategy of first use of nuclear weapons. All in all, the vital strategic relationship between the United States and the U.S.S.R. was in flux.

Moreover, there was no political framework to begin rebuilding a military equilibrium. In 1972 SALT I was supported by a structure of political agreements—the German treaties, the Berlin agreements. In 1979 when SALT II was signed there was no such supporting structure and the treaty was highly vulnerable. In 1981 the gloomy outlook for arms control reflected the pessimistic outlook for political progress. As far as the Reagan Administration was concerned Moscow remained poised on the brink of a new geopolitical advance.

III

The Reagan Administration inherited what seemed to be a series of crises, beginning in the Middle East and the Persian Gulf and stretching as far as El Salvador and Cambodia. The approach advocated by the new Administration flowed from an analysis that was almost the reverse of Carter's priorities. Whereas the old Administration had initially attempted to relegate the Soviet problem to a secondary position, the Reagan Administration ostentatiously restored Soviet relations to the central position. Indeed, it tended to assign Moscow a pervasive responsibility for international disorder. Even some fundamental North-South issues were seen as an indirect Soviet challenge, and old issues such as the Arab-Israeli dispute were re-examined on the basis of a need for a broad anti-Soviet "consensus." Finally, in the initial phase "linkage" was heavily stressed on the grounds that restraint in Soviet behavior was a prerequisite to real relaxation of tensions.

The Soviets, of course, brusquely dismissed any notion of preconditions. In April, Brezhnev said that the Soviets would be "simpletons" if they were to insist that Washington abandon all foreign bases before talks could begin. Yet for a number of reasons the Soviets have been cautious and circumspect in their behavior.

Of course, the opportunities were narrow. There was nothing resembling the openings in Angola in 1975 or Ethiopia in 1977–78. Throughout 1981, in each of the minor crises—Syrian missiles in Lebanon, the shootdown of the Libyan aircraft, the Sudanese-

Chad-Libyan dispute, even El Salvador and Nicaragua—the Soviets did not continue the broad offensive of the late 1970s, but stopped well short of their capabilities for exploitation.

It may be that the Reagan position on linkage had some deterrent value; some Soviet officials indicated that it was desirable to insulate regional conflicts from broad U.S.-Soviet relations, thus acknowledging the practical impact of linkage. But probably the most important reason for Soviet caution was the need for a period of consolidation. The problems of Afghanistan and Poland, the inability to formulate a new five-year plan (finally published nine months late), and the need to evaluate carefully the Reagan policies, all combined to recommend a Soviet holding action, a watching brief. And this, indeed, seems to have been the main characteristic of Soviet policy in 1981.

Developments in the Middle East and Persian Gulf were additional reasons for Soviet caution. The Iraqi attack against Iran in late 1980 created a new situation: should Moscow support its treaty partner in Baghdad or play for larger stakes to influence the future alignment of Iran? In effect, the Soviets chose to hold the door open to Iran. This meant they could act with restraint in the war and even claim some international credit for doing so. Despite the bloody record of the Iranian regime, Moscow refrained from virtually any criticism, even though many of its sympathizers and supporters were being put to death. The Iranian revolution remained anti-imperialist "in essence" and thus was still a major prize to be won over.

Moreover, Pakistan was showing the signs of prolonged strain under the pressures emanating from Afghanistan, Moscow and New Delhi. Though all of the various efforts to open genuine negotiations over Afghanistan proved abortive, Western and Pakistani persistence in pursuing them may well have suggested to Moscow that it really had little to fear. (Whether it could somehow bring the Afghan rebellion under control was a different matter.) Added to the potential for significant gains in Iran and perhaps in Pakistan, there was a potential for further upheavals following the death of Sadat, the new alliance of Libya, South Yemen and Ethiopia, and the struggle for Chad and the Sudan. All of this turmoil probably encouraged Moscow to wait for new opportunities—a style well-suited to Soviet policy in any case.

This period of relative restraint facilitated a dialogue of sorts between Washington and Moscow. Despite some stringent qualifications, both sides indicated that it might be worthwhile to explore some ground rules to regulate their competition. Secretary

Haig alluded to such an effort early in the year, Brezhnev took it up in April, and later in September President Reagan in his note to Brezhnev made it an agenda item. The President took the position that Soviet-American relations could not really improve without clear Soviet restraint in the Third World. Foreign Minister Gromyko responded by proposing to Haig negotiations on a set of principles of U.S.-Soviet relations. Whether drafting such principles remains on the agenda is not known, but the issues such a process would raise would strike at the heart of the relationship.

In May 1972 the two superpowers agreed on a set of principles which its principal architect, Henry Kissinger, described as expressing the "necessity of responsible political conduct." Their principal defect was that they lent themselves to varying and even contradictory interpretations (which the drafters, of course, recognized). The United States basically wanted to preserve the status quo, or at least regulate change in a measured fashion. It sought Soviet cooperation. The U.S.S.R., however, wanted to challenge if not assault the existing order whenever and wherever it was relatively safe to do so. A spheres of influence agreement might have resolved the conflict, but this was impossible. Therefore, a large area of the world has remained open to competition, because a code of conduct could not be translated into a meaningful set of understandings and agreements.

This issue, of course, has yet to be resolved. To reject out of hand any code of conduct would be an invitation to anarchy, if not confrontation. But to agree on generalities might also invite an inadvertent clash. Both sides seem well aware of the alternatives, and have been proceeding without much fanfare, but probably without any great expectations.

The issues are by no means abstract ones. In the Persian Gulf, the United States would have to seek guarantees that the U.S.S.R. would not pursue "unilateral advantage" by exploiting growing instabilities to occupy northern Iran. A similar guarantee for Pakistan from both the Soviet Union and India would be desirable if the area is to achieve any long-term stability. Similarly, Soviet restraint in the Arab-Israeli dispute is a condition to any durable long-term settlement. But Soviet statements suggest Moscow would, in return, be seeking the reduction or withdrawal of American influence and power in the Middle East and the Persian Gulf, as well as a political neutralization of Southwest Asia. It is difficult to foresee the basis for any fundamental settlement between the two powers. Continued conflict seems far more likely.

On the one issue—ending the occupation of Afghanistan—

where progress had at one time seemed to be a prerequisite, American policy under the new Administration proved increasingly indifferent. Lifting the grain embargo without any progress on Afghanistan was tantamount to writing an end to the policy of sanctions inaugurated by President Carter. Apparently some help has been flowing to the freedom fighters in Afghanistan, but on a modest scale. Washington has deferred too much to the Europeans and others who were pressing for a diplomatic solution on the dubious reasoning that the Soviet invasion had been a costly mistake that Moscow was eager to liquidate. Despite three separate U.N. condemnations, the U.S.S.R. suffered no lasting retribution, other than that inflicted on the field of combat. The resumption of arms control negotiations, the lifting of the grain embargo, and the gradual development of a high-level Soviet-American dialogue made the international condemnation of Soviet behavior irrelevant. Perhaps there is no solution. By the end of 1981, in any case, Afghanistan was well on its way to becoming the forgotten war. Whether the United States and its Western partners would eventually have to pay a price for this weakness remained to be seen.

Despite the withering away of the Afghan crisis as a major Soviet-American issue, the general impression was that little or no progress had been made on any of the major geopolitical issues dividing Washington and Moscow. The Soviet "threat" to the Persian Gulf remained, and American policy was increasingly oriented toward countering Soviet military action (e.g., operation Bright Star in Egypt, U.S.-Israeli "strategic cooperation," the provision of Saudi AWACS). Soviet influence among the more radical elements in the Middle East and Africa was growing, manifest in the new triple alliance of its clients, Libya, South Yemen and Ethiopia. Similarly its support for the Palestine Liberation Organization was demonstrably strengthened by the opening of an official representation in Moscow. For the first time since 1973 there was a possibility that the collapse of the Camp David process might lead to reentry of the U.S.S.R. in the diplomacy of the Arab-Israeli conflict. Moscow still provided the necessary support to Vietnam and the phony Cambodian regime. And, finally, the Soviet Union (and Cuba) and the United States seemed to be edging toward a serious confrontation over the Caribbean and Central America. The Soviets were giving Nicaragua more and more political and material support, including new arms shipments through Cuba. And the United States seemed intent on drawing a line against Cuban encroachments.

The potential for conflict, thus, remains high. But in one area Soviet-American strains might have actually been slightly reduced—China. The new Administration did, of course, carry the old policies a step further by openly (though in a confusing manner) offering to supply some arms and new technology to China during Secretary Haig's visit in June 1981. By the time it occurred, the Soviets had probably largely discounted the move. Gromyko (on August 8) said Moscow could not "remain indifferent," but China was not even mentioned in the litany of complaints to visiting American senators a few weeks later. Yet the underlying Soviet apprehensions must still be there.

American underwriting of a Chinese military buildup with what Gromyko called "up-to-date American weapons" could not be accepted in Moscow. But this no longer seemed likely, at least not in the short run. China was worried about the resolution of the new Administration, and was engaged in its usual maneuvering. The dispatch of a Chinese military mission to Washington was repeatedly and deliberately delayed. The reason, clearly, was that Peking wanted to pressure Washington to back away from its commitments to Taiwan. The U.S.S.R., ever sensitive to the nuances of triangular politics, responded with a new offer to settle the Sino-Soviet border dispute. While this particular issue remains dormant, the Chinese have moved to reopen border negotiations with India. The signal seems clear. The door to the Soviet Union was not slammed tightly shut. The real target of this Chinese maneuver, however, was Washington's nerves.

IV

In his message to Leonid Brezhnev on September 22, President Reagan indicated that one objective of American policy would be "to expand trade and to increase contacts at all levels of our societies." (This was before the imposition of martial law in Poland and the announcement of economic sanctions by the President.) But, in any case, American and Western policy toward trade and other economic relations with the East was a shambles— which the Polish crisis illuminated. A decade ago it was generally believed that economic relations would be a key, if not the key, to a political accommodation with Moscow. This theory was tried briefly during the period of détente, when an expansion of the scope of economic relations was held out as an incentive for better political relations. Over the past ten years, however, in the United States the policy has undergone an almost complete turnaround. Now, economic relations are seen primarily as a punitive sanction.

Thus Secretary Haig on July 28 testified that "our trade relations and our broader economic relations must reinforce our efforts to counter the Soviet military buildup and its irresponsible conduct...." He announced that as a result of a policy review, the United States had concluded that tightening of restrictions on "goods and technology which could upgrade production in areas relevant to Soviet military strength was both desirable and necessary." The problem was that before this policy review the Administration had already damaged its own rationale by lifting the grain embargo on April 24. Its claim at that time that its position could not be "mistaken" by the Soviets was a weak one.

But probably of more long-term significance, the Administration failed to obtain an allied consensus at the Ottawa economic summit. Even the Secretary of State had to acknowledge that "Some countries have more extensive commercial links with the East than the United States, and others believe that economic ties moderate political behavior." Finally, it was fairly clear that the use of economic relations as a retaliatory measure was far from agreed Western policy. Thus, when the Polish crisis broke in December 1981, Western policy was in disarray.

The weaknesses of the Western approach were nowhere more evident than in the abortive American effort to stave off the much publicized European-Soviet natural gas agreements that were finally consummated on November 20, just before Leonid Brezhnev visited Bonn. To be sure, the United States had a complicated hand to play. The United States had justified lifting grain sanctions on the very theory—commercialism—that the Reagan Administration was now arguing against with the Europeans. It thus found itself in the difficult position of proposing that the Europeans should make economic sacrifices lest they create a political dependency on Moscow, when the United States was selling over 23 million tons of grain to the Soviet Union and extending for one year the grain sales agreement of 1976.

Even the relevant security warnings against Soviet blackmail potential carried no great weight. The overall West German dependency on the Soviet Union for energy supplies (five percent) was not nearly as great as the European dependency on oil imports from the Middle East (or the U.S. dependency, for that matter). In any case, the growing web of economic relationships between East and West raised a serious question for American policy: could the United States afford to stand on the sidelines criticizing and carping while this relationship developed? Or should it modify its own position as the basis for attempting to forge a new

Western consensus? The crisis over Polish sanctions made such a consensus mandatory.

Even the policy of restricting the transfer of technology raises questions. The Soviet Union is highly vulnerable to the perennial failings of its own agricultural sector. Twenty-five years after the opening of the virgin lands and the adoption of a policy of massive investment in agriculture, the Soviet Union is still importing sizable amounts of grain and paying for it with scarce hard currency (including gold sales). Any alleviation of this problem clearly has some strategic significance for the U.S.S.R. So it could scarcely be argued that denying other technology was imposing a truly significant strategic burden, as long as grain sales were virtually open-ended.

Yet it is undeniable that the U.S.S.R. benefits from access to high technology, since a major Soviet economic problem is declining productivity. But most technologies are by and large available on standard commercial markets in the industrialized countries. Tightening technology transfers is no easy matter. It was one of the sanctions announced by President Carter in January 1980; the new Administration announced a further tightening, and then it was one of the sanctions invoked during the Polish crisis. Halfway measures, such as selling some pipelaying equipment and then suspending it, or selling a complete tractor-combine plant, created an image of a confused and uncertain policy. The main beneficiaries were in Moscow.

V

The issue of greatest long-term significance in 1981 was the Polish crisis. The political and institutional changes in Poland since July 1980 were the most important development within the communist system since the split between China and the U.S.S.R., as well as potentially the most far-reaching development in European politics since the formation of the two military alliances. The outcome could profoundly alter the relations between the U.S.S.R. and the United States. A Soviet invasion would deal a sharp blow to any near-term chances for détente, for arms control, or for an alleviation of global tensions. The evolution of a pluralist political order, on the other hand, could not fail to have an historic impact on both the East and West in Europe. The consequences of such a phenomenon were difficult to foresee because the Polish crisis was genuinely unique. A third alternative, an internal crackdown, seemed initially to be ruled out by the weakness of the Communist Party structure and the dubious reliability of the armed forces.

In the waning days of the Carter Administration when it seemed possible that the Soviet forces would intervene, stern warnings were issued. Some Carter officials take credit for deterring a Soviet move, which Moscow of course denied was intended. Whatever the actual situation had been in December 1980, the situation was still tense when the new Administration took office. Within a few days Secretary Haig, in a letter to Andrei Gromyko, warned against Soviet interference. This prompted Gromyko to reply on January 28 that the situation in Poland "cannot be a subject of discussion between third countries, including the U.S.S.R. and the U.S.A." He was wrong. Poland was the essence of the East-West discussion because it raised the fundamental questions about the nature of European détente: was Moscow prepared to permit peaceful political change in Eastern Europe? Or would it insist on some form of the Brezhnev Doctrine?

In essence, until mid-December the matter rested where the initial Haig-Gromyko exchange left it. The Soviets presumably needed no Western warnings to appreciate the repercussions of a bloody finish to the Polish crisis. Indeed, their behavior had been astonishingly restrained, so much so that some observers concluded there had been a loss of nerve in the Kremlin. More likely was a keen sense in Moscow of the high costs of direct intervention, matched by an equally deep apprehension over the consequences of a collapse of communist authority in Poland.

The primary Soviet maneuver was to try to strengthen the intestinal fortitude of the Polish party leaders. In April the Soviets toyed with a coup, but found no palace guard in the Polish Politburo. In exasperation, an attempt was apparently made to arrange the overthrow of Stanislaw Kania in June—an attempt which also failed. The Polish Party Congress which followed in July made matters worse: the Central Committee was almost completely purged and Kania's faction barely survived in the new politburo. After the Congress, the Soviets insisted on a "clear-cut program of extrication," and Kania's days appeared to be numbered. Steady Soviet pressure, including sporadic military maneuvers, and a vicious public letter in September succeeded in overthrowing him and installing General Jaruzelski on October 17, 1981. It was to be the penultimate move.

On December 13, Jaruzelski moved dramatically to impose martial law and to suspend, if not reverse, the whole process of change and reform that had evolved since July 1980. Tactically, the coup was executed with a precision and discipline that obviously reflected careful and long preparations, with Soviet coaching likely. It took completely by surprise the leaders of the Solidarity movement, which had by then obtained sweeping concessions even to the point of having a real share in power. Opposition was widespread but ineffective, with communications cut both within the country and externally. And although there were a number of strikes and outbreaks of violence, the Jaruzelski regime was apparently successful in maintaining control.

By the end of 1981 the situation seemed temporarily to have settled down, with the possibility of some form of negotiation involving the government, the Catholic Church and leaders of Solidarity, perhaps including Lech Walesa. The regime's special militia forces had proved reliable, but there had been no real test of how the army would perform if it had to deal with really serious resistance. And the economic situation remained desperate, with any improvement apparently dependent on some kind of compromise under which the Polish people would be willing to return to work on an effective basis, and on eventual financial and other assistance from the West.

Throughout the year, American opposition to Soviet military intervention had been straightforward. But beyond the worst contingencies, the Reagan Administration appeared divided over the proper response to the upheaval in Poland. Prior to Jaruzelski's imposition of martial law, the Administration had been wary of providing economic assistance, because it would relieve the Soviets of the responsibility or culpability for the failure of the communist system in Poland.

The other view was that Poland was drifting toward a disaster and needed Western assistance. If the economy continued to deteriorate, the inevitable result would be disorder and Soviet intervention. Assistance in stabilizing the situation was a gamble well worth taking and would ultimately benefit Solidarity. Reform of the economy could not even be contemplated in the midst of a crisis. This view did not prevail until shortly before Jaruzelski's coup. In failing to adopt a more positive approach to the Polish issue, the United States risked recriminations for watching and waiting too long.[4]

The Jaruzelski coup caught the West completely underprepared, and the initial reactions were largely improvised. Two general options seemed possible: to retaliate swiftly and strongly, even going so far as to freeze all East-West negotiations, or to

---

[4] Murrey Marder, "U.S. Never Met the Test Poland Presented," *The Washington Post*, January 2, 1981.

defer the more drastic measures for use if the situation worsened. The Reagan Administration settled on a course between these alternatives. It was well out in front of its allies in announcing sanctions against both Poland and the Soviet Union, but the content of its measures was modest. The prospect for going further—such as denouncing the Helsinki accords—was not ruled out, but dependent on allied agreement which was very unlikely.

Beyond immediate reactions, a more fundamental question remained to be addressed by the West and by the United States in particular. Could a viable relationship with the Soviet Union, especially in Europe, continue to be based on a divisible détente in which the Soviets dominated every aspect of Eastern Europe, while the West continued to expand economic relations and other contacts, conclude arms control agreements, and promote a general political relaxation? For most of the postwar period the West accepted European spheres of influence without an official acknowledgment. Thus the Soviet position was never challenged in any of the Eastern crises. Why, then, should Poland be an exception? It was, after all, virtually at the center of the Soviet security zone.

Some in Europe argued that this was in fact the situation, and that it was only realistic to accept it. It was naïve to believe that the Soviets would permit the situation to go so far as to challenge their position of dominance. And, they argued, a Polish solution was preferable to a Soviet solution. Hence, the West should proceed with great care, condemning the actions of Jaruzelski, but not drawing any drastic consequences for the general course of East-West relations. Direct Soviet military intervention, of course, would alter the situation; short of that, sanctions would only push the Polish regime closer to Moscow.

The Reagan Administration seemed to accept some of this reasoning in practice; at least its sanctions were carefully calibrated, and it had to give priority to protecting the Western alliance against new divisions. But Washington also seemed to be groping for a new position that challenged the postwar tradition. This interpretation held that Poland was in fact unique because it has occurred *after* the German treaties with Moscow and Warsaw and *after* the Helsinki conference of 1975. The 1970s thus marked a fundamental change in the European situation. Yalta was overtaken. A new political framework had been created: a sort of World War II peace treaty, in which the West recognized the territorial status quo in the East, and, in return, the East accepted certain principles of relations that implied a greater toleration of diversity and autonomy. Thus, an equilibrium was created between legitimate Soviet security interests and legitimate Western aspirations for a more relaxed European order. This general view was reflected in some of the statements of the Secretary of State in an interview with *The Washington Post* on December 26.

This interpretation—that Helsinki created a "whole new framework of international relations"—was bound to become an area of conflict not only with the the Soviet Union but within NATO. The Polish crisis exposed a serious Western disagreement over the concept of European security. The United States was boycotting a Soviet gas pipeline financed by its European allies. Both the United States and Europe accused Moscow of violating the Helsinki accords, but only the United States applied sanctions. Moreover, the Europeans still considered arms control agreement on missiles "imperative," while Washington contemplated ending the talks. A common approach to East-West issues had become mandatory. For the first time in at least a decade, serious concerns were raised in the United States about the viability of the Western alliance, a trend Moscow was certain to exploit.

VI

In relations with the Soviet Union, Ronald Reagan is rapidly approaching a crossroads. There is still a mutual Soviet-American interest in improving relations and some incentive to do so. From a domestic standpoint the President is supported by a favorable constellation of political forces. Just as Nixon had the anti-communist credentials to develop an opening to Peking, so Reagan has the credentials to initiate a new relationship with the U.S.S.R. And he is creating the prerequisite military base. He will have to make some political concessions to Moscow, but he can expect and obtain some concessions in return. He does not have to embrace détente. He can learn from his predecessors the dangers of overselling (Nixon), as well as undercommitting (Carter).

The President seems to be a perceptive student. When it was appropriate early in his first year to sound a strong theme of rearmament, he eschewed some of the softer rhetoric. But as the realities of alliance responsibilities and the pressure of domestic politics began to congeal, he was more than willing to move in surprisingly unanticipated directions: the MX decision in October and the arms control speech of November 18. That speech may well have marked the end of the opening phase of the Reagan foreign policy, but the Polish crisis intervened and introduced new uncertainties.

What the President needs now is a strategy to see him through the next two years.

In their dealing with Moscow, Nixon and Kissinger brought a number of diverse forces and issues to bear at roughly the right time; after demonstrating resistance to Soviet-sponsored forays in Cuba and negotiating their way through the Jordanian and India-Pakistan crises, Nixon gained significant leverage when he decided to bomb Haiphong in May 1972. His summit strategy was saved not because the Soviets flinched, but because they did not want to jettison the German treaties and the Berlin agreements still pending in the West German Bundestag, or provide a new opening for China, or, for that matter, to endure an anti-ballistic missile race. Similarly, détente began to collapse when Washington was unable to turn back adverse trends: the collapse in Saigon, Soviet intervention in Angola, or the constant infighting over defense and SALT (to say nothing of the consequences of Watergate).

For Reagan the lesson should not merely be that he needs to impose penalites for Soviet misconduct: this is his natural inclination in any case. He also needs to create some incentives for the Soviets, and, above all, he must begin to relate issues to each other. Restraint and reciprocity are valid but inert slogans. They must be applied in some meaningful manner. Where do we want reciprocity: in European arms control? Where do we want restraint: Poland, Iran, Saudi Arabia? What do we offer in return: restraint in Chinese arms sales? Spelling out these equations is the essence of diplomacy. Deciding to do so is the essence of statesmanship.

The Reagan Administration has not done so in 1981. Indeed, it probably could not do so before straightening out its domestic economic programs, including its defense and strategic weapons programs. But in 1982 it should begin to untangle a number of internal divisions and to indicate to our allies and the Soviet leaders a clearer sense of the alternatives. At some point in the process, a summit meeting may be necessary.

Which brings up the Soviet side. It is a great temptation, but usually an error, to gear American policy to the intricacies of Kremlin politics. We will never really know the array of Soviet internal forces—when it is a propitious time to move, and when it is not. Following American interests is obviously a better guide. But the Soviet side is not irrelevant. And the role of Leonid Brezhnev is still quite central.

Brezhnev has staked much of his stewardship on improving relations with the United States and West Germany. One reason certainly has been his abiding concern about China. Another may be the economic benefits he had hoped for and has, in part, received. In any case, what and who will follow him is a mystery. The best case would be a period of internal consolidation, the worst case an aggressive thrust to cash in on a new strategic balance. It is probably in the interest of the United States and of the Reagan Administration to explore the possibility of restoring a better relationship with the Soviet Union while Brezhnev can still put it through the Politburo. Some of the post-Mao difficulties in Sino-American relations might be an object lesson.

No outside observer can sketch out the numerous intermediate steps involved in restoring some balance to Soviet-American relations. There has been too great an accumulation of serious conflicts not to be pessimistic about the chances for much change. But given the many difficulties confronting the Soviet Union, there may still be an opportunity for American diplomacy to work out acceptable terms. One question is whether the Administration of Ronald Reagan has any real interest in moving toward a new relationship. Despite the Polish crisis, such a desire seemed to be still alive at the end of the year. In his message of December 29 announcing sanctions against the Soviet Union, the President stated:

The United States wants a constructive and mutually beneficial relationship with the Soviet Union. We intend to maintain a high level dialogue. But we are prepared to proceed in whatever direction the Soviet Union decides upon—towards great mutual restraint and cooperation, or further down a harsh and less rewarding path.

It was an appropriately ambivalent note on which to end 1981.

Flora Lewis

ALARM BELLS IN THE WEST

Europrean leaders were pleased to start 1981 with a new American President and looked forward to steadier Atlantic relations rather than to a bumpy, unpredictable course with Jimmy Carter. Not that they agreed more with Ronald Reagan; they knew very little about him. But they had come to dislike and disdain Mr. Carter so much that it was assumed a change must be for the better, and Mr. Reagan's general projection of a newly vigorous, confident, purposeful America, after a disheartening decade, was most welcome.

By late in the year, however, the common theme on both sides of the political spectrum, and on both sides of the Atlantic, was that the Alliance had never been so gravely troubled and so uncertainly led. The tone of complaint was no longer familiar grumbles about disarray or lack of consultation, the cyclical quarrels and reconciliations which have been characteristic of the unusual bonds between Western Europe and the United States for nearly two generations. The direction was only down. Some people have even begun to question the value of a partnership established to correct the failures of the 1930s by establishing a joint security system in a world so enormously changed. The unthinkable—a rupture—was being thought.

As the gloom deepened, the usual calls for reviews of procedures, new mechanisms to strengthen policy planning and crisis management, faded away. It was as though people sensed there was too much danger in any kind of tinkering lest something collapse. Europe as a whole was called "semi-Gaullist," in the sense that President Charles de Gaulle sought to silhouette France against the United States. But those who looked back and judged that de Gaulle's maneuvers to identify France as a power between the United States and the Soviet Union were not only right but prophetic forgot how much he had done to prevent the consolidation of Europe. There still wasn't any European "pillar" to fit President Kennedy's image of a more equal Atlantic relationship, and less prospect than ever of a united European defense to reduce dependence on America's protection.

And, for much of the year, there was a discomfiting new

Flora Lewis writes the column "Foreign Affairs" for *The New York Times*.

vacuum. Soviet-American relations seemed to have vanished. There was neither confrontation nor exchange. There was rhetoric, at first conciliatory from President Leonid Brezhnev seeking a meeting with Mr. Reagan, then increasingly harsh as the year wore on. The U.S. policy toward Moscow was unclear and perhaps unsettled. There was no agenda, except a decision in the fall to start talks on intermediate-range Euromissiles at the end of November. Later, it was announced that the U.S. and Soviet Foreign Ministers would meet in January to see about launching new talks on long-range strategic weapons; SALT II had never been ratified and was losing relevance with time. The result would be crucial, since both sides had come to expect that no useful agreement could be hoped for on intermediate-range weapons except within the framework of limitations on the biggest missiles. Any dividing line between the two areas was necessarily arbitrary, controversial, and, in the end, probably unworkable, given the French and British nuclear arsenals. But beyond these first steps, there were no clear sign posts on what kind of East-West relations Washington was seeking, what it expected from the U.S.S.R. beyond not taking advantage of weak spots on the earth's political crust. There was no visible plan for developing new relations with Moscow, only denunciation of the way things had been going.

Some Administration members, though it was not known whether they were expressing their own views or reflecting considered policy, told Europeans privately that the vacuum was deliberate. Their thesis was that nothing could be achieved with the aging Brezhnev regime, and that nothing should be attempted for several years until the U.S. rearmament program had produced enough added force to back up Washington's words. Then, they maintained, some future Soviet regime might see that it must change its ways to get on in the world and shift attention to its frozen home front.

Late in the year, Secretary of State Alexander M. Haig, Jr. told a congressional committee that the United States sought "restraint and reciprocity" from Moscow. That was the first sign that Washington was beginning to think of proceeding with Soviet-American relations. But it wasn't spelled out and there were no specific areas outlined as possible subjects on which future diplomatic exchanges might be engaged.

Then suddenly, on November 18, President Reagan reversed the barometer. After a period of seemingly haphazard and sometimes contradictory U.S. public statements about the possibility of a limited nuclear war in Europe and whether there were plans for an atomic "demonstration blast" should war start, accompanied by a burgeoning European peace movement with mammoth demonstrations in several countries, Mr. Reagan made his first major foreign policy speech. He stressed America's dedication to peace and her desire for effective arms control. It was a few days before Soviet leader Leonid Brezhnev was to visit Bonn and little more than a week before the opening of the Soviet-American talks in Geneva on intermediate-range arms in Europe. Mr. Reagan announced that the United States would seek removal of all such land-based weapons, the "zero-option" which West German Chancellor Helmut Schmidt had been urging as the negotiated alternative to deployment of 572 new U.S. missiles in Western Europe capable of reaching the Soviet Union.

Echoes of continuing argument within the American Administration left many in doubt whether this was just a speech, America entering the propaganda war as some called it, and an all-or-nothing offer meant to be rejected; or whether it was a policy envisaging renewal of dialogue with Moscow on a broad range of issues looking toward restarting détente. NATO chose to take Mr. Reagan at his word and was cheered. A speech can force creation of policy, even if it does not represent the climax of a period of thoughtful study and conclusion enriched with specific plans.

In any case, the speech and the offer did reflect Washington's acknowledgment of European distress at the way things had been drifting. Europeans simply could not accept the idea of just sitting out a few years with their backs turned to the Soviet Union. Public opinion had been putting rapidly mounting pressure on the leaders. The apparent policy freeze in Washington had added substantially to the strains in U.S.-European relations.

On December 13, the military coup in Poland added a new element. The West had been watching for so long to see whether or not there would be a direct takeover by the Red Army that it was unprepared to react to the use of Polish force against Poles. At first, many wished to believe assurances from the head of the new military junta, General Wojciech Jaruzelski, that he was only curbing extremists and that the process of "renewal" would continue in partnership with the Solidarity union as soon as "normalization" was achieved. Even the first Polish Pope, John Paul II, warned, above all, against the shedding of more Polish blood. Washington quickly understood the essential Soviet role in the decision to impose a strict order wiping out liberties won in 17 months of struggle in Poland. As more and more bits of information trickled West, the European governments also came to realize that the Polish attempt to liberalize communist society had been quashed. It was not easy to reach a joint Western decision on what to do about it, but the shock to public opinion brought a sharp change in the Western climate. Once again, the basic East-West differences in society and the basic attitudes common to the West and underlying its alliance were clearly visible. The pendulum shifted.

How long it would last and how suppression of the Polish workers would affect relations in the longer term depended on volatile developments. Nonetheless, the strains between Europe and America over the meaning and hopes of East-West détente were not simply washed away. Of course, they had not developed in a single year. Current perceptions of divergence on the core issue of security and survival tend to set the Soviet invasion of Afghanistan in late 1979 as the marker. But there was a deeper tension. For the first time, the meaning of nuclear parity was sinking in. The argument about the possibility of a limited nuclear war in Europe revealed a basic, historic change in the world's strategic situation. Twice, the United States had watched war rage in Europe and finally decided to intervene. The North Atlantic Treaty was signed to settle that painful question beforehand. A European war would also be America's war, and that certainty had prevented fighting in Europe since 1945. Nuclear parity and modern missiles created a new question. Would an American war necessarily also be Europe's war, perhaps limited to Europe's soil?

Sober heads were convinced that the underlying reason for the Atlantic relationship had not changed despite a certain sense of Europe as a buffer between two global powers. Neither the United States nor Western Europe would be safe in a world where one couldn't rely on the other. They do share political and social values which they want to preserve and, despite malicious gibes, their systems permit cooperation and abhor domination. Though some people were thinking about the possibility of rupture, the very thought sent chills of dread in the hearts of leaders and the responsible public. The necessity of alliance and partnership remains.

II

If the atmosphere had so deteriorated, however, it was because these foundations found little expression during most of the year. The public discourse was focused on fears and threats. In Europe, the Reagan Administration's assertions of stoutheartedness and its images of danger to justify a vast but not clearly coherent military program seemed like bravura, the kind that could bumble into disaster. More missiles of all kinds, weapons as the tender of diplomacy, reluctance to engage the adversary in earnest negotiation, reverberated as an increased risk of war. That provoked the upsurge in neutralist and pacifist sentiment and a degree of anti-Americanism. The plan to deploy cruise and Pershing II missiles in Europe to counter Soviet SS-20s became the magnetic pole to attract and organize an outpouring of these feelings, with huge demonstrations in West Germany, Holland, Italy, Britain. The U.S. leadership was surprised and at first contemptuous. It had expected warm support from Europe for its new boldness; its concentration on communism as the source of all the world's evil led it to ascribe the reaction to outside agitation and a wobbly resolve. Washington answered with hints of a new "Mans-fieldism," a threat to withdraw U.S. troops from Europe and by implication to leave the Europeans to fend for themselves.

Throughout the year, Administration officials, legislators and American commentators had been warning that if the American public perceived a lack of European interest in joint defense or too much divergence in judging and sharing the tasks of the Alliance, American public opinion would lose patience with supporting 300,000 men in Europe, mostly in the front line of possible attack. Sometimes this was expressed as a dangerous possibility which European leaders should help to avert. Sometimes, it sounded almost like a threat. On the one side neutralism, on the other unilateralism or even isolationism: the retorts provoked each other, never at the highest level but insistent enough to aggravate irritabilities.

The deepening recession was part of the darkening mood. A world depression had led to World War II. There is no logical link now between sagging economies and a threat to peace, but the unavowed memory was ominous. In any case, economic troubles turn countries inward and enhance nationalist tendencies which complicate foreign relations. There was no particular quarrel with President Reagan's economic program at first. Whether they believed in his methods or not, the Europeans hoped for a U.S. recovery to ease their own difficulties. But when Reagan's economics produced exorbitant interest rates, they were affected and complained bitterly. To fight inflation at home, the Reagan Administration severely curtailed the supply of credit, driving up its price. This attracted a flow of money from abroad to take advantage of high U.S. interest rates and forced a relative devaluation of European currencies as the dollar floated upward. Europeans had complained about President Carter's "benign neglect" of the dollar, but President Reagan's over-muscular dollar hurt even more and they began to talk of a "third oil shock," the added cost of paying fuel bills in expensive dollars. Then, toward the end of the year when it became increasingly evident that Reaganomics wasn't going to deliver renewed prosperity soon—the social cost for Americans had never been a European concern—the worries grew.

The dollar, the American economy, has been an immediate European problem since World War II. In the 1950s, it was said that "when the U.S. economy sneezes, Europe catches pneumonia." Successive U.S. governments have insisted on their sovereign right to run the economy as they think best. But it adds to Europe's sense of impotence, and resentment, when changes of policy it cannot influence aggravate its own less than satisfying attempts at economic management. This has been particularly true since the breakdown of the Bretton Woods system in 1971 and the volatility it introduced in currencies. At the end of World War II when the dollar reigned alone, the United States and its friends had established an international monetary system intended to prevent the rival devaluations, blockages and uncertainties which had deepened the Great Depression in the 1930s and had been factors leading to war. It was based on full convertibility of the dollar firmly pegged to gold at $35 an ounce. Inflation, fueled by the American refusal to take account of the economic drain of the Vietnam War, and Europe's economic revival and trade, led to continuing U.S. balance-of-payments deficits. President Nixon loosened and then cut the dollar's tie to gold, allowing it to move with the market's forces and permitting broad fluctuations in exchange rates. From time to time, pleas were advanced for establishment of a new, more orderly and predictable system. But it has never been possible to agree on more than temporary patchwork.

On top of all this, there was the irritating spectacle of public backbiting, feuding and contradictions in Washington. Not that the same things do not happen in other capitals, but the size of the issues was so much greater. When American Cabinet members toss brickbats at each other, they're talking about war and peace. President Reagan had met all the major European leaders by the end of the year and the personal chemistry was fine, but he had yet to cross the Atlantic. There had been none of the abrasion that marked President Carter's encounters. But nothing much came of the meetings either. Mr. Reagan listened, smiled a lot, repeated his message on the advantages of private enterprise and his determination not to be pushed around by Russians, and went his own way, apparently unmoved. Gradually, Europeans wondered what role he actually played in his Administration, indeed, whether he was even running his own government.

The result of all this was a mounting sense that the Western world was running out of control, that the levers were disconnected. That queasy feeling was more responsible for the strains between Europe and the United States than any decision or pronouncement. It made people feel that they must do something to catch hold or get out of the way. But they didn't know quite what. The trouble was that the European countries were in no better control, together or, many of them, domestically. And there were no international leaders admired and trusted beyond their borders as giants able to bear the woeful world and to guide it.

The sense of community was draining out of the European Economic Community. It was surviving, but, as one ardently supportive senior diplomat observed, its primary impact had become its "negative value," that is, as a bulwark against pressures for even greater protectionism and for national advantage among the member states. For market reasons, the feared deadline when financial resources and budget demands would produce an absolute deficit did not arrive in 1980. But no one doubted that the crisis would soon come, and nothing was being done to avert it. The two major issues were the Common Agricultural Policy, now generally admitted to be an unmanageable deformation of economic sense, and financial obligations which have grossly overburdened West Germany and Britain without the balancing sense of redistribution to overall communal advantage which makes such inequities tolerable in a federal system. Britain's *The Economist* summed up the situation after the year's last Common Market summit failed to budge any of the disputes. Its cover showed Britain's Thatcher, West Germany's Schmidt and France's Mitterrand holding their heads in various gestures of distress under the title, "Why Did We Ever Invent the EEC?"

The three largest members were following domestic economic and social policies bound to widen the gaps. At one extreme, Britain stuck to controlling the money supply and deflation while unemployment rose to postwar records. At the other, France focused on employment and social change, sharply raising government spending and leaning on business to break what its socialist theoreticians called the "the power of money" in society. France's future interest in the Community, these ideologists said, depended on whether it can be converted into a "social space" with a dominant concern for workers' rights and welfare, or would remain what they consider a protectorate of multinational capital. West Germany was somewhere in between, no longer the model of economic success, moderately in trouble, trying moderate solutions, but scarcely less politically exacerbated. Meanwhile, some smaller countries added pique to the gloom. Greece's new Socialist Premier Andreas Papandreou seemed intent on taking over the familiar role of spoiler, once played in turn by France and Britain, threatening a referendum on continuing membership but apparently seeking leverage to extract more benefits. France maintained its opposition to early membership for Spain, mainly to keep out competitive foodstuffs, and sharpened the divisive effect by offering extra support for Portugal to join ahead of Spain. Most governments were weak, or almost nonexistent (Belgium and Denmark, for example), more than ever concerned with local troubles at the expense of a broader vision.

III

The most secure European leader turned out to be one of the newest, France's François Mitterrand. With his election on May 10, the Fifth Republic turned out Charles de Gaulle's heirs and installed the Left opposition for the first time. New parliamentary elections gave Mitterrand's Socialists a solid majority. He took his fractious Communist allies into the government, but was not dependent on them. With the next legislative election not due until 1986, and the presidential election scheduled for 1988, the French government was free of political risk.

Nonetheless, the initial euphoria of change and proof that the constitution could survive a transfer of power gave way to unease as France waited to see what kind of socialism the new rulers had in mind. The promised quick reversal of economic decline did not materialize. Both unemployment and inflation continued to grow. Some of Mr. Mitterrand's associates began to blame the failure of their formulas on "sabotage" by "the power of money," the business community which had largely supported and benefited from previous governments. They spoke alarmingly of the "*ancien régime*," as though they really intended to overturn society abruptly and irreversibly. The climate did nothing to encourage investment in the private sector, and that reticence brought threats of further radicalization. The public sector, enlarged by nationalization of the 11 biggest firms and all remaining private banks, did not revive a sense that good times were on the way.

Although there was nothing like the open display of dispute that characterized Washington, there was a tug-of-war between the theorists of socialism and the pragmatists on Mr. Mitterrand's assorted team. That added to uncertainties. Conflicting economic policies frayed the close partnership with West Germany, and there was no replacement by some other special intimacy in Europe. Despite ideological differences, a tougher French position toward the Soviets warmed relations with America on East-West issues. But that was somewhat offset by the clash between Washington and Paris on North-South problems, with the French advancing their championship of the Third World, including elements such as the Salvadoran insurgents whom the Reagan Administration considered Soviet-backed proxies. Altogether, the stability of her government did not translate into an expectation of enhanced solidity for France.

In West Germany, prospects for political smooth sailing after Chancellor Helmut Schmidt's handy reelection in 1980 drained away rapidly and his hold on power came to look fragile. About a third of his Social Democratic Party (SPD) moved well to his left, and part of the Free Democratic Party, his minor but essential coalition partners, began to grumble and think of switching sides.

A new mood, impossible to measure and hard to define, was swelling in the Federal Republic. Some called it left-wing nationalism, others called it anti-politics, the search for an "alternative," which was the name chosen by a group which did surprisingly well in West Berlin elections and took enough votes from the Socialists to install a Christian Democratic mayor in that old SPD stronghold. Without a change of leadership, West Germany was also changing climate. A book by Peter Bender, called *The Europeanization of Europe*, became the bible of the discontent. Its advocates said it meant that people in both Eastern and Western Europe want to get rid of their superpowers and make their own new way of life. The churches, the Left, the environmentalists, and the simply uneasy contributed to a fuzzy movement without a program but with a conviction that something was profoundly wrong and something should be done about it. Their language was reminiscent of the counterculture movement of 1968, and they provoked some of the same reaction from stolid burghers. But the lines were vague and the direction unclear.

In this atmosphere, but not essentially because of it, Chancellor Schmidt incarnated West Germany's new role as a major political as well as economic power. That is likely to be the most important and long-range European development of the year with effects far beyond the horizon. The milestone was Mr. Brezhnev's visit to Bonn. Mr. Schmidt cast himself as "interpreter" between Moscow and Washington, to help the two superpowers renew a dialogue and get back to the effort of controlling arms. Mr. Brezhnev called West Germany "a partner for peace" and spoke of common sufferings in World War II without a hint of the old Russian fear and suspicion of Germans. Mr. Schmidt made clear that although he was eager for renewal of general détente, there could be no question about West Germany's firm anchorage in NATO and its special ties with the United States. Still, the striking advance of West German-Soviet reconciliation and the unknown implications for West German-East German relations echoed distant rumblings which might or might not signal an earthquake in Europe's political terrain well after both leaders have gone from the scene. The partition of Germany was fixed in the 1975 Helsinki accord, but even the stars move.

The apparent paradox of Mr. Schmidt's attempt to preempt the political stage, while his very hold on power was being undermined by a stridently hostile left-wing faction of his SPD and a swelling peace movement, did not really change the meaning of Germany's evolution. The opposition Christian Democrats are more solidly pro-NATO, but in power they would face an even stronger critique of their foreign policy and perhaps more temptation to indulge the nationalist sentiments of much of the discontent. The CDU has shown no real unhappiness with the new German-Soviet relationship, and should not be expected to reverse the underlying trend.

The problem of national identity and significance in the world of powers remains profound for West Germans, and probably for East Germans, too, though they have little chance for self-expression. Even Mr. Schmidt's harshest critics welcome the fact that when "he talks to the big ones of the world, it makes us somebody again." France has begun to feel uneasy, and that must be read as the basic purpose of her attempt to revive the moribund Western European Union as a forum in which to discuss "European defense solidarity." This time, however, it is not to draw Germany away from its American ties but rather to anchor it more firmly. As the conservative commentator Alfred Fabre-Luce said in December, France has shifted from fear of German revanchism to fear of German neutralism.

Britain, too, passed a milestone on an uncertain road. Prime Minister Margaret Thatcher's version of monetarism and old-style conservative economics, launched two years ahead of Mr. Reagan's economic program, was also well ahead with bad results. Industrial production was down to the level of 1975, unemployment continued rising at 11.4 percent in November compared to 8.4 percent in 1980, and the advertised beginning of recovery was yet to be seen. The Tories were restive, the public impatient with what no longer looked like a new idea worth a try. The opposition Labour Party mirrored the move toward ideological fundamentalism. The Labour Party conference rejected the leadership bid of moderate Denis Healey in favor of the Left's candidate, Michael Foot. The choice reflected the growing power of the constituency apparatus, dominated by the ideological Left and ever more assertive in its demand for controls, over the traditional leadership of Labour's parliamentary bloc with its greater sensitivity to the broad sweep of public sentiment. Even Mr. Foot, recognizing the electorate's distaste for so much radicalism, later moved away from the most adamant leftists and managed to block Anthony Benn's attempt to become Deputy Leader.

The widening gap between Right and Left, in the homeland of restraint and civility, made way for a new Social Democratic Party. Its leaders, breakaways from Labour, made an alliance with the tattered Liberals in the belief that the electorate was predominantly Center-Left. The response in by-elections was phenomenal, and the British political landscape was thoroughly jarred. Compared to France and Germany, that created a modest uncertainty which had no international repercussions. But, eventually, it could force changed assumptions about Britain's sturdy support for current U.S. policies and its ineffective role in the European Community, which Mrs. Thatcher seemed to see as a greedy gang to be held at bay. The three parties offered three truly divergent choices for Britain, both domestically and internationally.

But the rise of the newborn Social Democrats presented at least the chance of a moderate solution in a few years. The Social Democrats, whose Shirley Williams won triumphantly in the Crosby suburb of Liverpool, showing the new party could draw from Tory voters as effectively as from Labourites, stood firmly for the Common Market and NATO. Their goal of becoming the swing force with their Liberal allies in the next general election, preventing either a Conservative or Labour majority, no longer seemed implausible. Both traditional parties were bound to be deeply affected, though neither was yet able to absorb the conclusions and translate them into changed positions. Mrs. Thatcher has until early 1984 to call elections. But it seemed unlikely that either major party could sufficiently change by then to squelch the new party's threat.

IV

Other countries in northern Europe, in their cooler way, were equally bedeviled in kicking the shins of those in power. Belgium was the worst case, with Europe's highest unemployment (12 percent), an ominously mounting debt, and still almost total political paralysis from its language feud. No longer were Belgium or the other small countries providing the brilliant spokesmen free to voice the larger concerns of Europe from a limited but sturdy podium. Doméstic squabbles kept rending coalitions, and internal affairs devoured all energies.

The Netherlands consumed governments like herrings, though the diagnosis of "Hollanditis" did give it some international impact. That referred not so much to instability of leadership as to protest movements in the name of moralizing the country and the world. Two neutralist slogans, quoted by veteran diplomat and businessman Ernst van der Beugel, were so similar to prewar Dutch themes that he wondered whether Holland's participation in the Alliance was just one generation's aberration from an old tradition. "I fear the worst," he said in a speech. Another slogan was unique, and uniquely armored against logic. But it echoed among West Germans usually resistant to the pleasure of paradox. It called for "neutralization within NATO," and whatever that meant was meant seriously. Holland's natural gas kept the economy afloat, the currency strong, and inflation low. But the country is totally dependent on trade (89 percent of gross national product compared to 43 percent in Germany, 31 percent in France and 16 percent in the United States). Huge social expenditures are coming to be recognized as substantially beyond its productive means.

Italy remained engulfed in its own cheerful disorder, with almost no impact on larger European or Atlantic affairs. Even the Euromissile issue provoked relatively little fuss, although acceptance of cruise missiles to be based in Sicily was an important matter for the Alliance. West Germany's condition for deployment from the start, apart from an effort at negotiations, was that at least one other continental country serve as a base. Belgium and Holland remained uncertain candidates, so Italy could be decisive. But international affairs attracted little attention there and the rest of Europe paid little attention to Italy, a grave concern just a few years ago when its society seemed to be disintegrating.

For the first time since the war, a premier who was not a

Christian Democrat took office. He was the small Republican Party's Giovanni Spadolini, an amiable man who made the breakthrough seem painless and therefore not a drastic change. There were still no clear signs whether the new coalition heralded a more durable equilibrium in place of the now traditional musical chairs system of changing governments, whether the Christian Democrats would be able to use a period of diminished responsibility to achieve their long promised internal renewal, whether Italian politics were really evolving or continuing their rhythm of minor variations on a single theme.

Spain had a far more dramatic and worrisome year. An attempted putsch on February 23 explosively disclosed the intensity of nostalgia among parts of the army and the Franco loyalists in business and high society. It failed because of prompt and clear action by King Juan Carlos, whose determination to maintain democratic structures was evidently underestimated by the Right. (His Queen, Sofia, is the sister of ex-King Constantine of Greece and whether his conviction stemmed from character or from the negative example of how his brother-in-law lost a throne was problematical. It was probably both.) His guidance eased but by no means dispelled the difficulties Spain was having in establishing the habit of democracy, and Spaniards themselves did not take the future of the regime for certain. Terrorism, aimed largely at the army and the police, and its impulse, regionalism, which the military considered a threat to national unity, were the main reasons advanced for their challenges to the new system. But underneath, there was a tangible resistance by the old elite and its beneficiaries to change and liberalism, for them equivalent to disorder.

The Union of the Democratic Center, an amalgam put together for the first parliamentary elections in 1977, remained in power with a new Premier, Leopoldo Calvo Sotelo, but it was crumbling. Political tolerance and cooperation are not easy to install at any time, and a period of recession adds obstacles. The Spanish conservatives were losing their cohesion. But so were the Communists, who won only nine percent in their national debut, and they, too, had a series of internal quarrels threatening a split. Common expectation was that the Socialists will come to power in the next election, a prospect that the military traditionalists find "unacceptable."

Repeated plots were bruited about to prevent any such thing. Socialist leader Felipe Gonzalez, young and handsomely reassuring, is a confirmed social-democrat but none could be sure how his untried party would manage to govern. He had told some people that he felt obliged to oppose Spain's entry into NATO, but would be glad enough to have the issue out of the way before assuming responsibility. Gradually, however, his public opposition stiffened, and he said the Socialists would resubmit any ratified decision to a popular referendum when they take charge.

The major importance of Spain's joining the Atlantic Alliance, incomplete but on the way at the end of the year, was more domestic than international. The Spanish-American treaty already provided the military requirements in terms of Europe's defense needs. But the Spanish army has had little to do beyond dominating politics since the Civil War, and it was adjusting poorly to the loss of the old role without acquiring a new one. Absorption in Alliance machinery, new tasks justifying new organization and promotion lists, could help it move into the more normal position of a defense establishment under civilian controls, and everyday involvement of its officers with allies who take democracy for granted could shift attitudes. It was important for Western Europe, too, that Spain's emergence from its long isolation prove stable and politically sympathetic. The effect of Spain's civil war and its dictatorship had not been forgotten.

The other Spanish effort to rejoin the Continent, membership in the European Economic Community, was not going well. Its fruits and vegetables were seen as devastating potential competition in France and indirectly in Italy. Common Market political support for the new Spain was not strong enough to override national economic lobbies and extend an early welcome to Madrid, a source of resentment on the peninsula since stalling also affected Portugal.

Still, though threats to stability were greater than anywhere in Europe, Spain deserved a judgment of cautious optimism. Despite the stereotype of hot blood and volatility, its people had calmly gone a long way in a short time along the most difficult road for any society—establishment of orderly freedom after revolution, war and dictatorship. Though participants in the Civil War were dying out, there is such a thing as social memory and social education to the folly of fratricide. The loyalty of the King to the parliamentary regime and the steadfast refusal of the great majority of people to be diverted from a democratic goal remained dominant.

The position of Greece in Europe was almost the obverse of Spain's. It did join the European Community, and its military ties with NATO were reestablished after a long sulk to protest what Athens considered better treatment of Turkey. Then, in the fall, the conservative government established after military rule had collapsed in 1974 was ousted by Andreas Papandreou's Socialists.

The election was as spectacular as Mr. Mitterrand's in France and posed even more questions. Premier Papandreou withheld his most far-reaching campaign threats on taking office. But he announced that the United States would be required to remove its nuclear weapons from Greek territory, a unilateral step aimed at establishing a future Balkan nuclear-free zone; negotiations would be sought for the removal of U.S. bases; the new military agreement with NATO would be reviewed; and the Common Market would be asked to give Greece a special, preferential status.

As though to demonstrate that Greece had no intention of playing the docile newcomer to the Community, Mr. Papandreou imposed a veto on the plan for the Ten to endorse the dispatch of British, French, Italian and Dutch troops for the multinational force to separate Israel and Egypt in the Sinai. There were even greater problems involving the force, primarily between Britain and Israel, and Greece couldn't veto national decisions; but Athens' recognition of the Palestine Liberation Organization (PLO), and its readiness to challenge a political move by its nine European partners, added to the signs of an activist foreign policy by the new Greek government.

Mr. Papandreou went a step further at the NATO Defense Minister's Council (he is also Defense Minister) and, for the first time in Alliance history, prevented the issuing of a communiqué by demanding an expression of guarantees for Greece that was unacceptable to Turkey. The U.S. Secretaries of State and Defense held meetings with him, which he called "sympathetic," but they obviously made no promises and nobody knew how far Mr. Papandreou's ploy was serious threat and how much was bluff.

To what extent the Greek government was now going to be anti-American was a matter of how to measure, but it was clearly going to be anti-Turk. Nationalism had been as important in the campaign as socialism. One reason given by Mr. Papandreou for his dissatisfaction with NATO was that it failed to guarantee Greece's border with Turkey, presumably including disputed Aegean air and sea space. The "southern flank," as Greece and Turkey are designated in NATO jargon, was in for more trouble.

Turkey was relatively quiet, compared to the murderous period of gang warfare between Left and Right which had brought the military to depose civilian government once again. But the promised return of power to the politicians kept receding. The Generals were finding that trying to run a government as well as an army accumulated the same intransigent problems which had frustrated them before. Violence was repressed, but Turkey's troubles were no nearer solution. Moreover, West European opinion was stirring against prolonged military rule, and warnings multiplied that apparently unequivocal U.S. support for the junta was provoking the same kind of anti-American resentment within Turkey as support for the Colonels had produced during their seven-year reign in Greece.

But Washington was determined to think strategically, brushing aside issues of democracy and political prisoners. That showed in the establishment of a new U.S.-Turkish joint defense board and a request for a large increase in military aid to Turkey in current and future U.S. budgets. It was the familiar dilemma, most dramatically exposed in Iran in recent years, between current U.S. global concerns and longer term appreciation of popular feelings. Turkish journalists returning from the United States told Swedish Social Democrat Pierre Schori, with evident disgust, that Americans argued to them, "In Europe, your religion is democracy. Ours is stability." Because of continued turmoil in Iran and lack of progress in resolving Middle East tensions, Turkey's strategic importance had been much enhanced. But that acknowledgment from Washington could in no way guarantee stability, and its approach could actually help undermine it.

Altogether, the pattern of political change showed that neither the "red tide" proclaimed in the mid-1970s, nor the conservative tide announced a few years later, had been the real trend. Rather, it was the "outs" overtaking the "ins," even in Scandinavia with its habit of generations of social democracy. It has been a time of rejection, of fitful trial and error, of waning confidence both in familiar national authority and in the mighty directors of the world. Uncertainties were pronounced with vehemence, but that made them no more steadying.

The European Community continued to hover like a lightning bug, real, visible, but unable to set a direction. Jean Monnet's initial idea that the small countries would work together to offset divisive national demands of the larger ones wasn't working. To the extent they looked to Europe, each sought its own specific advantage. Lowered expenditures postponed the absolute budget crisis, but none of the urgent reforms was made and the next foreign ministers' meeting, the next summit, was adjured to tackle them. The directly elected European Parliament, expected to provide fresh and more popular momentum, turned out to be no better at mobilizing energies than its predecessor. The cry of impending disaster has been heard too often to make it credible that the Community is really going to fall apart. But neither is it moving in a way that could elicit hope and enthusiasm, so that "Europe" cannot satisfy the yearning for a reassurance which is missing on both the lesser and the grander scale.

It is true that governments in the Community further developed the custom of political consultation and a search for consensus in foreign policy. That is often noted as a countersign to the massive evidence of immobilism in its own affair of "building Europe." Its members have achieved a certain coherence which gives shape and weight to their views in the rest of the world. But this applies only to external issues, usually declaratory, such as a United Nations vote or a patently sterile "initiative" telling the Middle East what it ought to do to resolve its problems. The new Commission President, Gaston Thorn, derided the idea that the Community can generate effectiveness by agreeing on statements to be made to the outside world and avoiding decisions.

V

Eastern Europe looked no more firmly established in its mold nor more predictable. The Soviet Union, indeed, remained remarkably congealed, with no change in leadership, no noticeable change in the mysterious relation of forces in the Kremlin, or in policy. Leonid Brezhnev passed his 75th birthday, obviously ill, with his puffy face and his wooden walk, but still apparently very much in charge. His long unmoving rule, evidently based on a delicate balance of rival pressures, only intensified the question of what will happen when the battle for succession breaks into the open. There was no visible preparation for handing on power, and therefore no hint of whether the long containment of ambitions will explode with ferocity or just continue containing itself for fear of an explosion. It is known that there are groups, at least in the middle leadership, who are worried about the lack of any notions of reform and structural modernization, particularly in agriculture. They complain, privately, that 64 years after the revolution, the Soviet superpower is less able than ever to feed itself. Brezhnev aired some of these concerns himself in a speech to the Central Committee, noting the failings of Soviet agriculture and admitting they can no longer be blamed on bad luck and bad weather alone. But what all this might presage is sheerest guesswork.

Meanwhile, the Soviet leader continued to show keen interest in renewing exchanges with the United States and in meeting President Reagan, although in harsher, less inviting terms than early in the year. West German officials said that a comparison of transcripts showed Mr. Brezhnev using the same angry, impatient phrases in private conversation about Mr. Reagan in the second half of 1981 that he had used about President Carter in 1980.

The problem of food supplies had become general throughout the Eastern bloc, with Hungary and Bulgaria the relative successes. Bread, sugar and oil rationing had to be imposed in Romania, and there were reports that its dynastic ruler Nicolae Ceauşescu was stoned during visits to mining areas. Before the Polish crisis came to a climax and while peace demonstrations were sprouting all over Western Europe, the Romanian leadership organized a huge, unusual anti-nuclear march of its own in Bucharest. The illusion of making common cause with Western protestors did not last long, however. After the Polish coup, lines were more tightly drawn again. Czechoslovakia was in a state of tangible decline. A flourishing black market became crucial to reasonable distribution in the cities. A leader was reported to have declared sarcastically that border signs should read: "Welcome to Czechoslovakia, an industrial museum." Apocryphal or not, the point was confirmed in aging factories and drooping productivity. East Germany remained the most effective economy. But it depended on the enormous advantages of its large trade with West Germany and the special arrangements which give it almost equal access to the Common Market, without any of the responsibilities of membership.

It was lack of food and overall economic wastage which provoked the Polish crisis in the summer of 1980. The spontaneous creation of the union, Solidarity, which amassed a membership of ten million almost overnight, totally changed the situation in Poland and sent muted but piercing signals through the bloc. The ruling Communist Party, bewildered and yet aware that new attempts at repression against such massive resistance could only bring disaster, temporized and seesawed. It was never ready to accept what at first were modest Solidarity demands. But, as it conceded one after the other under threat of total national paralysis, the workers' disgust and audacity mounted. In December of 1980, Soviet troops mobilized ominously. The Poles refused to be cowed. It was the Russians who backed down, though we may never know whether they were really on the brink of direct occupation as in Afghanistan in 1979 and Czechoslovakia in 1968 or had only hoped to intimidate.

Through most of 1981, the question of Soviet intentions toward Poland remained perilously unclear. It seemed that Moscow had finally decided to let Poland stew in its own juice until its people grew tired of defiance, but no one could be sure. In any event, Moscow appeared to welcome the continued flow of Western aid and credit which kept Poland limping on its tightrope and made no objection when Poland, following Hungary by special Comecon agreement, applied to join the International Monetary Fund with all the openings to the West which that implies.

Arguments, strikes, negotiations, and further deterioration of the economy went on all year. After an inconclusive Party Congress in July, which had been anticipated with excitement as the moment when renewal and reform would be launched, the new First Secretary, Stanislaw Kania, was ousted and replaced by his Premier and Defense Minister, Wojciech Jaruzelski. The resort to an army leader reflected how far the Party's authority had collapsed. A strange triad of Party (government), Union and Church (the revered Cardinal Wyszynski died and was replaced by the relatively unknown Monsignor Joseph Glemp) emerged at the head of the nation, though how far they could be said to rule was something else. No governing communist party had ever submitted to such a division of control; no communist country had ever lived under such peculiar conditions of individual freedom (secured quite simply by assertion) and national constraint (secured by geography).

It came to an end on December 13. There were massive arrests, including almost all the Solidarity leadership conveniently gathered in a meeting hall in Gdansk, and proclamation of martial law with suspension of all civil rights. The security police, never dismantled though scarcely functioning during the period of struggle, and the army took control. Reportedly, General Jaruzelski, who was already First Secretary, Prime Minister and Defense Minister, had received an ultimatum that the Soviet armed forces would move if the Poles did not. The traditional nationalism of the army at first gave an ambiguous aura to the new Military Council of National Salvation which he established. It was the first time that military authority had been erected above Communist Party authority in a communist-ruled country. But, gradually, resistance developed, and it appeared that the old communist structures were to be reestablished, with some changes of personnel. The regime announced ominously that it "would not retreat because it had nowhere to retreat to," and that was blazingly clear. The Union was decapitated and could not conceivably become a willing partner in reviving the economy. The Church, at first hesitant before what seemed a danger of civil war, slid back into its millennial role of embodying Poland's national aspirations and seemed to be taking the long view. The people mourned, mostly in silence, here and there in desperate anger which could still ignite violence.

In the circumstances, any hope of economic recovery appeared to recede further and further. Jaruzelski's base, perhaps even in the army, was precarious, and overt Soviet action remained an imminent threat. There was little likelihood that Western state and private banks would continue to pour funds down a Polish drain which had already consumed $27 billion in debt. But the idea of proclaiming default was equally unsettling. In any case, Poland probably marked a watershed in East-West economic relations, bringing a more severe look at other hopeless debtors, such as Czechoslovakia and Romania, and setting a long-term caveat against more loans to state-run economies with so little prospect of repayment. Ironically, the Soviet Union was in a better position because of its high-priced oil and gas exports. But it presumably would have to bear much more of the burden of sustaining production in Poland, and it was unclear to what extent Moscow might accept some responsibility for Polish debts in order to protect its own and Soviet-bloc credit.

The most profound blow was to hopes, both East and West, that somehow gradual reform of communist societies could develop to ease their cumulative pressures. Italy's Communist leader Enrico Berlinguer spoke out most explicitly, saying it was no longer possible to look to the East. Uncertainties about just what was happening in Poland, with internal as well as foreign communications cut, and what the end of the crisis would bring made it difficult to draw the likely historical consequences. But it was already clear that they would have the greatest importance to the future of the whole communist movement and to the search for East-West equilibrium.

VI

The outlook is uncertain and dangerous on both sides of Europe. But alarm bells are ringing loudly in the West now, and that may be the most encouraging sign. There is a wide understanding, developed over the year, that the trouble isn't a grippe best left to cure itself. Thoughtful people were beginning to reexamine basics and look for new policy proposals. My own view is not that policy has many different ways, but that the facts of the world have changed and the ideas which served so well in the postwar period have to be adapted to new circumstances.

First, because it is the focus of dissension and the source of greatest fear, is defense policy. NATO doctrine has relied on nuclear superiority to balance conventional weakness and thus to deter war. It worked very well. But there is no longer nuclear superiority. The atomic arsenal has changed its meaning. It no longer guarantees security but it could bring about apocalypse. Enlarging it adds no defense that couldn't be far better achieved by mutual reductions. Instead of being well equipped for a quick response to a massive Soviet attack, what the Alliance now needs is assurance of time to expose the adversary to weaknesses behind its own lines and force it to share in the awesome decisions of escalation. That means serious new attention to conventional defense. Europeans who have always resisted the cost may think differently when they realize it would downgrade the nuclear substitute and raise the nuclear threshold. France's François de Rose has suggested a new integrated doctrine that would not only permit sharp reduction of atomic weaponry in Europe (and, in truth, in the United States as well) but remove the dread obligation of having to initiate a nuclear exchange or accept defeat. Doctrine revised to actual circumstance could provide a coherent, and therefore credible, arms procurement and manpower policy, now lacking.

The Europeans have become set in the habit of objecting when the United States has failed to set an Alliance line and objecting when it insisted on compliance. They greatly underestimate the influence they could have in Washington if they made constructive proposals to the common benefit. President Reagan's acceptance not only of Euromissile negotiations, but his offer to negotiate on the whole nuclear spectrum showed they can help shape U.S. policy.

Second, if the approach to the Middle East cannot be better harmonized, at least it could be less frenetic and impulsive. The United States needs to be more attentive to the political issues and less fascinated by arms supplies as the way to soothe worried or irritable clients. Max Kohnstamm, former aide to Jean Monnet, has proposed that life problems in all of Palestine and surrounding areas—water, food, energy supplies—should be the way to engage Palestinians and Israelis in talks. This was tried and it failed several times in the past, but the Middle East has changed too. The Europeans haven't really drawn any advantage, or made any contribution, with declamations. They could be more supportive of Egypt, which has made peace, and more cooperative with the United States in developing practical policies.

Third, decolonization is over but nonindustrial countries remain vital as markets and suppliers to the industrial states, and especially to Europe. The new countries' politics are varied and unpredictable. That shouldn't get in the way of a fruitful development and trading partnership. Europe will insist on it, and the United States will lose both in terms of strains with the allies and opportunities in the North-South relationship if it tries to impose political or economic conditions based on ideological preference.

Fourth, a decade after the collapse of Bretton Woods, there is still no adequate world currency system. The tremendous multiplication of trade makes reliability of exchange far more necessary, and without it the surge of investment essential to development will be hampered and distorted. Cooperative economics is as essential to the U.S.-European alliance now as the Marshall Plan was to the success of NATO.

Fifth, U.S.-Soviet relations have gone awry and cannot be mended either by reverting to the cold war or pretending détente didn't stumble. This is primordial to the U.S.-European connection. A sense of timing has been vital. The new U.S. Administration sought a recess while America rearmed and considered its possibilities. That was a dubious idea, not only because Western Europe can't wait. There is no way at all to foresee the tilt in Kremlin policies after Brezhnev. But it seems obvious that while Brezhnev has the power to negotiate with the United States and to accept mutual restraints, once he goes his successors will be preoccupied for some years with their own struggle for power and scarcely in a position to make any concessions. They could be tempted, for internal reasons, to be more adventurous.

The problem of dealing with the Soviets was the reason for the Western alliance in the first place. Comfortable coexistence, without danger, is not yet possible but confrontation can no longer be envisaged. Together, the United States and Europe need to reconsider an overall policy toward Moscow, what they can reasonably expect from the Soviets, and what they are prepared to contribute to put the inevitable rivalry on a basis of least possible risk and the best prospects for lowered tension.

Robert Solomon

"THE ELEPHANT IN THE BOAT?": THE UNITED STATES AND THE WORLD ECONOMY

Although the weight of the United States in the world economy is less overwhelming than in earlier years, economic events, economic policies, and economic ideology in this country continue to have a substantial impact on the rest of the world, as was demonstrated again in the year just ended.

The most important event, from the viewpoint of other countries, was the steep and sustained climb in American interest rates, which contributed to but was not the sole cause of a dramatic appreciation of the dollar in foreign exchange markets. The corresponding depreciation of other currencies posed serious policy problems for a number of countries and gave rise to numerous complaints in the spring and summer of 1981.

The economic policy mainly responsible was the monetary policy of the Federal Reserve, carried out with the general, if occasionally backsliding, support of the Reagan Administration. With the Federal Reserve's growth targets for the money supply much below the growth of GNP (gross national product) in current dollars, the immediate reconciliation between money growth and GNP growth came through an escalation of interest rates to levels not seen in living memory. Later, GNP growth slowed as the economy slid into recession. The Federal Reserve's objective, about which there is virtually no dispute here or abroad, is to reduce the rate of inflation, with the impact on the rest of the world a by-product of the pursuit of this domestic objective. But coming as it did when the economies of most other industrial countries were already in a sluggish condition, still reeling from the effects of the oil shock of 1979–80, the U.S. impact was far from welcome.

Among the non-oil developing countries, those few that are

Robert Solomon is a Guest Scholar at The Brookings Institution and formerly was Adviser to the Board of Governors of the Federal Reserve System. He is the author of *The International Monetary System, 1945–1976: An Insider's View.* The quoted phrase in his title is based on a remark by Otmar Emminger, former President of the West German Bundesbank.

heavy borrowers from the world's commercial banks experienced a significant increase in the burden of servicing debt, as interest rates skyrocketed. Some of these found it necessary to cut back their rates of economic growth, which had been remarkably rapid in recent years, in order to contain their balance-of-payments deficits. The large number of developing countries that are producers mainly of raw materials and food were not affected so directly by high interest rates in major financial markets, but both the volume and prices of their exports were depressed by stagnation in the industrial countries. And all developing countries were thrown into uncertainty by the apparent ideological approach of the Reagan Administration to development assistance and the role of the multilateral financial institutions, especially the World Bank and International Monetary Fund (IMF).

II

What happened to U.S. interest rates in 1981 has often been characterized as the result of a "collision" between fiscal and monetary policies, which were said to be pushing the economy in opposite directions and thus aggravating the interest-rate consequences of monetary policy. Such a policy conflict may well occur in late 1982 and beyond, as the Reagan tax cuts interact with increasing defense outlays and hard-to-compress non-defense government programs. The result could be an excessively stimulative fiscal policy and, assuming the Federal Reserve continues on its course of restraining the supply of money and credit, increased upward pressure on interest rates.

During 1981, however, fiscal policy actually became more restrictive. With cuts in non-defense spending counterbalanced by defense increases and the impact of the Reagan tax cuts not yet fully felt, total federal spending in real terms (that is, adjusted for inflation) was unchanged from the previous year, while tax revenues increased. (Although the actual budget deficit changed little, the budget adjusted for the effects of recession—technically known as the high employment budget—shifted significantly toward surplus.) It was thus a combination of tighter fiscal *and* monetary policies that helped to create the recession that began in the latter half of 1981. (The widespread misconception about the direction of fiscal policy in 1981 itself is understandable in view of the lengthy debate over the budgets for future years.)

In any event, before the recession took hold, U.S. interest rates rose to very high levels, with the prime rate at 20.5 percent and three-month Treasury bills at almost 16 percent. Since inflation was running at 10 to 11 percent in the summer of 1981, the inflation-adjusted or real rate of interest was probably higher than at any time since the late eighteenth century.

High interest rates were a principal cause of the rapid upward movement of the dollar in relation to the currencies of many other countries. The average value of the dollar in terms of the currencies of the ten major industrial countries (as measured by the Federal Reserve Board) rose 30 percent from August 1980 to August 1981. This was by far the largest swing in the dollar, up or down, since exchange rates began to float in March 1973. But it was not uniform among foreign currencies. In terms of the German mark and other currencies in the European Monetary System (EMS), the dollar rose 40 percent or more, while in terms of the pound sterling and Swiss franc the appreciation was about 30 percent. In Japanese yen, however, the dollar went up only four percent over this period, as the yen first rose against the tide until early 1981 and then declined more gradually than other currencies. Because the effect of U.S. interest rates on the yen was counterbalanced by Japan's rapidly strengthening current-account position, Japan's average exchange rate changed little in 1981. For this reason we focus on the European currencies in what follows.

From the viewpoint of most foreign countries, escalating interest rates in the United States attracted funds from money and capital markets at home into dollar-denominated deposits and securities abroad. Such shifts of funds into dollars, either in the Eurodollar market or in the United States, drove down the dollar value of foreign currencies.

Rising U.S. interest rates, however, were not the only reason for the depreciation of other currencies and the appreciation of the dollar. Two other forces, one economic and the other political, were at work.

In 1979–80, there was a strong improvement in the U.S. trade balance, and more broadly in the balance on current account (which measures the surplus or deficit in transactions involving merchandise trade, services, dividends and interest, and remittances to foreign residents and governments). This improvement was partially masked by the substantial increase in the price of imported oil that took place in 1979–80 and affected the balance-of-payments positions of all oil-importing countries. Although the dollar value of U.S. oil imports rose by more than $35 billion, or 85 percent, between 1978 and 1980 (while the quantity of oil imports fell nearly one-fifth), the U.S. balance on current account shifted from a deficit of more than $14 billion to a surplus of more than $3 billion. Over the same period the other industrial countries as a group experienced a shift from a current-account surplus of $27 billion to a deficit of $71 billion. In particular, West Germany and Japan moved from large surplus in 1978 to large deficit in 1980.

The strong balance-of-payments position of the United States and the corresponding deficits abroad, which persisted into the early part of 1981, affected exchange rates both directly via the financing of the payments imbalances and indirectly via the expectation that the imbalances would have to be corrected by exchange-rate adjustments. In foreign exchange markets widely held expectations tend to be quickly self-fulfilling. Hence the dollar appreciated while the currencies of countries in substantial current-account deficit depreciated.

Moreover, some currencies in Europe were influenced by political factors in 1981. At times, when the situation in Poland appeared particularly unstable, the German mark tended to weaken, as investors moved out of that currency on the basis of fear of the unknown. In France, the election of President Mitterrand and of a Socialist majority in the National Assembly led to downward pressure on the franc as both French citizens and foreigners felt motivated to get their funds out of France while they could. Thus the mark and the franc depreciated more than the currencies of other European countries—for example, Sweden and Switzerland—which were more immune to political events.

Another influence on exchange rates, and one that has traditionally been regarded as the major influence, is differing rates of inflation. This factor played no discernible role, as far as the dollar was concerned, in 1981: the mark and the yen, for example, both depreciated against the dollar though Germany and Japan had lower inflation rates than the United States. (In contrast, the realignment of exchange rates in the European Monetary System in October, when the mark and the Dutch guilder were raised by 5.5 percent and the French franc and Italian lira were lowered by three percent, was more reflective of differences in inflation rates.)

The average exchange rate of the dollar reached its peak and turned down in August, shortly after U.S. short-term interest rates began to fall. By late December about one-fourth of the dollar's appreciation in the year to August 1981 had been reversed.

Once again, not only interest rates were at work. Germany's current-account deficit was contracting rapidly and Japan was in substantial surplus. As we shall discuss in greater detail below, this was, from the viewpoint of other countries, the silver lining in the depreciation of their currencies against the dollar in 1980–81. Their competitive positions improved, with positive effects on their current-account balances.

III

The sharp rise in U.S. interest rates in 1981 compounded a policy dilemma in which most industrial countries already found themselves in trying to cope with the dual effects of the near-tripling of the price of oil in 1979–80. As had become evident after the first oil shock in late 1973, a large advance in the OPEC oil price acts on oil-importing countries like a huge sales tax. On the one hand, it drives up the price of the taxed product and through it the overall price level; on the other, it drains off purchasing power that might have been spent on other goods and services, thereby depressing the economy.

The average rate of inflation in the industrial countries had accelerated from seven percent in 1978 to 12 percent in 1980. But industrial production peaked in the first quarter of 1980 and then fell off, while unemployment rose rapidly to record post-World War II levels. In the circumstances, interest rates began to decline in the second half of 1980 in a number of European countries and in Japan.

Meanwhile, inflation decelerated somewhat but was sustained by the momentum of advancing wages, which were in turn reacting to rising prices. The desire to bring inflation down further kept central banks from easing monetary policy despite the sluggishness of output and employment. This was the dilemma in the minds of policymakers in a number of countries even before the sharp run-up of interest rates in the United States.

The dilemma became more acute as the dollar appreciated, first gradually in the autumn of 1980 and then more rapidly in the first eight months of 1981. To countries in Europe especially, currency depreciation—the mirror image of the dollar's appreciation—threatened to worsen inflation again at a time when industrial output was stagnating at a level five percent below the early 1980 peak. Depreciation against the dollar meant rising costs of imports not only from the United States but from all countries whose exports are denominated in dollars, including OPEC members and other oil-exporting nations. Rising import costs, it was feared, would affect all prices in industrial countries and provoke demands for more rapid wage increases.

In order to dampen these effects, many countries attempted to cushion the decline of their exchange rates by raising interest rates and by intervening in foreign exchange markets to support their own currencies by selling dollars. Germany's central bank took strong steps in February, which lifted the three-month money market rate from 9.5 to 13.5 percent. Similar, if less drastic, measures were adopted elsewhere.

There is no way to estimate the effect of these actions on exchange rates. It is hard to believe that they did not slow down the rate of depreciation of European currencies. Yet that depreciation was very rapid in the spring and summer of 1981. From March to August the dollar value of the mark fell almost 16 percent.

It is a fair question whether the European countries would not have been better off in 1981 to have kept their interest rates lower—in order to improve the performance of their lackluster domestic economies—and let their dollar exchange rates go. The rate of depreciation might have been faster, but this in itself might have brought an earlier reversal of exchange rates, as expectations developed that the trough had been reached. This approach never had a chance, however, since it would have required the participation, if not the leadership, of the West German Bundesbank. Through most of the year, while officials of the German government—from Chancellor Helmut Schmidt on down—were expressing unhappiness about U.S. interest rates, the Bundesbank was concerned about Germany's current-account deficit. It justified its stringent policy by the need to reduce this deficit as well as to counteract the price-increasing effects of depreciation and to sustain foreign confidence in the D-mark.

Another alternative would have been for European governments to have borrowed more heavily abroad and used the proceeds to support their exchange rates in the markets. The German authorities, for example, did borrow DM 20.6 billion (more than $9 billion) in the first ten months of 1981, but there is no doubt about Germany's creditworthiness and ability to borrow more.

In any event, European policymakers chose to combat the depreciation of their currencies with rising interest rates as well as sales of dollars. As they did so, a swelling chorus of complaints was directed westward across the Atlantic, and the term "benign neglect" was revived to characterize the posture of the U.S. authorities. Since no one wished to oppose American efforts to reduce inflation, criticism focused on excessive reliance on monetary policy in the United States and the Reagan Administration's announced policy of refraining from intervention in foreign exchange markets except in dire emergencies. (The ill-chosen illustration of such an emergency was the attempt in March on the life of the President, when in fact a small amount of market support was given to the dollar.)

The annual report of the Bank for International Settlements, published in June, strongly recommended that governments should reinforce anti-inflationary monetary policy with greater restraint in fiscal policy and also suggested that incomes policy—that is, direct action, by regulation or tax incentives, to influence wage and price behavior—should not be ruled out. Although these proposals were directed at industrial countries in general, press reports interpreted them as being aimed especially at the United States. More pointedly, France's new Minister of Economy and Finance, Jacques Delors, characterized high American interest rates and the appreciation of the dollar as comparable to a "third oil shock."

As the Ottawa summit meeting approached in July, the press featured reports about the coming confrontation between President Reagan and the other leaders over U.S. economic policies. By the time the meeting convened, however, it was evident that the Americans had no intention of yielding, and the communiqué papered over any differences that may have been expressed. But, on his return to Bonn, Chancellor Schmidt announced that he would propose a reduction in planned defense expenditures, in view of the high interest rates prevailing in the United States. The economic logic was not apparent. If Germany's economy was being depressed by the necessity to maintain high interest rates, wouldn't the decline in government expenditures depress it even more? Not for the first time, an economic rationale was used to support a politically convenient decision.

Meanwhile, central bankers were either silent or openly supportive of the Federal Reserve. It is not surprising that the president of the German central bank, Karl Otto Poehl, denied that "in present circumstances Germany could have very low interest rates if only rates in the United States were lower." The fact that few if any central bankers joined their government colleagues in public disapproval of U.S. policies is probably explained in part by esprit de corps in the central banking fraternity, but also by a strong belief, right or wrong, that they could not rid their own countries of inflation unless the United States led the way.

Those who expressed dissatisfaction with U.S. policies claimed that stagnation, if not recession, was being forced on Europe through the high real interest rates it had to maintain in order to combat currency depreciation. This complaint had a familiar ring. In 1977–78, when the dollar was going down rather than up, stagnation in other industrial countries was often blamed on the falling dollar, on the grounds that appreciating currencies were hurting exports. In 1981, stagnation was blamed on the rising dollar. While there may have been some merit in both views—paradoxical though it seems—it is also true that politicians abroad have for many years found it convenient to blame the United States when their own economies were not performing satisfactorily.

This unsatisfactory performance was aggravated by a tendency in some countries of Europe to use fiscal policy in a perverse way. As is normal in a modern economy, budget deficits increased as output, incomes and employment sagged. This familiar process, involving lower tax receipts and higher unemployment benefits, has long been referred to as a built-in stabilizer. But governments in some countries, most notably the United Kingdom, had become so preoccupied with public sector deficits that they adopted measures to offset the automatic enlargement of deficits. British Chancellor of the Exchequer Sir Geoffrey Howe, in his March budget, raised tax rates in an economy in its worst recession since the 1930s.

Although other cases were less flagrant, the OECD (Organization for Economic Cooperation and Development) has shown that fiscal policy became more restrictive in 1981 in Japan, France and Germany as well as in Britain and the United States. Thus, the major countries were raising their interest rates in response to the U.S. impact at a time when their own fiscal policies were tending to depress their already-sluggish economies. But it was American policies they complained about.

Moreover, what seemed to be ignored in all the complaints was that the exchange-rate changes in 1980–81 were setting the stage for a substantial improvement in the balance of payments of Europe at the expense of the strong surplus of the United States. Germany's current-account deficit fell from $19 billion at an annual rate in the first quarter of 1981 to $10 billion in the third quarter. In October and November, the current account was in surplus. For the ten countries of the European Community, the current-account deficit is estimated by the OECD to have declined from $40 billion in 1980 to about $21 billion in 1981.

More broadly, stagnating economies, in which both monetary and fiscal policies had become more restrictive, were getting a lift from their export sectors, which had become more competitive thanks to exchange-rate depreciation. How much further this process could go was an open question in early 1981. With the

United States in recession and the non-oil developing countries under balance-of-payments pressure, as is discussed below, the only buoyant markets appeared to be in some of the OPEC countries.

IV

In the economic conditions prevailing in 1981, trade policies in the industrial countries tended to become more protectionist.

The Reagan Administration's free-market philosophy was a force working against trade barriers. Early on, it acted to abolish quotas on shoe imports. But with its political constituency in economic trouble and members of Congress in a position to bargain over the domestic economic program, convenience as well as tradition called for the ills of the automobile, steel and textile industries to be blamed on imports. Tradition has also called for Americans to rant against Japan whenever that country is in large surplus in its bilateral trade with the United States, even at times, as in 1981, when the United States has a bilateral surplus with Europe.

Thus the Administration surmounted its free-market ideology in the spring and persuaded Japan to limit automobile exports to the United States. Also disturbing was American acquiescence to European protectionism in the late-1981 negotiations over renewal of the multifiber arrangement, under which the industrial countries had agreed, in 1973 and again in 1977, to accept "orderly" increases in their imports of textiles and apparel from developing countries. Under the renewed arrangement, signed in Geneva in December, industrial countries are permitted, in bilateral agreements implementing the general arrangement, to reduce imports. This was an ironic sequel to President Reagan's lectures to developing-country officials, in Washington in September and at Cancún in October, about the virtues of relying on free markets to generate economic development.

At the same time, Administration officials were following the time-honored practice of threatening Japan with congressional action against its exports if it did not reduce its trade surplus with the United States. Japan's imports of manufactured goods are very low indeed, as compared with the import composition of other industrial countries. The explanation is not very clear, but there is every reason to keep the pressure on Japan to see to it that obstacles to imports, whatever their nature, are removed. Such pressure would come with more grace and perhaps would yield more results if the United States and Europe were moving away from, rather than toward, protectionism.

V

Up to now, this article has focused on the economic performance and policies of the industrial countries. The past year was not a stellar one for the developing countries either.

Since the time of the 1973 jump in oil prices, a small group of so-called non-oil developing countries have become major borrowers from commercial banks in the industrial world. Eight countries in this category (Argentina, Brazil, Chile, Mexico, Peru, the Philippines, South Korea and Thailand) account for 70 percent of the external bank debt and half of the total debt of all non-oil developing countries. This small group also accounts for nearly half of the GNP of all non-oil developing countries. Its membership is not identical with the group that has been dubbed "newly industrialized" countries; the overlap is substantial but it is not complete because some of the latter countries, such as Hong Kong and Taiwan, are not—or are no longer—heavy borrowers, and a couple of the heavy borrowers are not far along on the road to industrialization.

These facts confirm that what is so often characterized as "the Third World" or "the South" consists, as Roger Hansen has put it, of "states of enormous diversity by all economic measures." Furthermore, "the economic 'gaps' growing most dramatically in the past decade have not been between the North and the South, but rather within the South itself—between the oil-rich and the industrially developed countries and the vast majority of their predominantly poor and significantly less industrialized diplomatic partners."[1]

The eight countries that were such large borrowers used the borrowed resources mainly to help finance current-account deficits. Such deficits supplement domestic savings and thereby permit a high rate of capital formation. This in turn has facilitated rapid export expansion and rates of economic growth considerably above the average for all developing countries. Even in 1979–80, when the second oil shock was having its effects, these eight countries had an average rate of growth of 5.5 percent per year compared with 1.5 percent for the industrial countries.

This virtuous circle of investment, growth and export expansion based in part on external borrowing had been encouraged in the 1970s by very low and at times even negative real rates of interest

[1] Roger D. Hansen, "North-South Policy—What's the Problem?" *Foreign Affairs*, Summer 1980, p. 1105.

(i.e., rates below the inflation rate).[2] This favorable circumstance has changed markedly in the past two years. The excess of the interest rate on three-month Eurodollar loans over inflation (of consumer prices) in industrial countries rose from 1.5 percent in 1978 to 2.5 percent in 1980 to 8.7 percent in the third quarter of 1981. In late December, it was back to about four percent.

Even if real interest rates had not risen to abnormal levels, the advance of nominal interest rates in step with inflation would have added to the current debt burden of developing countries. To be sure, this kind of enlargement of the debt burden would have been matched by a reduction in the real value of the debt with inflation, making future debt repayments lighter in real terms. But the effect, if interest rates keep up with rising prices, is to accelerate debt repayment, so that the traditional benefits that debtors derive from inflation are removed.

As it happens, the interest rates that prevailed in 1981, until August, went well beyond compensating for the erosion of debt because of inflation. They imposed a substantial burden on debtors. And, it is safe to say, they were a threat to economic progress in industrial as well as developing countries.

Among the ways in which the restrictive effects of the high interest rates showed up was in an increase in the current-account deficits of developing countries. Since the reduction in debt owing to inflation is not reflected in the reported current-account deficits, the latter tend to exaggerate the plight of the debtor countries. Nevertheless, the interest burden was heavy. For the eight countries we have been looking at, interest payments in 1980 came to $16.5 billion, a sum greater than their total current-account deficit in 1978. The increase in interest payments abroad from 1978 to 1980 accounted for more than one-third of the increase in the current-account deficits of these countries.

Similar data are not available for 1981, but in view of the fact that a substantial portion of the bank debt carries floating interest rates, there can be no doubt that interest payments rose sharply as the average rate on Eurodollar loans advanced from 14.4 percent in 1980 to 17.4 percent in the first three quarters of 1981.

The result, as might have been expected, was a determined effort by a number of these countries to compress their balance-of-payments deficits to magnitudes that could be financed and would preserve their appearance of creditworthiness. In the pro-

---

[2] See, for example, Robert Solomon, "The Debt of Developing Countries: Another Look," *Brookings Papers on Economic Activity*, 2: 1981.

cess, economic growth was sacrificed. Brazil, the largest debtor among developing countries, adopted severely restrictive domestic policies and experienced a substantial decline in industrial production. Its real GNP, which expanded eight percent in 1980, is estimated to have grown little in 1981. Mexico, despite the advantage of oil resources, also cut its growth rate in 1981 because of concern over its balance of payments.

This is, of course, an unfavorable turn of events for the development and political stability of the countries involved. Moreover, the consequent slowdown in imports by these and other developing countries will affect the exports of industrial countries and thereby add to the downward pressures on their economic activity.

VI

The overwhelming majority of developing countries were not strongly affected, in a direct way, by what happened to interest rates and exchange rates in 1981. What they were vulnerable to was slack demand for imports by industrial countries. This showed up in both the volume and prices of their exports of raw materials. And they, too, were still feeling the effects of the increase in oil prices of 1979–80. For those developing countries classified in the "low income" category by the International Monetary Fund, import prices rose an estimated 53 percent from 1978 to 1981, while export prices went up less than 23 percent. In the circumstances, the latest annual report of the Fund, an institution whose publications do not feature colorful language, characterized the impact of these events on the low-income countries as "almost devastating."

Furthermore, these countries are for the most part dependent on official development assistance (ODA)—bilateral aid from donors among the industrial and oil-exporting countries and loans on a concessionary basis from the soft-loan windows of the World Bank and the regional development banks. The size of these aid flows determines the capacity of the low-income countries to incur current-account deficits. In contrast to most industrial countries, low-income developing countries cannot count on finding the means to finance any given external deficit that they might incur as the result of developments in their own economies and those abroad. In technical jargon, their current-account deficits cannot be treated as autonomous. Rather, the amount of external funds available has to be taken as given, and the current-account deficit has to be limited accordingly.

Between 1978 and 1980, ODA increased about $10 billion, or 40 percent, to somewhat more than $35 billion.[3] Although this represented a welcome acceleration in such assistance, it was nearly matched by the rise in the cost of oil imported by the low-income developing countries. The OECD countries as a group are expected to increase ODA by perhaps four percent per year, in real terms, in the next several years. In the United States, however, the prospects for foreign aid and contributions to multilateral development banks are uncertain. Moreover, the slow growth likely to prevail in the industrial countries will hold down the export proceeds of developing countries, especially the poorer ones dependent on exports of primary products.

VII

The doubts about U.S. development assistance stem in part from general budgetary stringency as the Reagan Administration attempts to restrain non-defense outlays. And, despite the passage of a foreign aid bill in December, members of the Congress are unlikely to be generous to foreigners when they are being asked to cut back assistance programs to their own constituents.

Apart from the budgetary constraint, the economic ideology of the Reagan Administration raises questions about the future of the international institutions that provide funds to developing countries. The ideology was deftly summarized by the President, in his welcoming address to the annual meeting of the International Monetary Fund and the World Bank in September, as reliance on "the magic of the marketplace."

Although the Administration's policy stance is still in process of formulation, the broad outline is clear.[4] With respect to the World Bank and the regional banks, it is being suggested that too much lending has gone to finance public sector projects and not enough to private enterprises. The obvious answer to this charge is that much of the development lending is designed to provide the infrastructure necessary for economic development: roads, railways, harbors, dams and other projects for this purpose are inherently in the public sector. But in recent years the World Bank in particular has shifted its lending toward programs designed to develop energy sources and to improve the productivity

[3] World Bank, *Annual Report, 1981.* p. 26.

[4] It is set forth in "Assessment of U.S. Participation in the Multilateral Development Banks in the 1980s," Consultation Draft, Department of the Treasury, September 21, 1981, especially the section entitled Conclusions and Recommendations.

of the rural and urban poor, and this is likely to mean the provision of funds for both public and private projects.

In the same vein, the Administration's new approach would emphasize the role of the development banks as catalysts for private investment flows rather than as sources of capital. The unwillingness to go along with the proposed energy affiliate of the World Bank, in the face of widespread support for it by industrial and developing countries, was an early concrete expression of this principle.

Beyond the nature of lending by the development banks, the American Administration's objective appears to be to reduce and ultimately eliminate government financing and guaranties of their capital increases. In particular, U.S. budgetary contributions to the International Development Association (IDA)—the World Bank's affiliate that lends three to four billion dollars per year to low-income countries at minimal interest rates and with long maturities—as well as to the "soft loan windows" of the regional development banks would be reduced in real terms. It is noteworthy that A. W. Clausen, the new president of the World Bank (and former head of the Bank of America), made a special plea for IDA in his address at the annual meeting:

> What is it worth to the wealthy nations to be able to count on a reasonable degree of political and social stability, based on prospects for economic progress, in the poorest countries of the world? Does that touch on the affluent nations' self-interest, on their trading patterns; on the assured supply of this or that commodity; on their relations with other countries in the region? Should affluent countries worry that hunger and hopelessness in an urban slum of a poor society can drive jobless young people to irrational violence? Or can the rich countries afford, in the security of their wealth, not to care?

While IDA depends entirely on governmental contributions, the effect of the new approach, if it is implemented, on the World Bank itself and on the regional banks, is less clear. In particular, any removal of government guaranties of the banks' capital increases would raise serious questions. In the past, the ability of the banks to issue securities successfully in major capital markets has depended at least in part on the investors' assurance that the capital of the banks—callable from governments—stood behind the banks' liabilities.

Thus, if the Reagan Administration were to carry out to the full its rhetoric that the multilateral banks should henceforth depend on their success in the "marketplace" of private financing, the effect could indeed be drastic. How far the existing capital could be stretched could then become a serious problem.

American ideology was also focused on the International Monetary Fund, though in a rather awkward way. In a press interview before the annual meeting, Secretary of the Treasury Donald Regan stated that the United States wants the IMF to impose tougher policy conditions on borrowing countries. Apparently the Secretary was speaking from an out-of-date brief, and at the meeting itself all was sweetness and light and the Fund's "conditionality," as it is called, was not criticized. Nevertheless, a while later, the U.S. Executive Director abstained when the IMF was passing on a loan of more than five billion dollars to India and again when it was approving a further installment of a loan to Pakistan. The strength of U.S. support for the Fund is in doubt.

The highlight, at least as measured by theatrics, in what are called North-South relations, came at a summit meeting of 22 nations at Cancún, Mexico in October. This meeting had been recommended by the Brandt Commission, and President López Portillo persuaded President Reagan to attend. In two days at the plush resort of Cancún, the leaders failed even to identify specific issues on which concrete progress could eventually be made. Instead the representatives of the industrial countries accepted the proposed "global negotiations" in the United Nations. What this means or where it will lead is not at all clear. How can 150 nations negotiate? Whatever was agreed procedurally at Cancún, there is no chance that issues pertaining to the IMF and World Bank, where weighted voting prevails, will be permitted by the industrial countries to be decided at the United Nations.

Here was an instance of ideology in the developing world— where demands for a "New International Economic Order" and "global negotiations" are exceeded in their vagueness only by their lack of realism—prevailing over the ideology that the Reagan Administration has been expressing. But little is likely to come from this procedural victory. As *The Economist* put it, "words will speak louder than actions."

Yet issues exist on which cooperation between industrialized and developing countries could yield concrete benefits to both groups. Rodrigo Botero, former Finance Minister of Colombia and a member of the Brandt Commission, has identified these topics: increased energy production in developing countries, improved mechanisms for financial recycling, promotion of food production in developing countries, encouragement of exports by developing countries, and alleviation of poverty in the least-developed countries.[5]

[5] *Newsweek*, October 26, 1981, p. 43.

VIII

The outlook for the world economy in early 1982 is rather gloomy. One of the few rays of brightness is that the oil-importing countries have not had to endure still another hike in oil prices, as has happened so often after year-end meetings of OPEC. In fact, OPEC prices are edging down as the premiums other countries have been charging over the Saudi Arabian base price are trimmed. Of greater significance, 1981 saw a determined and successful Saudi effort to use its production potential to force down the prices of some of its OPEC partners; Sheikh Yamani pointedly announced that OPEC prices can go down as well as up. It seems more evident than ever that Saudi Arabia, with oil reserves that will last well into the next century, is concerned about the future value of those reserves, as conservation and alternative sources of oil and other energy are stimulated by present OPEC price levels. (President Reagan's early move to deregulate oil eliminated perverse incentives to import, and now keeps the U.S. oil price on a par with the world price. This is all to the good. What is questionable is the apparent tendency of the Administration to leave energy policy completely to the market by cutting tax inducements to undertake conservation measures and by de-emphasizing the synthetic fuels program. One would have thought that such efforts were part of the raison d'être of the Saudi policy on prices.)

There are few other rays of brightness. The inelegant term "stagflation," coined in the 1970s to capture the unhappy combination of sluggish output and employment combined with inflation, is still apposite as regards the industrial countries in the early 1980s. The United States is unlikely to meet the optimistic targets for growth, unemployment and inflation announced by the Reagan Administration in its early heady weeks. The other industrial countries, although affected by U.S. policies, cannot avoid looking to their own policy failures for an explanation of poor economic performance. And the diverse groups of developing countries cannot help being affected by what happens in the industrial countries.

In what follows, we shall put some analytical flesh on the bare bones of these concluding generalizations and offer a policy prescription.

The U.S. economy, whatever the precise timing of recovery from the recession into which it plunged in 1981, is unlikely to expand very far before once again running into monetary restraint. And now the federal budget and monetary policy are likely indeed to be on a "collision course," unless the prospective deficits are reduced drastically by tax hikes, smaller increases in defense outlays, larger cuts in non-defense spending, or some combination of these possibilities.

The three-year tax cut embraced by President Reagan relied heavily on the case put by supply-side economists, who claim that lower marginal tax rates increase incentives to work, to save and to invest. While these effects on economic behavior remain to be tested, it can be assumed with confidence that those whose taxes are lowered will increase their spending. Demand and supply are the bread and butter of economists, but the supply-siders would like us to ignore the demand effects of tax cuts. This would be myopic.

In an economy in recession, some degree of demand stimulus should be welcome. The problem is that a vigorously expanding economy will once again run into the ceiling imposed by monetary policy, whether the expansion is propelled by loose fiscal policy or by strong private spending.

The only way to reconcile sustained expansion of the real economy with the Federal Reserve's monetary targets is to bring about a significant reduction in the rate of inflation. The Federal Reserve's policies are consistent with a certain rate of growth of current-dollar GNP. The slower the rate of price advance, the more scope there is for that GNP growth to take the form of output expansion.

This is a message that Federal Reserve Chairman Paul Volcker proclaims almost every time he makes a speech or testifies before a congressional committee. Specifically, he pleads for moderation in wage settlements and price increases.

In a way, then, the Federal Reserve is operating an incomes policy—a policy that recognizes and tries to deal with the self-sustaining nature of the interaction of wages and prices. It cannot be claimed that the inflation still present in the United States— or, as discussed below, in Europe—is the result of excess demand, of too much money chasing too few goods. With unemployment above seven percent and capacity utilization in manufacturing below 80 percent even before the recession, more goods and services could have been produced. What explains the persistence of inflation is the inertia involved in the reaction of wages to prices and of prices to wages, both past and expected. Once a wage-price cycle starts, it tends to go on.

The classical remedy is a lengthy recession, in which workers accept lower wage increases out of fear of losing their jobs and producers trim price increases in consequence of the smaller wage advances as well as of the pressure of heavy inventories and idle capacity. Some of this is happening but it is a slow process, as Mrs. Thatcher's experiment demonstrates.

The alternative is an overt incomes policy, which acts directly on prices and wages. Incomes policy can take a variety of forms. One is governmental regulation of wage and price advances, as was done by the Nixon Administration in 1971–73. Another is provision of tax incentives or penalties to induce wage and price behavior in accordance with established norms.[6] Any type of incomes policy would clash with the philosophy of the present Administration. Nevertheless, if one or another form of this approach were adopted, as a temporary complement to—not a substitute for—monetary policy, it would accelerate the process of disinflation and make possible a sustained period of economic expansion and a reduction in the level of unemployment.

In the absence of such direct action on prices and wages, the economy is all too likely to fluctuate in a narrow band, lurching between aborted recoveries and frequent recessions. In time, inflation could come down to a tolerable rate, since the progress toward lower inflation in recessions is unlikely to be fully lost in the short-lived and incomplete recoveries. Still, one must ask, are these hardships necessary?

Furthermore, is such an economy likely to be conducive to an adequate rate of investment? The need to embody technological progress and to restore a decent rate of productivity growth is widely recognized. But the required capital formation is unlikely to occur in an economic environment in which either recession or astronomical interest rates are always just around the corner.

Most other industrial countries face similar problems, though the severity varies. In Europe, unemployment has passed 8.5 percent of the labor force, and idle youth pose serious political difficulties. The poor outlook is exemplified by a recent report of Germany's council of economic advisers—the so-called wise men—who proposed a program to boost investment in 1982 so as to increase the economy's rate of growth from 0.5 percent without the program to one percent with it. Japan has the best record on inflation, but its huge trade surplus is a reflection, at least in part, of inadequate growth of domestic demand. And the budget proposed by Prime Minister Zenko Suzuki for the next fiscal year

---

[6] The pros and cons of tax-based incomes policies are discussed in *Brookings Papers on Economic Activity*, 2: 1978.

will, despite the increase in defense expenditures, weaken domestic demand further.

The prescription set forth above, adoption of an incomes policy, also applies to most countries in Europe. Even before they found it necessary to dampen depreciation of their currencies against the strengthening dollar, they were using monetary policy to combat inflation that was not the result of too much demand but, as in the United States, was of the cost-push variety. And when monetary policy created sluggish economies that generated fewer tax revenues and required higher unemployment benefits, they tried to reduce the enlarged budget deficits, thereby aggravating economic stagnation.

What is needed in the industrial world is a determined attack on persistent inflation based on its essential nature—and almost everywhere today that is a self-sustaining wage-price cycle. Monetary policy is a very blunt instrument for damping such a cycle in economies suffering from insufficient demand. If the political bias and political obstacles to incomes policies could be overcome, the industrial countries would be in a position to restore a better rate of real growth. This would bring tangible benefits to their own citizens, in the form of lower unemployment and faster growing real incomes. It would provide an environment in which the developing countries, in all their diversity, would be more able to achieve or, for the lucky few, continue to enjoy rapid economic progress. And it would discourage protectionism, which always gathers strength when unemployment is high and factories are idle.

The lower inflation rates brought about by successful incomes policies would take much of the burden off monetary policy in the industrial countries. This in turn would permit significantly lower rates of interest. While exchange rates would continue to fluctuate over time, the extreme movements of the recent past would be less likely to occur.

At the risk of repetition, I would like to conclude by anticipating my critics. I am not proposing the abandonment of anti-inflation policy in favor of "pump-priming" or "Keynesian expansionism." Nor am I suggesting permanent controls. What I am proposing are anti-inflation policies that are more suited to the nature of the inflation that the United States and most other industrial countries are now suffering from. Even with present fiscal and monetary policies, a deceleration of inflation would result in faster real growth almost everywhere. In those countries that have tightened monetary policy in order to resist currency depreciation, some monetary relaxation would be possible. And in those countries that have tightened fiscal policy to combat recession-induced increases in budget deficits, some fiscal relaxation would be possible.

The sorry state of the world economy and the unpromising outlook call for new approaches. What many will regard as naïve or unworkable is worth a try. He who sleeps on the floor cannot fall off the bed.

John C. Campbell

THE MIDDLE EAST: A HOUSE OF CONTAINMENT BUILT ON SHIFTING SANDS

I f either Jimmy Carter or Ronald Reagan needed any special persuasion to become convinced of the centrality of the Middle East in the total picture of American foreign policy, harsh experience provided it. The former had some notable diplomatic successes in the region, the Camp David accords and the Israel-Egypt peace treaty, but he struggled through the final year of his presidency under the impact of two shattering events—the seizure of the American Embassy in Tehran and the Soviet invasion of Afghanistan. However history may judge his efforts to cope with them, there was no avoiding the impression of a humiliated and frustrated America which must have contributed to his electoral defeat in November 1980. President Reagan came into office determined to restore American strength and prestige, but one year later his Administration, shocked by the assassination of President Anwar el-Sadat of Egypt, at odds with Israel after a series of disputes culminating in the barbed exchange following Israel's de facto annexation of the Golan Heights, and unable either to put aside the Palestine problem or make any progress toward settling it, was still groping for a political structure on which to build the position of strength deemed necessary to hold off the Russians and protect vital oil supplies.

President Carter bequeathed to his successor a policy of containment: a commitment publicly declared in January 1980 to repel, by force if necessary, any Soviet attempt to gain control of the Persian Gulf region; a decision to build up U.S. military power, including a Rapid Deployment Force (RDF) which could be brought to bear in that region; and a hope of gaining for the containment policy strong support from other nations. He also bequeathed an American role, as partner, in the continuing negotiation between Israel and Egypt under the Camp David accords. The making of peace between those two countries was

---

John C. Campbell is former Director of Studies of the Council on Foreign Relations, and author of, among other books, *Defense of the Middle East* and *The West and the Middle East*.

going well and was to be completed by Israel's withdrawal from the remainder of the Sinai peninsula in April 1982. The other part of the Camp David process, the establishment of autonomy for the Palestinians in the West Bank and Gaza Strip, was not going well at all; in fact, the negotiations had made no real progress for more than a year. President Sadat had counted on a tripartite summit meeting—himself, Prime Minister Begin and President Carter—to be held late in 1980 to revive them with a better chance of success. But Carter's defeat at the polls put an abrupt end to that idea.

Elsewhere in the Middle East, American policy at the end of the Carter term was a patchwork of bits and pieces and blank spots. Relations with Iran had been dominated by the question of the American hostages, who were not released until the President's last day in office. As long as the Ayatollah Khomeini and the Islamic Republican Party (IRP) should remain in power, the prospects for a government with which the United States could have even minimal relations would be remote. Iran, moreover, was at war with Iraq, with obvious dangers to American interests, but America had no cards to play with either side. Neighboring Pakistan, vulnerable to external pressure and plagued by internal disaffection, was a candidate for U.S. aid, but President Zia ul-Haq had found the Carter Administration's offer not worth the risks of accepting it.

As for Saudi Arabia, the leading oil producer and key to any American policy in the Gulf, the royal house of al-Saud was saying, as usual, very little. The Saudis seemed to be worried by America's weakness and lack of resolve but at the same time distrustful of U.S. diplomacy and desirous of keeping U.S. power at arm's length. The attack on the Grand Mosque of Mecca by a band of fanatics in 1979 and other internal events, moreover, had raised questions about the long-term stability of the kingdom to which it was not clear that Riyadh, much less Washington, had the answers. Syria was as hostile as ever to the United States. Jordan, a traditional friend, was reserved. Lebanon was in chaos, prey to its own warring factions and the ambitions of outsiders.

The Middle East "arc of crisis" was definitely still in crisis at the beginning of 1981. The outgoing Administration, with its mixed record, had nevertheless tried to build its policies on national interests generally recognized and followed by every American President since World War II. The new Administration would not be likely to change the aims, but would have to decide whether the means were adequate and the strategy right.

II

Ronald Reagan brought no ready-made policy for the Middle East with him when he took over the White House. His campaign themes had been general: America had been weak, had failed to stand up to the Russians and would have to build up her strength and her international standing, in the Middle East as elsewhere, so that there would be no more Irans, no more Afghanistans, symbols of American humiliation and defeat. His specific references were to Israel, as is customary in presidential campaigns, but they went beyond the standard pledges of friendship and support to describe Israel as a strategic asset for the United States, a potential bulwark of a new and stronger security in the region.

In the first months of 1981 the emphasis was on increasing military power, which meant carrying on the Carter program but with more speed and more muscle. The new Administration kept in place the two carrier task forces already in the Indian Ocean and moved ahead with the planned Rapid Deployment Force, which was to be bigger and more effective. It continued the search and the negotiations for facilities—in Oman, Somalia, Egypt and elsewhere—which U.S. forces could use regularly or in time of crisis, and also the expansion of the base at Diego Garcia in the Indian Ocean. The chief aim of these early decisions was to impress the Soviets with America's seriousness of purpose and capacity to act. They were also intended to convince the governments and peoples of the Middle East that America would be strong of arm and firm of will, a steadfast friend and a redoubtable foe. If leaders such as Anwar Sadat, King Hussein of Jordan or the Saudi rulers harbored doubts as to American constancy or dependability—as, in varying degrees, they did—the Reagan Administration wished to dispel those doubts.

Military power in the region was important as a deterrent to overt military moves by the Soviet Union. That proposition does not assume that the Soviet leaders had the intention of moving into Iran or Pakistan or seizing the oil fields of the Gulf, or that they will decide to do so in the future. It has always been the conundrum of a successful policy of containment that the containing power rarely knows if the result would have been the same whether or not the measures of deterrence were taken. But it was clear to both the Carter and Reagan Administrations that, after Afghanistan, America could not risk *not* having visible and substantial power in or near the region. The RDF, certainly at the outset of 1981 and probably at any later time, would not be able to contain at the border a full-scale Soviet invasion of Iran or

Pakistan. But it could still give pause to the men in the Kremlin in that it would face them with the fact, if they should move, of a conflict with America, one that would not be cheaply won in the Middle East and might not be confined there. Furthermore, the building of American strength, as Washington saw it, could deprive the Soviets of the means of bending local states to their will by the exercise of crude political pressure backed by uncontested military superiority. It was, therefore, a necessary backdrop to whatever political and diplomatic strategy Washington might choose to pursue.

The key question, of course, was what the strategy would be. By what its spokesmen said or left unsaid, the new Administration laid itself open to the charge of equating military power with policy and counting on it to turn unfavorable situations into favorable ones. What had happened in Iran, where for so many years the United States had relied on the Shah to maintain order and stability and help defend American interests, held for the new foreign policy "team" a salutary lesson: for the protection of vital interests there was no substitute for American power. But that was not the only lesson. In any event, if they were not ready with a defined or definable political strategy, they had, at the very least, to examine the political requirements of the proposed military posture. What relations with the local states—such as commitments, alliances, forms of military cooperation and planning, arms transfers, use of bases and other facilities—were necessary to create the desired position of strength against the U.S.S.R.? With what states in particular? On what basis of common concern could cooperation be built? Were Washington's priorities those of its presumed and potential friends in the region? As those questions were answered, or not answered, in the course of the year, the outlines of a political strategy might appear.

When Secretary of State Alexander Haig made his initial visit to the region in April those questions were surely in the minds of his hosts even though they apparently received no extended discussion. Secretary Haig's guiding idea was that of "strategic consensus" as a basis for defense of the area. It was a new phrase for an old concept. For three decades Haig's predecessors had been trying to organize the defense of the Middle East against the Soviet threat, with mixed results. In 1953, soon after taking office, John Foster Dulles had made a trip to the region on a similar quest for friends and allies. He came away with the idea that those who were ready to cooperate with each other and with the West should form a security organization. The resultant northern tier alliance or Baghdad Pact (later the Central Treaty Organization or CENTO) was enthusiastically welcomed, and its members armed, by the United States. However, although it maintained an existence of sorts for many years, the alliance could not withstand the stresses of internal revolution, regional conflict, and differing priorities. One by one the regional members (except Turkey) dropped away: first Iraq, then Pakistan, then Iran, leaving only the decision for formal burial in 1979.

It was a measure of the retreat of American power and influence over the years that Secretary Haig would have to look for his strategic consensus mainly in the southern tier, with Israel, Egypt, Jordan, Saudi Arabia and Oman, possibly linked in some way with Turkey and with Pakistan.

Those various nations, however, had very little or no consensus with each other. Arab states which had thrown Egypt out of the Arab League because Sadat had made peace with Israel with American encouragement and help would not be willing to join Egypt in a new alignment under American sponsorship. Nor could they even think of association with Israel. Pakistan was preoccupied with its own special situation in relation to India. Turkey was standing firmly by its NATO alignment, but Turkey was not accepted as a leader or partner by the Arab states despite her efforts to move in that direction.

Secretary Haig was well aware of these differences, but he sensed that all the countries were, or should be, exercised about the Soviet threat. The Islamic states had formally condemned the Soviet invasion of Afghanistan at the United Nations and at three meetings of the Islamic Conference, the most recent in January 1981, and had expressed the same fears and concerns through diplomatic channels. Israel's anti-Soviet convictions were beyond question. There might be, therefore, a basis for consensus between each of the states individually and the United States, from which the latter could somehow fashion a structure serving the security of all.

That would be no simple task. American diplomats, in setting about it, were bound to run into all the unsolved and unsolvable problems with which they had been contending for years. What could be done about them, even with greater military power and a firmer will, was not subject to dramatic change. Talk of new initiatives in the Middle East invariably accompanies a change from one party to another in the seats of power in Washington, and 1981 was no exception. But, just as invariably, the elements of continuity based on generally accepted ideas of the national interest tend to assert themselves as a new Administration gets to the business at hand. So it was with Alexander Haig and his new team, which on the professional level was not without representation from former teams.

In brief, the basic aims of the United States in the Middle East were: first, *security*, denial of the area to Soviet control, maintenance of the independence of the Middle East nations, and prevention of situations which could lead to nuclear war; second, *oil supply*, the continued availability of Middle East oil to the rest of the world in adequate quantity and on bearable terms; and third, *relative stability*, or more accurately, the containment of instability which could jeopardize attainment of the first two aims. Purposes had not changed very much from Truman to Carter, and would not change very much under Reagan.

The new look, to the extent that it was more than cosmetic, had to do largely with perceptions of the Soviet Union and of Middle East politics and with the choice of means to pursue the established ends. The Administration could choose its own means and set its course, but, as with its predecessors, the range of choice and the chances of success were constricted by the policies and decisions of other states, the availability of resources, the interaction with policies in other parts of the world, the demands of domestic politics, and the unpredictability of events in the Middle East; indeed, the only certainty was that unexpected and upsetting events would occur there. It was against this background that Washington began its efforts to find strategic consensus and establish a position of greater strength and stability in the region. Perhaps the best way to describe those efforts is to look at the individual countries and areas where aims had to be translated into practice, noting how American policies shaped, or were shaped by, the unfolding events of the year.

III

From the moment of the Soviet invasion of Afghanistan in December 1979, Washington began to talk of "Southwest Asia" instead of the Middle East as the area of crisis and of American concern. Whatever the geographic terms, the focus of attention was the Gulf and its oil. The "Carter Doctrine," the declaration by the President in his State of the Union message in January 1980, warned the Soviets that any further advance beyond Afghanistan threatening the vital oil region would run into American resistance using all means necessary, not excluding armed force. President Reagan was not about to declare his espousal of a doctrine bearing Jimmy Carter's name—the term, in any case, was an invention of the press—but the policy remained the same: America would not remain indifferent to the advance of Soviet power into Iran or Pakistan. But how could such a policy be made effective?

In the case of Iran, the United States in the eyes of Tehran was the "Great Satan," responsible for all the ills and problems of that country. Therefore, the actual America, however distinct it might be from the Ayatollah Khomeini's image of America, could not change or even affect Iran's future international orientation. The internal struggle between the clerical Islamic Republican Party and the more secular elements represented by President Bani-Sadr, Mehdi Bazargan and others had been decided by early 1981, in favor of the former. Ultimate power remained with Khomeini, whose outlook left not the slightest opening for normal relations with the United States. The hostage crisis was over, as of the first day of the Reagan Administration, but neither side was ready even to look at common interests the two countries might have in holding off the Russians or in rebuilding the Iranian economy from the turmoil and the wreckage of the revolution and the war with Iraq. The only consolation for Americans was that Iran was almost as negative in her relations with the "lesser Satan," the U.S.S.R.

Washington was, however, as aware as Moscow of the key geographical position of Iran. While neither power exercised significant influence on what was going on inside that country, each had warned the other against intervention on penalty of being faced with military countermeasures. Each tried to figure out, meanwhile, how to make the best, or avoid the worst, of whatever the results of Iran's internal travail might be. Moscow's bets, for the present, seemed to be not on the militant secular and socialist factions, such as the *Mujahedeen* and *Fedayeen*, but on Khomeini and the Islamic dogmatists, who had gained the upper hand. The Iranian Communists, the Tudeh, presumably on Moscow's orders, were cooperating with the IRP, taking the risk that if the clerical regime were overthrown, the Tudeh would go down with it. Washington's bets were on a change or evolution of the regime taking place without dissolution of public order or fragmentation of the country, with the hope that any regime in power in Tehran would hold to the idea of Iran's vital interest in the integrity of the country against any Soviet attempts to interfere. The contemplated buildup of American military power in the region was intended to convey the message that the United States could prevent such interference, even though the Ayatollah might see the buildup more as a menace than a protection.

This muted duel was evident in the attitudes which both powers adopted toward the Iraq-Iran war. The Soviets had a security treaty with Iraq but were already disillusioned with President Saddam Hussein's independent policies, including the decision to go to war, which seemed to ignore Soviet interests. They took a public position of neutrality but accompanied it with unobtrusive measures representing a definite tilt in favor of Iran. In Russian strategy over the years Iran had always held a position of higher priority, and still did. For the United States as well, having no diplomatic relations and few means of persuasion with either side—although each in its propaganda proclaimed the other to be an American tool—neutrality was the indicated course. It was not politic to alienate Arab friends, principally Saudi Arabia and Jordan, by taking sides against a sister Arab state which they were helping. Nor was it wise to open doors to the Soviets by appearing to support Iraq against Iran.

For Washington the war was a nuisance and could become a disaster if it spread to other lands or cut down oil exports from the Gulf to the point where the West's needs could not be met. Neither eventuality happened. The war settled down to a stalemate throughout 1981, and the fall in oil exports from the two belligerent states was more than matched by the decline in world demand for oil. In Iran the clerical regime displayed a remarkable capacity for survival in the face of both foreign and civil war, armed revolt in the Kurdish areas, the ousting of President Bani-Sadr, loss of part of the main oil-producing area to Iraqi occupation, the assassination of many key leaders of the dominant IRP, and the disruption and decline of the economy. Toward Khomeini's Iran the United States did not find it possible to have a policy, but the vital American strategic interest in the country remained. It was a time for the analysts and the planners, not for active diplomacy.

The other country immediately threatened by the Soviet move into Afghanistan, and therefore of great concern to the United States, was Pakistan. The government of President Zia ul-Haq, already insecure as a result of Iran's revolution and of political troubles at home, let it be known that the door was open to offers of American support. The Carter Administration had demonstrated its interest through the President's strong "Carter Doctrine" statement in January 1980, and a bilateral security agreement dating from 1959 and providing for joint consultation in time of crisis was still in force. Pakistan had long since lost her enthusiasm for formal alignment with America, however. What Zia and his generals desired above all was up-to-date weaponry to use as they saw fit.

The Carter Administration's effort to strike a deal was frustrated by Zia's contemptuous rejection of its proposal of $400 million in military and economic aid as insufficient ("peanuts," in his phrase) and apparently not worth incurring increased pressure from the Russians; and, on the American side, by the contrast between Pakistan's record on the issues of human rights and nuclear nonproliferation and the international standards Carter was trying to establish. From the standpoint of Reagan and Haig, Pakistan was so important to the policy of containing Soviet power that these remnants of the Carter philosophy should not be allowed to thwart the higher security interest. Consequently, they offered a much larger aid package on a longer term basis and without setting conditions objectionable to Pakistan. The deal was then negotiated and concluded in June for $3.2 billion in economic and military aid over six years, plus the sale and delivery of 40 F-16 aircraft (which the Pakistanis hoped to pay for with their own and Saudi funds).

The aid to Pakistan was not aimed primarily at enabling that country to fight off a major Soviet invasion, although it might contribute to making an invasion less likely, but at meeting the existing dangerous situation on the northwest frontier. That frontier was being crossed by Afghan refugees and by resistance fighters intent on carrying on the struggle against the Soviets and their puppet Afghan regime, and also occasionally by Soviet forces pursuing their foes to their base areas. A porous border also increased the potential for Soviet troublemaking among disaffected ethnic groups in Pakistan. Zia's interest in getting U.S. weapons to help in inducing Soviet restraint, keeping control of the border, and maintaining with other Islamic countries, within safe limits, a posture of support for Afghan resistance to Soviet rule was clear enough. If the aid should be insufficient, then it would merely expose Pakistan to Soviet intimidation and pressure without adequate assurance of American backing to justify the risks. For that reason the Administration was inclined to give Zia more or less what he wanted, and was prepared to make a strong case to the Congress, which had to vote the funds.

Opponents of the deal raised a number of objections. Their most persistent criticism was of the failure of the U.S. government to insist on safeguards against Pakistan's making nuclear weapons.

On the political side critics, citing the baleful example of the Shah's Iran, pointed to Zia's regime as an unstable and unpopular dictatorship which denied civil and political rights to its citizens and self-expression to its national minorities, faults and weaknesses which arms would not remedy but just make worse. On the military side they held that whatever the quantity and quality of the arms provided, Pakistan would be no better able to defend herself against the Russians; and besides, the F-16 aircraft were too advanced for the Pakistanis and were needed by U.S. and NATO forces. Finally, there was the old complaint, proved by prior experience, that Pakistan was seeking arms primarily against India, and that by "tilting" in favor of Pakistan the United States would alienate India and thrust her more decisively to the side of the Soviet Union.

The Administration could hardly succeed in satisfying all its critics. But it could argue plausibly that the security factor, in the light of what had happened in Afghanistan, tipped the balance in favor of making the deal. This meant, since Zia wrapped himself in the mantle of sovereignty and nonalignment, that the United States could not dictate to him conditions limiting his domestic or foreign policies. On the nonproliferation issue the Administration not only had to give way to Pakistan but, having done so, had to try to persuade the Congress to waive the provisions of the Symington Amendment to the Foreign Assistance Act, which barred aid in such instances. The decision represented a confession of failure, but prior efforts to control Pakistan's nuclear program had been unavailing, and it was at least possible that large-scale aid in conventional weapons would give Pakistan a greater sense of security with less inclination to count on the nuclear option. The closer the nexus of U.S.-Pakistani military cooperation, the greater the element of constraint, since Pakistan would know that setting off a nuclear explosion would almost certainly bring that cooperation to an end. The Congress, in passing new foreign aid legislation in December, gave the President the right to waive the termination of the Symington Amendment, but only for a 30-day period after the detonation, during which time Congress would have to authorize any extension of the waiver.

Perhaps the most valid criticism to be made of the policy toward Pakistan was of the limited focus of a six-year agreement made with one country, and with a government having dubious credentials and prospects, without any wider strategic and political thinking embracing a larger area. Pakistan is connected with India in the subcontinent; both are deeply affected by Soviet control of Afghanistan, though they have reacted to it in different ways. If India and Pakistan take as the overriding premise of foreign policy their enmity for each other, then an outside power will have to make the same assumption. But events which change the global or regional patterns of power also crack habitual patterns of thought and policy.

Both countries understand that by itself Pakistan is no longer a threat to India's preeminent position in the subcontinent, and that Soviet power on the Khyber Pass and the possibility of Soviet domination of Pakistan cannot fail to concern India. A Chinese-Indian rapprochement, some signs of which have appeared, can help to reduce Indian fear of Pakistan as a Chinese surrogate. The once familiar picture of polarization, with a U.S.S.R.-India bloc and a China-Pakistan-America bloc in armed confrontation, may not be the picture of the future.

The United States, to be sure, has to act in the world as it is. Pakistan was vulnerable, Pakistan wanted aid, and so the decision was taken to provide it, without waiting for democracy or nuclear sanity in Pakistan or for changes of mind and heart in Indo-Pakistani relations. The absence of a broader approach, however, may have its negative effects in the future, if only in the tendency of a long-term bilateral program to create its own momentum, its own vested interests and adverse reactions, and to shut off other opportunities. For if one thing is certain, it is that no strategy for the security of Pakistan can succeed over the long run unless it also serves the security, and gains the cooperation, of India.

Pakistan does, however, face west as well as east, and her connections with the Gulf states and with the Arab world give added relevance to her place in American efforts to protect the sources of oil vital to the West. This theme can be exaggerated, of course, as it was when the Western powers in the 1950s tried to make Pakistan the eastern anchor, matching Turkey in the west, of the northern-tier barrier against the Russians. Yet it has had much more substance in the past few years than in that earlier time. Pakistan's shared concern with other Islamic states about the Soviet Union (about both superpowers, for that matter) and about issues such as Palestine and Jerusalem has led to increasing ties with Arab states, including cooperation in the military field, especially with Saudi Arabia. Pakistan is benevolently inclined toward the Gulf Cooperation Council, a fledgling organization including Saudi Arabia and the smaller Arab states of the Gulf. These connections are developing without U.S. initiative or management—and perhaps all the more significant on that account—

but may well be given added strength and durability by continuing American aid to Pakistan.

IV

After the loss of Iran, the remaining "pillar" of U.S. strategy in the 1970s, Saudia Arabia, was more important than ever in American eyes, indispensable to any viable policy. She was the one major state in the Gulf with which the United States had friendly relations, the only hope for maintaining a political and military position there. She gave the lead to the smaller Gulf states, from Kuwait to Oman, and retained links with Iraq, which still had no diplomatic relations with Washington but was increasing ties with the West to balance the Soviet connection. Saudi Arabia had weight in the Arab world, not in the military dimension but through oil wealth and financial diplomacy, and also because of the prestige that went with being the land of Mohammed and guardian of the holiest places of Islam. As a moderate Arab state able to communicate with both the radical and the more traditional or pro-Western regimes, Saudi Arabia was able to exert considerable influence in calming inter-Arab disputes, as in Lebanon.

American hopes for broadening the Arab-Israeli peace process also rested mainly on the Saudis despite their rejection of Camp David and their break with Sadat for dealing separately with Israel. Saudi Arabia might bring its influence to bear on the Palestine Liberation Organization (PLO) to accept the existence of Israel and thus break down the barriers to a more realistic negotiation about the Palestinian future than the narrow and unproductive "autonomy talks" going on between Egypt and Israel. And there was little chance of getting Jordan to participate in negotiations unless King Hussein had Saudi encouragement and support to do so.

Finally, and most important, Saudi Arabia was by far the Middle East's leading producer and exporter of oil. With the sharp fall in exports from Iran and Iraq, Saudi oil was absolutely essential to the West, and Saudi oil policy was crucial because that country accounted for close to half of the production of the Organization of Petroleum Exporting Countries (OPEC). By keeping the level in the neighborhood of 10 million barrels per day, the Saudis could play the leading role in OPEC and exert downward pressure on world prices. They did so primarily for their own reasons rather than to help the Western economies or to please the Americans, but whatever the reasons, the latter had a vital interest in maintenance of Saudi production at current high levels, and therefore in the security of Saudi Arabia and the good-will of her rulers.

Saudi Arabia was an American friend of long standing, from the time when King Abdul Aziz first granted an oil concession to Standard Oil of California in the 1930s. Yet the bases of that friendship had never been established beyond questioning on both sides, and its course was not uniformly smooth. The problems faced by Washington in 1981, like those of the past, revolved around (1) how to reconcile U.S. interests in security and oil with Saudi Arabian interests as seen by the Saudis; and (2) how to handle the whole complex of Israel, the Palestinians, and the Arab-Israeli conflict and settlement in the light of Saudi and American attitudes marked not just by misunderstanding but by fundamental differences in outlook. Moreover, no matter how hard the United States might try to do so, it was impossible to keep the question of security in the Gulf separate from that of Palestine.

All these points came to the surface in 1981, and were subjected to heated debate in the United States, in connection with the proposed sale of five Airborne Warning and Control System (AWACS) aircraft and additional military equipment to Saudi Arabia. Before discussing that affair, let us look briefly at Saudi Arabia herself, her internal strength and weakness and her international role, for those matters were always underlying the policy debate and often on its surface. It may provide a means of judging how far Saudi Arabia could or would play the part envisaged for her by policy planners in Washington.

She is not a strong state in the usual sense, having a very small population on a very large territory poor in useful resources except petroleum. Still close to its pre-modern past, Saudi society has been shaken by rapid economic and social change accompanying sudden oil wealth, a vast and frenzied development program, and multiplying contacts with the outside world including an influx of foreign labor and other elements not sharing the Saudi heritage or institutions. Unsettling as they are, these phenomena do not lead to categorical conclusions about the stability of the system. Disaffection exists among conservatives who fear the erosion of traditional values, among the Shi'a minority in the eastern part of the country who were stirred by the revolution in Iran, among officers in the armed forces, and also among Western-educated Saudi citizens rising within the economic system but generally excluded from political power and responsibility.

The situation, however, is not like that of the Shah's Iran, in which an increasingly isolated monarch behaved more and more imperiously and alienated large segments of the population. The Saudi royal family, some 4,000 strong, is rooted in the society, and its members are everywhere. It has shown great flexibility and adaptability to changing conditions and to times of crisis. It was able to manage the succession when one King (Saud) proved incompetent and when another (Faisal) was assassinated. It does not have to contend with a politically ambitious class of mullahs such as exists in Iran and it has maintained the close connection between Islam and the house of al-Saud that dates from the beginning of the state.

Saudi Arabia's foreign policies have been constrained by the basic weaknesses of the country and by the natural caution of her rulers. Nevertheless, Saudi Arabia automatically acquired influence by virtue of vast oil reserves, sovereign control over production levels and prices, buying power and appetite for Western goods and services, and surplus oil revenues capable of helping other countries and also of disrupting the international financial system. In these economic matters the Saudis, in the American view, had behaved circumspectly and responsibly. Much of their oil money went to buy American equipment, technology and management for their development program, and some was invested in U.S. Treasury obligations. They always had at their disposal, of course, the "oil weapon," which they could use for political purposes, as in 1973, if they thought circumstances demanded it; but in recent years they have given no sign of such an intention.

In the more limited and familiar area of the Middle East the Saudi rulers employed their financial power to more specific political advantage. They could use it traditionally, if crudely, in trying to buy the allegiance of tribal leaders in this or that smaller state on the periphery of the Arabian peninsula. Or they could put their hand into the larger game of inter-Arab politics. Having influence with Jordan and with Syria, for example, because they provided subsidies to both, they were able to calm a Syrian-Jordanian dispute which reached the brink of open warfare in December 1980. They also had influence over the leadership of the PLO, though not of its more radical components, and were instrumental in bringing Yasir Arafat to accept a truce with Israeli and Israeli-supported forces in Lebanon in July 1981.

This aspect of Saudi foreign policy was especially prized by the United States as a contribution to stability and to the prospects for an Arab-Israeli settlement. Saudi leadership in the Arab world, however, was neither generally recognized nor consistently effective. At bottom, it was defensive. The Saudi leaders made public protestations of crusading against communism and zionism, seen as twin evils. But above all they were fearful of radicalism which might reach their country from Iran, Iraq, Syria, or Libya, or through the extremists of the PLO. Their defense was not to meet it head-on and thus promote division and struggle in the Arab world, but to smother the conflicts with talk of Arab solidarity, to placate the radical Arab regimes rather than to challenge them, and to support and finance the PLO instead of trying to suppress it. When Sadat made his choice for negotiation with Israel, the Saudis pointedly did not join him, and when he signed the Camp David accords, they joined the radicals in condemning him, breaking relations and cutting off financial aid.

Similar ambiguities and contradictions marked Saudi Arabia's relations with the United States. A special relationship based on mutual security had grown up over a long period. In the early years after World War II the Saudis had made the Dhahran airfield available to the U.S. Strategic Air Command. The United States, through a series of presidential letters and official statements though not by formal treaty, had given assurances of protection of the independence and integrity of the kingdom, and at various times had given substance to that commitment by diplomatic action or military demonstration. President Reagan made the most far-reaching pledge of all when he told the press that the United States would not permit Saudi Arabia "to be an Iran,"[1] a guarantee, apparently, of protection against internal revolution as well as external attack.

The historical record of this security relationship, however, also illustrates its limitations. The American commitments were low-key, even secret, not advertised by either government. The Saudis always avoided formal alignment with the United States. They did not hesitate to cut off oil exports in 1967 and again in 1973 when they judged American actions to be trampling on Arab and Saudi interests. They were disturbed by Soviet gains in the Horn of Africa, by the emergence on their border of a self-styled Marxist state closely tied to the U.S.S.R. (the People's Democratic Republic of Yemen), by the fall of the Shah and the revolutionary militance of Khomeini, and by the Soviet takeover of Afghanistan. But even those shifts in the balance did not bring them running to the United States for a more formal security relationship.

[1] *The New York Times*, October 2, 1981

They wanted American power to balance and deter that of the U.S.S.R. and her client states in the area, but not to have that power on or too close to the territory of Saudi Arabia. They wanted U.S. arms and training missions. They did not want U.S. troops, bases, prepositioned matériel or a system of close strategic cooperation. They did not go nearly as far as Sadat in this direction, either in statement or in action. If American pressure should become too strong, or the American presence overweening, the most likely result would be an internal shift of power within the royal family at the expense of those closely associated with the American connection.

Saudi unwillingness to appear to compromise the principles of independence and nonalignment, on grounds of fidelity to the nation's own traditions and its position in the Arab world, was strengthened by the central importance given to the question of Palestine. Saudi attachment to the cause of the Palestinians had a number of motives: Arab solidarity, intense feeling for Jerusalem as a holy place of Islam, influence of Palestinians within Saudi Arabia, and fear of radicalism or revolution sparked by the PLO or others. Whatever specific weight one may give to each motive, the United States was not able to change any of them as long as the Saudis saw U.S. policy as totally supportive of Israel and deaf to Palestinian rights. Palestine thus cast a very large shadow on U.S.-Saudi relations.

Rightly or wrongly, the Saudis felt they were taking considerable account of American interests and that America, in failing to move Israel on the Palestine question, was taking less account of theirs. They felt quite justified, since they desired modern arms, in making Washington's willingness to sell such arms a test of American friendship. So it was in 1978, when they asked for F-15 aircraft. President Carter complied, paying the price of Israeli displeasure and getting the proposal through Congress by joining to it a package of arms for Israel. That was considered a watershed decision, showing that U.S. policy toward an Arab state was not subject to veto by Israel's supporters in the United States. But it was a watershed that had to be crossed again, for Saudi Arabia was interested in buying additional equipment for the F-15s, previously denied, to increase their range, and also five AWACS planes for better intelligence and defense. Accordingly, one of the first items on President Reagan's foreign policy agenda was a new test of the special relationship.

The decision to go ahead was made early. It was immediately denounced by the Begin government as a direct threat to Israel.

The task of getting congressional approval was difficult enough without mismanagement, which the executive branch provided in generous measure. That is not the main story here, except as the whole affair affected U.S. relations with Israel and with Saudi Arabia, and thus the ability of the United States to act effectively in the Middle East. The White House did not gird itself for the inevitable battle until opponents had lined up a majority of Senators against the proposal. In the House the Administration knew it had no chance to win; it therefore concentrated on the Senate, as under the legislation the sale could not be blocked unless both houses voted against it.

It was not strictly a referendum on Israel, although that was the central issue. Some Senators had reservations having nothing to do with Israel, such as why sophisticated equipment should go to a backward country which would not have the competence to use it; why the United States should not insist on joint control of the AWACS planes; and whether those planes, delivered to a regime which could be overthrown any day, might wind up in the hands of the Soviet Union. The Administration went as far as it could in giving assurances to Senators, but the Saudis were not prepared to oblige by accepting restrictions on their sovereignty. Much of the debate bordered on the unreal, as the AWACS planes were not to be delivered until 1986, and anything could happen in the Middle East in five years.

In the end the President had to appeal to the argument that repudiation of the deal would strike at his ability to conduct the foreign policy of the United States, and had to use all the power of his position to persuade individual Senators to support him. The final vote, taken on October 28, showed a 52–48 margin against the resolution that would have blocked the sale. The come-from-behind victory was not achieved without cost. It had roiled relations with many in Congress, drawn down the President's political capital, and strained relations with both Saudi Arabia and Israel.

Despite the final outcome and the President's demonstrated willingness to go all out to save the deal, all was not sugar and spice with the Saudis. They felt humiliated and insulted by the long process in which their stability, competence and trustworthiness were questioned day after day. They must have expected some of it, given a minimal understanding of the American constitutional system. But the way in which the whole matter was handled practically guaranteed that the U.S. political gain with Saudi Arabia would be marginal. The Saudis were not going to rush into military cooperation for defense of the oil fields, as the Pentagon had hoped, just because of the AWACS decision. Their role as a moderate force for Arab-Israeli peace, praised by the Administration and denigrated by opponents of the sale, remained to be tested.

As for U.S.-Israeli relations, the deterioration was palpable. When Prime Minister Begin visited Washington in early September, he made his case against the AWACS and the equipment for the F-15s to the President and to Secretary Haig. They apparently understood that he would not openly join the fray as the Senate approached the time of decision. He had, however, already made public statements, giving the cue to American Jewish organizations mounting a vigorous effort aimed at the Congress, and continued to make them. He also delivered himself of vitriolic verbal assaults on Saudi Arabia, calling the royal family, *inter alia*, medieval, despotic, corrupt and a supporter of terrorism. His Foreign Minister, Yitzhak Shamir, gave a speech on American soil expanding Begin's themes in even more pungent words. All this, at a time when the President was trying to convince the Senate that Saudi Arabia was a constructive force for peace in the Middle East, did not sit well with Washington. Reagan's press conference remark that no foreign country was going to dictate the foreign policy of the United States bore witness to the tension, evident also in muffled talk of "Reagan or Begin" as the real issue of the AWACS vote and in allegations of anti-Semitism. The Administration did not want it that way, but saw the AWACS watershed as one that had to be crossed if American prestige and position in the area were not to suffer a disastrous loss.

After the battle was over, Washington was looking for ways to heal the wounds and be responsive to Israeli desires for U.S. support, whether in the form of additional arms, plans for strategic cooperation, votes and vetoes in the United Nations, or statements for the Camp David process and against the PLO. On the military balance, Secretary Haig pledged that America would make sure that Israel maintained a "qualitative edge" over the Arabs. Hastening to make up, however, did not do much to appease Israel. It also tended to fudge the issues brought out by the AWACS affair and to set the stage for future conflicts of interest clouded by misunderstanding. These would certainly come, perhaps not far in the future, for both countries now had to face the fact of the stalemate in the Camp David negotiations on the West Bank and Gaza, in short, the Palestine question.

V

For some time American diplomacy on the Arab-Israeli question had been relatively inactive. By the time of the 1980 election campaign President Carter had run out of miracles and confined himself to preaching the virtues of the Camp David process. Then, after the November election, uncertainty continued through the interregnum and beyond, as the new Administration examined its choices and waited for the results of Secretary Haig's projected trip to the Middle East and the expected visits of Sadat and Begin to Washington.

At that point the state of play was, briefly, the following: (1) the Egypt-Israel peace treaty of 1979 was being carried out by both sides, with the final Israeli withdrawal from the eastern part of Sinai set for April 1982; (2) the negotiations on autonomy for the West Bank and Gaza had not attracted Palestinian or Jordanian participation and had made very little progress, with Israel determined strictly to limit the functions of the future Palestinian authority and Egypt standing on a broad interpretation of the "full autonomy" agreed upon at Camp David; (3) the question of Jerusalem had been put aside at Camp David by an agreement to disagree, but was never far beneath the surface and came up in the discussion of such matters as whether Jerusalem Arabs would vote in the election for the proposed Palestinian authority; (4) tension was growing on all Israel's frontiers except the one with Egypt, exacerbated by Arab unrest and Israeli repression in the occupied territories, PLO militancy, and a chaotic situation in Lebanon.

It was clear that Haig did not intend to plunge into these matters. His and the President's priority was the military balance with the Soviet Union. Since Southwest Asia was the region where the worst erosion of Western power had taken place, strategic realities and increasing Soviet intervention, said Haig, were more important than isolated issues such as the Arab-Israeli dispute. Why rush into discussions on the West Bank problem, which was obviously an obstacle to strategic consensus, when it could be left in the background for a while? Anyway, the Israeli election due to take place later in the year might change the negotiating picture.

The difficulty with that approach was that the problem would not stay in the background. The governments of Saudi Arabia and Jordan brought it up, and not in terms favorable to Camp David, whenever American diplomats talked to them about strategic cooperation. And the more America talked about strategic cooperation with Israel, the more difficult it was for Arab leaders to offer cooperation of any kind. Sadat was the exception, but even he was coming under criticism and pressure at home because of the inflexibility of Israel's positions in the autonomy talks and policies in the occupied territories. The United States might wish to arm them all against the Russians, but the recipients looked at the flow of weapons in terms of the local balance and of who would use them against whom. There was no evading the political factors that underlay how the Middle East governments regarded America's new strategy.

Before long, events and decisions outside the Camp David negotiations were pushing American diplomacy into thickets it would have preferred to avoid. They led to a deterioration of U.S. relations with Israel in the first half of 1981, all the sharper because both sides had expected something different. Reagan came into office after a pro-Israel campaign, with many advisers who subscribed to the idea of Israel as a strategic asset. The early statements of high officials, including the President himself, referred to the PLO as a terrorist organization and expressed understanding of Israel's policies on such matters as pursuit of Arab guerrillas across the borders. The result was to strengthen the Begin government in the belief it could count on a more favorable American attitude toward measures taken for Israel's security.

Disillusion came fairly rapidly on both sides, largely because Begin took ever more drastic measures to strike at the PLO in Lebanon and to suppress Arab opposition and increase Israeli settlements in the West Bank. American reactions grew sharper, reverting to the established State Department line that such measures were illegal and an obstacle to peace. America's announced intention to sell AWACS planes to Saudi Arabia and Begin's immediate and total opposition to it made relations worse. Then in June came the shock of the daring raid in which Israeli aircraft flew across Saudi Arabia to bomb and destroy an Iraqi nuclear reactor near Baghdad. No other state could accept Israel's argument that this was an act of legitimate self-defense. The United States condemned it both in official statements and in voting for a resolution to that effect in the U.N. Security Council, and suspended (temporarily, it turned out) shipment of F-16 aircraft. A few weeks later Israel carried out an air raid on Beirut, aimed at PLO headquarters there but killing over 300 Lebanese civilians. Again Washington was issuing statements of shock and disapproval.

Begin, running for reelection, was more interested in impressing

Israeli voters than American officials. He was also acting consistently with deeply held convictions and with policies he had pursued since taking office in 1977. Israel was at war with the PLO because the PLO was dedicated to the destruction of Israel. That war was being fought in many places, but nowhere more violently than in Lebanon, where Israel was carrying out raids by air, sea and land in reply to PLO attacks on villages in northern Israel.

Lebanon was a battlefield of many simultaneous struggles because the nominal Lebanese government and army had no effective control over the country. Armed factions of Christians and Muslims, Left and Right, Sunni and Shi'a and Druse, Palestinians and Lebanese, fought against each other and among themselves, with religion and ideology often counting for less than personal ambition, revenge and available firepower. Syrian troops, designated as a peacekeeping "Arab Deterrent Force" by decision of the Arab League, occupied much of the country. The PLO, with well armed units of its own, controlled certain areas and acknowledged no higher authority although several of its factions had ties to individual Arab countries such as Syria, Iraq and Libya. Syria and Israel used Lebanese territory to test each other and to protect their respective interests. Their confrontation and the incidents which punctuated it carried the continuing menace of a real war.

Israel's involvement in Lebanon included support of Christian forces which, as opponents of the PLO and of the Syrians, served Israel's interests in serving their own. One such force controlled territory on the southern border adjacent to Israel. The main Christian-held territory was in the north, and it was here that fighting between Christian Phalangists and Syrians in the spring of 1981 grew into a full-blown crisis, as Israel declared she would not permit the Christians to be crushed and Syria introduced into Lebanon surface-to-air missiles (SAMs) capable of shooting down Israeli planes, which had been flying at will all over Lebanese territory. Prime Minister Begin announced that the missiles must be removed or Israel would destroy them.

At this point the United States took on the role of pacifier, sending Philip Habib, a veteran diplomat, on a mission of multiple visits to Beirut, Damascus, Riyadh and Jerusalem, counseling restraint as he tried to find a formula that would prevent war. Begin held off a strike at the Syrian missiles to give Habib's mission time to achieve that result by other means. But in all other respects the conflict in Lebanon, and particularly between Israel and the PLO, grew in intensity. Habib's mission was broadened into an effort to establish a cease-fire and truce. Ultimately, through Saudi and U.N. as well as U.S. diplomacy, because neither the United States nor Israel could talk with the PLO, a cease-fire was arranged and accepted in late July.

Meanwhile, on the last day of June Menachem Begin's party, Likud, probably helped by the atmosphere of crisis, squeaked through to victory in the Israeli election, and he was able to form a coalition government with a majority of one vote in the Knesset. Thus it was Begin, and not Shimon Peres and Labor, with whom Washington would have to deal, and as head of a government more nationalist than before and less likely to consider compromise on control and eventual annexation of the West Bank; the more moderate figures in the old government—Moshe Dayan, Ezer Weizmann, Yigal Yadin—had all resigned before the election.

President Sadat made his visit to Washington in August, hit it off well with Reagan, and declared his intention to go ahead with the Camp David peace process. He cannot have had much hope that Israel would be more forthcoming than before, even if more American weight were thrown into the balance on his side, but his main objective was still to maintain the Egypt-Israel peace treaty, vital provisions of which, especially the Israeli withdrawal from the rest of the Sinai, remained to be carried out. He appeared to be more concerned about Libyan threats to Sudan and by evidence of increased danger from the Soviet Union and its friends and clients in the area. Libya, Ethiopia and the People's Democratic Republic of Yemen were drawing together in military cooperation that could only be aimed at Sudan, Egypt and Saudi Arabia. Egypt was already getting U.S. help in building base facilities at Ras Banas on the Red Sea and would permit the United States to use them in time of crisis. Sadat's offers of military cooperation and his request for more arms for Sudan struck a responsive note with his hosts, who were looking for ways to counter any Soviet moves and to deflate and defeat Libya's Colonel Qaddafi.

Prime Minister Begin, following Sadat to Washington, also got a friendly reception. He came with the prestige of an electoral victory—one-vote margin or not, he was definitely in charge—and the truce in Lebanon was still holding. Washington decided to accentuate the positive at this get-acquainted meeting, celebrating traditional friendship and future cooperation. Apparently no effort was made to stress American reservations about many of Israel's actions or the seriousness of the President's determination to put through the AWACS sale, or to discuss in concrete terms how the autonomy talks could move ahead. Instead, most of the talk was about strategic cooperation between the two countries, which could hardly convey an impression other than of continued U.S. support for Israel's policies for her own security.

After the two visits, with their repeated genuflection to the Camp David process, it was time for resumption of the autonomy talks, but none of the three parties put a high priority on it or had a specific plan that might bring progress. Israel held the territories and could continue to hold them without violating the Camp David accords, since autonomy could not come into being until the parties agreed on what autonomy was. Meanwhile, Ariel Sharon, an advocate of creating new facts in the form of Jewish settlements, now held the post of Minister of Defense and was putting his own ideas on autonomy into practice. Egypt could put her ideas on autonomy into negotiating papers but could do nothing to get them accepted. Sadat's attention was turning more to his position at home, now being challenged to the point that he found it necessary in September to crack down hard on a variety of critics and opponents. But he still felt he should keep the talks going and avoid a crisis with Israel.

Into this situation of latent danger came the news of the assassination of Sadat on October 6. The shock was greatest, perhaps, in Israel and in America, for both had built their own policies very substantially on the policies he had forged for Egypt and, to what degree they could not be sure, on the continued presence at the helm in Cairo of Sadat himself. Not only the autonomy talks but the Egypt-Israel peace treaty might now come into question, and also the key role of Egypt as a political and military partner of the United States in the Middle East and Africa. Hence the extreme concern in Washington that the assassination might unloose a political earthquake in Egypt, an attack by Libya on Egypt or Sudan, or a rupture of the peace process with Israel.

The United States quickly declared its support for the Egyptian government and for Sudan, warned Libya, and assigned two AWACS planes to the area to patrol borders, gather intelligence and demonstrate support. Each day's news seemed to bring a new threat and a new U.S. commitment. But Sadat's successor, Hosni Mubarak, took charge according to constitutional procedures, established order, and announced that his government would carry on the policies of Sadat, including the Camp David accords.

Sadat had not, however, set Egypt's course for all time, and changes were inevitable although not likely to be apparent at once. Mubarak was not Sadat and would not have his personal touch nor all of his assets and his liabilities. It was not clear whether Mubarak would be challenged in Egypt, and by whom, or whether he would seek different elements of domestic support (in addition to the officer corps, the essential prop of every Egyptian government since 1952) or a different complex of foreign relations. Domestically he would be tough against the Muslim fanatics who wanted revolution, but he soon showed readiness to conciliate some whom Sadat had persecuted, including critics of the close embrace with America. In foreign policy he was not likely to fall in with the concept of Israel, Egypt and America together against the world.

With other Arab rulers Mubarak did not have the vindictive personal feuds that Sadat seemed to enjoy, although he was associated with Sadat's policies which had brought about Egypt's ostracism from the Arab community. It seemed inevitable that Egypt would seek ways to mend relations with other Arab states, and vice versa, and that Israel would try to prevent it. Reconciliation with Saudi Arabia, in particular, would be of advantage to both, for their strengths—Saudi Arabia's wealth and Egypt's historic political and cultural weight in the Arab world—are complementary. The key question in Egyptian-Arab rapprochement is how, and on whose terms, it can take place. It is not likely that others will fall in with Egypt's peace with Israel, nor that Egypt will abandon it. The terms, most likely, would have less to do with the common defense of the region against the Soviets than with Arab solidarity and support of the Palestinians, and in that event the Camp David "Framework for Peace in the Middle East" might well be a casualty.

The new situation after the death of Sadat, in any case, made new thinking on the Palestine question necessary, both in the region and in Washington. Two American ex-presidents, Ford and Carter, returning from Sadat's funeral, stated to the press that the United States would have to come to the point of opening communication with the PLO. Neither had said that while in office, and President Reagan, being in office, did not say it. But their remarks were indicative of a growing view that peace could not be made in Palestine without bringing Palestinians into the game, and that this could not be done without the PLO.

After the AWACS vote in late October a "peace plan" which Crown Prince Fahd of Saudi Arabia had put forward in August as a basis for settlement, without causing a great stir, began to move into the center of active diplomacy. The plan called for

Israeli withdrawal from all occupied territories, the right of Palestinians to repatriation, a temporary U.N. trusteeship over the West Bank and Gaza Strip, and then the establishment of a Palestinian state there with East Jerusalem as its capital. A further point, which could be taken as a promise of acceptance and recognition of Israel, said that all states in the area had the right to live in peace (although Israel was not mentioned by name). Statements made by high U.S. officials, including the President, took note of that point in calling the Fahd initiative an encouraging development. The Israeli reaction to both the Saudi proposal and the American comments on it was negative. Begin called it a plan for the gradual liquidation of Israel. The State Department then gave assurances that the United States was not turning away from Camp David.

The ill-defined and partially self-contradictory position of the United States owed something to the American habit of making frequent and sometimes off-hand official comments on current events, and something also to a combination of not entirely consistent purposes. U.S. officials wished to keep Egypt and Israel on the Camp David track, to give a boost to the autonomy talks, to capitalize on supposed Saudi good-will following the AWACS vote, and to encourage Saudi Arabia to come into the settlement process.

Prince Fahd's plan did not move very far toward middle ground. It was, in general terms, a restatement of the standard Arab interpretation of U.N. Resolution 242, with the addition of the specific demand for a Palestinian state, the same position Sadat had taken when he went to Jerusalem in October 1977. It was also, as Fahd himself stated, not a means of bringing the Arab states and the PLO into the Camp David process but an alternative to Camp David. As a basis for negotiation, setting forth conditions for settlement, it was obviously unacceptable to the United States as it was to Israel, but as a statement of initial Arab positions on points which could serve as the agenda for negotiation without conditions, it might be a breakthrough. From that standpoint, although it was not the declared standpoint of the Saudi government, the favorable American comments were understandable.

Those few and faint favorable comments, however, coupled with assurances to Israel and renewed dedication to Camp David, were not sufficient to help Saudi Arabia in her efforts to sell the plan to fellow Arabs. The moderates were generally sympathetic but the radical rejectionists were not. Arafat, who at first supported it, changed his tune when other PLO factions and even some within his own Fatah organization spoke out against it. Syrian endorsement might have given the plan momentum, but Hafez al-Assad did not even show up at the Arab League summit meeting convened to consider it in Fez, Morocco, in late November. That meeting was hastily adjourned without any decision.

The debacle at Fez was an embarrassment for Saudi Arabia and a disappointment for Americans who had seen the Saudi initiative as positive and constructive. The disarray of the Arab world was a source of satisfaction to Israel, which could now point to the Arab states and the PLO as having rejected even a one-sided peace plan of Arab origin. But the failure of the Fahd plan did not do anything to enhance the prospects of the Camp David negotiations. On the contrary, the strengthening of hard-line views in Israel and on the Arab side made them dimmer than ever.

The waters were muddied further, at the end of November, as the United States and Israel decided the time had come to put their talk of strategic cooperation into the form of a written agreement. It was, for Washington, partly a means of repairing relations with Israel, strained by so many recent events, partly a demonstration that the movement for strategic consensus was proceeding apace with Israel as it was with Egypt, which was just then collaborating with U.S. forces in extensive joint maneuvers, "Operation Bright Star," on and around Egyptian territory. For the government of Israel, wishing to associate itself with American strategy so that America would be associated with Israeli strategy, the agreement was welcome but disappointing in that it did not go far enough. It provided for exchange of intelligence (which was going on anyway), stockpiling of U.S. medical supplies in Israel for use in an emergency (such as a small war in the Persian Gulf), and joint naval exercises; nothing very extensive, but the main significance of the accord was the fact of its formal conclusion.

The underlying idea of Israeli participation in defense of the region (of Arab oil fields, for example) strained credulity and raised objections even in Israel, where the Labor opposition called for a vote of confidence on it in the Knesset and barely lost. As for the Arabs, the effect was to justify the hard-liners and weaken those friendly to America. To all of them, strategic cooperation between Israel and the United States meant only one thing and was best illustrated by what happened in October 1973. The U.S. government, presumably, had counted the political costs when it made the agreement with Israel, but might have to count them again later.

Inevitably, the year's developments were reinforcing in Israel a kind of siege mentality, and Menachem Begin's style was always to take the offensive, even when it provoked objection and protest from Israel's one friend in the international community. American objections, experience showed, tended to be pro forma and temporary. The extreme nature of Arab reactions to Israel's moves could be counted on to bring America to Israel's defense. Begin, moreover, had never left any doubt that he would take measures he believed necessary to defend Israel's rights and interests, no matter what any outsider thought about it. Such a measure was the extension of Israeli civil law to the Golan Heights, a de facto annexation, rushed through the Knesset in a few hours on December 14. That he had long intended the eventual incorporation into Israel of that territory, under military occupation since it was taken from Syria in the war of 1967, was well known. It was the timing and the method, with no prior notice to the Israeli public or to Washington, that caused surprise and anger.

The Begin government anticipated a negative American reaction, but not the degree of Washington's outrage or the harshness of the reprisals. The United States declared the Israeli measure a violation of Resolution 242 on which the Camp David accords were based, joined in the unanimous resolution of the U.N. Security Council, initiated by Syria, calling it legally null and void, and then took the step of suspending the recently concluded U.S.-Israel agreement on strategic cooperation and of informing Begin that future cooperation in that field depended on Israel's policies in the peace negotiations and military restraint in Lebanon. Begin's angry reply, couched in bitter and insulting terms and railing against attempts to "punish" Israel, was that he took the American action to mean cancellation of the agreement. Begin's surprise move had thus dealt a new and severe blow to Israel's standing in America, to Israel's own objective of closer military cooperation with the United States, and perhaps also to the strategic conceptions which the Reagan Administration had held when it entered office less than a year before.

VI

This narrative has made almost no mention of America's European and Japanese allies, whose interests in the Middle East are extensive, their dependence on its oil being greater than that of the United States. The omission not only reflects the reduced power of the Europeans to influence the course of events and the reluctance of Japan to engage in global power politics, but also the prevailing American view that only the United States has the means to protect Western interests in the Gulf and to bring about an Arab-Israeli settlement. American officials wanted Europe to help in the effort to build a military barrier to Soviet expansion and not to interfere in the process of peacemaking following Camp David; dissatisfied with Europe's performance on both counts, they were not inclined to listen intently to European advice either on defense strategy or on the diplomacy of Arab-Israeli peace.

In one respect, however, the Europeans did put in an appearance in 1981, and with American encouragement. Bickering and deadlock in the autonomy talks posed a potential threat to the one solid accomplishment in peacemaking, the Egypt-Israel treaty, especially in the atmosphere of uncertainty created by the death of Sadat. Israel might refuse to go through with the final evacuation of Sinai, and some voices in Israel were urging precisely that. Begin said he would carry out the obligations of the treaty, but it could not be ruled out that changed circumstances would change his mind. To remove as much uncertainty as possible, it was necessary to make the final arrangements for the international observer force which was to be stationed in evacuated territory after the Israeli withdrawal.

Because a U.N. force, as specified in the treaty, could not be formed owing to a predictable Soviet veto in the Security Council, the United States was obliged to find individual states willing to contribute military units. Through casting the net far and wide, the American effort had turned up, by the fall of 1981, only three states (Colombia, Uruguay and Fiji) prepared to send units to serve alongside those of the United States, which would make up about one-half of the proposed force. What Washington wanted was a broader base indicating substantial world backing for the peace settlement; hence, the satisfaction and relief when four members of the European Community (Britain, France, Italy and the Netherlands) agreed to participate, with the prospect that Canada, Australia and New Zealand would also join.

The composition of the international force had to be agreed to by Israel and Egypt, however, and the former was quite negative about the Europeans. Israel had never wanted to have Western European countries associated with the peace process, regarding them as blatantly pro-Arab and soft on the PLO, especially after the European Community's June 1980 declaration at Venice, endorsing Palestinian self-determination in the West Bank and Gaza and PLO participation in negotiations for a settlement. In announcing their willingness to take part in the international force in Sinai, moreover, the Europeans gratuitously repeated their position taken at Venice, putting on record their view that the Palestinian half of the Camp David accords was a failure, even as they were all for making the other half, the peace treaty, a success. But for Israel it had to be Camp David, all of Camp David, and nothing but Camp David.

It took persistence and a bit of legerdemain on the part of American diplomacy to find the formulas by which the United States, Israel and the Europeans could keep their respective positions more or less intact and still agree, as they finally did in December, on European participation in the international force in Sinai. The episode was significant not just for the overcoming of a difficult problem, but for the fact that America, at long last, saw some merit in bringing her allies into the Middle East peace process. It was no more than the beginning of an approach to the problem of how the Western alliance, under strain in other areas as well, should look to its common interests in the Middle East. That was a problem with a long history.

Ever since the Suez crisis of 1956, which marked the demise of British and French aspirations to maintain a leading role in the Middle East and the clear predominance of the United States as the major Western power there, a gap had existed between European and American policies, serious enough to shake the foundations of the alliance in times of crisis such as that of 1973, even though their primary interests were identical or parallel.[2] The differences owed a great deal in the 1960s to Charles de Gaulle's insistence on the independent role of France (and of Europe), and in the 1970s to Henry Kissinger's insistence on American primacy. They were too deep and persistent, however, to be purely a matter of dominant personalities. They reflected separate national approaches, differing estimates of how European and American interests, even where parallel, could best be protected, and interpretations of each other's motives that came close to caricature: the Europeans as Munich-type appeasers of the Arabs or of the Russians, the Americans as enfeoffed to Israel and the Jewish lobby and obsessed by the Soviet threat.

The price of misunderstanding and non-cooperation has placed a mortgage on the future. In the absence of a common Western energy strategy, each country has sought to make its own deals with individual oil-producing states, deals which ignored or prej-

[2] I have described and analyzed these developments in "Les Etats-Unis et l'Europe au Moyen-Orient: intérêts communs et politiques divergentes," *Politique Internationale*, No. 7, printemps 1980, pp. 165–86. See also Dominique Moïsi, "L'Europe et le conflit israélo-arabe," *Politique Etrangère*, décembre 1980, pp. 835–47.

udiced the interests of other consumers, soured relations among them, and did not provide any real security as to the supply and price of oil. Without an effective long-term policy to reduce dependence on Middle East oil, and to maintain access while doing so, the Western countries and Japan will be at the mercy of the wars and revolutions, and of the political decisions and whims of rulers, in one of the most volatile areas of the world.

In political and military cooperation the record was no better. The revolution in Iran and the Soviet move into Afghanistan, which shocked Europe as well as America and posed the same threat to sources of oil vital to both, actually widened the gap between them. What Americans saw as necessary defensive action—economic sanctions, a military buildup—Europeans saw as overreaction. Where America was writing off global détente with the U.S.S.R., her West European allies wished to preserve détente where it really counted for them, in Europe, almost regardless of what happened in Afghanistan and the Middle East. The differences, which in the last year of the Carter Presidency were eroding the cohesion of the alliance, increased as the new Administration's statements and actions were seen in Europe as overly concerned with military power and heedless of European views and interests.

And so, the military buildup in the Indian Ocean went forward as an American enterprise, although France did maintain naval forces in the area. Aid to Pakistan and to Egypt was undertaken by the United States alone. Strategic cooperation with Israel was strictly an American policy, just another obstacle, as Europeans saw it, to good relations between the West and the Arab world. The Europeans were not, however, holding themselves out of the Middle East picture. They were bargaining for oil, engaging in trade and in development projects, and, with the French in the lead, selling arms where they could, all with a view to helping their own economies and securing political advantage. And the European Community, continuing to promote its own line on the question of a Palestinian settlement, was praising Prince Fahd's plan and taking diplomatic soundings in Arab capitals, which was the kind of help Haig indicated he would gladly do without. It was, to put it bluntly, absurd that the members of the Atlantic Alliance, all of whom supported the continued independence and security of Israel and were for a settlement that would give the Palestine Arabs a self-governing homeland in the West Bank and the Gaza Strip, could not harmonize their policies.

An exception to the general record of policies at cross purposes in 1981 was provided by American and European participation in a major program of aid to Turkey. As a NATO ally vital to the defense of Europe, Turkey had a special claim on such aid. But since she was important, for geographical reasons, to the defense of the Middle East, European-American collaboration in her support was a good example for that area—although even that example was clouded when the Europeans held up their assistance because of the Turkish military regime's dubious record on human rights and slowness in returning the country to democracy, while the United States, putting priority on security and defense, went full speed ahead with military aid.

The hue and cry over Libya at the close of the year spread a few more clouds over U.S.-European relations. America's right and need to react directly and forcefully to attacks on her armed forces (as in replying with fire to fire from Libyan aircraft over the Mediterranean in August) or to conspiracies to assassinate high officials cannot be legitimately questioned. Nor can international terrorism be condoned. What European opinion questioned was the timing, the methods, the overblown publicity, and the engagement of the President of the United States in a shouting match with such as Muammar Qaddafi.

In the prevailing European view, Qaddafi had been supporting terrorism for a good many years, but he was reducing rather than increasing that support; he was exporting oil to the West; he was not a Soviet agent even though he had a lot of Soviet arms to play with; he had withdrawn his forces from Chad; he was a nuisance to the West but a nuisance also to other states in the Middle East and in Africa, and it was their job to deal with him, slow as the process might be. Meanwhile, why build him up as an Arab and Third-World hero standing up to the superpower of the Western world?

It was the familiar picture: on one side, an Administration in Washington unable to compromise its absolutes in order to find common ground; on the other, a group of allies primarily concerned with their own interests and convinced of their own wisdom, doing little to help.

VII

In considering the year's events, the most valid criticism to be made of U.S. policy may be that in concentrating on a stronger military posture it neglected political foundations.[3] The Soviets

---

[3] Such a critique is forcefully made by Christopher Van Hollen, "Don't Engulf the Gulf," *Foreign Affairs*, Summer 1981, pp. 1064–78.

had made no new territorial gains, but the house of containment was built on the shifting sands of regional instability and the Arab-Israeli conflict, with no general acceptance of American leadership. If the nations of the Middle East were to be defended and their oil kept available to the West, they would have to be convinced that American and Western policies were consistent with their interests as they saw them. That is the kind of proposition, referring to an area prone to violent change and crisscrossed with conflicts of its own, that hardly gives useful guidance to a Secretary of State. A policy attempting to accommodate everybody's interests will end up being no policy at all. Nevertheless, the events of 1981, seen against the background of previous history, point to a number of continuing factors which have had a bearing on the success or failure of policies and may condition those of the future.

1. American military power is necessary to balance that of the U.S.S.R., and the Middle East nations, in greater or less degree, rely on that balance for their security. The power to provide the balance must be nearby because Soviet power is also nearby. From the standpoint of most Middle East nations, it should be "over the horizon" (e.g., in the Mediterranean and the Indian Ocean), not on their soil. Thus, plans which make military sense to Americans in terms of the requirements for deterring or defending against a Soviet attack on the region may be infeasible for lack of political support in the countries to be defended. To insist on the best possible military posture may reduce the political cooperation that already exists.

2. The Soviet Union pursues a policy of seeking and seizing opportunities to expand its influence and control while simultaneously putting forward proposals for regional security, nuclear-free zones, and Arab-Israeli peace, to be achieved with Soviet participation and cooperation. Primarily propaganda rather than serious negotiating propositions, such proposals have a potential appeal to the peoples of the region. The West, as it builds up its military power to deter Soviet military action, also has the task of exposing and countering that appeal. The West should not refuse dialogue or negotiation with the Soviets as a means of clarifying respective interests and positions, managing crises that may be dangerous to all, and so testing the Kremlin's willingness to cooperate. But the West will not serve its own interests by accepting (a) a facade of cooperation behind which the Soviets continue to expand their influence and control; (b) a division of the region into spheres of influence; or (c) a Soviet veto over decisions

necessary for peace, stability and access to oil.

3. The two superpowers are and will continue to be present in the region. The local states accommodate to the facts of power; they look to America or to Russia, and sometimes to both, for arms, for the goods and technology they need, and for support in conflicts with their neighbors; they may play on the global Soviet-American competition for their own advantage. The comparison to the Balkans before World War I is an apt one. Not all the regional issues and conflicts, however, are or should be related to the global competition; nor are many of them subject to American control and management. Even major regional conflicts like the Iran-Iraq war may find their own level and outcomes without intervention by the superpowers or shifts in the global balance, as long as deterrence works. To take another example, a Marxist regime, such as exists in South Yemen, may be more effectively tamed or removed by action of Arab neighbors or of its own people than by operations with a made-in-U.S.A. label; that is, of course, unless the Soviet Union uses force to save its protégé.

4. It is natural for the United States to seek friends and allies in the region, to reward with arms and other favors governments which are cooperative. The advantages are evident, but experience has shown the need to be aware of the hazards of overcommitment, such as (a) the impermanence of ties with states which can change their rulers or change their friends without notice; (b) the dominance of local issues and conflicts, so that if one government chooses the American connection, its domestic opponents or foreign rivals are likely to choose or to deepen the Soviet connection; and (c) the risks of identification with a regime which is wrapped, or wraps itself, in the mantle of American protection and then may go down taking American prestige and influence with it. Iran was not a success story. Egypt or Saudi Arabia may not be either, and the way to prevent failure does not lie wholly in American determination to stand by friendly governments.

5. The urge for nonalignment is real, for it stems from the experience of peoples long subject to domination by outsiders. Organizations like the Islamic Conference, the Arab League and the Gulf Cooperation Council, which exclude outside powers, are important expressions of popular sentiment and political solidarity even though they are militarily impotent. The strongest ideological-political forces in the region are nationalism and Islam, to which both elites and masses turn as these societies are strained and torn by rapid economic and social change. The challenge of "fundamentalism" and the reconciliation of Islam with the de-

mands of modern society are for those peoples to work out. The forces of nationalism and militant Islam can be diverse and divisive within the region, as we have seen, but they almost invariably contain strong anti-Western currents.

The West, though it may have to react against extreme and fanatical actions, cannot in the long run protect its interests in confrontation and conflict with nationalism and religion. If the West can nurture a basis for cooperation with the Middle East that exists in mutual economic interest, independence and respect for cultural differences, it may avoid that conflict or reduce its dimensions. If so, those same elemental forces of nationalism and religion may serve effectively as a bulwark against Soviet imperialism and communism, with which they are incompatible.

6. In general, the above considerations do not apply to Israel and the Arab-Israeli conflict. Here, the United States is directly involved. It has commitments to Israel and a special relationship with Israel, which is a stable democracy. American diplomacy has spent years searching for Arab-Israeli settlements and must continue to do so. The Egypt-Israel peace treaty was a giant step forward. It has eliminated, unless there is a startling reversal in Egypt, the danger of another Arab-Israeli war on the scale of 1973. But it appears to have made more difficult the achievement of peace between Israel and her other Arab neighbors.

Although the Camp David peace process is still held to by the U.S. government as the only route to take, it is difficult to see any hope in that course in the light of fixed Israeli and Arab positions, limited participation, and the unreality of the proposed five-year interim period of autonomy in the absence of basic decisions. As the situation deteriorates, with damage to American and Western interests in the entire area, a reappraisal of policy cannot be avoided.

7. The Palestine question remains a formidable obstacle and burden to U.S. relations with the Arab world. It undermines the moderates and strengthens the wild men. It plays into the hands of the Soviet Union. It threatens to isolate the United States with Israel as the only friend in the region. A settlement may not be possible; nor can we assume that a settlement, if reached, would end Arab-Israeli tension or transform America's relations with the Arab world. Nevertheless, the effort must be made. The terms, of course, have to be negotiated by the parties, principally Israel, Jordan and representatives of the Palestinians (not excluding the PLO), and that requires a major endeavor to get those parties talking to each other.

In any case, the time has come for the United States to take a stand on the principles of settlement that were left ambiguous in U.N. Resolution 242 and bypassed by the complex formulas of Camp David but have wide international support. They are, briefly, Israeli withdrawal from the West Bank and the Gaza Strip to the lines of 1949–1967, with minor modifications to be negotiated by the parties; self-determination by the inhabitants of those territories, not including Jerusalem, whether the choice is for an independent state, union with Jordan, or whatever; special arrangements for East Jerusalem to be negotiated; Palestinian acceptance of Israel; Israeli acceptance of Palestinian self-determination; and peace between them guaranteed by the great powers and the United Nations. These principles are not new. If the State Department looks in its files, it will find something very similar in the now forgotten "Rogers plan" of December 1969.[4]

Such proposals were not acceptable to Israel in 1969; nor are they acceptable today. They are not acceptable to the Arab side either, even if one takes the plan of Prince Fahd as the Arab position. But they may offer the only possibility of a settlement, and the dangers and damages of no settlement are being felt by the United States and many other nations far from the immediate area of Palestine. A settlement that holds the promise of reconciliation rather than total and indefinite confrontation is also the only long-term answer to Israel's security problem.

8. The United States, standing on the above principles, would face difficult times in its relations with Israel. No American President would relish the task of pressing Israel to modify her positions. Yet there has always been a distinction between America's commitment to Israel's independent existence, which is firm and unchanging, and America's support for Israel's security needs as defined by the Israeli government, with which the U.S. government may differ. There is room for a clarifying exchange and debate here, within and between both countries, difficult as it may be.

9. Finally, a point already made, America needs her Western allies in the Middle East, and they need America. An earlier essay in these pages, covering the year 1978, referred to the burdens of empire in the Middle East, suggesting that America had taken on tasks beyond her means and ability to perform.[5] Since that time,

[4] Described in detail in William B. Quandt, *Decade of Decisions: American Policy Toward the Arab-Israeli Conflict, 1967–1976*, Berkeley: University of California Press, 1977, pp. 89–92.

[5] John C. Campbell, "The Middle East: Burdens of Empire," *Foreign Affairs: America and the World 1978*, pp. 613–32.

with events in Iran and elsewhere, the American empire has shrunk but the burdens have not. The obligations, military and other, grow rather than diminish. Western interests require a Western response, the use of diversity in unity. America is both too small and too big to do it alone. Too small, because her resources are not limitless, her political influence is not all-pervasive, her diplomacy not all-wise. Too big, because as the Western superpower she is the main target, the imperialist enemy, the "great Satan," when governments and leaders in the Middle East feel the need of such an enemy. At such times it is useful to have less satanic friends who can maintain lines of communication and influence and use them for common ends.

Every new Administration needs time to find its footing in foreign affairs, especially in a complex and changing area like the Middle East, and the Reagan team has taken as much or more time than its predecessors. It may be unwarranted, not to say unfair, to make hasty judgments, or to set up a list of points like those above, against which to compare the record of the year. Earlier Administrations, after all, broke their heads on these same issues. Other observers would have quite different checklists. This one, if it has any validity, may serve better to judge the later years of the Reagan Administration than the first. In any event, it may stimulate both policymaker and critic, as they struggle to find answers to swiftly moving events and crises, at least to ask the right questions.

Paul E. Sigmund

LATIN AMERICA: CHANGE OR CONTINUITY?

The election of Ronald Reagan in November 1980 may not have actually led to victory parties in the capitals of the more conservative military regimes of Latin America, but it seemed clearly to indicate that there would be a significant change in U.S. policy toward that area. While Jimmy Carter's Latin American policy was not a central issue in the 1980 campaign, it appeared from statements by Reagan's advisers and from the conservative "think tanks" that prepared policy papers during the transition period, that there was likely to be a shift in Latin American policy as dramatic as the one that marked the early days of the Carter Administration—in an exactly opposite direction. While the furtherance of human rights would not be completely abandoned as an objective of U.S. policy (Roger Fontaine, one of Reagan's Latin American advisers, had told a Chilean audience in September that "a concern for human rights did not begin with the Carter administration nor will it end with it"), it was to receive a much lower priority; and with friendly governments it was to be promoted through "quiet diplomacy" behind the scenes rather than through public denunciations and aid cutoffs.

A second shift that seemed likely to affect U.S.-Latin American relations was a renewed emphasis on the East-West conflict and a corresponding lessening of attention to so-called North-South questions such as development assistance and the demands for changes in the economic relations of developed and developing countries, summed up in the so-called New International Economic Order. The number one issue affecting contemporary international relations was considered to be the spread of Soviet expansionism, not the development needs of the Third World.

The shift on the part of a new Republican Adminstration to a greater emphasis on "realism" in U.S.-Latin American relations, in contrast to the more idealistic programs of the Democrats, followed a long tradition. Franklin Roosevelt's Good Neighbor

Paul E. Sigmund is Professor of Politics and Director of the Latin American Studies Program at Princeton University. His most recent books are *The Overthrow of Allende and the Politics of Chile, 1964–1976* and *Multinationals in Latin America: The Politics of Nationalization.*

Policy and the development of the institutions of hemispheric collective security under the Truman Administration had followed the "dollar diplomacy" and direct military interventions of earlier Republican Administrations. John F. Kennedy's Alliance for Progress, even in its watered-down form under Lyndon Johnson, was abandoned by Richard Nixon in favor of a "low profile" in Latin America, and (with the exception of the Chilean covert interventions of 1970–73 and a half-hearted attempt to develop a "New Dialogue" with Latin America in the mid-1970s) an almost total disregard of the area by Henry Kissinger during his tenure as Secretary of State under Presidents Nixon and Ford. Then in 1977 the Carter Administration took up the banner of human rights, already being promoted as a result of congressional legislation, appointed an activist Assistant Secretary of State for Human Rights and Humanitarian Affairs, and used cutoffs of military aid and loan support to indicate U.S. disapproval of a number of the more repressive military and authoritarian governments of Latin America.

Perhaps the most important of the criticisms of the Carter policies were written by a former Democrat, Jeane Kirkpatrick, then associated with Georgetown University and the American Enterprise Institute. In a widely discussed article in *Commentary* (November 1979), "Dictatorships and Double Standards," Kirkpatrick distinguished between authoritarian and totalitarian regimes, and argued that friendly "non-democratic" autocrats in countries such as Iran and Nicaragua had been undermined by U.S. policy, which was "led by its own misunderstanding of the situation to assist actively in deposing an erstwhile friend and ally and installing a government hostile to American interests and policies in the world." The article is supposed to have brought her to the attention of Ronald Reagan and influenced her selection as his Ambassador to the United Nations. Before she took up her post, however, a second article was published in *Commentary* (January 1981) that focused the criticisms more specifically on the Carter policy toward Latin America. In "U.S. Security and Latin America" she argued that the Carter policies:

not only proved incapable of dealing with the problems of Soviet/Cuban expansion in the area, they have positively contributed to them and to the alienation of major nations, the growth of neutralism, the destabilization of friendly governments, the spread of Cuban influence, and the decline of U.S. power in the region. Hence one of the first and most urgent tasks of the Reagan administration will be to review and revise the U.S. approach to Latin America and the Caribbean.

The supporting evidence for Mrs. Kirkpatrick's argument was drawn mainly from the Nicaraguan case where, it was asserted, the Carter Administration "acted repeatedly and at critical junctures to weaken the government of Anastasio Somoza and to strengthen his opponents" in the service of a "globalist utopian" approach, promoted by a book written a decade earlier by Zbigniew Brzezinski under the auspices of the Council on Foreign Relations, the two reports of the Linowitz Commission on U.S.-Latin American Relations, and the conclusions of a study group of the Institute for Policy Studies—the last demonstrating "how strong had become the affinity between the views of the foreign policy establishment and the New Left." The remedy, Kirkpatrick concluded, for the errors of the Carter Administration was, like their cause, intellectual. It was necessary to abandon the ideological globalism of the previous Administration, to build on the concrete circumstances of each foreign policy case, and to assess alternative policies in terms of their impact on "the security of the United States and on the safety and autonomy of the other nations of the hemisphere."

The Kirkpatrick approach was typical of the thinking of the new Administration.[1] Reagan and his advisers came into office determined to alter significantly what they perceived to be the deleterious direction of the previous Administration's policy toward Latin America (and the world) in two areas—the relation of human rights to security considerations, and the priority given to the communist threat. Every new Administration comes to office convinced that it will correct the mistakes of its predecessors. In this case, however, this involved more than a shift in emphasis back toward a more traditional balance-of-power diplomacy of the Kissinger variety. National security was to be redefined as a militant anti-communism, and the U.S. stance in Latin America and the world was to be one of strength, rejecting the "gun-shy" attitudes of the previous policy. A military man—although one whose career had been as much political as military—was made Secretary of State and took office determined to "draw the line" against the Soviet Union and Cuba after the "losses" in Iran and Nicaragua.

---

[1] For other examples of attacks on Carter Administration policies by Reagan campaign advisers on Latin America, see the articles by Roger Fontaine *et al.* and by Pedro San Juan in *The Washington Quarterly*, Autumn 1980. These attacks also mention the Brzezinski book (*Between Two Ages*, New York: Viking, 1970), the Linowitz reports (published as *The Americas in a Changing World*, New York: Quadrangle, 1975, and *The United States and Latin America: Next Steps*, New York: Center for InterAmerican Relations, 1976), and the study by the Institute for Policy Studies' Working Group on Latin America, *The Southern Connection*.

Now, a year later, it may be possible to assess the impact of this determination. In what ways has U.S. policy toward Latin America changed, and in what ways have there been significant continuities in that policy despite the change in Administrations?

II

El Salvador was the first area in Latin America where the new Administration attempted to demonstrate that it was following a different policy from that of its predecessor. Long a backwater in an area of the world to which the United States paid little attention, Central America had been catapulted onto the front pages in 1978 and 1979 with the national uprising in Nicaragua against the 40-year reign of the Somoza family which culminated in the victory of the Sandinista-led revolutionaries on July 19, 1979. In neighboring El Salvador, a tiny overpopulated statelet the size of Massachusetts which had been ruled by the military and "the fourteen families," the shock waves of the Somoza overthrow had sparked a reformist coup in October 1979, led by army colonels in league with civilian politicians who established a junta to carry out long-overdue social and economic reforms. Several civilian members of the original junta resigned three months later, citing the lack of progress on reform and continuing repression by the armed forces and security services, but the military managed to strike a deal with the largest Salvadoran political party, the Christian Democrats, whose presidential candidate, José Napoleón Duarte, had been arrested, tortured and exiled after an apparent victory in the 1972 presidential elections. The new regime called for continued implementation of a reform program which included nationalization of banks and foreign trade, and an ambitious agrarian reform.

The Carter Administration had maintained cool relations with the regime of General Carlos Romero before his overthrow in October 1979. Along with Guatemala and Brazil, Romero had rejected U.S. military aid in 1977 just before the United States itself cut off Salvadoran military assistance because of human rights violations. After the reformist coup, "non-lethal" military aid involving transportation and communications equipment was resumed in 1980, then in December it was cut off again, following the murder of three American nuns and a lay social worker. In early January 1981, two U.S. representatives of the American Institute for Free Labor Development and the head of the Salvadoran land reform program were murdered in the Sheraton Hotel of San Salvador, but as the Carter Administration received increasing intelligence evidence of the shipment of U.S. weapons from communist sources through Cuba to the Salvadoran guerrilla movement, it authorized the renewal of military aid without the lethal vs. non-lethal distinction.

The presidential authorization of the aid renewal on January 16, 1981, four days before Ronald Reagan took office, came in the midst of a ten-day "final offensive" by the guerrilla opposition aimed at overthrowing the Salvadoran government before Reagan took power. The offensive and the accompanying call for a general strike were unsuccessful in securing popular support, but the new Administration decided to make El Salvador an example of its new approach to what it described as a "textbook case of indirect aggression by Communist powers through Cuba." That description was the conclusion of a collection of documents, *Communist Interference in El Salvador* (often referred to as the State Department White Paper on El Salvador), and an accompanying summary Special Report published on February 23, 1981. Three days earlier Secretary of State Alexander Haig conducted a briefing in which he referred to the flow of several hundred tons of military equipment to the Salvadoran guerrillas from "the Soviet bloc, Vietnam, Ethiopia, and radical Arabs," with "most of this equipment, not all but most," entering via Nicaragua (*New York Times*, February 21, 1981). Haig also referred in his briefing to the need "to deal with the source of the problem and that is Cuba," but did not specify what actions were to be taken in pursuit of that goal. The State Department documents, discovered in El Salvador in November 1980 and January 1981, included a detailed account of a trip in May and June by Shafik Handal, head of the Salvadoran Communist Party, to Eastern Europe, the Soviet Union, Vietnam and Ethiopia in search of arms—preferably those of Western make—as well as subsequent discussions in Havana and Managua to arrange the transshipment of the arms to El Salvador.[2]

---

[2] The White Paper seems to have been put together hastily, and it was subsequently subjected to critical scrutiny by *The Wall Street Journal* (June 8, 1981) and *The Washington Post* (June 9, 1981). They noted that the Spanish documents were sometimes inaccurately translated and summarized and that the figures as to the amounts of arms (800 tons committed, and 200 tons actually shipped to El Salvador) were exaggerated estimates not supported by the documentation. In addition, close scrutiny of the published documents showed an initial reluctance by the Soviet Union to support the guerrillas, as well as complaints in July 1980 on the Salvadorans' part of the lack of enthusiasm for their cause by the Nicaraguans, who were bent on protecting their own revolution. Nevertheless no one has denied that the trip was made, or that substantial arms of American manufacture traceable by serial number to Vietnam and Ethiopia did suddenly appear in, or en route to, El Salvador in late 1980. Nicaraguan and Cuban government officials have also admitted privately to third country representatives that such arms shipments were made. See U.S. Department of State, *Response to Stories about Special Report No. 80*, June 17, 1981. A follow-up State Department study, *El Salvador: The Search for Peace*, was published in September 1981. For evaluations of U.S. policy from a variety of points of view, see "Struggle in Central America," *Foreign Policy*, Summer 1981, and Richard E. Feinberg, "Central America: No Easy Answers," *Foreign Affairs*, Summer 1981.

The State Department publications and the announcement that U.S. economic and military aid would be increased, and advisers sent to train the Salvadorans in the use of the helicopters and patrol boats provided, set off an intense public debate in the media, with cover stories in *Time* and *Newsweek* on the background and nature of the Salvadoran conflict. Congress received a barrage of letters, many of them from church-affiliated groups, opposing U.S. military aid to El Salvador, and the press publicized the continuing killings of innocent civilians by both sides—with the majority of the killing being carried out by those associated with the government security forces. Church and human rights lobbyists pressured the congressional committees that were considering the Administration's request for an increase in military and economic aid to El Salvador.[3] In El Salvador itself, the junta, now headed by Duarte as president, announced that it planned to hold elections for a constitutional assembly in March 1982, with presidential elections scheduled for 1983. When Colonel Roberto d'Aubuisson, a rightist military man who had been living in exile, returned with the announced intention of overthrowing the junta, the U.S. Embassy took an active role in discouraging him, and President Reagan surprised some of his conservative supporters by endorsing the Salvadoran agrarian reform program, including its successful effort to transform the 350 largest landholdings into agricultural cooperatives.

The public debate and heavy constituent mail on El Salvador had a direct impact on the actions of the two congressional committees considering the Administration's request for $26 million in military aid and $87.7 million in economic assistance in the coming fiscal year. Over Secretary Haig's objections both committees voted to place conditions on U.S. aid requiring that the President certify every six months that the Salvadoran government was making "a concerted and significant" effort to control human rights violations including those by its own armed forces, and was committed to holding free elections and agrarian reform, and to negotiation with opposition groups for a peaceful settlement. The House version originally included an authorization of a congressional veto of further aid within 30 days of the presidential report, but that was later dropped, and the final version adopted by the full Senate in September also provided that the government was only required to be willing to negotiate

---

[3] For estimates by members of Congress on the strong constituent opposition to military aid to El Salvador, see *The New York Times*, March 26, 1981. The House subcommittee vote in March on shifting $5 million to Salvadoran military assistance was 8–7.

with "groups which renounce and refrain from further military or paramilitary opposition activity."

The unanimity of the organized church groups in Washington in their opposition to military aid to El Salvador was something of a foreign policy first. Unlike Bishop Rivera y Damas who in his weekly homilies in San Salvador was careful to emphasize that both sides were guilty of human rights violations and impeding a peaceful solution, the U.S. churchmen, in calling for a cutoff of all U.S. military aid to El Salvador, emphasized only the well-reported abuses of the government security forces, giving little or no attention to the problems of the outside arms being supplied to the guerrillas and the murder and assassinations which they carried out.[4]

The opponents of U.S. military aid, including 35 members of the House of Representatives led by Gerry Studds of Massachusetts, argued that the level of violence by the regime's security forces and by paramilitary groups associated with them fell within section 502B of the Foreign Assistance Act, which provides for a cutoff of aid to any government engaged in "a consistent pattern of gross violations of internationally recognized human rights." They also claimed that an aid cutoff would force the junta to negotiate a cease-fire and coalition government with the Frente Democrático Revolucionario (FDR), the exile opposition alliance of Social Democrats, former Christian Democrats, and other groups, linked since mid-1980 to the Marxist guerrilla Farabundo Martí National Liberation Front (FMLN). (The credibility of FDR-FMLN offers to negotiate was somewhat undermined by the publication of a document, subsequently admitted to be authentic, entitled Proposal for International Mediation and dated February 3, which described the policy of support for negotiations as aimed at gaining "time to improve our internal military situation" following the defeat of the final offensive.)

West Europeans were divided in their reactions to the U.S. policy in El Salvador. Christian Democrats generally supported Duarte, while Social Democrats favored negotiations with the FDR, which was headed by a fellow party member, Guillermo Ungo. Concern about the European attitudes led to the dispatch of

[4] In the midst of the January final offensive, Bishop Rivera y Damas drew on Catholic moral teaching on the just war to set forth the four requirements for insurrection—serious abuse of political power, the exhaustion of peaceful alternatives, a positive balance between the evils of the insurrection and the good that could result, and the likelihood of success. Only the first condition, he said, was met in the current situation—thus imposing a moral obligation to continue to search for a peaceful solution. See Kerry Ptacek, *The Catholic Church in El Salvador*, Washington: The Institute on Religion and Democracy, 1981, p. 5.

Lawrence Eagleburger, the new Assistant Secretary of State for European Affairs, on a mission to Europe to explain and defend the U.S. position.

In El Salvador, the Duarte proposal for constituent assembly elections was undercut by the continuing violence on both sides, and the likelihood that opposition leaders returning from exile would soon meet with assassination. Nevertheless the proposal for elections was endorsed by the United States, and when, following a lengthy behind-the-scenes ideological struggle, Thomas Enders, a career Foreign Service Officer, was appointed Assistant Secretary of State for Latin America, he made a public speech in July asserting that only a "political solution" could heal that divided country. That solution was the 1982 and 1983 elections, "open to all who are willing to renounce violence and abide by the procedures of democracy." Enders ruled out negotiations with the FDR-FMLN since "we should recognize that El Salvador's leaders will not and should not grant the insurgents through negotiations a share of power the rebels have not been able to win on the battlefield." (*New York Times*, July 17, 1981.)

It was precisely a negotiated solution of the kind Enders opposed that the French and Mexican governments seemed to be aiming at, a month later, when they recognized the FDR-FMLN as "a representative political force"—while not breaking their diplomatic relations with the Salvadoran junta. The Mexican-French initiative did not seem to move the Salvadoran situation closer to a solution, although it received the editorial endorsement of *The New York Times*. Led by Venezuela's Christian Democratic government, nine Latin American countries denounced the statement as favoring those "who through violence are trying to twist the democratic destiny and the free self-determination of the people of El Salvador"; five others also indicated their opposition, leaving only Nicaragua aligned with Mexico, and Panama uncommitted.

By fall, the Salvadoran war seemed to have reached a stalemate. The rebels took over a small provincial town for a few days in late August, and were in control of the countryside in parts of the north and center of the country, but their principal efforts were now devoted to economic sabotage culminating in the dynamiting of one of the two major bridges linking the eastern third of El Salvador with the rest of the country. The test case of the new Administration's resolve to "draw the line" and contain the spread of communism had simmered down to grudging and conditional support for continued economic and military aid by a reluctant Congress, occasional aggressive remarks by the Secretary of State about Cuban and Nicaraguan support for the guerrillas, and a general lack of enthusiasm for a civil war that seemed to have no solution. In September, when President Duarte came to argue his case on American television and in Congress, he received surprisingly little attention.

Later in the year the United States withdrew some of its 52 advisers but also announced that 1,500 Salvadorans would receive training in the United States or Panama. In December the Organization of American States voted 22 to 3, with Mexico, Nicaragua and Granada voting in the negative, to support the March 1982 elections, and to send observers if requested to guarantee the "purity" of the vote. Yet critics like Mexico noted that without the participation of the Left opposition the elections were unlikely to resolve what appeared to be an interminable civil war.

The Reagan Administration after nearly a year of deep involvement in El Salvador had not achieved the quick military victory it had sought. Indeed, its policy did not seem to differ much, except in its rhetorical emphasis on the external aspects of the problem, from that of the Carter Adminstration. It too supported the political center, free elections and social reform, as a way to prevent a takeover by the Left, and it seemed no more capable than was Carter of helping Duarte and the Christian Democrats to control the excesses of the security forces and paramilitary groups, whose continued indiscriminate killings undermined the U.S. argument that it was defending democracy against totalitarianism.[5]

The problem seemed intractable. As the leading presidential candidate in Costa Rica, Luis Alberto Monge, told a U.S. congressional delegation in September, "Those who hold the real power on both sides are beyond the reach of the democratic forces on both sides." An international peacekeeping force was suggested to guarantee the security of the opposition in the March elections, but the Salvadoran armed forces rejected this as a violation of national sovereignty. A victory by the FDR-FMLN might produce the mixed economy and pluralistic democracy that the Social Democratic leader of the FDR, Guillermo Ungo, promised, but— in contrast to the Nicaraguan Sandinista guerrillas two years earlier—no one had a real understanding of the intentions of the

---

[5] Carter defenders argue that his Administration was more willing to use aid as leverage to induce reform. See, for example, Richard E. Feinberg's essay on the Carter policy of "Creative Evolutionism" in Richard E. Feinberg (ed.), *Central America: International Dimensions of the Crisis*, New York: Holmes and Meier (forthcoming).

leadership of the guerrilla FMLN except that they were Marxist-Leninists and that one of their representatives, Salvador Cayetano Carpio, had made statements that elicited invidious comparisons to Pol Pot in Kampuchea. Others, rejecting the Pol Pot analogy, talked of a "Zimbabwe solution," but there was neither leadership of the stature of Robert Mugabe, nor a neutral military like the British army.[6] As the year ended, the House Foreign Affairs Committee called on the President to press for "unconditional discussions among the major political factions" but both sides maintained their previous positions—the Duarte government demanding a renunciation of violence by the Left, and the FDR-FMLN calling for negotiations which would give priority attention to a restructuring of the armed forces.

III

Nicaragua was the second country where the Administration was determined to pursue a different policy. The 1980 Republican Party platform had deplored "the Marxist-Sandinista takeover in Nicaragua" and spoken of "support of the efforts of the Nicaraguan people to establish a free and independent government." Yet it was unclear what policy initiatives would be taken by the new Administration to achieve that goal.

As in the case of El Salvador, the Carter Administration had already toughened its policy toward Nicaragua before the inauguration of Ronald Reagan. In January 1981, faced with the evidence of a substantial increase in arms shipments through Nicaragua to El Salvador just before the final offensive there, the Carter Administration delayed the projected disbursement of the remaining $15 million of the $75 million U.S. aid program voted by Congress in 1980, and cancelled authorization of negotiations for the renewal of Public Law 480 long-term low interest loans for the sale of wheat and cooking oil. In September 1980, President Carter had certified, as required by Congress, that Nicaragua was not "aiding or abetting or supporting acts of violence or terrorism in other countries," but in January, with new evidence of Nicaraguan government involvement in the supply of arms to the Salvadoran rebels, the new aid was not extended.

The Reagan Administration continued the review of Nicaragua

<hr>

[6] The Pol Pot comparison had been used by Jeane Kirkpatrick in the January 1981 article discussed above. On the Zimbabwe solution, see William LeoGrande, "A Splendid Little War," *International Security*, Summer 1981. For a discussion of the possibilities of international observer teams for the March election, see Robert Leiken, *Prepared Statement*, Subcommittee on Inter-American Affairs, House Foreign Affairs Committee, September 24, 1981, p. 13.

aid policy and despite a reported cutoff of arms flows from Nicaragua to El Salvador for three weeks in March a formal decision by the President to suspend the aid was announced on April 1. Yet Reagan did not demand repayment of the $60 million already expended (as authorized by the congressional legislation), previously contracted aid disbursements continued, and at the end of 1981 seven million dllars in unexpended but contracted aid still remained. The Nicaraguan government carried out a national and international propaganda campaign against the attempt to "starve Nicaragua into submission," and secured donations of wheat from Argentina, the Soviet Union and Bulgaria as well as a long-term credit sale of $15 million for wheat and oil from Canada.[7] In April, Libya announced a cash loan of $100 million and Mexico extended credit for all the petroleum it sold to Nicaragua during 1981, rather than providing a 30 percent loan as previously agreed upon. While the U.S. aid extended to Nicaragua during the first year of the Reagan Administration dropped sharply from the $110 million spent during the last 18 months of the Carter Administration, "pipeline" aid continued, assistance to the private sector amounted to $6.9 million between January and August, and aid from other countries more than offset the reductions in U.S. assistance. Nicaragua's economic prospects for 1982 were not bright, but the U.S. aid cutoff was not likely to be in itself decisive. However, as a symbolic act it communicated the continuing hostility of the American Administration, while not achieving any effect on arms flows.

Press reports began to appear of a training camp outside Miami of Cuban, Panamanian and Nicaraguan exiles as well as of raids into Nicaragua by exiles based in southern Honduras. The Sandinista government pointed to these groups to justify the expansion of its army to a projected 50,000 soldiers, plus a 200,000-man militia. The inflow of an estimated $28 million of Cuban and Soviet arms and an increase to 1,500 in the number of Cuban military and security advisers, along with renewed Nicaraguan government pressures on opposition party leaders, unions, radio stations and press (*La Prensa*, the respected newspaper that had spearheaded the opposition to Somoza, was closed on various pretexts five times between June and November) were cited by Secretary Haig to justify the need to take countermeasures against the military buildup. News leaked out about a Haig order to

---

[7] U.S. Agency for International Development, Nicaraguan Desk, Washington, D.C. It was reported that Nicaragua's campaign to secure foreign wheat was so successful that it sold surplus wheat to Costa Rica later in the year.

prepare papers on policy options that included a naval blockade against Nicaragua (*New York Times*, November 5, 1981). Reports were circulated—quickly denied by Cuba—about the dispatch of 600 Cuban troops to the Salvadoran rebels—and the Secretary of State spoke ominously about the need to arrest the "drift toward totalitarianism" in Nicaragua. Yet Haig's statements were privately criticized in press leaks by other government officials (especially in the Defense Department, which feared the domestic and international impact of a "Bay of Pigs" in Nicaragua) or were publicly questioned by other governments with which the United States maintained good relations—such as Mexico and Venezuela. At a press conference in November, President Reagan declared that there were "no plans" for the use of American troops "anywhere in the world."[8]

The verbal escalation, it was later revealed (*Washington Post*, December 10, 1981), followed two months of secret negotiations between Assistant Secretary of State Enders and the Nicaraguan government. Enders apparently offered a joint reaffirmation of both countries' OAS obligations to refrain from aggression or interference, a renewal of economic and technical assistance, and U.S. action against anti-Sandinista exiles on its soil—in return for Nicaraguan termination of arms flows to the Salvadoran rebels and de-escalation of its military buildup. The exchanges ended with a note from Nicaragua on October 31 calling on the United States to enforce its own laws against the exile training camps and to cease generating military tension in Central America and the Caribbean. In November, U.S. influence seems to have been exercised to prevent a $30 million Nicaraguan loan from appearing on the agenda of the Executive Board of the Inter-American Development Bank. Yet the Administration requested $33 million in new aid for Nicaragua for 1982 (over Administration objections, the House restricted it to the private sector, with aid for the public sector permitted only if there is "progress" toward free elections), and the announcement in early January 1982 that France had agreed to a $17 million program of "nonoffensive" military aid to Nicaragua weakened the argument that it had become a military outpost of Cuba and the Soviet Union

Vigorous criticism of the proposals for action against Nicaragua came from the opposition groups within Nicaragua, since they

---

[8] Under the War Powers Act of 1973, such actions would require congressional authorization or a notification by the President to the Congress of an emergency involving a threat to American security. In the latter case the Congress by concurrent resolution can require the troops to be withdrawn. The troops must be withdrawn within 60 days unless Congress specifically authorizes their continuing presence.

realized that such actions would destroy the very groups that the Administration was purportedly attempting to save. While the imprisonment in October of three leaders of the Private Enterprise Council (COSEP) for accusing the government of engaging in "a Marxist-Leninist adventure that will only bring more bloodshed," and the apparently related resignation of the Nicaraguan Ambassador to Washington, seemed to confirm the Haig assertions, the Nicaraguan opposition continued to treat with the Sandinista government: after the government published a draft Political Parties Law, two opposition parties rejoined the quasi-legislative Council of State to discuss it. *La Prensa* was still being published (with a larger circulation than the two pro-government papers combined), there was no mass exodus by the middle and entrepreneurial classes, the church made public criticisms of the regime's policies in statements by the bishops' conference and the archbishop's Sunday homilies, and the Marxist-dominated Sandinista regime continued to permit a situation of "harassed pluralism" that contrasted with the Administration talk of totalitarianism.

At the end of the year the continuing flow of arms and advisers to Nicaragua from Cuba and the reported training of Nicaraguans in Bulgaria to fly Soviet MiG fighters led to Administration concern that Nicaragua would become, in Secretary Haig's words, a "platform for terror and war." In his speech to the OAS Assembly in St. Lucia in December, Haig indicated that the United States was "prepared to join others" to prevent a Central American arms race. Yet, he also spoke of U.S. efforts to normalize relations with Nicaragua, and said: "If Nicaragua addresses our concerns about interventionism and militarization, we are prepared to address their concerns. We do not close the door to the search for proper relations." (*New York Times*, December 5, 1981.)

In an interview on his return from the meeting, Haig again ruled out the use of U.S. troops in Central America but discussed increased military and economic cooperation with other Central American countries, and seemed concerned to allay fears of unilateral U.S. actions of the type that had been discussed in press reports in November. Once again strong words had been followed by a relative restraint in policy—conduct that one press observer described as the Administration's "Caribbean Climbdown" (*Washington Post*, December 8, 1981.)

A similar pattern can be discerned in two other Central American countries. In May, Acting Assistant Secretary of State John Bushnell testified to Congress that the Administration planned to resume military aid to Guatemala to combat the spread of insurgency there, if the Guatemalan government gave evidence of attempting to control the violence perpetrated by military and paramilitary forces (estimated by the U.S. Embassy at 300 deaths a month). In June, it classified a shipment of jeeps to Guatemala as nonmilitary in character in order to circumvent a congressional ban on military aid to that country. Yet when retired Lieutenant General Vernon Walters visited Guatemala as Ambassador at Large to suggest an effort to control the violence and support for a civilian candidate in the scheduled March 1982 elections, the Guatemalans were unresponsive. The maneuver with the jeeps also provoked such criticism from Congress and the media, and the continuing stories of atrocities from Guatemala (including the assassination in July of a priest from Oklahoma who had earlier received death threats from right-wing groups) were so horrifying that no further movement in the direction of closer cooperation with the Guatemalan military was politically possible.

The March 1982 elections did not offer hope for a change. Unlike the situation in El Salvador, assassination and intimidation had effectively destroyed the Center and the Left within Guatemala; only one of the four presidential candidates was a civilian, and all were identified with the Right or extreme Right. Yet despite the increase in guerrilla activities, especially among the Indians who comprise 52 percent of the population, the insurgents were divided, the Indians themselves spoke different languages, and the Guatemalans were able to secure arms from other countries—notably Israel—so that it was difficult to make a case for an urgent need for U.S. military aid. Thus the Carter policy toward Guatemala remained essentially in effect.

Similarly, the existing policy in Honduras of support for a transition to civilian rule after 18 years of military domination remained unchanged, as the Hondurans elected a civilian president and congress from the Liberal Party on November 29th. Military aid was increased to ten million dollars, more advisers sent, and "small-scale" naval maneuvers held off the coast, but it is difficult to see in what important respect the policy was different from that of the Carter Administration. Democracy and free elections remained the U.S.-supported alternative to extremists on the Left and Right.

Democracy, free elections and anti-militarism have a long history in another key Central American country—Costa Rica—which dissolved its army in 1948. In August, when Jeane Kirkpatrick in a press interview in Lima suggested that the United

States might aid Costa Rica against terrorism and subversion by offering special police training, her statement was denounced in public letters by the Costa Rica president, who stated categorically that "Costa Rica does not want military aid." (*Miami Herald*, August 13, 1981; *New York Times*, August 19, 1981.) While the arrest of a Costa Rican terrorist group in June had shocked Costa Rican opinion, it was more upset by the 500 percent devaluation of its currency and the soaring unemployment rate. The likely victor in the February 1982 presidential elections, Luis Alberto Monge, suggested that the best way the United States could help would be with economic assistance for the sagging Costa Rican economy. New funds for low-interest food loans were made available, and when the Costa Rican aid appropriation came up before Congress, an extra emergency appropriation of $25 million was voted by the House, but the combination of declining coffee prices and the increased cost of imported oil produced a continuing balance-of-payments problem that did not seem amenable to any short-term solution.

IV

In September Belize, the former British Honduras, became independent, joining the many other mini-states of the Caribbean that had recently achieved that status. It was in the Caribbean that the new Administration took its most significant step in its relationship with the rest of the hemisphere—the so-called Caribbean Basin Initiative. Like so many other Administration policies in the area it was initially conceived as an explicitly anti-communist effort, but again like others it was considerably modified in application. (As in other cases it marked a further development of initiatives taken by the Carter Administration, which had supported the establishment of the World Bank group on the Caribbean that resulted in a quadrupling of external aid to the region.)

Reagan Administration attention was focused on the Caribbean by the stunning victory in October 1980 of Edward Seaga's Jamaica Labor Party over Michael Manley's People's National Party. Seaga represented private enterprise, anti-communism, and a welcome to foreign investment, after years of rule by a Manley government which had been socialist in philosophy, friendly to Cuba in foreign policy, and critical of the leading foreign investors, particularly the U.S. and Canadian bauxite companies. After his election Seaga called for a "mini-Marshall Plan" for the Caribbean, and from the outset he echoed the militant anti-communism of the new U.S. Administration. As a showcase for the Reagan philosophy of encouragement of private investment, Jamaica received support from the new Administration for a $600 million loan from the International Monetary Fund with only mild conditions attached, Reagan appointed a U.S. Business Committee on Jamaica chaired by David Rockefeller to promote foreign investment in that country, and the Administration's foreign aid request for Jamaica was nearly doubled to $90 million.

For Castro and his new satellite, the tiny Caribbean island of Grenada, a very different set of policies was adopted. The United States attempted unsuccessfully to restrict its donation to the Caribbean Development Bank to prohibit its use for Grenada; the existing aid program to Grenada was terminated; and it tried to persuade the Europeans not to finance an airport extension in that island, arguing that it would be used to transport and supply Cuban troops engaged in intervention abroad. As for Cuba, legislation was introduced to establish Radio Martí, an exile propaganda station similar to Radio Free Europe; the Administration began to enforce the legislative restrictions on trade with Cuba more strictly, even to the extent of requiring licenses for the import of Cuban publications; and in November Secretary Haig's earlier statements about getting at "the source" of Salvadoran guerrilla arms were given concrete focus with news reports that in June the Pentagon had been asked to prepare an option paper on Cuba which included such possible steps as an arms blockade and even an invasion.

In mid-December Assistant Secretary of State Enders testified to the Western Hemisphere Affairs Subcommittee of the Senate Foreign Relations Committee about what he called "a new Cuban strategy for uniting the Left" in the countries of the Caribbean Basin. Tracing a pattern of action beginning with Nicaragua in 1978 and continuing in El Salvador, Guatemala, Colombia, and currently in Honduras, Enders argued that the new Cuban approach was to bring together the various feuding leftist guerrilla groups and promise them arms and training if they agreed to unite and adopt a common strategy of armed struggle under Cuban guidance. The newly unified groups were instructed to attempt to form alliances with democratic movements on the Left, especially the social democrats, and to use them to get support from their counterparts in Europe. In addition, their guerrilla campaigns typically included economic sabotage aimed at undermining the deteriorating economies and tourist trade in order to exacerbate social unrest.

Enders' testimony was buttressed by a report submitted to the Committee on "Cuba's Renewed Support for Violence in Latin America." Besides reviewing the evidence on Cuba's military aid to Nicaragua and the Salvadoran guerrillas, it detailed current Cuban efforts to subvert democratically elected governments in Colombia (an effort to unify the leftist opposition, and the training of 100 to 200 "M-19" guerrillas whose capture in February had led to the suspension of relations between Colombia and Cuba), in Costa Rica (the use, documented by a Costa Rican congressional committee, of Costa Rican territory to smuggle arms to El Salvador, and the training in the Soviet Union and Cuba of Costa Ricans involved in terrorism), in Jamaica (smuggling of arms used in attacks against the opposition during the 1980 elections, as well as covert military training of Jamaican students in Cuba), and in Honduras (attempts to unify the Left, Honduran attendance at training courses in Cuba, and the discovery of three "safehouses" in November with sizable arms caches).[9]

Enders concluded that "we must communicate to Cuba that the costs of escalating its intervention in the region will be very high." But the only specific measures he mentioned were the exile radio station and a tightening of the economic embargo and refugee controls. At the end of the year countermeasures against Poland became more important than action against Cuba and once again tough talk was not followed up by corresponding action.

There was action, however, on a variation on the Seaga proposal designed to strengthen the weak and dependent economies of the Caribbean states—and by extension to give multilateral support to the troubled Central American economies (thus El Salvador magically became a Caribbean and not a Pacific state). The Caribbean Basin Initiative, as it was called, was not a Marshall Plan at all. It was a program to promote trade, investment, and aid to the Caribbean and Central America by the United States, Canada, Mexico and Venezuela (and later possibly Europe and Japan) on a bilateral basis (thus bypassing the thorny issue of aid to Cuba and Grenada), and encouraging each of the four donor countries to increase their economic support for the area. The proposal tied in with existing programs such as the Mexican-

---

[9] "Cuba's Renewed Support for Violence in Latin America," Special Report No. 90, Washington: Department of State, Bureau of Public Affairs, December 14, 1981. The Enders statement has been published as "Strategic Situation in Central America and the Caribbean," *Current Policy* No. 352, Washington: Department of State, Bureau of Public Affairs, December 14, 1981.

Venezuelan 30 percent discount loans on petroleum for Central America, as well as Canada's already announced increased aid to the English-speaking Caribbean, while focusing attention on the weak economies of the Caribbean and Central American states with the hope that such steps as a regional investment insurance program and the lowering or elimination of tariff barriers could promote development and create jobs throughout the area.

The United States planned to make available to the countries in the area only a little more than a tenth of Seaga's original request—and this included the Central American countries as well as the Caribbean—so that it was not an ambitious program. However, it included some new elements, such as proposals for a temporary one-way elimination of tariffs for Caribbean exports (without the restrictions of the Generalized System of Preferences from which they already benefit) and the extension of special tax credits to investors. Whether the program could make much of an impact on the massive unemployment in the area, resolve the problem of declining export revenues from sugar and coffee or produce the takeoff in economic development outlined by its backers remained doubtful. However, it dramatized the Administration's concern with the area, and did so in a way which, because of the necessity of bringing in the other countries, including Mexico and Canada, could not take on the cold war role that had originally been assigned to it.

v

The fact that countries with as different policies in the area as Mexico and the United States could cooperate in the program shows how flexible it was and how cordial the relationship between the United States and Mexico had become. Shortly after his election Reagan had taken the unusual step of meeting the Mexican President on Mexican territory, and during 1981 Presidents Reagan and López Portillo met four times. Those meetings indicated a dramatic turnaround in U.S.-Mexican relations, based more on the personal relationship which the two leaders developed than on any agreement on policy. On Cuba, El Salvador and Nicaragua they remained far apart, and significant differences remained in the areas of Mexican undocumented workers in the United States, fishing rights, and Mexico's refusal to join the General Agreement on Tariffs and Trade, but the two countries seemed to be able to transcend their differences and maintain cordial relations even when their policy positions were far apart.

A striking example of this was the North-South meeting of eight developed and 14 developing countries organized by Mexico at Cancún at the end of October. The Mexicans respected U.S. insistence that Cuba not be invited—despite Mexico's long-standing close relations with Castro. President Reagan agreed to participate despite U.S. opposition to the basic thrust of the Third World countries' demands, especially the attempt to give the one nation-one vote General Assembly the power to overrule the specialized economic agencies such as the International Monetary Fund and the World Bank where voting is weighted according to economic contributions. At the two-day meeting in Cancún the U.S. President again demonstrated his talent for disarming those who disagree with him with his personal charm, and the meeting concluded with an agreement that global negotiations to aid the poor nations should be held at the United Nations "on a basis to be mutually agreed and in circumstances offering the prospect of meaningful progress with a sense of urgency." The question of how decisions were to be made was simply sidestepped, and while President Reagan was correct in asserting on his return that "we did not waste time on unrealistic rhetoric or unattainable objectives" (*New York Times*, October 25, 1981), the meeting did not achieve any concrete results except to allow an informal exchange of views between North and South on such issues as agricultural development, energy, and international financial relations.

On the continuing problem of illegal Mexican migrants, some changes in U.S. policy were expected since Reagan as a candidate had spoken of the need for stricter controls coupled with an expanded "guest worker" program. In February a Commission appointed by President Carter and headed by Father Theodore Hesburgh issued a report recommending a one-time amnesty for illegal aliens already in the country, somewhat enlarged ceilings for legal immigrants from Mexico and the adoption of civil and criminal penalties for U.S. employers who knowingly hire illegal workers. President Reagan appointed his own Cabinet Task Force and in July the Administration announced that it planned to introduce legislation providing for conditional amnesty for illegal immigrants living in the United States for ten years, an experimental "guest worker" program involving 50,000 Mexicans a year over the next two years, as well as employer penalties.[10] As in the case of earlier recommendations to deal with the problem, it seemed far from clear that the Administration proposals would produce any concrete action on the part of Congress, but near the

---

[10] For a detailed analysis of the Administration's immigration proposals, see Sylvia Ann Hewlett, "Coping with Illegal Immigrants," *Foreign Affairs*, Winter 1981/82, pp. 355–78.

end of the year the death of 16 members of a boatload of Haitians seeking to enter Florida illegally focused renewed attention on the problem.

Behind the public disagreements on international policy, immigration and fisheries is the reality of the increasing economic interpenetration of the Mexican and U.S. economies. Seventy percent of Mexico's exports and 60 percent of its imports are to and from the United States, and trade between the two countries has increased 50 percent a year in recent years. Despite a battery of Mexican regulatory legislation, U.S. investment in Mexico increased from $4.4 billion to nearly $6 billion in 1980 (*Survey of Current Business*, August 1981), and 70 percent of Mexico's oil exports go to the United States. As a candidate Ronald Reagan had endorsed a further integration of the two economies along with that of Canada in a North American Common Market, but both Canada and Mexico publicly rejected the proposal in January. Mexico saw the proposal as the institutionalization of a dependent relationship, giving the United States preferential access to its energy supplies and cheap labor, while preventing Mexico from promoting its exports and regulating foreign investment in support of domestic industry. Existing Mexican regulatory measures and subsidies have created charges of unfair practices in international trade that have already led to the imposition by the United States of a countervailing duty on some leather goods, but for the present Mexico seems to have the best of both worlds, benefiting from special tariff arrangements for border assembly plants, and from exemptions for many of its exports under the Generalized System of Preferences for Third World countries, while continuing to implement legislation that limits and discriminates against foreign—usually U.S.—trade and investment.

VI

The other major policy area where the new Administration was determined to alter the Carter approach was the relative priority given to human rights in relation to security considerations. The previous Administration had not been oblivious to security considerations or unwilling to allow them to override human rights concerns in its relations with such countries as the Philippines and South Korea. But in Latin America those considerations appeared to be less salient, and the repression by certain governments, notably in the Southern Cone (Chile, Argentina and Uruguay), so serious that the Carter human rights policy had its most evident impact in relations with those countries. Already before Carter's election, the Congress had established a separate Human Rights Bureau in the Department of State and required annual reports from the State Department on the human rights situation of all recipients of U.S. aid. But at the beginning of the Carter Administration the Executive took further initiatives, reducing or eliminating U.S. aid to several Latin American governments, voting against loans from international financial institutions on explicit human rights grounds, and supporting action by the Organization of American States and the United Nations condemning human rights violations.

Chile was the first and most frequent object of these sanctions. Congress adopted increasingly severe restrictions on military aid and sales between 1974 and 1976; loans to Chile by the World Bank and the Inter-American Development Bank were opposed by Carter appointees; and a series of sanctions including exclusion from joint naval maneuvers and prohibition of Export-Import Bank credits were adopted after Chile failed to extradite those involved in the 1976 murder in Washington of Orlando Letelier, Allende's former ambassador to the United States.

As for Argentina, as a result of human rights violations following the overthrow of Isabel Perón, Congress adopted the Humphrey-Hawkins amendment barring U.S. arms aid or sales, and Carter emissaries, including the Assistant Secretary of State for Human Rights and Secretary of State Cyrus Vance himself, raised the human rights issue directly during visits to that country. Most striking was the change in relations with Brazil, where the earlier Kissinger policy of promoting a special U.S.-Brazilian relationship was replaced by increasingly distant relations, both because of the human rights issue (Brazil rejected U.S. military aid in reaction to the 1977 human rights report) and because of Carter Administration efforts to persuade the West German government not to supply Brazil with a nuclear reactor without full safeguards that it would be used only for peaceful purposes.

In the last two years of the Carter Administration there was a significant reduction in repression in the countries of the Southern Cone. In Chile, DINA, the intelligence organization which had become almost a state within a state, was reorganized, its successor organization given more limited powers of detention, and confirmed cases of disappearance ceased—although torture, several killings, and short-term detentions and expulsions continued. In Argentina, where the number of disappeared persons between 1976 and 1979 was estimated at 5,600 by the Argentine Human Rights Assembly, the 1980 State Department human rights report

estimated the number of disappearances at between 12 and 28—
although 900 political prisoners remained "at the disposition of
the executive power" under legislation enacted before the 1976
coup. In Brazil since the mid-1970s, but especially with the
promulgation of an amnesty in 1979, the process of political
opening ("abertura") had meant that except for occasional con-
fiscation of publications, and legal action against strikers, the
human rights violations of the early 1970s had ceased. In Uruguay,
while there were still 1,219 political "detainees," no disappearances had taken place since 1978, and in 1980 the military had
made an unsuccessful attempt to impose a constitution which
would have permitted a transition to civilian rule while retaining
wide powers for the military.[11]

In these circumstances it was easy for the new Administration
to argue for a shift in priorities, and to assert that public condemnations of governments with which the United States was allied
militarily (through the Rio Treaty of Mutual Assistance) and
politically (through the OAS) damaged the U.S. international
position. Shortly after coming to power the Administration lifted
the ban on Chilean access to Export-Import Bank loans and
participation in joint naval exercises, and introduced legislation
to remove the congressional prohibition on Argentine military
aid. Similar legislation to lift the ban on Chilean military sales
was proposed later in the year.

Despite denials by Administration spokesmen—Secretary of
State Haig at his confirmation hearings said that "other than in
the most exceptional circumstances" the United States should not
provide aid to regimes that "consistently and in the harshest
manner" violate human rights—there were many who suspected
that the new approach meant abandonment of a concern with
human rights except when they were violated by communist
regimes. Their fears seemed to be confirmed by the nomination of
Ernest Lefever as Assistant Secretary of State for Human Rights.
In July 1979, Lefever had testified to a congressional committee
in opposition to human rights conditions on U.S. aid, and his
Center for Ethics in Public Policy had been identified with a
conservative position in international affairs. When his name was
first mentioned in February, it elicited media criticism, but the
debate over the new "tilt" in human rights was sharply intensified
by the publication in April, both in book form and in a substantial

[11] Department of State, *Country Reports on Human Rights Practices* (Report submitted to the
Senate Foreign Relations Committee and House Foreign Affairs Committee), February 2, 1981,
Washington: GPO, 1981, *passim.*

excerpt published in *The New Yorker*, of a deeply moving account of the repression in Argentina, *Prisoner without a Name, Cell without a Number*, by the exiled Argentine publisher Jacobo Timerman. Along with horrifying details on torture and executions during his two years of detention on charges that were never substantiated by Argentine courts or the military themselves, Timerman's book denounced the Argentine military regime as anti-Semitic and totalitarian, comparing it to the early years of Nazism. Appearing on U.S. television in connection with the publication of the book, Timerman attributed his release in 1979 to the Carter human rights policy, which for the first time since the Marshall Plan had "captured the imagination of the world," and asserted that at one point the U.S. Embassy was the only source of legal advice for the families of those who had disappeared.

Conservative and neo-conservative writers attacked Timerman for not mentioning his financial connection with the late David Graiver, accused of acting as banker for the left-wing guerrillas, and for exaggerating the plight of Argentine Jews, but the debate focussed attention on human rights in Argentina and the U.S. role there.[12] In May both the Senate Foreign Relations Committee and the House Foreign Affairs Committee conditioned the repeal of the ban on U.S. military sales or aid to Argentina on significant progress in the area of human rights as well as an accounting by the government for the "disappeared" persons—in spite of letters from the Secretary of State urging them not to do so. (The conditions were later softened to direct the President "to pay particular attention" to them.) When Lefever's nomination came before the Senate Foreign Relations Committee for approval in late May he was subjected to intense questioning about his earlier views on human right issues as well as his Center's sources of financial support. Describing himself as a "compassionate realist," Lefever insisted that he had a long history of defense of human rights, although in a veiled reference to his predecessor's activism he did not see himself in a "Sir Galahad role going around the world on personal missions." Possibly the most damaging part of his testimony was his willingness to denounce the Soviet Union as "the gravest violator of human rights" in the contemporary world, while refusing to name any non-communist violators because that is "not my style" (*New York Times*, May 19, 1981). In early June, the Republican-controlled Committee voted 13-4 against his confirmation and he withdrew his name from consideration.

[12] See, for example, Irving Kristol, "The Timerman Affair," *The Wall Street Journal*, May 29, 1981, and Mark Falcoff, "The Timerman Case," *Commentary*, July 1981.

For a time it was reported that the Administration was considering abolishing the Human Rights Bureau, but this would have required congressional action. After a lengthy interval, Elliott Abrams, then Assistant Secretary of State for International Organizations, was named to the post, and concurrently a State Department memorandum on human rights was published that called for application of the policy "evenhandedly" and on the basis of "a balancing of pertinent interests." It recognized that "A human rights policy means trouble, for it means hard choices which may adversely affect certain bilateral interests. At the very least we will have to speak honestly about our friends' human rights violations and justify any decision wherein other considerations (economic, military) are determinative." (*New York Times*, November 5, 1981.) The memorandum proposed the appointment of three deputies to the Assistant Secretary and an expansion of the Bureau's coordinating role with other agencies, including defense attachés in U.S. embassies.

Abrams, who described his obligations as Assistant Secretary as "to speak the truth" and "be effective," easily won confirmation and, if the memorandum is an indication of future policy, once again an attempt to carry out a substantial alteration in existing policy had been modified by the pressure of Congress and public opinion. Whether the announced policy would be followed up by genuine action in the area of human rights depended on the degree of commitment of the new Assistant Secretary and the bureaucratic politics of the Administration. In view of its earlier stance, human rights activists were not optimistic that the memorandum and new appointment marked a genuine shift in policy.

Despite the original intent of the change in human rights policy to remove what had become a persistent irritant to bilateral relations with the regimes of the Southern Cone, there was no immediate or striking improvement in relations with those regimes. In the case of Argentina there remained a difference in policy toward the Soviet Union; since the post-Afghanistan reduction of U.S. wheat sales, Argentina had become a principal supplier of wheat to the Soviet Union. In the case of Brazil as well, soybean sales to the U.S.S.R. soared and the regime seemed much less willing than in the early 1970s to play the role of principal U.S. partner in South America—if only because its own problems with finding secure energy sources meant that friendly relations with Iraq, Libya and Nigeria were more vital to its national interest as it conceived it. On the other principal subject of controversy between the United States and Brazil, nuclear proliferation, Vice President Bush announced on a visit to Brazil in October that Brazil would be given a special exemption to allow it to purchase enriched uranium for its U.S.-built reactor. There remained little prospect, however, of the reestablishment of the partnership between the United States and Brazil that Secretary Kissinger had begun to build in the last year of the Ford Administration.

In the case of Chile, there were also continuing obstacles to improved relations—mostly of the making of the Pinochet regime. A new Chilean constitution, approved in a hastily-called plebiscite in September 1980 and implemented in March 1981, not only gave Pinochet eight more years as president, but in its "transitional" provisions gave him power to censor all new publications, forbid public meetings, and expel or sentence to internal exile those who propagate subversive doctrines "or have the reputation of being activists for such doctrines, and those who carry out acts contrary to the interests of Chile or constitute a danger for internal peace." Two days after a visit by Mrs. Kirkpatrick in August in which she announced the U.S. intention to "normalize completely its relations with Chile," Pinochet used his constitutional powers to order the immediate expulsion of Jaime Castillo, the chairman of the Chilean Human Rights Commission and Minister of Justice under former President Eduardo Frei, as well as three other prominent former political leaders who had signed a declaration criticizing the government's imprisonment of the leaders of a newly-formed National Trade Union Coordinating Committee.

The expulsions, the continuing reports of the detention of regime opponents by police and the intelligence agency, and the refusal of Chilean courts to take action against those implicated in the Letelier case made it more difficult for the Administration to move to lift the sanctions imposed by Congress in 1976 against military aid to Chile. The House initially refused to do so, and in October when the Republican-controlled Senate voted to lift the ban, it accepted an amendment offered by Senator Percy, the chairman of the Foreign Relations Committee, providing that no military aid, credits or support assistance were to be provided until the President had supplied Congress with a report certifying that Chile had made "significant progress" in human rights, neither "aided nor abetted" international terrorism, and was taking steps to bring to justice those involved in the Letelier murder. Percy also agreed with Senator Edward Kennedy's request to hold full Committee hearings on any such presidential certification. The objective of full normalization of relations with Chile still faced obstacles from the Congress and from the media (which published accounts of the importation of poison nerve gas from Chile by Letelier's murderers just as Congress was making final decisions on Chilean aid).

Neither the media nor the Reagan policymakers paid much attention to a more important process that was taking place in Latin America. In contrast to Central America, most South American countries—some by imposition and some by consent— had achieved a certain basic stability and self-confidence. Four of them—Venezuela, Colombia, Ecuador and Peru—were functioning constitutional democracies, in the case of the last two after extended periods of military rule and despite a brief border war early in the year. Uruguay was beginning again with negotiations between the military and the civilian politicians on a return to constitutionalism, and Brazil was debating the modalities of state elections in the fall of 1982—although the rules the government laid down seemed to assure that the official government party would win. Besides scheduled votes in El Salvador and Guatemala under circumstances which severely limited the freedom of choice of the voters, elections were scheduled in 1982 for the Dominican Republic, Mexico, Colombia, Costa Rica and Brazil, while in Honduras the first civilian president in many years was to be inaugurated in January 1982. If, as many have argued, the United States has an interest in the establishment and maintenance of regimes in the Americas which share its values, this may be as significant a shift in Latin America as the radicalization of Central America and the independence of the mini-states of the Caribbean. Aside from a proposal at the December OAS meeting to establish a research institute on democracy, the policy initiatives of the new Administration did not seem to respond to these developments—possibly because of its belief that the previous Administration had placed too much emphasis upon them. It also paid no attention to the important economic changes in the region, especially the increasingly serious problem of the sizeable international debts that Brazil ($64 billion), Mexico ($48 billion, up $5 billion in 1981), Chile ($15 billion), and Costa Rica ($2.6 billion, in technical default) had incurred—preferring here as elsewhere to leave Latin America's economic problems to the private sector.

VII

Has U.S. policy towards Latin America changed under the new Administration? Yes, but not as much as those who articulated it at the outset indicated that it would. It began with the assertion of a dramatic turnaround of policy but found that domestic constraints in Congress and public opinion, as well as its international relationships, forced it to adopt policies that were in many cases not very different in substance from those of the previous Administration.

In Central America, support for elections and reform and avoidance of identification with regimes that engage in systematic repression were prerequisities for the support of Congress and public opinion. Direct military intervention was exceedingly difficult because of the War Powers Act, and Congress still showed an assertiveness in foreign policy that limited presidential action. Human rights legislation remained on the books, including an Assistant Secretary of State with that special responsibility, as well as a congressional mandate for annual reports on the subject. Despite what looked like an ideological purge of some top career foreign service personnel, the permanent bureaucracy continued to exert an influence in favor of existing policies. Relationships with important Latin American allies such as Mexico and Venezuela required that policy be formulated in consultation with them, and their views taken into account. Before unilateral action could be undertaken, the impact of actions in Latin America upon U.S. worldwide responsibilities and relationships and on domestic opinion had to be considered.

Yet there were changes too. The new Administration continued to use aggressive rhetoric (often not matched by its subsequent actions) that emphasized the possibility of military solutions. Whether this was seen as a way to induce changes in the conduct of adversaries, or was meant to justify its conduct to its conservative constituency at home, was not clear. It was more interested in improving relations with Latin American military governments— and despite the talk of using "quiet diplomacy" to promote human rights seemed less willing to use any leverage the United States might have for the promotion of civil and personal liberties in friendly countries. This was a change of emphasis rather than a complete shift from moralism to militarism—but the message was delivered to Latin America that the earlier concern with democracy and liberty was being replaced by the mixture of traditional security considerations and militant anti-communism that Latin American intellectuals and democrats had criticized in U.S. policy for so many decades.

Given the increased Cuban presence in Central America and the political openings and decline in repression that were taking place in many parts of Latin America, some movement in this direction would probably have taken place under any Administration. What was disturbing about the new stance was that in its determination to demonstrate that it did in fact represent a different approach, the new Administration might in a crisis situation take actions that might harm U.S. interests in the world and lead to the opposition of most of the hemisphere and the alienation of its European allies, who have become increasingly involved in Latin America over the past decade. Cuba remained an obsession, and from the time just before Ronald Reagan's inauguration when Castro attacked him as "fascist," "genocidal," and "covered with blood," it was clear that relations with that country were likely to deteriorate. In addition the flow of Cuban arms to Nicaragua meant that there was continuing pressure within the Administration for forceful action against that country.

So far this has not happened—both because of the arguments of the domestic and foreign opponents against a policy based exclusively on force and on "the hegemonic presumption,"[13] and because of the constraints built into the American system of government. And this is as the Founding Fathers, who called for "energy in the executive" especially in the area of foreign affairs, but also established a system of checks and balances, intended it to be.

VIII

The divergent approaches that the Carter and Reagan Administrations have taken to Latin America suggest a number of continuing questions about U.S. policy in the Western hemisphere.

1. Should policy continue to be conducted as if it were a morality play—within one case Soviet expansionism, and in the other repressive governments, as the devils? Is it not possible to take a more pragmatic view of U.S. interests in the area?

2. As part of such a view, are not U.S. interests clearly greater in some parts of Latin America than in others? Crises or not, is it not time to recognize that in Mexico, the Caribbean and Central America, a special set of factors—notably geographic proximity and links of economics, energy and migration—argue for continuing U.S. concern for their defense from external subversion, and for the promotion of social justice, democracy and development?

3. What are the most appropriate means to achieve those

---

[13] See Abraham Lowenthal, "The United States and Latin America: Ending the Hegemonic Presumption," *Foreign Affairs*, October 1976, pp. 199–213.

goals—particularly when they are in tension or conflict with one another? Are cutoffs in military aid an effective or useful way to achieve justice and freedom or simply a way of satisfying our consciences? Is a prohibition of military sales an appropriate way to influence the conduct of other nations when they can acquire what they need from other countries allied with us—notably France and Israel? How useful are cutoffs in economic assistance if they lead to greater suffering for the poor in the countries involved?

4. How can the United States best adjust to the development of divergent interests and relationships on the part of the countries of Latin America—in particular with Europe and Japan?

5. Why, except for a short period under the Alliance for Progress 20 years ago, have we not applied the policy recommendation made by Milton Eisenhower in the late 1950s—a handshake for the dictators, whether of the Right or Left, and an *abrazo* for the democratic governments?

Perhaps most important: the debate on Latin American policy reflects a larger philosophical disagreement between those who regard force and national security as the central elements in international relations and those who believe that, at least in a democracy seeking to secure international and domestic support for its policies, the values and ideals of the United States must have an important role in the conduct of foreign policy. Is it not time to recognize that in practice neither view is sufficient in itself and that there are powerful constraints limiting any attempt to replace one conception with the other?

David Anderson

AMERICA IN AFRICA, 1981

One should approach the subject of Africa with caution. Like a horse, it is dangerous at both ends and uncomfortable in the middle. 1981 has been dominated by continuing conflicts in southern Africa and in the Western Sahara, Chad and Eritrea. In northeastern Africa, past and present conflict has swollen the flood of African refugees to almost half the total number of refugees in the world, at a time when a gravely worsening economic crisis, exacerbated by unusual climatic conditions stretching over a period of years, has brought to millions in sub-Saharan Africa the prospect of death by starvation. The assassination of President Anwar el-Sadat in October was a dramatic reminder that Africa's troubles cannot be insulated from the rest of the world, that external dependence which ignores internal political and economic realities is dangerous—that there are limits to America's ability to control events in Africa.

It was a depressing scene for the new American Administration as it began to fit Africa into its global policies, but as the year progressed some shafts of light were breaking through. In African eyes by far the most crucial issue was, and remains, the independence of Namibia. After a faltering start American diplomacy was instrumental in putting the negotiations to this end back on track, so that by the end of the year international agreement on arrangements to bring Namibia to independence as a unitary state seemed once more to be in prospect. The outcome, however, remains dependent on decisions by a South African government that has swung during the year to a more hard-line posture both on internal affairs and in its actions toward its neighbors.

Elsewhere in southern Africa, Angola remains torn by civil war, and its future depends heavily on a successful outcome of the Namibia negotiations. The new government of Zimbabwe, however, continued to win respect—and some financial assistance—from the international community for the skill and compassion

---

David Anderson is Assistant Secretary-General in the Commonwealth Secretariat in London, and Managing Director of the Commonwealth Fund for Technical Cooperation. He has worked and travelled widely in Africa for over 30 years. The views expressed in this article are entirely personal.

with which it tackled its delicate internal adjustments and the mature responsibility with which it recognized the sensitivity of the southern African situation, despite recurrent provocations from neighboring South Africa.

In northern Africa, U.S. policy was dominated by an obsession with the behavior of Colonel Muammar el-Qaddafi in Libya. Reacting against his irresponsible adventurism in Africa, and also reflecting the anti-Soviet tone that tended to dominate its approach to African issues, the Reagan Administration developed during the year an ever stronger policy of confrontation with Libya, while at the same time acting to buttress Egypt and the Sudan, on the one hand, and Tunisia on the other. Meanwhile the struggle by the Polisario insurgent forces in the Western Sahara continued unresolved, with the Organization of African Unity (OAU) attempting to take an active role in the face of mounting criticism of its effectiveness in dealing with the major internal African disputes.

On the political front, 1981 was marked, for the first time in many years, by the absence of any substantial successful coup until the Rawlings takeover in Ghana in late December. (The ouster of David Dacko from the presidency of the Central African Republic scarcely merits that title.) Moreover, limited progress was made toward more open government in Nigeria, Tunisia, Senegal, Uganda and even Liberia. Though some oppressive authoritarian regimes remain, there are signs that African societies are recovering their equilibrium after the traumas of independence, when they inherited systems of government divorced from their culture and tradition and for which many of their leaders had had insufficient training. It is hopeful too that at last the OAU feels confident enough to show greatly increased concern about the violation of basic human rights by some of its members. From the standpoint of American policy, however, the tendency of the new Administration to associate itself more strongly with authoritarian regimes, for geopolitical reasons, may raise increasingly serious problems.

In the face of the most difficult economic situation for more than 20 years, and anticipating the exhortations toward greater self-reliance in the latest World Bank Report, "Accelerated Development in Africa," there has been a resurgence of regional cooperation for economic development, with an emphasis on increased intra-African trade. The United States played its part in supporting new efforts in this direction, but again its tendency to act selectively on geopolitical grounds may place serious constraints on the Administration's ability to cooperate fully in these initiatives.

As 1982 opens, the reputation and effectiveness of the United States in Africa depend above all on the outcome in Namibia. Let us therefore examine first the course of events and the prospects there.

II

Namibia has been an issue for the United Nations, Africa and the West at least since 1966, when a resolution of the U.N. General Assembly declared South Africa's League of Nations mandate over the territory to be terminated.[1] For all practical purposes the territory has until recently been governed as an integral part of the Republic. Its public services are provided by South African civil servants (mostly Afrikaners), its revenues flow to Pretoria, its official language is Afrikaans, its economy and its somewhat sparse physical infrastructure are integrated with the Republic's, and some 80,000 South African citizens are resident there. Its long Atlantic coastline extends strategic protection to the heartland. Its rich fishing grounds (until ruined by uncontrolled overfishing), its cattle and karakul, and its enormously valuable mineral resources have until recently more than compensated South Africa for the cost of administering and defending the territory.

Since 1978 the U.N. contact group of five Western powers (the United States, Britain, Canada, France and West Germany) has been engaged in tortuous negotiations with the South African government to find a formula for independence. Initiated by a group of U.N. diplomats headed by U.S. Ambassador Donald McHenry, negotiations were held against a background of escalating conflict between the South African forces and the liberation army of SWAPO (South West African People's Organization), operating from bases in Angola. At the same time, South Africa was hurriedly putting together an internal government for the territory, with a white-dominated center and regional ethnic governments.

By the fall of 1980 the U.N. plan for holding elections in Namibia, under Resolution 435 adopted in September 1978, was

---

[1] In 1971 the International Court of Justice handed down its opinion that South Africa's presence in Namibia was illegal. The legal position is important both in regard to the military actions by South Africa in Angola (can any actions taken to defend an illegal occupation be other than illegal in themselves?) and also, as Namibia moves toward independence, in regard to the legal rights of corporations like Rio Tinto Zinc which have been exploiting the country's mineral resources in agreements with the South African government concluded after the 1966 termination of the mandate.

already in trouble. Prior to the election of President Reagan, South Africa had endorsed the idea of a working conference at Geneva in January 1981, and initially appeared to welcome that conference as a means to give legitimacy to the internal political parties within Namibia and to open up the question of constitutional principles—essentially measures to protect the white population—which the U.N. plan had stipulated should be discussed only after the elections. In the event, however, the South Africans and the leading internal party, the Democratic Turnhalle Alliance (DTA), used the conference to complain about U.N. partiality toward SWAPO. On this ground the South Africans declared that it was premature to fix a date for a cease-fire and elections in the territory. It seems likely that the South Africans had, even in advance of the conference, decided to delay further progress on the negotiations until the new American Administration's policies were clear and also until after their general elections due in April. The conference gave them an opportunity to expose the internal Namibian parties to some international recognition. They were not impressive.

There followed a period of uncertainty when it seemed as if the West had run out of initiatives. In fact everybody was waiting for signals from the new American Administration. When they began to come they were not reassuring either to the black African countries or to the European allies, but on the contrary seemed to justify the South African government's expectation that the new Administration would be more sympathetic to its view.

The Carter Administration, with its general helpfulness on the Rhodesia and Namibia negotiations and with the efforts of Andrew Young to place American policy decisions in the context of African concerns, had raised American-African relations to a level of trust and confidence not achieved since the pre-independence era of the 1950s. Unfortunately, the new Administration, both in its campaign rhetoric and in its initial moves, showed no interest in building on this foundation. It emphasized the discontinuity of American policy on Africa by an apparent "tilt" in favor of South Africa and by failing for the first six months to enunciate a clear policy on Namibia.

Thus, in a General Assembly debate on Namibia in March, the United States (and its European allies) voted against the rejection of the South African delegation's credentials, and abstained (again with its European allies) on a resolution calling for economic sanctions. This was followed almost immediately by more or less surreptitious, but well publicized, visits to the United States by a number of senior South African military officers and by Dirk Mudge, leader of the DTA. Statements by President Reagan about being "helpful" to South Africa, whose minerals are "strategically essential to the Free World," and of his intention to ask Congress to repeal the Clark Amendment (forbidding arms supplies to insurgent groups in Angola) did nothing to allay the growing alarm in African countries. On one occasion President Reagan even sought to reassure South Africa by referring to it as a "wartime ally," a remark that displayed a remarkable lack both of sensitivity and of knowledge about history.[2] Moreover, at the beginning of March, six American citizens were expelled from Mozambique on the ground that they were supplying intelligence to the South African security forces. In response, the Reagan Administration suspended food aid to Mozambique for six months.

These and other insensitivities, the growing evidence of the strategic importance America gives to South African resources and facilities, the hardening of its attitudes to the Marxist-inclined states and the absence of any clear policy statement on Africa created the gravest suspicions among African leaders. At the beginning of the year it was not so much what the Administration was doing which gave offense, but its style.

The diplomatic gaucherie of this concatenation of *obiter dicta*, official pronouncements, and diplomatic signals may have been due in part to inexperience. It may also have been connected with problems the Administration was having in securing Chester Crocker's confirmation as Assistant Secretary of State for African Affairs. His nomination was vigorously attacked by Senator Jesse Helms, and the outcome remained in doubt until May.

Then the South African elections in April produced an unprecedented vote for the right-wing Herstigte Nasionale Party (as well as a much less significant erosion of government support toward the liberal Progressive Federal Party). The palpable threat from the Right boded ill both for Prime Minister P.W. Botha's promises

---

[2] As the SWAPO leader Herman Toivo Ja Toivo pointed out at his trial in Pretoria in 1968, the present ruling party of South Africa was on the other side during the war against Nazism. Toivo said to the South African court: "During the Second World War, when it became evident that my country and your country were threatened by dark clouds of Nazism, I risked my life to defend both of them, wearing a uniform with orange bands on it. But some of your countrymen when called to battle to defend civilization resorted to sabotage against their own fatherland ... today they are our masters."

There may be good reasons of policy for the American government to assure the South African leaders of its friendship, but their performance in the Second World War is not one. Africans, who have suffered so many humiliations in the distortion of history by the white people, might have been spared this gratuitous insult. Toivo is still in a South African prison.

of internal reform and for a Namibia settlement.[3] Although South Africa has always said it would abide by a free and fair election, during the campaign Botha categorically stated that "as long as there is a National Party government, we would not give over South West Africa to the authority of SWAPO."

Nonetheless, even before his confirmation as Assistant Secretary, Chester Crocker undertook a two-week tour of ten African capitals, to consult on a plan to break the Namibia deadlock. It was the beginning of a new serious American effort, albeit one which had been developed with minimum consultation with the other members of the contact group. From the leaked memorandum of Crocker's conversations in South Africa, America's objectives appeared to be to link any Namibia settlement to the withdrawal of Cuban military forces from Angola, an issue on which Angola's Foreign Minister, Paolo Jorge, stated about that time that when Namibia became independent and the aggression from South Africa ceased, the Cuban troops would no longer be needed and would go home. Crocker also appeared to be trying to clear the way to include South Africa in the U.S. security framework.

By then the African Frontline states were not interested in motives but in results. Provided that Resolution 435 remained the basis of the plan, they were willing to accept reasonable supplementations short of an imposed constitution, and they did not inquire what pressures or inducements the Americans had used in their negotiations with the South Africans. The SWAPO leader, Sam Nujoma, who had already agreed in January to a cease-fire under U.N. supervision, now stated that SWAPO "are prepared to give guarantees and safeguards to all white settlers in Namibia."

The explorations continued when the South African Foreign Minister, Pik Botha, visited the United States in May and was given assurances that the Administration would pursue a policy of "constructive engagement" with South Africa rather than one of "confrontation" in the search for a settlement on Namibia. In return South Africa was asked for a clear "statement of commitment" to cooperate in efforts to reach an internationally accepted independence settlement for Namibia, and for "a definitive statement of their core concerns." Foreign Minister Botha is reported during that visit to have rejected the use of a U.N. military force during the transition to independence but to have said he saw "a real possibility of progress" on a negotiated settlement within the new framework proposed by the United States.

[3] See John de St. Jorre, "South Africa: Is Change Coming?," *Foreign Affairs*, Fall 1981, pp. 106–22.

Then, in June, Mr. Crocker and Deputy Secretary of State William Clark held further talks on Namibia in both South Africa and Zimbabwe. Concurrently the OAU, meeting in Nairobi, sharply criticized U.S. policy, and during the same period, the importance of a Namibia settlement was also insistently pushed by America's European allies, and particularly the members of the contact group. Notably, the only significant statement on a non-economic issue emerging from the July Ottawa Conference of the Western and Japanese heads of state concerned the importance of negotiations on Namibia.

By August it seemed that a "two-track" American policy was emerging with the dual aims of achieving a settlement in Namibia and getting the Cubans out of Angola. But the direct linkage between the two was gradually downplayed, as the European members of the contact group reportedly signed on to U.S. proposals for constitutional principles to be agreed by all parties, and Washington reaffirmed the U.S. commitment to Resolution 435 as the necessary framework for an internationally agreed settlement.

At just this point, however, South Africa elected to conduct a major military incursion into Angola. Confronted with a U.N. resolution condemning South Africa for the invasion, the United States elected to cast a veto. It was a low point for the year in U.S.-African relations.

Nonetheless, the U.S. veto must have gone some way to allay the "deep South African distrust of the United States" which Foreign Minister Botha had expressed to President Reagan and Secretary of State Alexander Haig in May. Moreover, as an inducement to South African cooperation on Namibia, the United States was by then promising future cooperation with Pretoria, and had stated that a settlement would involve withdrawal of the Cubans from Namibia; had clearly excluded Walvis Bay from the negotiations; and had emphasized the importance of South Africa to the maintenance of regional stability—and consequent limitation of Soviet opportunities. This cooperation could only be achieved if South Africa similarly cooperated in arrangements for an independence settlement in Namibia.

At any rate, in late September there was a dramatic breakthrough, with the United States obtaining the agreement of South Africa and the contact group for a new approach that abandoned any direct link to the Cubans in Angola but did provide for negotiations on constitutional principles as an element in the revised plan. From an inauspicious beginning the Administration had made a creditable recovery in establishing that American actions in Africa, based on a perception of America's national interests and global responsibilities, are not necessarily or invariably antipathetic to the needs and aspirations of African states. When it had made up its mind, the Administration moved on the Namibia issue with a decisive leadership which has hitherto been lacking in the U.N. contact group, showing a willingness to take risks and to exercise power.

In concrete terms U.S. Namibia tactics reportedly call for the separation of negotiations into two phases. In Phase 1, all parties are to subscribe to the statement of constitutional principles put forward by the United States and the contact group. In Phase 2, agreement will be reached on the modalities of the transition period, leading up to elections. The outline of the constitutional proposals are known. They include popular election to a constituent assembly which will approve by a two-thirds vote a constitution providing for a unitary, multiparty, nonracial democratic state with separate executive, legislative and judicial branches. There will be a bill of basic rights for individuals enforceable in law. By the end of 1981, agreement appeared to have been reached on most of these proposals with SWAPO, the Frontline states (plus Nigeria) and the less extreme of the Namibian political parties. A possible sticking point, however, is a provision for proportional representation—which could lead to a proliferation of parties and obstruct decision-making—and a call for representation of "different political groups"—which could encourage the entrenchment of ethnic separateness in the country.

If the constitutional principles are agreed this winter (as in the informal Administration timetable), the way would be open for detailed discussions on modalities, leading to the beginning of implementation of Resolution 435 in 1982. The outstanding issues have been the subject of discussion with South Africa since the beginning of its negotiations with the contact group in 1978. As laid out in Resolution 435, the agreement calls for a cease-fire, to be followed by the phasing out of most South African forces and the phasing in of a U.N. peacekeeping force that would be stationed mainly in a demilitarized zone on the territory's northern border with Angola. (The South African administration is to continue to govern the territory during the transition period, under international supervision.) The size of the U.N. force (now set at 7,500), the number of South African troops remaining, the time period for the drawdown of these troops, and for the electoral campaign will all be in contention.

Another main source of future problems is the South African government's insistence that the United Nations is not an impartial arbiter, and that the international organization should cease to recognize SWAPO as the sole legitimate representative of the Namibian people. Then the DTA may insist that a certain period of time elapse between U.N. dissociation from SWAPO and the implementation process. If South Africa wishes to move forward, these issues may be resolved fairly quickly, but if not, they may, as in the past, offer the occasion for lengthy delays.

Clearly, South Africa's intention—to obstruct or accede—is the key to the outcome of the American strategy. The signs can be read both ways. As noted, the South African government has maintained publicly and privately that SWAPO control of Namibia would be intolerable, and has demanded an agreed constitution giving cast-iron guarantees to the minority groups (mainly the whites) before an election. In no public statement has there yet been any withdrawal by the South African government from these positions, though Foreign Minister Botha has also stated that if SWAPO won a free and fair election the result would have to be accepted.

There are, however, some signals that South Africa recognizes that it has come to the end of the road. One such possible signal, paradoxically, was the invasion of Angola in August, which provided a counter to any accusations of softness by the right wing of the National Party or by the HNP opposition party. Demonstrations of machismo, externally and internally, appear to be necessary in South Africa from time to time to provide psychological reassurance to what is basically a very insecure society. If the government is about to agree to elections in Namibia, the result of which they cannot control, they must not be seen to do so from a position of weakness.[4] (Significantly, the raid was similar to those into Zambia and Mozambique by the Rhodesian forces just before the cease-fire and elections there.) The Angolan raid was also designed to inflict maximum destruction on the SWAPO organization and communications with Namibia. In South African eyes, a military defeat would lower the reputation of SWAPO with the Namibian people. Moreover, the disruption of communications should reduce their activities within Namibia at

[4] The raid was also perhaps a final gesture toward an army which has for a long time been fighting shadows in a hot desolate country far from home. This way they could feel when withdrawn that there had been some military purpose in the long drawn-out exercise. The army, moreover, harbors a sense of humiliation at its forced withdrawal from Angola when it intervened in favor of UNITA in 1975.

a crucial time.[5] The August raid, and a further deep incursion lasting 18 days in December, may have had a supplementary objective of strengthening UNITA's capacity to occupy territory in southern Angola in the hope of creating a buffer zone between part of Angola and Namibia, possibly leading to the installation of a more amenable regime in Luanda or the establishment of a puppet breakaway state.

Another hopeful sign was the visit by Pik Botha to Namibia's capital, Windhoek, prior to the arrival of the U.N. contact group in October. The purpose of his trip seemed to be to lay it on the line with the internal groups that this time around was the real thing. His message was not well received by the local political parties (who must have a lively appreciation of their likely performance in a free election). Reportedly Botha stated at the end of October that the latest initiative could bring a settlement, and that a failure could strain South Africa's relations with Washington. Finally, South Africa apparently has not yet raised any major objections to the proposed constitutional guidelines presented by the Western five.

A third portent of South African acquiescence is that Namibia is becoming more and more of an economic liability to Pretoria. The mounting cost of the war (defense expenditures were up 40 percent in 1981) now exceeds the revenues from the territory. At a time when South Africa's own economy is in recession, the drain of manpower to the frontier war is having increasingly adverse effects on industry, and the military are worried about the demands made on their resources by the rising level of internal unrest.

Yet there is still a long way to go, and time, once again, for the South African government to pull out of the process as it has done before. Much will depend on the reaction among the Afrikaner people in South Africa when the terms of the arrangements become known. Prime Minister Botha has developed a style of government which bypasses the consultative organs of his party on sensitive political change. There certainly has been no clear indication yet to the party or to the people that the government may be about to agree to a settlement in Namibia which is likely to bring to power a SWAPO government there.

---

[5] Many independent observers believe that SWAPO's appeal in Namibia and indeed its physical presence there as a politicizing agent are not dependent on military bases in Angola, and that the demonstrated incapacity of the DTA internal government to achieve change in the face of stubborn conservative opposition is much more likely to affect the voting in a free election.

If Pretoria does go ahead with the settlement, the ramifications for future developments within South Africa itself should be significant. If the loss of Namibia proves a bitter pill for South Africans to swallow, the result may be increasingly hard-line and authoritarian governance within South Africa itself. More optimistically, a peaceful settlement in Namibia which permits blacks and whites to live on terms of political equality might have an important positive effect on South African attitudes about their own condition. In any event, the direction of future internal developments within South Africa will of course affect the willingness and ability of the West to carry through on a policy of constructive engagement with South Africa.

If South Africa finally obstructs this significant effort by a conservative American Administration, it would bring down on its head the obloquy of the entire international community and create a demand for coercive action that would be difficult to withstand. Such an action by South Africa would create even more difficult problems for the United States. Unless America were to join with the international community in exerting the utmost coercive pressure on South Africa, it would stand accused of collusion with Pretoria. The alleged "tilt" toward South Africa, which can be justified as part of a strategy for change, would have to be clearly repudiated if change were not forthcoming. Thus, unless the United States could show that South Africa is being made to pay a price for its intransigence, U.S. relations with the rest of Africa would suffer enormous damage. U.S. withdrawal from further participation in the Namibia dispute, as promised by Mr. Crocker, will in no way assuage African anger. Such a course would be disastrous, not only for the future of southern Africa, but for U.S. relations with Africa.

On the other hand, because these negotiations are rightly regarded as an American initiative, if they succeed the United States will be accorded that measure of respect which Britain earned when it succeeded in bringing Zimbabwe to independence. It will provide an opportunity for a new and more constructive relationship between America and black African countries, which has been at a low ebb much of this year. It is not likely that warm relations of partnership based on shared objectives and values will ever emerge between the present Administration and the black countries of southern Africa. But a relationship based on mutual respect and open communication is possible and indeed necessary for the avoidance of costly misunderstandings when the post-Namibia situation in southern Africa is appraised. Let us return to the need for such communication in the concluding section of this article.

III

During the year the tilt by the Reagan Administration toward South Africa has been reflected in a tilt toward the Right in Prime Minister Botha's internal policies and a more activist hard line toward neighboring countries.

The internal security situation deteriorated substantially during the year. The closure of black newspapers and the banning, arrests and detentions of journalists, students and trade union leaders did not staunch demonstrations of dissent expressed in protest rallies, school boycotts, strikes (often politically motivated), rejection of participation in constitutional mechanisms (the President's Advisory Council and the election for the Indian Council), and a black boycott (with accompanying violence) of the celebration of the 20th anniversary of the Republic. Nor did the relentless pursuit of the program of forced relocation of peoples to the homelands convincingly avert the threatened breakdown of the influx control system which is the keystone of the apartheid policy. Heavy police action taken to control these events has led to greatly increased alienation of the non-white population, an ever growing proportion of whom (as reflected in recent opinion polls) believe violence is necessary to achieve desired change in society. Meanwhile the African National Congress (ANC) has stepped up its program of sabotage and attacks on government installations and police personnel (the Defense Minister admitted that acts of sabotage trebled in the first half of the year).

The business community, straddling the Afrikaner/English divide, watched these developments with great unease. In 1979 Prime Minister Botha had promised movement toward the internal reforms the business community considered necessary in the interests of an expanding economy—improved housing facilities, job access, black trade unions, realistic wage policies. In November this year the Prime Minister made it clear to the business community that internal reform is in cold storage. Said Harry Oppenheimer after the meeting, "The high hopes of two years ago have been followed by a general sense of disillusion."

There seems little doubt that violent racial conflict will grow in South Africa. For many years to come the government has the means to contain it—at increasing cost. However, it is likely that the conflict will spill over into neighboring countries leading to internationalization in a most dangerous fashion.

Already toward the end of the year there were signs that South Africa had decided on a policy of preemptive actions against neighboring black-ruled states. The raids by South African uniformed forces into Mozambique and Angola apart, the escalation of sabotage activities by the Mozambican anti-government guerrillas, the blowing up of oil refineries in Luanda, bombings in Lesotho, and a bomb explosion at the ZANU (PF) headquarters in Salisbury all had South African links, and, in the minds of most black Africans, at least South African government connivance if not direct participation. As the year drew to a close, the South African pro-government press had started a campaign accusing Botswana of being the "Southern African Cuba," which seemed to portend the extension of preemptive actions to that country.

The Reagan Administration has made opposition to international terrorism a central theme in its foreign policy, and African states find the lack of any condemnation of these acts of international terrorism by the U.S. government quite inconsistent with its own asserted principles. They believe moreover that the new U.S. policies toward South Africa have encouraged that government to believe that it can with impunity undertake violent intervention against the stability of neighboring Marxist-inclined states.

The festering unrest within South Africa and the government's connivance at (where not actually engaged in) attempts at sabotage and subversion in neighboring countries cast doubt on the reliability of South Africa as an ally or source of strategic raw materials for the West in any long-term global perspective, unless there can be a commitment to uninterrupted social and political reform. There is no indication from events of 1981 that such a commitment is on the agenda of the ruling party of the country.

IV

In the rest of southern Africa, U.S. relations with the Frontline states continued to be important both as regards a settlement in Namibia and U.S. opposition to left-wing regimes. The major focus of Administration attention has of course been Angola. During the year the Administration repeatedly advocated the removal of the Clark Amendment prohibiting covert aid to groups in Angola opposed to the government. The Senate agreed in October, but the proposal was later withdrawn by the Administration when the House appeared likely to defeat it—or to vote down the foreign aid bill to which the measure was attached. In addition, Jonas Savimbi was permitted to visit the United States in November and December, and reportedly talked to officials at the Pentagon as well as the State Department.

However, the Administration insisted that its stand on the Clark Amendment did not mean that it was planning to send covert aid to UNITA, and stated that it did not see UNITA as an alternative to the present government, but rather as a factor which should be included in the Angolan political process. The pressure of U.S. oil companies in Angola also appeared significant in moderating the Administration's stance. In August, the U.S. Export-Import Bank approved some $80 million for U.S. investment in oil development in that country.

On the Cuban question, the Administration appears to have paid some attention to Angolan assertions of their need for the Cuban troops in light of their vulnerability to attack by South Africa. Though there appeared few signs by year's end of any intention on the part of the Angolan government to negotiate with Jonas Savimbi, the U.S. Administration voiced optimism that the parallel strategies of settling Namibia and ousting the Cubans would come to fruition simultaneously, with the Namibia settlement providing the spur for a Cuban exodus, and the prospect of Cuban departure providing additional reassurance to the South Africans. Because the extent of the linkage between the two issues—both for the Administration and for the South Africans—continued to be ambiguous, the issue could not be ruled out, by year's end, as a further potential obstruction to a Namibia settlement.

The other key country in this area for the Reagan Administration is Zimbabwe. The Republican Administration has embraced Zimbabwe from the outset as a potentially hopeful "moderate" biracial democracy. At the Zimbabwe Aid Donors Conference in March, the Administration committed $75 million a year over the next three years to the Salisbury government. While not hesitating to point out disagreements with certain U.S. policies, Prime Minister Mugabe has indicated his continued desire for good relations with the United States and cooperated closely with the Namibia initiative.

During the year Mugabe's ability to walk a tightrope between blacks and whites, radicals and moderates was put to severe tests by the South African government, which has been pursuing an increasingly harsh policy toward Zimbabwe, aimed, some observers feel, at the destabilization of the black-ruled state. Although the Zimbabwe government has not allowed the ANC to establish official representation or bases there, the South Africans are alleged to have organized the assassination of a prominent ANC official outside his home in Salisbury. Pretoria also unilaterally terminated a long–standing preferential trade agreement that gave Zimbabwean manufactured goods a guaranteed market in South Africa; refused to extend a lease on a Boeing jet for Air Zimbabwe; gave notice that work permits of 20,000 Zimbabweans working in South Africa would not be renewed when they expire; placed severe restrictions on the supply of diesel fuel; and began requiring visas for Zimbabweans, a process which requires 14 days. Most seriously, South African Railways withdrew 25 of its diesel locomotives in service with Zimbabwe's railways when their leases ran out, just when they were desperately needed to transport a record maize crop. A South African-aided rebel movement in Mozambique has also disrupted railways which transport oil to Zimbabwe.[6]

The failure of the white Republican Front Party to join in condemning these actions has led to a serious deterioration in relations between whites and blacks in the country, exacerbated by allegations of involvement by whites in planned subversion and sabotage—including the bombing of the ZANU (PF) headquarters in Salisbury in December. A number of whites including one Member of Parliament have been detained without charges and toward the end of December legislation was published which would enable the government to seize the properties of persons suspected of subversive activities. There has also been renewed talk of a one-party state.

It is too early to see in these developments the breakdown of interracial cooperation in Zimbabwe, but the white exodus has increased. If Mugabe is to maintain the precarious equilibrium established at independence, he will need a full measure of understanding and support from the Western countries which alone have leverage to influence South Africa's policies. Meanwhile the worsening racial situation in Zimbabwe may complicate negotiations on Namibia.

U.S. relations with Tanzania during this year have become

---

[6] The danger to small states in Africa from the violence inherent in South African society and its government's obsessive fear of "communism" was also made vividly evident in December by the patent South African involvement in the bizarre attempt by a handful of white mercenaries to overthrow the leftist government of the Seychelles islands. Although the United States deplored both the raid and South Africa's lenient handling of those involved, the fact that it was necessary for Washington to issue an official disclaimer of involvement in that event sadly reflects the Administration's own assessment of the degree of suspicion of U.S. actions that continues to exist in Africa.

exceedingly chilly. Possibly regarding Tanzania as a favorite of the Carter Administration as well as an unattractively "leftist" and ideologically hostile regime, the United States has displayed its pique by cutting its aid allocations in half, and leaving Dar es Salaam without a U.S. Ambassador for five months during the summer and fall of the year. The U.S. stance may be regarded by the Administration as a cost-free display of its ideological likes and dislikes toward a country where the United States has no real interest. Tanzania has, nonetheless, cooperated fully in the Namibia initiative.

The use of the U.S. veto in the fall to block the election of the Tanzanian candidate for the U.N. Secretary-Generalship was widely regarded as an extension into the international arena of the Administration's anti-Tanzanian posture. Mr. Salim's candidacy was unanimously supported by the OAU members and also by other Third World groupings, and the U.S. blocking action caused resentment spreading beyond Tanzania. The main beneficiary of this episode seems ironically to have been Russia, which is believed to have been equally opposed to Salim's appointment but which did not have to act publicly against the Third World nomination.

Finally, the United States has provided some support for the Southern African Development Coordination Conference (SADCC), which aims at economic development of South Africa's neighbors. The SADCC group brings together nine black-ruled states of southern Africa of widely differing political hues in a series of cooperative endeavors aimed at developing their resources and their markets on a regional basis wherever this can be shown to be economically advantageous. In little more than two years the group has been remarkably effective in raising international interest and funds (more than $670 million to date) and in preparing and implementing programs (particularly for reorienting patterns of transportation in the region). Their success in enhancing their internal economic self-sufficiency could be an important factor in reducing instability and resulting conflict during the period— undoubtedly troubled—of South Africa's transition to majority rule. SADCC could provide a catalyst for positive change and a focus for Western links with the countries of southern Africa during the difficult times that lie ahead.

The Administration's ambivalence toward the group's key goal of reducing economic dependence on South Africa, however, makes a more enthusiastic American effort in support of the group unlikely in the near future. Moreover, the Administration's country-by-country assessment of eligibility for aid seriously inhibits its capacity to play the leading role it might otherwise have in international cooperation with the group.

v

In North Africa, the Administration expressed its opposition to Soviet and leftist adventurism by squaring off with Colonel Qaddafi. During the year the Libyan strongman, who in June was elected next year's president of the OAU, continued to pursue an erratic foreign policy dominated by anti-Zionism, idiosyncratic revolutionary socialism, pan-Arabism, and the search for a greater Islamic republic. Supported by oil revenues received from America and Europe, he functioned very opportunistically, offering a kaleidoscope of financial aid, military defense agreements, political unions, and military hardware and training to governments, opposition groups and liberation movements.

Clearly, Qaddafi's political activities vigorously oppose U.S. interests in every theater where he operates—in Egypt, Sudan, Morocco, Tunisia, Chad, Somalia, Liberia, Angola. He has been an enthusiastic participant in the anti-Camp David "rejectionist front," and patron of various Palestinian groups, as well as of revolutionaries and anarchists in Europe and the Third World. He is also a member, with Ethiopia and South Yemen, of a new, anti-U.S. military pact, and has a wide range of ties to the Soviet Union. His military establishment is formidable in African terms and includes sophisticated equipment purchased largely from the U.S.S.R. but also from the West.

Only in Chad, however, has Qaddafi achieved a tangible military success, when in 1980 he intervened on behalf of President Goukouni Oueddei in the Chadian civil war. This was followed by the now familiar offer of a union between the two countries. (A similar proposal was made to and rejected by President Ould Haidalla of Mauritania early in 1981 when Qaddafi helped thwart an attempted coup d'état in that country.) Even though his intervention brought an uneasy peace in Chad and enabled a government recognized by the OAU to establish a measure of authority, this adventure, like so many others, is adding to Quaddafi's isolation in Africa as a dangerous dreamer and meddler, without advancing in any way his foreign policy objectives. His troops were too close for comfort to other fragile states and throughout the year there was agitation among the West African states for the withdrawal of Libyan forces from Chad. This objective was not facilitated by the support provided by the United States and its allies, Egypt and Sudan, to Chad's dissident ex-Defense Minister, Hissene Habré, operating from bases in Sudan—a situation not unlike that prevailing in Angola.

Rather, it was the decisiveness of the French that broke the logjam late in 1981. They offered logistic support for an OAU force to replace the Libyans and, at a Franco-African meeting in Paris persuaded President Goukouni to request the Libyans to withdraw. The Libyan response was impeccable. They withdrew (except from the uranium-rich strip of territory in the north of Chad which they have occupied since 1973) with an alacrity which was embarrassing to the OAU. Whether this will enable peace to be maintained will depend on the ability of the OAU to muster and maintain a peacekeeping force and on the withdrawal of external support for Habré.

For its part, the Reagan Administration has pursued a course of all-out opposition to Qaddafi since the spring of the year, when it expelled the Libyan diplomatic mission from Washington. Arguing that Libya's penchant for "destabilizing" its neighbors and further-flung adversaries cannot be permitted given the present fragility of the international order, the Administration apparently seeks to penalize Qaddafi for his "general pattern of unacceptable conduct." While some observers feel that the United States has overreacted to what is really a minor international annoyance, it also appears that the Administration may view its Libya policy as a relatively cost-free demonstration of U.S. muscle and will to take on its adversaries. Throughout the year, the United States endeavored to isolate Qaddafi diplomatically, and to confront him in a number of concrete actions.

In August the United States shot down two Libyan war planes in the Gulf of Sirte. The action was taken in response to the Libyan planes' pursuit of U.S. aircraft flying over waters claimed by Libya as its territorial sea but defined by the United States (and others) as international waters. The incident provoked loud Libyan protests, somewhat perfunctorily supported by other members of the Arab League and OAU. If Qaddafi had not raised so many hackles throughout the region, the reaction probably would have been stronger. Many African and Arab members of the OAU did feel, though, that the show of strength by the American Mediterranean fleet was out of proportion to the Libyan threat. And they sympathized with Libya's weakness in the face of U.S. power. Former U.S. Senator William Fulbright may have been speaking for many African states who have no cause to support Libya when he said: "Destroying two inferior Russian-made planes of a small primitive country raises the question about how responsible and beneficent we are in the use of our great power."

Then in December, the United States moved again. Stopping short, at least for the time being, of an oil embargo, the Administration banned travel to Libya on the part of U.S. citizens and appealed to 2,000 American workers and dependents there to leave. Prior to the U.S. move, the major U.S. oil company in Libya, Exxon, had itself decided to pull out. Other American oil companies are remaining in Libya, but assisting their employees to depart. The U.S. action followed increasing concern about Libyan support for opposition movements in both Egypt and the Sudan, after the assassination of Egyptian President Sadat. It also came swiftly on the heels of U.S. accusations that Colonel Qaddafi had sent an assassination team to kill President Reagan and other senior officials. (America's European allies reacted largely negatively to the U.S. action, opposing U.S. efforts to isolate Libya, and particularly the idea of an oil embargo.)

Despite his accession to the OAU chairmanship, Qaddafi's political successes in Africa have been few. Thus it seems possible that his potential for creating serious trouble in the region has been exaggerated by the United States. Mr. Crocker has described Libya as "a leading Third World arsenal of Soviet-supplied hardware." Whether or not this is an accurate description, Qaddafi's lack of military success is notable. With a population of about three million, he just does not have the manpower commensurate with his ambitions, and in this respect is greatly overshadowed by the neighbors he confronts in Egypt and the Sudan. Despite his demonstrated readiness to exacerbate already disturbed situations, internal events are much more important than Qaddafi in destabilizing the countries of the region. Further, Qaddafi's link with the Soviet Union is hardly that of client. Though Russia may derive advantage from some of his disruptive activities, the Soviets find him too impulsive and unpredictable to be a reliable ally. Russian suggestions that he should depersonalize his power base and develop a party cadre in the country have gone unheeded.

If the U.S. stance toward Libya is seen by its European allies as exaggerated or counterproductive, strains within the Alliance could seriously weaken its impact. Furthermore, to the extent that Qaddafi is increasingly seen as a victim of superpower bullying, his support in Africa and the Middle East would correspondingly increase. Thus the U.S. campaign against Libya may not be without costs, and the United States should begin to count them realistically before proceeding too much further down this road. America may already have achieved all the advantage available from a show of force against its small "radical" adversary— particularly during the coming year while he holds the presidency of the OAU.

VI

Elsewhere in North Africa, the Administration's declared intention to support its friends against their foes seemed to be producing a shift in U.S. policy in a new "tilt" toward Morocco regarding its prosecution of the Sahara war. That war, pitting Morocco against the Algerian and Libyan-backed Polisario movement over control of the former Spanish territory of the Sahara (annexed by Morocco in 1975), saw both a flurry of peace politics and heightened military activity during the year. At the June OAU summit conference, Morocco's King Hassan agreed to an OAU-sponsored referendum on the future of the Western Saharan territory. Later, however, the King's commitment appeared questionable, in view of his characterization of the vote as a referendum of "confirmation" (of Moroccan sovereignty). The opposition within Morocco to any referendum which would separate the territory from Morocco is intense. The leadership of the King's main opposition on the Left, the Socialist Party, was brought to trial in October for its public opposition to the King's assent to a referendum.

In mid-October, the Polisario attacked the isolated Moroccan base of Guelta Zemmour in the southern Sahara, and downed five Moroccan aircraft, allegedly with new high-powered SAM-6 missile launchers. Clearly the Polisario's backers (either or both Algeria and Libya) had decided to escalate the military struggle.

The Moroccan losses were severe, and prompted a request to the United States for more advanced planes and weaponry to even the balance. U.S. Assistant Secretary of Defense Francis West, who visited Morocco in early November, reportedly promised to supply only what would be required to restore the balance on the battlefield (said to include training for Moroccan pilots and electronic countermeasures to help Moroccan jets evade the SAM-6 missiles). In the event that the United States does step up the quantity and quality of its arms exports to Morocco, it could be digging both itself and its ally into a deeper pit. For Morocco's claim to the Sahara is opposed by the membership of the OAU, which came close in 1980 to recognizing the Polisario as the government of the independent state of Sahara.

The OAU members view the Sahara as a remnant of colonialism, whose people have not yet been accorded the right of self-determination. Whether or not the Saharoui people (who and how many they are is a much-disputed issue) would vote for independence or integration into Morocco cannot be known in the absence of a referendum. In the present situation, however, both time and resources would seem to favor the Polisario. While Morocco can ill afford the drain of its meager resources (depleted by three successive harvest failures), the oil wealth of both Algeria and Libya enables them to finance the Polisario without undue strain. Unless U.S. arms aid is combined with urgent pressures on Morocco to move toward a peace settlement, the United States would appear, once more, to be committing itself on the wrong side of an open-ended conflict.

Again, in the Sudan, the United States has stepped up military and economic aid in response to allegations of destabilization by Qaddafi. The Sudan's mounting troubles closely parallel those of its neighbor and ally, Egypt. As internal opponents to the regime of President Gaffar Nimeiry multiply, the Sudanese economy has deteriorated into almost hopeless shambles. The U.S. commitment of $100 million in military aid and $100 million in other forms of assistance, the largest U.S. aid allocation in sub-Saharan Africa, would seem a drop in the Sudanese bucket.

In the Horn of Africa, the Administration has had some success in developing military facilities in the Sudan, Somalia, and Kenya to counter the potential threat to Persian Gulf oil from the presence of the Soviet Union in Ethiopia and South Yemen. To date the Administration has handled the situation with the delicacy it requires, notably in refusing to supply Somalia with offensive weapons which might be seen to threaten its neighbors, Ethiopia and Kenya.

These U.S. initiatives did not find much favor among most black African states, though many recognize that the establishment of the Soviets in Ethiopia makes the American response inevitable. On the other hand, regional radicals protested the U.S. policy by forming their new anti-U.S. alliance. At least on paper, the tripartite alliance among Libya, Ethiopia and South Yemen seemed to offer an increased threat to the Sudan and perhaps to Egypt.

For the most part, however, the Horn proved an area of unwonted calm in the region during 1981. Ethiopia apparently had taken control of the Eritrean population centers, driving the liberation forces into the surrounding hills, or in some cases, into the Sudan. It also retained firm military ascendancy in the Ogaden region claimed by Somalia. As a result of the Ogaden conflict, thousands more ethnic Somalis fled from Ethiopia into vast refugee camps (housing nearly 1.5 million people), where the hard-pressed Somalian government and international aid agencies struggled to maintain them. It is worth noting that during 1981 Cuban forces in Ethiopia have not participated in military activities in either the Ogaden or Eritrea.

Somalia's camps hold the largest group of refugees in Africa, but the continent as a whole (and particularly North Africa) contains about half the world's refugees—around five million. Compared with the stringent immigration controls of Western nations, African states have been remarkably generous to refugees, but this has resulted in sometimes overwhelming burdens being placed on fragile economies such as those of Somalia and the Sudan. Many aspects of national life have been transformed by vast influxes of alien refugees settling in rural areas or swelling the populations of already overcrowded towns. The security problem created by large numbers of armed refugees is particularly threatening to countries which can ill afford to increase their internal security expenditures, and it is sometimes compounded by the attitude of the countries of origin, which may regard the very presence of the disaffected refugees as a potential threat to their regimes.

The refugee situation is now of a magnitude and duration which can only be dealt with internationally. Thus in April the United Nations jointly with the oau sponsored a conference to raise emergency aid (targeted at $1.2 billion) for the African refugees. The Reagan Administration pledged $285 million at Geneva as part of a $470-million Western aid package, and declared that the United States was prepared to admit up to 8,300 African refugees into the United States through 1982. The Administration evidently looked upon the commitment as a way to assure Africans that their continent is a priority for the United States: U.N. Ambassador Jeane Kirkpatrick pointed out at the conference that while most domestic and foreign expenditures are being cut, the Administration recommended to Congress a 30 percent increase in overall aid for Africa.

VII

In the rest of the continent a measure of political stability reigned, despite worsening economic trends. All but a handful of sub-Saharan countries face intractable and severe economic crises. As the World Bank report shows, for sub-Saharan Africa as a whole the 1970s were economically harder than the 1960s.[7] This has been especially true of the late 1970s. The "second oil crisis" has hit a majority of African states harder than the first. In 1977–78 a pattern of recovery seemed to be emerging, but this was totally reversed during 1979–80.

There have been specific factors in many cases. Violent external or internal political confrontations have hampered many countries' economic performance. Droughts in a wide arc from the Sahel across to the Horn and down the east side of the continent to Swaziland and Botswana have been endemic. National economic strategies have often been overambitious or badly implemented.

But the dominant influences have been movements in the international economy. For a number of African states, by 1981 it took twice as many units of exports to buy a typical import basket as in 1977. For example, the World Bank study concludes that of Zambia's 50 percent fall in real purchasing power since the mid-1970s, at least two-thirds were quite beyond the influence of anything Zambia could have done.

The economic crises have generally flowed from external trade problems aggravated by poor agricultural performance, and take the form of foreign exchange shortages, food shortages, and breakdowns in transport. Resulting import cutbacks are leading in many cases to economic strangulation. For example, Tanzanian industrial capacity utilization has fallen from about 70 percent in 1977–78 to perhaps 35 percent in 1981, with parallel decreases in road and rail transport capacity due to shortage of fuel, vehicles and spares.

The problem does not seem to be resolvable by conventional aid programs, nor by strategies and programs reflecting the predilections of donor countries. First there needs to be recognition of the magnitude of the crisis. Thereafter, if the West is concerned with stability and human welfare in Africa, it will have to enter into urgent discussions on responsive programs calling for the total commitment of donor and recipient governments as well as the backing of African peasants, intellectuals, industrial workers and enterprises. It is not yet too late to do this, but it would need a substantial reorientation of Western thinking for which there is not much time.

African responses to the worsening economic climate since 1977

---

[7] Its title, "Accelerated Development in Africa," seems odd for a report which records a decline and projects worse to come.

have been laggard, but during 1980–81 a number of attempts at radical restructuring have been begun—mostly related to the International Monetary Fund (IMF) and World Bank as well as bilateral finance packages. The negotiations have been marked by tension and suspicion. The IMF's emphasis on cutting demand seems to most African states to promise indefinite stagnation, not recovery, and appears likely to lead to social and political apathy or chaos.

The European Economic Community through the Lomé Convention has a special role in economic cooperation with sub-Saharan Africa (with the exception of Mozambique and Angola), and in 1981 great efforts were made to overcome the disadvantages of its ponderous bureaucratic procedures in implementing a basically constructive and innovative approach to resource transfers. But in spite of some imaginative mechanisms for compensatory payments for loss of export earnings, the Lomé Convention is mainly based on project aid and is not designed to deal with the most acute features of the current economic crises in sub-Saharan Africa, which relate to shortages of fuel, vehicles, food, fertilizers and manufacturing inputs to maintain existing operational capacity. Bilateral assistance too (including USAID) has been largely project oriented.

Renewed efforts to make regional economic integration work (ECOWAS [Economic Community of West African States] in West Africa, SADCC in Southern Africa and the new Preferential Trade Area of Eastern and Southern Africa) are also in part a response to the crisis. Apart from SADCC, however, progress in getting programs under way has been disappointingly slow and apparently too late to contribute toward avoidance of the catastrophe which threatens.

So far deaths caused directly by famine have been held to a low level except in Uganda and the Horn of Africa. This may not continue. Low agricultural growth, worsening trade balances and rather sluggish growth of food aid suggest that further droughts may lead to a dramatic increase in deaths by starvation and associated diseases in many countries of sub-Saharan Africa.

Not all countries were in these dire economic straits. During the year, America's key African trade partner, Nigeria, struggled with both the institutional kinks in its fledgling democracy and the economic consequences of the oil glut. Relations with the United States continued cordial, as the new Administration acknowledged (like its predecessor) the importance of Nigeria as the most populous African state, member of OPEC, and a leading state of the Third World. The survival of Nigerian democracy, modeled on that of the United States, may also be considered a significant U.S. interest. During the year ethnic complexities and intricate balances placed great strain on the Nigerian administration, as the demand for new ethnic states proliferated far beyond the capacity of the Lagos government to meet. Because of the two countries' many common interests—including a dislike of Colonel Qaddafi's activities and a desire for political stability in Africa and the Middle East—Nigerian suspicions about U.S. initiatives in southern Africa were played in a low key.

Another country of traditional importance to the United States, Zaïre, continued to experience shaky political and economic fortunes. A perennial problem country for the Western nations with mining and financial commitments there, Zaïre did survive the year without another invasion or attempted coup. The defection in April of Premier Nguza Karl-I-Bond, however, further threatened Kinshasa's international credibility. Despite a new three-year credit of $1.2 billion extended by the International Monetary Fund in June, and about $500 million in aid for this year from the World Bank's Zaïre consultative group of major donors, the economic and political conditions of life for the Zaïrois populace continue to deteriorate; the resumption during the year of the persecution and imprisonment of church leaders for their criticism of public corruption is ominous. The continued U.S. commitment to the Mobutu regime may saddle Washington with major bills at some future time. Further conflicts involving Zaïre are likely to prove particularly troublesome for the United States now that the French Socialists have declared their intention of ending France's role as gendarme in Africa.

How sharply French policy in Africa may veer from its former pattern remains to be seen. Along with their heightened interest in southern Africa, the French have emphasized the priority of political and economic aid, rather than military relationships, in their traditional spheres of African influence. French Foreign Minister Claude Cheysson has more African experience than any other Western foreign minister; he also has a deep understanding of and sympathy with African aspirations. Under his leadership the center for European initiatives is likely to move to Paris, and the resulting policies will not placidly follow the American lead. Cheysson's capacity to generate action has already shown itself in the French initiative to roll back the Libyans in Chad. In the Central African Republic he has demonstrated prudent reservations about military intervention—an attitude which may signal future directions with regard to Zaïre.

French divergence from the American view of Africa was expressed pungently by President Mitterrand shortly after his election in May, when he said that U.S. policy saw the Third World merely as a series of strategic points on a military map and instanced the U.S. rapprochement with South Africa which, he said, "shows no concern for what goes on in the rest of black Africa." These criticisms will find a ready acceptance in Africa. They place France in an unaccustomed role as Africa's friend in the Western court. French-American differences on Africa are likely to emerge with particular intensity if the U.S. Namibia policy fails. More positively, U.S. support for a peaceful settlement of the Sahara dispute could be significantly assisted by the French, who have close historical, cultural and economic ties with Morocco and a new rapport with socialist Algeria.

VIII

In both of its widely differing policy initiatives—in southern and northern Africa—the new U.S. Administration demonstrated during 1981 that it sees its policy in Africa as a projection of its power struggle with the Soviet Union. Though this one-dimensional approach is not shared by Europeans, West or East, on the basis of considerable circumstantial evidence it seems a fair assumption that the Soviet Union itself shares the U.S. perception that Africa is a proxy theater for the global power struggle; that the U.S.S.R. seeks not to compete but to exclude the West from large areas of Africa; that its immediate objective is to break the Western monopoly of international relations with Africa; and that it may regard political stability in Africa as the maintenance of a status quo in which it is disadvantaged. Africans, however, watch with dismay as this scenario unfolds in Egypt, the Sudan, the Horn of Africa, Morocco, Angola and Mozambique. It may be helpful for U.S. leaders to take a closer look at African perceptions of this superpower struggle.

Although African countries wish to be seen as individual states in their own right, not as pawns in a cold war struggle, they recognize the West's concern with the extension of Soviet naval activities in the Indian Ocean and the South Atlantic. They recognize too that the West regards continued access to South Africa's mineral resources as a key strategic necessity, and believes that the presence of Cuban troops and Soviet advisers in southern Africa is a potential threat to Western interests.

Africans share the West's desire for peaceful change and mutually advantageous trading: Prime Minister Mugabe and others have made it abundantly clear that they want the West to have access on reasonable terms to their natural resources. But the West's concern for peaceful change, in their view, cannot be confined to South Africa—a necessary precondition is the economic well-being on which the stability of Pretoria's neighbors depends. This requires the cooperation of the West, first in demanding that South Africa desist from all attempts, military or economic, to destabilize its neighbors. Secondly, the West has been asked to cooperate in the development of the black African states to reduce their economic and infrastructure dependence on South Africa.

The 45 countries of Africa sought independence because they wished to make their own decisions about choice of friends, social values, and life patterns. Clearly no African state so far has given up these rights either under duress or in return for material inducements. Any policy which ignores this fundamental characteristic of the African situation, which seeks to enforce an external political will on any African state, or to divide by co-option, will arouse the strongest opposition and will be counterproductive in the long term. It is therefore timely that in November the U.S. State Department published a memorandum stating that "Human rights is at the core of our foreign policy because it is central to what America is and stands for. Human rights is not something we tack on to our foreign policy but is its very purpose: the defense and promotion of freedom in the world."

The incorporation of these sentiments into official policy would require a reappraisal of the Administration's relations with countries such as South Africa, Zaïre and Morocco, whose strategic importance and open-door economic policies have attracted American support, but whose record on human rights leaves much to be desired. Logically it would also lead to a fresh look at U.S. relations with socialist countries such as Tanzania which, domestically and externally, give human rights greater priority. It would be a major reversal of the trends apparent in 1981 if the Administration were to pursue that course. Nonetheless, such a significant change of emphasis would substantially increase the moral stature of America in the eyes of African people.

Further, it must be recognized that the "linkage" theme in American relations with Third World countries severely limits the Administration's ability to adapt to developing situations in Africa and gives rise to inconsistencies and occasional absurdities, all of which weaken the U.S. potential for constructive engagement. When Zambia and Botswana go to the East to buy weapons they have been unable to purchase from the West, when Zimbabwe buys military equipment and training more cheaply from North Korea than it can from the West, Pavlovian bells seem to ring in Washington. In another example, the exclusion of Mozambique and Angola from U.S. aid to the SADCC programs largely nullifies the Administration's generally positive response to that organization and raises suspicions of a U.S. intent to divide.

Although the United States condemns South Africa's internal policies, it nonetheless moves toward a closer future relationship; however, no similar separation is made between U.S. attitudes toward the internal (socialist) policies of Angola and Mozambique and U.S. longer term interests in relations with these countries. If the United States is to play a constructive role in crucial ongoing consultations with the black states of southern Africa, it needs now to begin to broaden the base of its relationships with them.

France and Britain have their own discrete, well-established arrangements for regular consultative meetings with African leaders. These consultations provide opportunities for personal exploration of core interests and of collective action. They are extremely valuable in developing mutual understanding and personal trust and in the avoidance of miscalculations. The United States is excluded, for historical reasons, from these consultations and its ability to contribute positively is accordingly diminished. The Cancún Summit was an attempt to replicate at an international level this kind of personal consultation. The Sahel disaster a few years ago stimulated efforts to create permanent consultative machinery. Neither of these initiatives has been entirely successful, but it may be that with the end of colonialism in the African continent (in Namibia) a propitious environment will be created for establishing new consultative machinery in which the United States can take its proper place.

Finance Minister Rui Baltazar Alves of Mozambique emphasized the need for a new approach to genuine consultation when he said in a speech to the Southern African Development Coordination Conference:

The establishment of cooperation in new moulds requires, on the part of the developed countries, a deeper knowledge of the African reality.... It equally requires the recognition that the African peoples have the capacity to manage their own interests without disagreeable pressures or interferences made against their dignity, freedom and independence.

This is the message from Africa in 1981.

Richard H. Solomon

EAST ASIA AND THE
GREAT POWER COALITIONS

For more than three decades East Asia has had its share of buffeting by the rivalry of the great powers. The region has been the site of America's two most recent wars—in Korea and Vietnam—which reflected the interplay between local conflicts and efforts of the Soviet Union, China, and the United States to safeguard vulnerable frontiers, establish alliances with which to countervail the expansion of rivals' influence, and secure the interests of allied states.

The U.S. position in East Asia, since the early 1950s, has been based on a core of stable alliance relationships with Japan, South Korea, the Philippines, and the ANZUS states of Australia and New Zealand. These ties have been strengthened in recent years by the normalization of relations with the People's Republic of China (P.R.C.) and by positive if informal dealings with the Association of Southeast Asian Nations (ASEAN), the economic development-oriented regional grouping composed of Thailand, Malaysia, Singapore, Indonesia and the Philippines.

This varied coalition has drawn its limited cohesion from a combination of the economic dynamics of the market-economy states, and a shared concern with the growth of Soviet military power in the region—either directly as in Moscow's buildup along the Sino-Soviet frontier, the garrisoning of the northern territories (claimed by Japan) which began in 1978, the expansion of the Soviet Pacific Fleet, and the 1980 occupation of Afghanistan, or indirectly through Moscow's support for Vietnam's 1979 invasion of Kampuchea (Cambodia). It is a loose entente which has given the United States some promise of countervailing the forceful expansion of Soviet influence and presenting Moscow with an inhospitable Asian frontier which would weigh heavily in its consideration of adventures in other parts of the world. It has

Richard H. Solomon directs The Rand Corporation's research program on International Security Policy issues. He previously served on the staff of the National Security Council (1971–1976) with particular responsibility for Asian Affairs. His latest publications include *Asian Security in the 1980s.* He was also editor and a major contributor to a 1981 volume, *The China Factor: Sino-American Relations and the Global Scene.*

required the Soviet Union to view East Asia as an insecure region in which its access is limited to bilateral alliances with Mongolia and Vietnam and an uncertain relationship with North Korea, supplemented by ties to India and Afghanistan in South and Southwest Asia.

Nineteen eighty-one saw no major upheavals in East Asia. The region was relatively calm when compared with the turmoil-ridden Middle East and Persian Gulf, and a Europe weakened by economic sluggishness and strained alliances. Yet the year did see developments in America's relations with key East Asian states which placed in some jeopardy the future U.S. position in the region. The major problem, which cast a shadow over other aspects of U.S. Asian policy, was serious tension in relations with Beijing (Peking) over the prospect of American arms sales to Taiwan. What had been a relationship with some positive momentum and strategic weight stagnated over the year in distrust and uncertainty.

Ironically, most of the states of Asia had welcomed the transition in Washington to the Reagan Administration. President Carter's policies, especially his shifting position on stationing of American troops in South Korea, had generated considerable uncertainty about the U.S. role in the region. President Reagan, shortly after his inauguration, sought to erase doubts about America's commitments to the security of its allies by a strong show of support for South Korea leader Chun Doo Hwan, one of the new President's first official visitors to Washington.

The deft handling of the Chun visit, however, contrasted with mixed signals on China policy. While the State Department reaffirmed support for the Carter Administration's 1978 normalization agreement and expressed interest in strengthening a strategic relationship with the P.R.C., White House spokesmen repeatedly emphasized the President's determination to implement the Taiwan Relations Act by selling arms to the now-derecognized island. Secretary of State Haig traveled to China in June to reactivate the Sino-American tie, revealing at the end of his visit that the P.R.C. would be eligible for purchase of lethal U.S. weaponry on a case-by-case basis. But in fact no arms sales developed over the year, as P.R.C. leaders sought clarification of the Administration's policy on arms sales to Taiwan. By year's end a quiet crisis had developed over the Taiwan issue, with a rupture or downgrading of the diplomatic relationship a possibility for 1982.

President Reagan and Japanese Prime Minister Suzuki held a

successful summit meeting in Washington in early May. In the weeks following the meeting, however, the U.S.-Japan security relationship was strained by a series of diplomatic and military incidents that revealed continuing Japanese sensitivities in defense matters. And as 1981 progressed, the Administration found itself no less frustrated than its predecessors in findings ways to induce the Japanese to increase their defense preparedness, and in managing economic tensions between the two countries that were heightened by a year-end U.S. trade deficit with Japan of more than $15 billion.

Early in the year, Prince Sihanouk emerged from his North Korea retreat to announce a willingness to explore the formation of a united resistance against the Vietnamese occupiers of Kampuchea with his former Prime Minister Son Sann and the "Democratic Kampuchea" Prime Minister Khieu Samphan. A meeting between the three leaders in Singapore in early September, however, did little more than expose the reluctance of the non-communist Khmers to work with the detested and distrusted Pol Pot resistance—and vice versa. A meeting of the ASEAN foreign ministers in Manila in June, and a United Nations conference a month later, produced a resolution calling for the withdrawal of Hanoi's troops from Kampuchea and the holding of U.N.-supervised elections; but the meetings also revealed tensions between the ASEAN states and China over Beijing's future role in Southeast Asia. The Soviets and Vietnamese ignored the U.N. resolution, and the Indochina conflict continued to fester with no clear outcome in sight.

Events in East Asia over the past year, and the policies of the new Administration, thus highlight difficult challenges ahead for the United States in managing its relations with Japan, China and ASEAN. They reveal problems in strengthening the loose regional coalition which could be part of a broader effort to counter the continuing global growth of Soviet military forces and Moscow's vigorous pursuit of its interests in the politically unstable Third World.

II

The growing Soviet military presence in the Far East has provided the common denominator of security concerns for the major states of East Asia. It has been an important impetus for the Sino-American rapprochement, Japan's halting steps toward rearmament, and—indirectly—the increasing cohesiveness of

ASEAN. Moscow's influence in Asia is projected almost exclusively through its military capabilities and its actions as an arms supplier, notably with Vietnam and India. Except for dominating the trade of its client states of Mongolia, Vietnam, and Afghanistan, and being a major trading partner of North Korea and India, the Soviet Union has very modest economic links to the region.[1] Soviet political influence is limited to those countries seeking a counterweight to the Chinese—primarily Vietnam and India, less so North Korea, and potentially Indonesia and Malaysia.

Moscow's military buildup in the Asian region has gone through two distinct stages since the mid-1960s. The first began shortly after Khrushchev's demise when the new Brezhnev leadership began to increase Soviet ground forces deployed against China from a little more than a dozen divisions in 1965 to over 40 a decade later. This trebling of Soviet forces arrayed against the P.R.C. seems to have reflected the judgment in Moscow that the feud with China—which to that date had been largely political in character—now constituted a long-term interstate conflict. The military buildup may have been intended, in part, to heighten the visible costs to China of Mao Zedong's domestic and foreign policies, and thus perhaps stimulate a political reaction within the Chinese leadership against the Chairman. But the Soviets were also insuring themselves against Beijing's assertion that large sections of Chinese territory had been unjustly acquired by Czarist authorities in the nineteenth century through military pressure and political manipulation.[2]

While today these Soviet ground combat forces deployed against the P.R.C. are less than half the "million men" claimed by the Chinese, their superior weaponry nonetheless constitutes a significant offensive conventional threat to China's northern tier of provinces and a nuclear challenge to the entire country. It is a

---

[1] Trade with the Soviet Union in 1979—the most recent year for which complete statistics are available—represented less than 4 percent of the imports and exports of 11 of the 19 states of East, Southeast, and South Asia (which together generate about 95 percent of the region's GNP). The exceptions are Mongolia (which had 85 percent of its two-way trade with the U.S.S.R.); North Korea (53.7 percent); Vietnam (62.3 percent); and India (8.4 percent). In contrast, commerce with the United States represented between 10 percent and 35 percent of the two-way trade of the 12 market economy states and China. See Richard H. Solomon, "Coalition Building or Condominium: The Soviet Presence in Asia and American Policy Alternatives," in a study of Soviet policy in East Asia, edited by Donald S. Zagoria, to be published by Yale University Press in 1982.

[2] China's position on the border dispute has been that it is willing to settle differences on the basis of the existing frontier demarcation if Moscow will publicly recognize that its present control over former Chinese territories was "unjustly" acquired. Beijing's position seems clearly political in purpose: to establish common cause with other states whose territories have been occupied or annexed by the Soviet Union, and with those who feel threatened by it.

force potent enough to do considerable damage to China's industry and urban centers, yet not large enough to occupy and govern the country.

A second stage in Moscow's Asian military buildup was initiated publicly in late March of 1978 when Communist Party leader Brezhnev toured industrial and military facilities in the Soviet Far East with Defense Minister Dimitri Ustinov. Following the Soviet leader's trip, a series of military developments oriented toward neutralizing U.S. forces in Asia proceeded apace. A new generation of mobile intermediate-range nuclear weapons was deployed in the Siberian and Transbaikal Military Districts—the now-familiar SS-20 intermediate-range ballistic missile and the "Backfire" bomber—thus creating a threat of missile and air attack not only on all of China but also on U.S. bases in Japan and the Philippines. The bombers also gave Moscow enhanced attack capabilities against ships of the U.S. Seventh Fleet. Increased effort was also given to completing construction of the second major land supply route to Soviet Asia, the Baikal-Amur Mainline Railroad.

Concurrently, the Soviet Pacific Fleet was given significant new assets for anti-submarine warfare and power projection—most notably in the 1979 deployment of the new ASW carrier *Minsk* and the amphibious assault ship *Ivan Rogov*. Submarines assigned to the fleet were also increased by 15 percent. The momentum behind this force buildup may have been slowed temporarily by the death in an airplane crash of Soviet Far East naval commander Admiral Emil Spiridanov and much of his staff in February 1981. But the process continues as Moscow upgrades both the quality of its weaponry deployed in the Far East and the manpower assigned to it, which now totals more than 50 divisions (including forces deployed in Mongolia). Moreover, the capacity of these forces to operate in coordinated fashion throughout the region was enhanced in 1978 by the creation of a Far East theater command at Ulan-Ude.

The objective of this force buildup is evident enough: to deter attacks on the Soviet Far East, and to neutralize militarily the coalition of the United States and its treaty partners and friendly countries. Moscow is now creating in East Asia—as in Europe—a nuclear and conventional military threat designed to intimidate U.S. and allied forces operating on Asian soil or in nearby waters, as well as the Chinese. It is a force which, before long, may have the capacity to interdict the Pacific sea and air lines of communication which link the United States to the region and enable it to sustain its security commitments to its allies.

While Moscow's current East Asian force posture is still relatively defensive if compared with Soviet capabilities in Europe and Central Asia, it takes on a more offensive cast if seen in global terms. The United States must defend the interests of its allies in Asia and the Middle East/Persian Gulf via long and vulnerable sea and air lines of communication both in the Pacific and Indian Oceans. The Soviet Union, by contrast, can "swing" its Far Eastern forces—which constitute about one-quarter of its ground and air strength—westward along relatively secure internal lines of communication for operations in the Middle East or Europe, or use these forces in East Asia to block American and allied responses to regional or global contingencies.

Soviet commentators have characterized such recent developments as the garrisoning of Japan's northern territories in 1978 as a response to the signing of a Sino-Japanese peace and friendship treaty in September of that year. In fact Soviet leaders, since the early 1970s, have *anticipated* the formation of an "anti-Soviet" coalition in East Asia by the Chinese, Japanese and Americans. They have taken steps to preempt it in a way that has only driven forward the process of coalescence, illustrating Moscow's penchant for creating threatening military deployments in a way that stimulates regional polarizations and exacerbates the rivalry of the great powers.

Concurrent with these military developments has been a series of Soviet political initiatives designed to head off the formation of a two-front "anti-Soviet" coalition, and more recently to establish a series of bilateral alliances. These alliances—with associated basing rights—would enable Soviet forces to operate far from their bases in the Soviet Far East and Central Asia south into the Persian Gulf and Indian Ocean, and into Southeast Asia.

The first of these initiatives was Brezhnev's call of June 1969— not long after the first of the major Sino-Soviet border clashes— for the formation of an "Asian Collective Security" grouping. This appeal found little acceptance in Asia or elsewhere; it was interpreted widely as little more than an effort to isolate the Chinese. Indeed it was an important factor, along with Moscow's invasion of Czechoslovakia the preceding year, in driving the Chinese toward improved relations with the United States.

Following initiation of the Sino-American normalization process in 1971, Brezhnev unsuccessfully sought to engage three successive U.S. presidents in discussion of issues related to China, or to build into U.S.-Soviet agreements understandings that were clearly anti-

Chinese in character.[3] Interpretations of these Soviet initiatives vary: at face value they suggest an effort to create a Soviet-American condominium over developments in Asia; in practical effect they would have generated considerable distrust in U.S. relations with allied governments in the region, and severely impeded the process of normalizing U.S.-P.R.C. relations. Yet Moscow's efforts along this line continue to this day, as in appeals by Soviet Asian scholars to their American counterparts that the United States and the U.S.S.R., as "the two major powers capable of influencing trends in Asia," have a particular shared responsibility to "shape regional problems together," and in allegations of Chinese "adventurism" and the "perfidiousness" of the Japanese.

By the mid-1970s, however, the Soviet leadership seems to have concluded that the diplomacy of détente was ineffectual either in drawing the United States into a broad collusive relationship or in slowing down the process of Sino-American normalization. Conversely, they appear to have sensed that prevention of further erosion of their position in the Middle East—resulting from their expulsion from Egypt in 1972—and countering the evolving ties between China, Japan, the United States, and Western Europe was best accomplished through the creation of a series of bilateral alliances and military basing facilities. These would enable the U.S.S.R. to project its growing military capabilities into Africa and Asia. Thus followed the now-familiar series of direct and proxy Soviet interventions in the Third World—from Angola in 1975, through Ethiopia, Somalia, and South Yemen in the Middle East, to support for the Vietnamese invasion of Kampuchea in late 1978 and Moscow's direct invasion of Afghanistan in early 1980.

There is room here to debate the time-honored issue of a Soviet "grand design," of a geopolitical strategy behind these initiatives—as opposed to the grasping of opportunities (as in Angola and Ethiopia) or the countering of threats to existing Soviet positions (as in Afghanistan). Yet the effect, if not the intent, of these actions has been to establish a series of forward operating positions for the U.S.S.R. in Africa and Asia which, in combination with enhanced Soviet military capabilities, places in jeopardy the security of the energy sources of Western Europe, Japan, South Korea and the United States, and which significantly

[3] See Henry A. Kissinger, *White House Years*, Boston: Little, Brown, 1979, esp. pp. 766, 835–840; Richard M. Nixon, *RN: The Memoirs of Richard Nixon*, New York: Grosset and Dunlap,1978, p. 1030; and William G. Hyland, *Soviet-American Relations: A New Cold War?*, Santa Monica: The Rand Corporation, R-2763-FF/RC (May 1981), pp. 26–28.

increases the capacity of the Soviets to challenge the security of the sea lanes.

Moscow has paid a price for these moves, however. Added stimulus has been given to the formation of a defensive counter-coalition—as in driving U.S.-P.R.C. relations into areas of low-level military cooperation following the invasion of Afghanistan, and in eliminating what little political credibility remained in détente.

A sustained Soviet military buildup and regional interventions, on the one hand, and the slow formation of a defensive coalition on the other—this is the interaction of the past decade which gives recent events in Asia their greatest meaning. Current tensions in Sino-U.S. and Japanese-American relations, and in U.S. dealings with other states of the region, reveal the difficulties facing the United States in its efforts to further strengthen this coalition. These include reluctance on the part of our East Asian allies to be drawn into a broader security entente, regional animosities based on events of decades past, and domestic political instabilities that could weaken U.S. ties to key governments.

III

How to manage U.S. China policy in the context of the ongoing Sino-Soviet feud has been a contentious issue in the American foreign policy community since the normalization process began. And 1981 saw divisions of opinion within the Reagan Administration about the place of China in American strategic planning and how to handle the "unofficial" post-normalization relationship with Taiwan.

The question of U.S. arms sales to Taiwan became a central issue in U.S.-P.R.C. relations during the year as a result of shifting priorities and perceptions in both Beijing and Washington. The normalization negotiations of late 1978 had only set aside resolution of the delicate Taiwan issue. The United States recognized the P.R.C. as the sole legal government of China and directly "acknowledged" Beijing's (and Taibei's) contention that Taiwan is a part of China. P.R.C. leaders expressed "hope" that the future status of the island could be resolved peacefully, but they refused to commit themselves to the United States to use only peaceful means in dealing with Taiwan, on the ground that to do so would be an infringement of sovereignty. As a result, the United States unilaterally reserved the right to sell arms of a defensive quality to Taiwan even after it had broken relations with the Nationalist government—a position that subsequently was given the force of

U.S. domestic law by Congress in the Taiwan Relations Act of April 1979.

Chinese leaders said at the time of normalization that they "absolutely could not agree" to such arms sales; they went ahead with normalization nonetheless because of the broader strategic significance of the U.S.-P.R.C. relationship and its value in the context of the imminent military confrontation with Moscow's new Asian treaty partner, Vietnam. In thus agreeing to disagree on the arms sales question, however, there remained between Washington and Beijing the clear potential for renewed conflict on the issue that had divided China and the United States since the early 1950s.

Throughout the 1970s the dominant theme in statements by P.R.C. leaders regarding Taiwan had been patience in resolving the island's future. Mao Zedong told Henry Kissinger in 1973 that, "We can do without [Taiwan] for the time being. Let it come after 100 years." Vice Premier Deng Xiaoping echoed this view on the eve of normalization in 1978 when he stated publicly in Japan that Taiwan's status "will inevitably be resolved—if not in ten years then in 100; if not in 100 years, then in 1,000." But in a speech to Communist Party cadres in January of 1980, Deng raised the urgency of the Taiwan question by stressing that "the return of Taiwan to the motherland" was one of three major tasks for the P.R.C. in the new decade.

The heightened salience of the Taiwan issue for Beijing was probably based on the expectation that the mainlander-domi-nated nationalist leadership on the island, now firmly in the hands of Chiang Kai-shek's son Chiang Chin-kuo, was likely to pass from the scene in the 1980s. Chiang Ching-kuo follows his father in an unwavering commitment to the principle of "one China." But the increasing "Taiwanization" of the island's economy and politics, and the prospect of a leadership succession in the 1980s that could lead to a less effective political authority in Taibei—and one perhaps less committed to the unity of China—must have given Deng a sense that Taiwan's reunification with the P.R.C. could only become more difficult with the passage of time. And as a leader with only a few more years on China's political stage, Deng himself no doubt wished to make progress on an issue of great emotional and nationalistic significance to the Chinese.

Beijing's concerns about Taiwan were given added stimulus during 1980 as the Carter Administration resumed sales of military equipment to the island and the presidential campaign gave added visibility to China policy issues. As candidates in the primaries, both Ronald Reagan and George Bush attacked the Carter Administration's agreement for normalizing relations with the P.R.C. And after his nomination Mr. Reagan, in a statement of August 25, 1980, stressed his intention to treat America's post-normalization relations with the island as having "official" character and to actively implement the provision of the Taiwan Relations Act that authorized sales of defensive arms to the island. At the same time, the eventually victorious Republican candidate parted company with Presidents Nixon, Ford, and Carter in placing little emphasis on the strategic value to the United States of normal relations with the P.R.C. Indeed, in a *Time* magazine interview on the eve of his inauguration, Mr. Reagan expressed doubts about the wisdom of U.S.-P.R.C. defense cooperation, noting that China "is a country whose government subscribes to an ideology based on a belief in destroying governments like ours."

Following Mr. Reagan's inauguration, however, the new Administration seemed to return China policy to the track established during the preceding decade. Efforts by several Congressmen in mid-January to invite a delegation of officials from Taiwan to Mr. Reagan's inauguration were downgraded—after a strong protest from Beijing—in a way that emphasized the unofficial character of their visit. Mr. Reagan's Secretary of State, Alexander Haig, repeatedly emphasized the strategic significance of normal U.S. relations with the P.R.C., and the State Department, in a statement of February 6, expressed the intention of the new Administration to base its China policy on the joint U.S.-P.R.C. normalization communiqué of December 15, 1978. Indeed, Secretary Haig attempted to move the U.S.-P.R.C. relationship a step forward when he announced, at the conclusion of a mid-June visit to Beijing, the willingness of the Reagan Administration to consider sales of lethal weaponry to the P.R.C. Yet the divisions of opinion within the Administration on China policy seemed to endure as each initiative of the State Department designed to keep the U.S.-P.R.C. relationship on course was paralleled by a White House reference to the President's determination to implement the Taiwan Relations Act.

In the Spring of 1981, American press commentary had speculated that Beijing would accept a continuing program of American arms sales to Taiwan if the P.R.C. were also able to purchase U.S. weaponry. In view of the Soviet threat, went the argument, China was sufficiently in need of the American connection that it would swallow its objections to continuing U.S. arms sales to Taiwan. In the second half of the year, however, P.R.C. leaders turned this argument around: progress in Sino-American security cooperation would be suspended, they said, until the Reagan Administration "clarified" its position on arms sales to the island. Thus, planning for General Liu Huaging's visit to Washington to discuss possible purchases of American arms and other forms of defense cooperation, announced at the end of Secretary Haig's June visit to Beijing, was suspended.

In the early fall the issue of U.S. sales of new combat aircraft to Taiwan again surfaced in public discussion and press commentary. There were multiple pressures for a decision. Taiwan authorities had been seeking permission to purchase such a new aircraft throughout the 1970s in order to replace their aging fleet of F-100s, F-104s, and F-5s, and thus prevent the erosion of the island's air defenses; and in mid-1980 the Carter Administration had authorized the Northrop Corporation and General Dynamics, contenders for the "F-X" export fighter, to discuss potential sales with Taiwan as well as with a number of other prospective foreign buyers.

The objectives of Taiwan's leaders in pressing for the sale seem to have been as much political as military. It was a way of encouraging Reagan to make good on his campaign intention to implement the Taiwan Relations Act and upgrade Taibei's contacts with the U.S. government. And improvements in the island's relationship with Washington, they must have assumed, were likely to slow down if not degrade the evolution of U.S.-P.R.C. relations. At the same time, the two U.S. aircraft manufacturers, who had invested considerable sums in developing the "F-X" fighter, were approaching the limits of how long they could cover their investment without purchase orders. And there were those in and around the Administration, and in Congress, who pressed the United States to make good on the domestic legal obligation, specified by the Taiwan Relations Act, to sustain the island's defenses.

In this context, Beijing attempted to seize the political initiative. Chinese authorities undertook a public propaganda campaign directed at both Taiwan and the United States designed to promote their terms for peaceful reunification, while also privately escalating their demands for a cessation of all U.S. arms sales to the island. Former President Carter and other officials of his Administration were invited to China during the summer and fall and were warned of the seriousness of the arms sale issue. There were dark hints that domestic political support for the newly consolidated Deng government, with its strong commitment to promoting strategic and economic relations with the West, would be undercut by U.S. arms sales to the island.[4] And it was asserted that the Carter Administration had committed itself during the normalization negotiations of 1978 to phase out such sales in two or three years. Mr. Carter, in a Beijing press conference at the end of his August visit, however, stressed that he supported the sale of defensive weapons to Taiwan (as well as to the P.R.C.), and that he had never agreed to limit the duration of such sales to the island.

On September 30 the official New China News Agency (NCNA) published a nine-point program for peaceful reunification with Taiwan under the name of Marshal Ye Jianying, Chairman of the National People's Congress. The document, which Secretary of State Haig later characterized as "remarkable" and a "not meaningless" proposal, called for reunification talks between Communist and Nationalist authorities. Taiwan was promised "a high degree of autonomy," including the right to retain its own armed forces and socio-economic system, and to sustain trade and cultural relations with foreign countries. Senior authorities on the island were invited to take up national political and administrative posts in the P.R.C. This proposal became the centerpiece of a celebration in Beijing on October 10 (Taiwan's national day) of the 70th anniversary of Sun Yat-sen's 1911 revolution, with Chinese from the P.R.C. and various foreign countries urging Nationalist authorities to initiate reunification talks.

Beijing's peaceful-reunification proposal and the issue of weapons sales to Taiwan also were the subject of discussions between President Reagan and P.R.C. Premier Zhao Ziyang at the Cancún "North-South" summit meeting in Mexico in late October. The Chinese Premier, according to press accounts, asserted to the President that in view of the P.R.C.'s proposal for peaceful reunification, any sales of U.S. arms to Taiwan would constitute an obstacle to peaceful reunification as well as interference in China's internal affairs. President Reagan, according to a senior Administration official, "didn't say anything [about the arms sales issue] because there's been no decision on that subject."

[4] During 1981 Deng Xiaoping finally succeeded in placing three long-time associates in key leadership positions, thus consummating an effort that began in the fall of 1976 when the "Gang of Four" was purged and Deng was rehabilitated for the third time. In early March 1981, Geng Biao—long considered a Deng loyalist—was appointed Minister of Defense. And in late June, the Chinese Communist Party's sixth plenum elevated Deng's long-time associate Hu Yaobang to the Party chairmanship, thus eliminating Chairman Mao's designated successor Hua Guofeng from that role. This development further strengthened the political standing of Politburo member Zhao Ziyang, another Deng supporter, who had replaced Hua Guofeng as Premier of the State Council in the fall of 1980.

The official added, "We hope to handle this vexing question with sensitivity and to successfully find our way through it without damage to our fundamentally important strategic relationship."[5]

Subsequent to the Cancún meeting, P.R.C. Foreign Minister Huang Hua visited Washington and reportedly again escalated Beijing's demands beyond the aircraft issue to include an end to all U.S. arms sales to Taiwan. An official NCNA commentary on November 25 seemed to rule out a compromise on the issue by stressing that any U.S. arms sales to the island were a violation of Chinese sovereignty and would only "gravely endanger the development of U.S. relations with China and lead to their retrogression."

Thus, by year's end U.S.-P.R.C. relations, while superficially normal, approached the brink of a major disruption.[6] Public discussion of the Taiwan arms sale issue in the United States during 1980 and 1981 had contributed to mobilizing the potent sentiment of Chinese nationalism. Deng Xiaoping and his colleagues had signaled the seriousness of their concern about the issue early in 1981 by downgrading relations with the Netherlands government in response to the sale of two Dutch submarines to Taiwan; they now seemed prepared (or compelled) to press the issue to the point of downgrading or even breaking diplomatic relations with the United States.

Prospects for a compromise are clouded by a combination of domestic political pressures on the Taiwan issue for the Chinese, and the Reagan Administration's determination to treat honorably a long-friendly government which has amply demonstrated the vitality of a market economy in Asia. However, both Washington and Beijing must face the great costs of a breakdown in normal ties.

For the Chinese, "abnormal" relations with the United States would remove American inhibitions over future arms sales to the island and raise the prospect of having to consider military alternatives to peaceful reunification at a time when the Soviet security challenge continues to grow. Moreover, a deterioration in U.S.-P.R.C. relations could undermine recent positive developments in P.R.C. contacts with Taiwan. An indirect trade of more than $300 million between the island and mainland has now developed, and Taiwanese businessmen are pressing for an expan-

---

[5] Jack Nelson, "Reagan Gets India, China Complaints," *Los Angeles Times*, October 11, 1981.
[6] It is notable that other aspects of the relationship were not affected by the arms sales issue in 1981. Cultural and educational exchanges proceeded apace, and trade for the year increased to approximately $5.7 billion, an 18.7 percent increase over 1980.

sion of the trade. Students and professionals from the island and mainland now routinely meet in the United States, Japan and Europe, at least building the human contacts that had been cut off for three decades. And Taiwan authorities in March 1981 made a small if significant step toward direct contacts with the P.R.C. by agreeing with the International Olympic Committee to field a team in 1984, to be organized by the "Chinese Taibei Olympic Committee," which would compete alongside the team from Beijing.

P.R.C. leaders seem to believe that their reunification drive will be facilitated if the United States undercuts the authority of the Chiang Ching-kuo government by both refusing its request for new aircraft and terminating all other sales of U.S. military equipment. Such an abrupt cutoff, however, could degrade the political stability of the island's leaders, undermine their confidence to enter into talks, or impel them to seek arms elsewhere. Pressure for termination of all arms sales to Taiwan also risks eroding American political support for the P.R.C., as there is strong bipartisan backing in Congress for prudent sales of defensive weaponry to the island. And countries such as Japan, which China encourages to maintain defense ties with the United States, would be disrupted by U.S. abandonment of its residual security link to the island.

For the Reagan Administration, Beijing's peaceful reunification campaign directly confronts the United States with the issue of how to relate to the prospect of negotiations between the island and mainland. P.R.C. leaders may harbor the suspicion that Taiwan's supporters in the United States are really working toward a two-China arrangement. Yet the Administration, like its three predecessors, has publicly committed itself to the results of the diplomacy of the 1970s: acceptance of "one China" and affirmation of U.S. interest in a peaceful settlement of the Taiwan question by the Chinese parties themselves. In this regard, it was notable that Republican Senator Hatfield returned to Washington from a visit to China in August and publicly called on the President to use his good offices in mediating between Beijing and Taibei. While most U.S. observers would reject the notion of the United States involving itself directly in the negotiating process, American interests would clearly be served if the two Chinese parties could resolve their differences through direct talks.

Resolution of the current impasse between Washington and Beijing on the highly emotional and politically loaded issue of arms sales to Taiwan can only come through reaffirmation by both sides of the understandings that since the early 1970s have been the foundation of the normalization process: that positive U.S.-P.R.C. relations have considerable strategic value to both sides; that there is a continuing U.S. interest in peaceful resolution of Taiwan's future that will be expressed through prudent sales of defense weaponry reflecting the actual threat the island faces; and that the United States will support any arrangement for reconciliation worked out by the two Chinese parties themselves without the threat of coercion. From this perspective, in current circumstances U.S. sales of military spare parts and maintenance of the island's air defenses—as by extending Taiwan's current F-5E fighter aircraft co-production arrangement—would maintain but not enhance the island's defenses. It would sustain the confidence and credibility of Taiwan's leaders to respond to new approaches to securing their futures through negotiations, yet not suggest either a lack of U.S. interest in their security or a commitment to a level of defense capability that might preclude any interest in a negotiated solution.

If the Taiwan issue is not to destroy normal U.S.-P.R.C. relations, both Beijing and Washington must weigh their handling of it in the strategic context which prompted the initiation of the normalization process a decade ago. Compared with 1971, the P.R.C. now faces a Soviet military presence on four frontiers rather than one. And Chinese leaders expressed renewed concern in 1981 about the weakening of NATO—which would give Moscow greater flexibility for initiatives in the Middle East and Asia—as well as over prospects for Soviet involvement in Iran and elsewhere in the Middle East. While P.R.C. leaders say they are prepared to go it alone again, as they did in the 1960s, with only their Third World friends, renewed Chinese isolation would only deal a serious blow to P.R.C. security and plans for economic modernization.

For the United States, while there is now a more realistic appraisal of the limits of the China connection as a supplement to traditional American alliance relationships than was the case in the heady early days of triangular diplomacy, there is also a growing awareness of the potential value to the United States of China as a security and trading partner.[7] What needs to be added to the balance is an assessment of the costs to the United States of a return to confrontation with the P.R.C. over the Taiwan issue: the renewed diversion of attention and resources needed to secure

[7] This point is elaborated in the chapters by Strobe Talbott, Dwight Perkins and William Hyland in Richard H. Solomon, ed., *The China Factor: Sino-American Relations and the Global Scene*, Englewood Cliffs, N.J.: Prentice-Hall, 1981.

the island by military means; the heightening of tensions with our Asian allies who, even if they look with concern at the prospect of U.S. weapons sales to the P.R.C., would be upset by renewed U.S.-P.R.C. hostility; and the gratuitous gains to Soviet strategic flexibility of a deterioration in the Washington-Beijing relationship. Neither the United States nor the P.R.C. can face with equanimity the costs of a return to "abnormal" relations.

IV

For the past three decades the U.S.-Japan relationship has been the anchor of America's economic and security presence in Asia. This past year saw the stability and future direction of that relationship seriously tested; indeed, use of the term "alliance" to describe it in the joint communiqué issued at the end of Prime Minister Suzuki's visit to Washington in May led to the resignation of Foreign Minister Ito because of Japanese sensitivities to the defense aspects of the relationships. Both the future form and level of military cooperation between the two countries and the management of increasingly acute economic tensions remained unresolved issues at year's end.

Japan's remarkable economic growth has been both the source of recurrent tensions with the United States and the impetus for the country to redefine its international role. In years past Japanese politicians could separate the country's economic activities abroad from its political role, while depending on the United States for security. This approach has now been outdated as a result of the global Soviet military challenge, the resulting over-commitment of U.S. defense capabilities, and the particular combination of Japan's economic strengths and vulnerabilities. There is now an intimate linkage between Japan's trade and security that has yet to be reconciled in Japanese foreign and defense policies.

Japan's security and economics are most obviously linked as a result of the political instabilities in the Middle East and Persian Gulf and the Soviet Union's involvement in the region, including its invasion of Afghanistan and use of naval and air bases in Indochina. Imported oil accounts for three-quarters of Japan's energy resources. In 1980, 70 percent of that oil came from the Persian Gulf and was transported by tankers to Japan through the critical maritime straits of Southeast Asia. A disruption in this oil flow would wreak havoc with the Japanese economy.

The U.S. role in the defense of Japan's home islands, in countering the Soviet challenge to the oil fields of the Persian Gulf, and in securing the sea lanes, is weighed by American officials against the limited character of Japan's own self-defense capabilities and the impact of Japanese exports on the U.S. economy. The Japanese, in contrast, focus particular attention on the regional sources of instability in the Middle East and Persian Gulf, and on an assumed American ability to help resolve the Arab-Israeli dispute. In these "perceptual gaps" lies much of the current tension in the relationship: Americans resent Japan's presumed "free ride" in defense matters, and are concerned over signs of independence in its foreign policy (as when Palestine Liberation Organization leader Yasir Arafat was invited to Japan this past September); Japanese fear that the United States is overemphasizing the Soviet threat while not pursuing a sufficiently flexible policy in the Middle East in order to stabilize the region and hold the support of the Arab oil-exporting nations.

Trade and security are also linked by Japan's heightened ability to provide economic assistance to countries essential to U.S. and Japanese interests. Tokyo has provided such assistance on a limited scale in recent years to Thailand, Pakistan, Turkey and Egypt; and in late January the Foreign Ministry announced a doubling of Japan's economic development aid in the period 1981-1985. The proposed five-year total of $21.4 billion would make the country the second largest donor after the United States. Japanese may soon be spending more on foreign aid in per capita terms than Americans.

Less immediate sources of potential conflict over trade and security issues lie in the interest of Japanese businessmen in developing natural resources in the Soviet Far East—investments that have been restrained to date as a result of tensions in U.S. and Japanese relations with the Soviet Union. Yet U.S. officials are concerned that the Japanese—as well as the Europeans— might become dependent on trade with the U.S.S.R or fail to use the potential for investment in Siberian development as an incentive for Soviet military restraint.

Japan's industrial strength and its ability to supplement U.S. defense research and production capabilities also became an issue in October 1981 when Deputy Secretary of Defense Frank Carlucci suggested in Tokyo that Japanese companies contribute to the common defense effort by supplying U.S. manufacturers with advanced technology. The Japanese have yet to think their way through this issue; but there is bound to be resistance from industrial firms anxious to preserve their competitive edge in advanced technology, and from officials opposed to modifying the self-imposed prohibition against arms exports.

The most basic linkage between defense and economics, of course, is Japan's ability (and willingness) to purchase military equipment and enlarge its defense capabilities. The country's modest level of defense spending relative to the United States and the NATO allies—less than one percent of GNP as compared with 5.5 percent and roughly three percent respectively—has been a primary focus of contention between Tokyo and Washington in recent years.

Under the National Defense Program Outline of 1976, Japan decided that its goal should be a self-defense force capable of repelling "limited, small-scale aggression," with primary emphasis given to the politically influential ground forces as opposed to the air force and navy. The Soviet invasion of Afghanistan, plus Moscow's garrisoning of the northern territories, prompted a serious reexamination in early 1980 of the country's defense needs. Then Prime Minister Ohira constituted a Comprehensive National Security Study Group, which urged early and significant increases in defense spending, beyond one percent of GNP, to give Japan a meaningful self-defense capability, with greater emphasis on air and naval force modernization. Concurrently, the annual White Paper of the Japan Defense Agency explicitly identified the "phenomenal" Soviet military buildup in Asia as "an increasing potential threat to the security of Japan."

Nonetheless, and despite a series of low-key efforts by the Carter Administration in 1980 to get Japan to move to substantial defense increases, the final budget for fiscal 1981 provided for only very small increases. This was the state of the play as the Reagan Administration took over.

Defense spending was a major subject when Prime Minister Suzuki visited Washington in May. In response to what were apparently fairly strong urgings by President Reagan and others that Japan increase the pace of its 1976 defense modernization program, Suzuki gave assurances that his government would "make even greater efforts" to improve Japan's defense capabilities, and would also assume a greater share of the financial burden of U.S. forces in Japan.

However, the visit was followed immediately by sharp controversy in Japan over the use in the communiqué of the term "alliance" to describe the basic bilateral security relationship. The implication that Japan itself had obligations under the Mutual Security Treaty of 1960—which is on its face a U.S. undertaking to defend Japan, with no reciprocal Japanese obligations spelled out—was strongly criticized in the Diet and press, and in the end the Foreign Minister took responsibility for the language and resigned.

If this were not enough to show how sensitive defense issues remain in Japan, it was quickly followed by a series of unrelated but reinforcing events which for a time severely agitated the Japanese. In mid-April the U.S. nuclear submarine *George Washington* collided with and sank a Japanese merchant ship. Two crewmen of the vessel drowned as a result of the accident, and Japanese public opinion was outraged because the submarine— later said to be unaware of the sinking because of dense fog—did not conduct a search and rescue operation. Not long thereafter, Japanese fishermen accused vessels of the U.S. Seventh Fleet of cutting their nets during training maneuvers. And in mid-May, former Ambassador Edwin Reischauer created a furor in the press and Diet with the revelation that in the 1960s U.S. warships had transited Japanese waters with nuclear weapons on board—and with the tacit understanding of Japanese officials—in apparent contravention of one of Japan's three "non-nuclear" principles (that there be no "introduction" of nuclear weapons into Japan). As a result of these incidents, Secretary of State Haig cancelled a visit to Tokyo scheduled for late June.

The outcry over these events proved to be short-lived, however. Public opinion polls conducted by the major Japanese newspapers—the *Asahi*, *Yomiuri*, and *Mainichi*—both before and after the events of the spring revealed undiminished majority support for maintenance of the U.S.-Japan Mutual Security Treaty, with opinion evenly divided over the acceptability of U.S. nuclear weapons transits through Japanese waters. By mid-summer the controversies had died down and Suzuki reaffirmed his May undertaking. Earlier in the year, the northern territories issue— and the Soviet threat—had been highlighted by a government-backed day of rallies in which petitions demanding the return of the islands were signed by more than 18 million citizens. In mid-September, Suzuki himself toured the northern shores of Hokkaido to dramatize Japanese concerns about the growing Soviet military presence just across the narrow Nemuro Strait.

At the official level, there is a growing consensus among Japanese and U.S. defense planners about the priority objectives of Japan's military modernization effort and the missions appropriate to the Self-Defense Forces: improved command and control capabilities to facilitate interservice coordination; increased combat supplies and logistical support to make possible sustained combined service operations; and air and naval force modernization to enable Japan to secure its own airspace and waters out to a distance of approximately 1,000 miles from the home islands.

American and Japanese defense analysts seem to agree that a military invasion of Honshu or Hokkaido is an unlikely contingency. They also share the concern that in an actual or threatened conflict in the Persian Gulf involving the United States and Soviet Union, the need to concentrate U.S. military forces in the Indian Ocean could enable the Soviet Union to intimidate a weakly defended Japan, if not to cut the air and sea lanes by which the United States would resupply American and Japanese forces and secure the oil so vital to Japan's economy. Where Japanese and American leaders part company is in the priority to be given to developing the military capabilities required to deal with such a contingency, in the face of Japan's current governmental budgetary deficit.

In the Japanese public at large, including some elements in the government itself, there remains substantial resistance to a large and rapid increase in the Self-Defense Forces. There are a number of mutually reinforcing reasons for this, including lingering distrust among older Japanese of the impact of the military on the country's social and political life. There is also some reluctance to directly confront the Soviet Union. Publication in late September 1981 of the Pentagon's study, *Soviet Military Power*, evoked a critical response from Prime Minister Suzuki, who instructed the Japan International Problems Research Institute to prepare an independent estimate of "the Soviet Union's overall national power." It is expected that this study will downplay the direct military threat to Japan posed by the U.S.S.R., while emphasizing Soviet economic and political vulnerabilities.

In short, by the end of 1981 there had not yet emerged that kind of new national consensus which, in Japan, is the prerequisite to an effective change in policy. Continuing exchanges between U.S. and Japanese defense officials made it clear that, for the time being at least, there would be no substantial acceleration of efforts to meet the goals of the Mid-Term Defense Program Estimate for the period 1980–84. The final Japanese budget for the next fiscal year, announced in December, did provide for a defense increase of 7.5 percent (with all other sectors of the budget held to roughly two percent increases). This was officially welcomed in Washington, but with the clear implication that much more was still hoped for in the future.

The other major source of tension in Japanese-American relations is trade, and 1981 saw a continuation of the pattern of recent years of official jawboning as part of efforts to reduce Japan's trade surplus with the United States. Throughout the spring there were pressures from Special Trade Representative William Brock and other Reagan Administration officials for Japanese restraints on automobile exports to the United States. On May 1, just prior to the Reagan-Suzuki meeting, Tokyo announced a voluntary 7.7-percent reduction in auto exports to the United States for the year. Tensions mounted again in September with the announcement of an anticipated U.S. trade deficit with Japan for the year of more than $15 billion, a figure that accounted for over 90 percent of the global American trade imbalance for the year. Congressmen attending the Fifth "Shimoda" Conference in September warned their Japanese counterparts that "Japan cannot continue to feast off the U.S. economy" while concurrently restraining imports of American goods, without eliciting a strong protectionist reaction. Similar pressures mounted in Europe, where the Economic Community faced an expected trade imbalance with Japan of over $12 billion.

Toward the end of the year Secretary of Commerce Malcolm Baldrige, warning of "unmanageable" problems stemming from the growing trade imbalance, urged the Japanese to lower import barriers on such items as data processing software and equipment, aluminum ingots, petrochemicals, fertilizers, pharmaceuticals, citrus fruit and beef. On November 30, Prime Minister Suzuki reshuffled his Cabinet to bring in officials deemed more capable of dealing with the growing trade and defense tensions with the United States. He also expressed the intention to consider early reduction of certain tariffs and simplification of import procedures.

Whatever tactical economic adjustments are made in Tokyo, however, will only fend off for a short time Japan's economic problems with the United States and Western Europe. Even larger Japanese trade surpluses are anticipated for 1982. What is needed on all sides is clearer understanding of the structural nature of these continuing economic problems, and institutional procedures that will facilitate the lengthy and difficult process of adjustment. For the United States and the Europeans, declining productivity in certain sectors must be remedied, and exporting firms must learn to adjust to an increasingly competitive international trading system. Reduction of inflation in the United States will help make American products more competitive in Japan, as a continued high value of the dollar will work to increase the cost of American goods sold overseas. And for Japan, remaining areas of tariff protection, the habit of "buying Japanese," and complex importing procedures must give way to greater economic openness.

Failure to manage these trade tensions will ultimately confront Japan with the most serious economic (and therefore security) challenge to the country's remarkable postwar growth—namely, the erection of tariff barriers or import quotas for Japanese exports and subsequent constriction of the country's trading economy. Protectionist political pressures in the Congress will mount in response to growing trade deficits (even though the U.S. "current account" with Japan—which includes such transactions as tourism, shipping. and insurance, as well as trade in manufactured goods—is more nearly in balance), and in reaction to the country's resistance to carrying a larger share of the burden of its own defense.

One of the constraints on U.S. adjustment to current economic problems is the larger proportion of the economy, relative to Japan, devoted to defense spending. In per capita terms, Americans will spend almost ten times more per person on defense in 1982 than the Japanese, and this ratio will only increase as American force modernization plans are implemented. Even if the Japanese notion of "comprehensive security" (which includes overseas economic development assistance as well as defense spending) is accepted as a basis of comparison, the substantial disparity between the American and Japanese efforts will be seen by U.S. officials and by Congress as inequitable—especially as Japan's trade surpluses continue to grow. What is required is a change in Japanese perceptions of their role in world affairs, and the adaptation of that new role to relations with the United States and other countries essential to Japan's economic well-being and security.

Finally, there is the major continuing problem of adequate consultations between the two governments. Failing a constant exchange of views on all issues of common concern—today embracing virtually all areas of the world—there is a constant danger of actions being taken by either party (but usually the United States) that surprise the other. An example of this was President Reagan's decision in April to end the U.S. partial embargo on grain sales to the Soviet Union; apparently there was no consultation with Japan, and while the Japanese were not directly affected, they at once felt exposed in their own post-Afghanistan economic sanctions against the U.S.S.R. Why, it was asked, should

Japan be left alone in policies that would only sustain tensions with the Soviet Union? And why, at any rate, could not the Japanese have been warned so that they could adjust their own policies without seeming to have been caught unawares?

Such problems of policy coordination only stimulate the Japanese to question the value of their relationships with the United States and the Europeans and to pursue a more independent foreign policy course. As a Foreign Ministry "Blue Book" published in the spring of 1981 observed, "Japan has now reached the stage at which it should participate, autonomously and in a positive way, in the maintenance and organization of international relations." While the document emphasized the importance of developing common perceptions and strategies with the "advanced democracies, including the United States, [this] does not necessarily mean that [Japan's] specific policies should be the same as those of other countries. The important thing for Japan is to play its due role commensurate with its own capability and circumstances."

The challenge facing the United States is to work with the complex combination of Japanese defense diffidence and economic strength to evolve a coordinated set of foreign and defense policies that are properly attuned to Japanese—as well as American—interests. The report of the Japan-United States Economic Relations Group (also known as the "wise men's" group), published this past October, stressed that an "effective Japan-U.S. partnership requires better mechanisms for consultation between the two governments." If the two countries cannot soon redefine their security relationship to mutual satisfaction, and develop institutions for managing their ongoing economic problems, there inevitably will be a political spillover that could seriously erode a relationship that since World War II has been fundamental to America's presence in Asia and Japan's economic development and security.

v

The two great areas of military conflict in East Asia in the postwar period have been Korea and Southeast Asia. In each case the communist half of a divided country has had ample reasons of its own to seek to take over the non-communist half. But the two conflicts inevitably became enmeshed in the rivalries of the great powers, with the Chinese playing a major role in the 1950s and 1960s, and—after Beijing's foreign policy realignment in the

1970s—the Soviet Union emerging as the backer of Vietnam in opposition to China.

In Northeast Asia the situation on the still-divided Korean peninsula remained stable during 1981. The Reagan Administration reaffirmed the U.S. commitment to the security of the Republic of Korea. And in wrestling with the dilemma of supporting a friendly government in the face of domestic pressures for political liberalization, it deliberately made a substantial break with the Carter policy of coolness toward the government of General Chun Hoo Dwan, the military leader who had taken power after the assassination of President Park Chung Hee in the fall of 1979.

This change was dramatized by what was obviously a carefully negotiated invitation to General Chun to visit Washington in February. Two days before the invitation was made public, General Chun commuted the death sentence imposed on opposition leader Kim Dae Jung and lifted the martial law that had been in force since President Park's death. During the General's visit, President Reagan emphasized his intention to maintain American troops in South Korea to insure the country's security in the face of the North Korean military challenge. On March 3, General Chun was sworn in as President for a seven-year term based on elections that had been conducted just days after his return from the United States.

The apparent tradeoff between General Chun's sparing of Kim Dae Jung's life and his reception in Washington eased South Korea's relations with the United States, and with Japan. Yet pressures from South Korea's students and public figures for progress in human rights and political liberalization are likely to increase in view of the disparity between the country's remarkable economic growth and its authoritarian political system. The latter continues to be rationalized in terms of the substantial North Korean military threat, which attracted brief but worldwide attention in late August when the North Koreans apparently fired a missile at an American reconnaisance aircraft patrolling the demilitarized zone (DMZ).

The military confrontation between the two Koreas is a matter of continuing concern, and a large North Korean military exercise in December highlighted the vulnerability of the South to a surprise attack on its industrial and political center just 30 miles south of the DMZ. Yet the confrontation seems basically stabilized as a result of Mr. Reagan's reaffirmation of U.S. support for the defense of the South, and lack of Soviet and Chinese interest in a

North Korean military attempt to reunify the peninsula. Indeed, North Korea revealed some interest in political approaches to easing its increasingly isolated position this year by inviting American scholars to Pyongyang in an effort to draw the United States into direct talks. The Kim Il Song government continues to resist direct dealings with the South Koreans, however, as was revealed when Pyongyang's official press promptly rejected Chun Doo Hwan's proposal of June 5 for a summit meeting between the two Korean leaderships.

South Korea's international position continues to be strengthened as a result of its remarkable economic growth. The country's GNP expanded by over 200 percent during the 1970s; and after a serious recession in 1980, the economy experienced modest but stable growth this past year. The country's economic strength is beginning to draw the attention of the major communist states, thus helping to blur the lines of confrontation in Northeast Asia that have existed since the early 1950s. *The Asian Wall Street Journal* reported in mid-February that an indirect trade in coal and agricultural products of more than $300 million has grown up between China and South Korea; and in late September representatives of world trade centers from the Soviet Union, China, and South Korea (among other states) met in Moscow to facilitate further economic contacts. And South Korea's international position was given a substantial boost in early October when the International Olympic Committee picked Seoul—over Nagoya—as the site of the 1988 summer games.

Thus, prospects seem favorable for stability in the conflict that has riven Northeast Asia for three decades. The interesting questions for the 1980s are whether the Chun Doo Huan government will be able to stabilize and broaden its base of domestic political support, and whether North Korea—itself faced with the prospect of a leadership succession—will finally accept the reality of the South Korean state, perhaps through some cross-recognition arrangement among the major powers, as a basis for broadening its presently narrow range of international contacts.

VI

At the ASEAN foreign ministers' meeting in Manila in June, Philippine Foreign Minister Romulo expressed the common concern of the Association when he noted that the conflict between China and Vietnam over Hanoi's occupation of Kampuchea "has projected the Sino-Soviet and Sino-Vietnamese disputes into the heart of Southeast Asia's regional politics." The dilemma for the United States is how to reconcile its shared interest with China in preventing the Soviet Union from consolidating its military presence in Vietnam with the concern of the Southeast Asians that China not become a major presence in their region. U.S. inability to devise a policy which will bridge these conflicting concerns could split ASEAN, as Malaysia and Indonesia see the P.R.C. as their primary security challenge while Singapore, Thailand, and the Philippines worry primarily about Vietnamese expansionism backed by the Soviet Union.

In dealing with the Kampuchean crisis, Malaysia and Indonesia hope to bring about a settlement which will leave an independent and viable Vietnam as a buffer against the Chinese. They thus seek a negotiated resolution of Hanoi's occupation of Kampuchea. The Chinese, in contrast, assert that only a long and debilitating period of military pressure against the Vietnamese— sustained by a united Khmer resistance to Hanoi's troops in Kampuchea and P.R.C. military pressures along the Sino-Vietnamese frontier—will bring about a fundamental change in Hanoi's foreign policy. The suspicion mounts in Southeast Asia, however, that China's support for the remnant military forces of Pol Pot's "Khmer Rouge" along the Thai border, and Beijing's determination to bring Hanoi to its knees, is designed not just to evict the Soviets from the region but to establish Chinese vassal states in Indochina.

Beijing is well aware of these ASEAN concerns, and in early February P.R.C. Premier Zhao Ziyang sought to ease them during a visit to Bangkok when he said, "We will try to take further actions to prevent our relations with the communist parties of the ASEAN countries from affecting friendly relations between China and ASEAN." Yet the Chinese continued to generate doubts about their intentions, as when Premier Zhao refused to repudiate P.R.C. backing for the Malaysian Communists during a visit to Kuala Lumpur in August. Moreover, Beijing's efforts of 1981 were designed to gain respectability for the Pol Pot resistance forces along the Thai-Kampuchean frontier. The Chinese urged a reluctant Prince Sihanouk and his former Prime Minister Son Sann to join in a united effort with the Khmer Rouge against the Vietnamese so as to gain support for the resistance from ASEAN and the United Nations.

China's effort to strengthen the resistance was intended to prevent Hanoi from stabilizing its control over Kampuchea. The situation "on the ground," in fact, was relatively quiet throughout

1981. Despite a brief Vietnamese incursion into Thailand along the Kampuchean frontier in early January, and a period of Sino-Vietnamese border clashes in May, there was no large-scale fighting. And although signs persisted of serious economic deprivation in Kampuchea and Vietnam, there were no large refugee flows on the scale of 1979–1980. Most of the conflict was played out at diplomatic convocations in Manila, New York and Singapore.

The ASEAN foreign ministers, at their June meeting in Manila, reached consensus on a political approach to resolving the Kampuchean conflict. After rejecting an Indonesian proposal calling for recognition of the Hanoi-backed Heng Samrin government in Phnom Penh, the group agreed on a three-step process of Vietnamese military disengagement from Kampuchea based on the introduction of a United Nations peacekeeping force which would disarm the various Khmer factions and establish conditions for free election of a government. Hanoi was urged to attend the United Nations conference on Kampuchea scheduled for New York in mid-July. The United States supported the ASEAN proposal, but Secretary of State Haig, who arrived in Manila from Beijing, sounded very "Chinese" to his ASEAN hosts in his forceful denunciation of the Vietnamese. The Secretary also was asked to explain American intentions behind the just-revealed decision to consider arms sales to the P.R.C.

The United Nations conference was intended by the ASEAN states to build support for a comprehensive settlement of the Kampuchea conflict. The mid-July meeting in New York was boycotted by the Soviets and Vietnamese; yet the 83 nations that did attend were able to agree on a unified appeal for a U.N.-supervised withdrawal of Vietnamese forces from Kampuchea and the holding of free elections. The Chinese initially blocked ASEAN efforts to extend an invitation to the Heng Samrin government, and they opposed draft language that would have called on the U.N. peacekeeping force to disarm Pol Pot's forces as well as the Vietnamese. But a compromise was worked out which called for measures to ensure that no armed faction would disrupt free election of a Khmer government. The United States expressed its support for the ASEAN position by backing the draft resolution worked out in Manila, and by walking out of the conference when the Pol Pot delegate rose to speak.

There was little expectation in any quarter that the Vietnamese would respond to the compromise U.N. resolution. Thus, following the conference parallel efforts were pursued by the Chinese, the United States, Thailand and Singapore, to fashion a more effective resistance force from the anti-Vietnamese Khmer factions in order to constitute an acceptable alternative to the Hanoi-backed Heng Samrin government and to sustain military pressures on the Vietnamese occupiers of Kampuchea. In early September, Singapore hosted a meeting between Prince Sihanouk, Son Sann, and the "Democratic Kampuchea" Prime Minister Khieu Samphan. The three leaders issued a joint statement expressing the desirability of forming a joint government, but they only established a committee to explore measures to form a coalition and rejected the idea of creating a unified military structure to lead the resistance. The significance of the meeting was further called into question when Khieu Samphan and his party prematurely left Singapore without naming a representative to the committee which was supposed to lay the groundwork for a coalition government.

Despite the lack of promise in these diplomatic maneuverings of the summer, the U.N. General Assembly voted in mid-September to sustain the Pol Pot regime as Kampuchea's representative in the United Nations—thus blocking recognition of the Heng Samrin government for the third year in a row. For the ASEAN states, however, there remained the problem that the only effective armed element resisting the Vietnamese continued to be the detested forces of Pol Pot—supported by the Chinese. In late November the Singaporeans took a step toward remedying the situation when they expressed willingness to supply arms to the non-communist Khmer groups if they would join in a loose coalition with the Pol Pot forces. Son Sann, leader of the best-organized of these groups, the Khmer People's National Liberation Front, subsequently departed Bangkok for the United States and Europe in search of military assistance for a non-communist "third force." At the same time, Pol Pot's "Democratic Kampuchea" regime sought to broaden its international acceptability by announcing, via the New China News Agency, that it was disbanding its communist party organization while sustaining the fight against the Vietnamese.

It is implausible that in the next few years either the non-communist resistance groups or the "Democratic Kampucheans" can form a force strong enough to expel the Vietnamese from Kampuchea. A situation of neither war nor peace is most likely to prevail in Indochina—which is the circumstance most favorable to the Soviets, as they will continue to be viewed by the Vietnamese as the only possible source of support for their ravaged economy and for security against the Chinese. The Soviet hand in

Indochina is not highly visible; yet Russian ships and aircraft continue to call at Danang and Cam Ranh Bay, and Moscow provides economic and military assistance to Hanoi estimated in value at $3-5 million a day. This fall there were strong indications that the Soviets were providing the Vietnamese with chemical weapons for use in Kampuchea and Laos, but a U.N. panel of experts found the evidence of "yellow rain" toxins to be inconclusive.

The most reasonable goal for the non-communist Khmer groups around Son Sann and Prince Sihanouk is to create a political organization and military force strong enough to be a credible alternative to both the Heng Samrin government and Pol Pot's "Democratic Kampucheans." In such circumstances there would be a continuing basis for resisting pressures within ASEAN for recognition of the Heng Samrin government; and the noncommunist Khmers would be able to protect themselves in some form of loose coalition with the Chinese-backed forces of Pol Pot. If such an alternative could be created, it is conceivable that opposition to the Vietnamese occupation of Kampuchea could be sustained long enough to see a change of policy in Hanoi.

The more likely outcome, however, is an inability of Son Sann and Prince Sihanouk to form an effective if limited political structure and fighting force. And with the passage of time, the voices within ASEAN fearful of China will press for recognition of the Vietnamese occupation of Kampuchea. In such circumstances, Southeast Asia would face the least promising outcome of the current chapter in the Indochina saga: consolidation of the Vietnamese position in Kampuchea; a serious split within ASEAN over regional security policy; unabated Sino-Vietnamese hostility; and a continuing Soviet presence in Indochina.

VII

Since the mid-1970s it has been conventional wisdom to observe that America's relations with the diverse countries of East Asia are strong and full of promise. Yet events of the past year indicate that there are real dangers for the United States if it mismanages its relations with the various states of the region: there could be a serious disruption in dealings with the People's Republic of China over Taiwan; there could be an erosion of the relationship with Japan as a result of tensions over trade and security planning; and there could be a split within ASEAN over policy toward the Indochina conflict.

The importance of an effective East Asian policy for American interests can hardly be overemphasized. U.S. trade with the region surpassed commerce with Europe in the mid-1970s. Economic dynamism remains our common good and our great advantage. In terms of collective GNP, the United States and its allies have more than three times the resource base of the Soviet Union and its allies to promote domestic modernization and contribute to the security and economic development of other countries. And East and Southeast Asia provide relatively secure communication routes for trade, access to the critical energy resources of the Persian Gulf and Middle East, and relationships with which to countervail the global Soviet military challenge.

The problem for the United States and its allies and friends is how best to mobilize the resources and relationships of Asia for common benefit. It is clear that there is no support in the region for Moscow's proposed collective security arrangement, or for a condominium of the superpowers. There is also great reluctance among our traditional allies to join with China in an explicitly anti-Soviet united front. While the United States no longer holds the dominant economic and military position in Asia that it enjoyed in decades past, it still has a key catalytic role to play in matters of both security and economic development. As the predominant "hub" power in the region with positive relations with virtually all its states, the United States provides the basic framework and resources for regional defense and trade. A strong American military, political, and economic presence in East Asia is critical to dampening the impact of the Sino-Soviet feud and mediating relationships still burdened with the legacy of past conflicts: Japan's slowly growing but delicate ties with South Korea; the concerns of the ASEAN states about the impact of China, Japan, and Vietnam on their economies and security; and the future of China's relations with Taiwan.

Given the diversity of Asia's cultures, economies, and security needs, there is no one concept that can provide a framework for U.S. dealings with the region as an entity. Discussion in recent years of the idea of a Pacific Basin Community to facilitate trade relations has revealed resistance on the part of the smaller states of Asia to being submerged in a structure which would reflect the weight of the Japanese and American economies. Yet some forum broader than a collection of bilateral relationships is needed to deal with common economic and security problems. It may be that the annual ASEAN foreign ministers meeting, which is also attended by observers from the United States, Japan, Australia,

New Zealand, and the European Economic Community, is the best context for discussion of regional issues and global concerns. But such a forum will focus primarily on political and economic matters. Security issues will continue to be dealt with primarily in a range of bilateral relationships in which the United States will provide the common coordinating presence.

From this perspective, America's Asian agenda in early 1982 holds the following priorities for the next several years:

U.S. policy planning for Asia must be kept in a global and strategic context. Our ability to respond to a security crisis in the Persian Gulf will be affected, in part, by the condition of our relations with Japan and the P.R.C. U.S. arms control negotiators in Geneva would hardly want to deal with their Soviet counterparts in circumstances where there had been a breakdown in the U.S.-P.R.C. relationship; and China and Japan will want assurances that a reduction in Soviet SS-20 IRBMs or tanks in the European theater will not just lead to the redeployment of these weapons to the Soviet Far East.

Events in the past year suggest that Soviet concerns about a headlong rush by the United States, China, and Japan to form an anti-Soviet coalition are inflated. The inhibitions against creation of such a security entente are substantial. Yet it would be unfortunate if Moscow did not see the *potential* for such a coalition in positive American relations with Japan and the P.R.C. Our challenge is to lay the basis for such relations with the Japanese and Chinese, and then to convince the Soviets that threats to the common interests of the three countries will evoke a common response—while restraint in Moscow will be reciprocated by restraint in Washington, Tokyo and Beijing.

The U.S.-P.R.C. confrontation over the Taiwan arms sales issue must be defused. Presumably both sides will see their interests served by a return to the understandings reached in late 1978 at the time of full normalization of relations. Prudent American sales of weaponry to the island must reflect the actual military threat faced by Taiwan, and be designed so as not to obstruct any process of political accommodation between Beijing and Taibei. If such a reaffirmation of the U.S.-P.R.C. relationship can be achieved, the strategic and trade possibilities in the Sino-American tie can be pursued.

Improved mechanisms for consultation and consensus-building in U.S.-Japan relations must be worked out at both the governmental level and in the private sector. Otherwise, it will be difficult to weather the adjustments that both sides must make in economic and defense matters if they are to build a "productive partnership" reflecting Japan's enhanced capabilities, responsibilities, and aspirations. The most effective approach to this process in the defense area seems to be one of the United States privately pressuring for steady improvements in Japanese military capabilities, commensurate with existing threats to Japan's security as well as the political and economic limitations faced by the Japanese government. This should be coupled with purposeful efforts by U.S. and Japanese defense planners to lay the basis for major long-term improvements that will gain political support only in response to some new challenge or security crisis. While there is the danger that such a strategy will be too slow to meet the needs of a crisis, it may be the only alternative to renewed U.S. public hectoring of the Japanese and a negative reaction in Japan that would undermine prospects for even gradual advances in U.S.-Japanese defense cooperation.

A similar pattern of incremental adjustments is likely to characterize management of the trade tensions between the two countries. But as the Japanese respond to American (and European) pressures to open up their domestic markets, due weight must be given by the American side to those factors in the trade imbalance which are beyond the control of the Japanese, and to those problems in the U.S. economy which affect the trading relationship.

In Southwest Asia, the primary U.S. effort must be to preserve the integrity of ASEAN. In the short run this may require more active efforts by the United States to support formation of a non-communist Khmer government in exile and to reinforce Thailand's security. The longer-term problem is to affirm to the ASEAN countries that the United States retains an active role in regional security which will buffer them against the impact of the Sino-Soviet conflict and Vietnamese regional ambitions.

In Korea, a stable military balance on the peninsula is a matter for continuing attention. Given North Korea's increasingly unfavorable circumstances, there is reason for concern that if the United States found its military assets diverted from Northeast Asia by crises in the Middle East or Europe, Kim Il Song might try to regain control over his future through a military gamble.

In the Philippines, as in Korea, the stability of the U.S. relationship will be affected by domestic political trends over which we have but modest influence. American support for the authority of the governments must be weighed against indigenous public backing of their leaders. U.S. interests endure beyond the tenure of individual leaders, yet we must beware of undercutting the authority of friendly governments where the alternative may well be political chaos. Vice President Bush highlighted this enduring dilemma for the United States in late June last year when he attended the inauguration of Philippine President Marcos, who had been reelected for a six-year term in an uncontested election. In his hyperbolic praise of Mr. Marcos for his "love of democracy," Mr. Bush was expressing Washington's hope for political stability and an eventual peaceful succession in a key allied country, if not the views of many Filipinos of their President's political instincts.

And, finally, U.S. management of its relations with Asia must preserve sufficient flexibility to grasp what may be new opportunities in the pattern of regional alignments. While at present circumstances are not right for new approaches to Vietnam or North Korea, the time may come when existing regional confrontations can be stablized through American initiatives coordinated with other interested parties. In this regard, it is worth noting efforts by India and China in mid-December to resolve their decades-old border dispute, as well as North Korean and Vietnamese attempts to engage private American citizens as a way of reaching the U.S. government. While such initiatives may not be well-intentioned, appropriately timed, or immediately successful, they represent possibilities for defusing the conflicts that continue to shape the coalitions of the great powers in East Asia.

Elaine P. Adam

CHRONOLOGY 1981

UNITED STATES
(*See also* country, regional and topical entries)

JAN. 1. Ninety-seventh Congress, 1st session convenes. Strom Thurmond named Senate Chairman pro tem; Thomas (Tip) O'Neill, Jr. reelected Speaker of House for 3rd term. Different parties control upper and lower houses for first time since 1932.

JAN. 6. Defense Secretary-designate Caspar W. Weinberger (confirmed 1/20) tells confirmation hearing US-USSR arms talks to be delayed pending policy review.

JAN. 14. President Jimmy Carter in farewell address stresses arms control, environment and human rights.

JAN. 15. Carter budget message asks $793.3 billion in FY 1982, with $27.5-billion deficit.

— Weinberger in *New York Times* interview says US to consider sea-based MX mobile intercontinental ballistic missile, backs Rapid Deployment Force (RDF).

JAN. 16. Carter final State of Union message stresses inflation and unemployment, ongoing USSR threat to Poland.

JAN. 20. Ronald Wilson Reagan inaugurated as 40th US President; pledges "era of renewal." American hostages in Iran freed minutes after Reagan takes office (*see* Middle East: Iran).

JAN. 21. Senate, 93-6, confirms Alexander M. Haig, Jr. as Secretary of State; sworn in 1/27.

JAN. 23. Economics professor Murray L. Weidenbaum named to succeed Charles L. Shultz as Chairman, Council of Economic Advisers.

JAN. 25. Fifty-two American hostages return home (*see* Middle East: Iran). In 1/27 White House welcome Reagan pledges quick "retribution" for any future such attack against US.

JAN. 28. Reagan abolishes remaining US oil price and allocation controls effective at once.

FEB. 5. Reagan address asks sweeping spending and tax cuts to avoid "economic calamity."

— State Department issues '80 human rights report (delayed until after visit of Republic of Korea (ROK) President Chun); singles out ROK and Vietnam, severely criticizes USSR.

FEB. 18. Reagan State of Union message asks $41.4-billion cut in FY '82 budget of $695.5 billion with $45-billion deficit, personal tax cuts of 10% per year for 3 years, and $181.5-billion defense outlay.

FEB. 26. Select Commission on Immigration and Refugee Policy (created in '78, headed by Rev. Theodore M. Hesburgh) delivers final report to Reagan.

FEB. 27. Office of Management and Budget Director David Stockman says Reagan has ordered additional $13-billion budget cut.

Mar. 8. Top)US aides to UN Law of the Sea Conference replaced without warning before 3/9 conference start.

Mar. 9. State Department says Reagan seeks $6.9 billion for security assistance in FY '82 ($900 million over Carter request); will include *inter alia* $350 million for foreign crises.

Mar. 10. Reagan sends Congress $695-billion FY '82 budget.

— State Department announces $982 million in low-interest loans for 15 strategically situated countries (part of $6.9-billion security aid bill).

Mar. 19. Haig at Senate Foreign Relations Committee (SFRC) hearing says US seeks "consensus strategy" to counter USSR threats.

— Under Secretary of State for Security Affairs James L. Buckley at House panel hearing urges repeal of Clark and Symington Amendments.

Mar. 24. White House names Vice President George Bush to head crisis-management team.

Mar. 30. Reagan, White House Press Secretary James S. Brady, Secret Service agent Timothy McCarthy, and police officer Thomas Delahanty seriously wounded in Washington by alleged gunman John W. Hinckley Jr.

Mar. 31. Reagan in excellent condition, confers with aides after 3/30 surgery; returns to White House 4/11.

Elaine P. Adam was the editor of the Council on Foreign Relations' *American Foreign Relations: A Documentary History*, from 1970 to 1978.

Apr. 18. Pentagon says Weinberger now stresses possibility of long conventional war in several areas over that of short nuclear war with USSR.

Apr. 20. *The New York Times* publishes Haig 3/31 speech to Trilateral Commission saying US should oppose all human rights violations but favor "authoritarian" over "totalitarian" regimes.

Apr. 22. Eugene V. Rostow named Director, Arms Control and Disarmament Agency (ACDA).

Apr. 30. SALT II foe Lt. Gen. Edward L. Rowney named chief ACDA negotiator.

May 20. House, 244-155, approves $695.5-billion budget; social programs cut by $36 billion, military outlays raised by $25 billion to $188 billion. Senate, 76-20, adopts budget 5/21.

May 21. In reversal of Carter position, Buckley calls foreign arms sales a "vital" tool of US foreign policy.

May 27. Reagan in West Point speech says "era of self-doubt" over, treaties no substitute for arms buildup; reaffirms commitment to volunteer army.

June 4. Reagan revised tax plan cuts business benefits by $50 billion over 6 years, adds breaks for individuals.

June 18. Associate Supreme Court Justice Potter Stewart announces retirement as of 7/3. Arizona Appeals Court Judge Sandra Day O'Connor named to vacancy 7/7.

June 29. Supreme Court rules, 7-2, US may revoke passports on national security grounds.

July 3. Senior Pentagon aides announce 5-year, $120-billion Navy modernization plan.

July 24. House, 206-186, approves $228 million more for $3.2 billion Clinch River Breeder Reactor authorized in 1970.

July 29. Senate, 89-11, and House, 238-195, approve slightly different versions of 3-year, 25% tax cut.

July 30. New US immigration policy proposes *inter alia* fines for employers of illegal aliens, trial 2-year Mexican "guest worker" plan, conditional amnesty for illegal aliens.

July 31. House in voice vote and Senate, 80-14, approve conferees' $35.2-billion FY '82 budget cut.

Aug. 3. Senate approves tax cut, 67-8. House passes bill on 8/4, 282-95.

Aug. 8. Reagan orders neutron bomb production (*see* East-West).

Aug. 13. Reagan signs tax and budget bills.

Sept 23. Weinberger outlines 3-year, $13-billion defense budget cuts.

Sept 24. Reagan's 5th national address on economy asks $3 billion more in revenues and added $13-billion spending cut in FY '82; agrees to trim request 10/18.

Sept 29. Reagan issues order allowing Coast Guard to intercept ships suspected of carrying illegal aliens.

— Debt ceiling exceeds $1-trillion mark for first time as Senate, 64-34, approves $1,079-billion limit.

— International Communication Agency title changed back to US Information Agency and US Information Service.

Sept. 30. Senate votes for repeal of Clark amendment; bill goes to House.

Oct. 2. Reagan announces 6-year, $180.3-billion defense program; includes stationary MX based in "hardened" silos, 100 B-1 bombers. Senate Armed Services Chairman John Tower says 10/4 that plan does not close "window of vulnerability."

Oct. 8. Reagan formally presents plan for commercial nuclear power; lifts '77 ban on reprocessing, asks faster plant licensing.

Oct. 22. Senate, 40-33, passes FY '82 $5.7-billion foreign aid bill.

Nov. 6. Senate in voice vote passes $130.7-billion defense authorization; delays consideration of B-1, MX funds until 11/18. House on 11/18 passes $197.4-billion bill (including B-1, MX funds), 335-61.

Nov. 11. *Ohio*, first Trident submarine, commissioned.

— Weinberger says Titan II missiles to be retired, MX sites to be chosen in 10/82.

Nov. 12. Reagan rejects Stockman resignation over remarks in *Atlantic Monthly* doubting efficacy of Reagan economic plan.

Nov. 13. Reagan orders retirement of Adm. Hyman G. Rickover.

Nov. 23. Reagan vetoes $428-billion omnibus spending bill (passed by both houses 11/22) as inflationary. House and Senate pass $413-billion bill through 3/31 on 12/10.

Dec. 4. Reagan executive order broadens CIA powers to conduct covert domestic operations.

— Reagan letter to House says $11-billion foreign aid appropriation and $12-billion authorization for FY '82 and '83 is "requisite element" of foreign policy.

Dec. 14. House-Senate conferees vote $11.4-billion foreign aid authorization; bill retains Clark amendment, lifts Chile, Argentina, Pakistan aid ban.

THE UNITED STATES AND THE WORLD ECONOMY

JAN. 1. Greece becomes 10th member of European Economic Community (EEC).

JAN. 6. Gaston Thorn (Luxembourg) succeeds Roy Jenkins (United Kingdom) for 4-year term as EEC Commission President.

JAN. 9. Major US banks set prime rate at 20%.

JAN. 15. US '80 oil imports at 5.2 million barrels a day (b/d), down from 6.4 million in '79.

FEB. 4–5. French President Valéry Giscard d'Estaing and West German Chancellor Helmut Schmidt meet in Paris, warn Japan on auto exports, reaffirm faith in European Monetary System (EMS).

FEB. 5. International Energy Agency (IEA) and Organization of Petroleum Exporting Countries (OPEC) report world oil supply and demand in balance at 48.6 million b/d. IEA Director Ulf Lantzke says '80 IEA oil use down 7.5% to 35.5 million b/d.

FEB. 8–13. Conference of 94 nonaligned nations meets in New Delhi.

FEB. 9. In policy shift, US announces it will buy 20,000 b/d on spot market to fill Strategic Petroleum Reserve.

FEB. 16–17. EEC finance ministers meet in Brussels, ask US cooperation on interest rates; stand by EMS despite 15% drop in German mark since Jan.

FEB. 19. US announces it will not join proposed International Bank for Reconstruction and Development (IBRD) energy agency for poor countries.

— Commerce Department reports '80 real gross national product (GNP) down 0.1% in first yearly decline since '75.

MAR. 2. Gold reaches $463/oz., lowest point since 12/75.

MAR. 4. Secretary of State Alexander M. Haig and Treasury Secretary Donald T. Regan oppose import curbs against Japanese automobiles.

— Chairman of Economic Advisors Murray L. Weidenbaum urges 25% cut in money supply growth rate in '81—most specific Administration statement so far on monetary policy.

MAR. 12. West German Economics Minister Count Otto Lansdorff in US warns rising protectionism is greatest world threat since World War II.

MAR. 13. US IBRD Director Colbert King resigns; criticizes stress on bilateral over multilateral development aid.

— North-South June summit delayed until Oct. 22–23 to give US time to formulate policy.

MAR. 19. US current accounts in '80 show $118-million surplus—first non-deficit year since '76.

MAR. 23. Cabinet task force on auto industry reaches "consensus position" to encourage, not ask, Japan to curb exports.

MAR. 23–24. EEC summit in Maastricht, Holland, asks coordinated drive to lower interest rates.

MAR. 27. International Monetary Fund (IMF) Managing Director Jacques de Larosière announces 2-year, $4.9-billion Saudi fund for developing lands' lending agency.

— Commerce Department reports $36.4 billion '80 trade deficit, down from $40.4 billion in '79.

MAR. 30. European steel companies end Luxembourg meeting, fail to meet EEC 4/1 deadline on voluntary output curbs to replace 10/1 compulsory quotas.

APR. 4. Mexico cuts oil price by $2.50 to $32/barrel; Kuwait 4/6 cuts output 400,000 b/d to 900,000 after oil firms refuse to pay $3 premium. On 4/14 Atlantic Richfield Company cancels order for 60,000 barrels Nigerian oil.

APR. 16. US ends '78–'80 intervention policy, will let dollar fluctuate except in emergencies.

APR. 19. Petroleum Minister Ahmad Zaki Yamani in US says Saudis will maintain current output and price until OPEC cuts oil price by 15%.

APR. 23. IMF to end reconstitution requirement 5/1 in move to make Special Drawing Rights centerpiece of world monetary system.

APR. 24. Reagan ends USSR grain and phosphate fertilizer embargo; keeps ban on fishing privileges and high technology products.

APR. 26–MAY 1. US Special Trade Representative William Brock and Japanese trade official Naohiro Amaya meet in Washington and Tokyo; on 5/1, announce 3-year, graduated auto export curbs through '83.

APR. 27. US and 14 creditor nations agree in Paris to reschedule $2.4-billion Polish debt in first such accord with a communist country.

MAY 1–4. Asian Development bank holds 14th annual meeting in Honolulu—first on US soil (*see* Southeast Asia).

MAY 4. Federal Reserve Board (FRB) raises interest rate to banks 1% to record 14%.

MAY 6. Regan sees higher interest rates for "several months"; says '81 US budget deficit up $2 billion to $5 billion since Mar.

MAY 7. Rich nations (not US) and Arab oil exporters pledge $25 billion to IMF for poor nations.

MAY 11. French franc and stock market drop, gold surges on news of French Socialist victory (*see* Western Europe).

MAY 11–12. Thatcher and Schmidt meet in England; will seek lower EEC budget share.

MAY 12. Kuwait cuts oil output 250,000 b/d to 1.25 million as of 4/1.

MAY 20. Yamani announces Saudis will seek oil price freeze through '82.

MAY 21. France announces exchange controls to stem capital flight; franc to stay in EMS.

MAY 25–26. OPEC 60th meeting held in Geneva; majority agrees on $36–$41/barrel price, with 10% or 1.5 million b/d output cut as of 6/1/81; Dr. Subroto (Indonesia) reelected as organization's president.

JUNE 8–9. US-USSR meet in London on grain sales; US to sell 6 million metric tons by 9/30 expiration of 5-year grain accord.

JUNE 9. FRB approves free banking zone as of 12/3.

JUNE 14. Bank for International Settlements in report warns strict US monetary strategy could lead to breakdown of economic cooperation.

— UN Population Fund report puts world population at 4.4 billion, sees 10.5 billion stable level in 2110.

JUNE 15. EEC finance ministers delay common stand on US interest rates for 3 months at French request.

JUNE 17–18. Six-member OPEC committee on long-term pricing formula meets in Geneva. Venezuela Oil Minister Humberto Calderón Berti on 3/19 calls for 2- to 3-year price freeze at current $36/barrel base.

JUNE 20. IBRD President Robert S. McNamara in *New York Times* interview warns Congress that cuts in $658.3-million IBRD and $3.2-million International Development Association funds would seriously harm US interests.

JUNE 22. Reagan names 17-member group, headed by Regan, to study role of gold in world monetary system.

JUNE 25. Reports say Saudi oil output to drop to 9.85 million b/d as of 7/1 (denied by Yamani 6/30); On 6/29 Nigeria cuts some prices by $2.50 to $37.50/barrel, Libya cuts prices by $1.10 to $39.90/barrel.

—EEC industry ministers in Luxembourg agree on steel subsidy phaseout plan; plan ratified 7/3.

JUNE 26. McNamara successor (as of 7/1) A. W. Clausen voices concern over congressional reluctance on funds for IBRD and affiliates, backs role of private sector in development.

JULY 1. Dollar at 36-year high against French franc and at 10-year high against 15 major currencies.

JULY 7. Mexico cuts oil output by 700,000 b/d after contract cancellations by five governments and several US oil concerns.

JULY 8. Brock and Commerce Secretary Malcolm Baldridge present strongly anti-protectionist trade policy to Congress, stressing commitment to free play of market forces in foreign trade.

— $800-million oil pipeline to move Alaska crude oil to western US and eastern Canada reported shelved because of oil glut.

JULY 12–13. French President François Mitterrand and Schmidt meet in Bonn, agree to oppose US interest rates policy at Ottawa.

JULY 13. In most serious critique yet of new US trade policy AFL/CIO head Lane Kirkland at Senate hearing calls it irresponsible, asks import curbs.

JULY 20–21. Seventh annual economic summit of 7 industrial nations held in Ottawa.

JULY 21. FRB Chairman Paul Volcker at House Banking Committee outlines more cutbacks in money supply growth, attributes high interest rates to inflation expectations.

JULY 24. Arab Monetary Fund announces expansion to $900 million in next 6 months.

— West German banks and USSR reach accord on $10-billion, Siberia-Europe pipeline.

JULY 27. Reagan report on East-West trade asks 3-year extension of most-favored-nation treatment for China, Hungary, Romania.

JULY 29. Canada moves to shore up 48-year low of its dollar. On 8/3 gold reaches 20-month low of $388.50 as US dollar continues record rise against Western currencies.

AUG. 3. Bonn Central Bank discounts US interest rates as factor in German recession, says stronger EMS would have little effect on rates.

AUG. 5. One-year US-USSR grain accord signed in Vienna, effective 10/1; commits USSR to buy 6 to 8 million tons a year.

Aug. 11. Senior US aide reports US-EEC-Japan early warning system to deal with trade, investment issues.

Aug. 13. Energy Department confirms US agreement to buy Mexican oil for Strategic Petroleum Reserve; 5-year, $3.5 billion accord signed 8/20.

Aug. 10–21. UN Conference on New and Renewable Sources of Energy meets in Nairobi; adopts action plan by consensus. US in reservation reasserts opposition to new energy affiliate.

Aug. 19–21. OPEC meeting in Geneva ends in deadlock over price and output reductions.

Aug. 26. Nigeria cuts oil price by $4 to $36/barrel.

Sept. 1. Ottawa and Alberta sign 5-year accord ending 16-month-old oil price dispute.

Sept. 1–14. UN Conference on Trade and Development meets in Paris on aid to 31 poorest nations.

Sept. 8. US stock market at 15-month low; Reagan on 9/10 urges Wall Street to back economic plan.

Sept. 11. IMF annual report finds world inflation slowing but says high interest rates, slower growth causing unemployment.

Sept. 14. Regan and Weidenbaum in separate remarks ask FRB to ease money supply growth slightly. Volcker on 9/16 says spending cuts best way to ease interest rates.

Sept. 15. EEC provisional 38% synthetic fiber duty on US imports becomes definite.

Sept. 21. Haig address to 36th UN General Assembly rebuffs new international economic order, urges reliance on free markets, private initiative.

Sept. 25. Stock and bond prices plunge over 9/24 Reagan proposals (see US); markets from London to Tokyo also drop.

Sept. 29–Oct. 2. IBRD/IMF 36th annual meeting held in Washington; Reagan opening address again stresses private enterprise role, tougher loan conditions.

Sept. 30–Oct. 1. US-USSR grain talks held in Moscow; 1-year sales extension signed.

Oct. 2. Japan announces import-increase plan to forestall protectionist barriers; on 10/12 reports trade surplus with US reached record $1.76 billion for Sept.

Oct. 4. EEC finance and economic ministers realign 4 major EMS currencies.

Oct. 14–16. General Agreement on Tariffs and Trade (GATT) Steering Committee ("Group of 18") meets in Geneva, unanimously backs '82 world trade conference.

Oct. 20. OECD members sign accord on export subsidy cuts of 20% to 25%.

Oct. 22–23. International Meeting for Cooperation and Development convenes in Cancún. Reagan, stressing role of private sector in development, calls meeting "positive."

Oct. 27. US and EEC agree, subject to GATT approval, to let US firms defer taxes on export earnings.

Oct. 28. Commerce Department reports $28.7-billion trade deficit for first 9 months of '81.

Oct. 29. OPEC meets in Geneva, agrees on unified price of $34/barrel through '82. On 10/30 Yamani says Saudi output to drop 500,000 b/d to 8.5 million as of 11/1.

Nov. 10. Poland applies for IBRD/IMF entry.

Nov. 11. GATT report says '80 oil use down 5%—a 4-year low; world output down 4%.

Nov. 12. Exxon announces end of all oil, gas production in Libya; Mobil on 11/13 says its operation stopped 11/1.

Nov. 13. Baldrige announces steel antidumping suits against Belgium, Brazil, France, Romania, South Africa (Canada, Spain added 11/19). EEC in Geneva meeting with US aides rejects allegations.

Nov. 18–Dec. 22. Fifty-one nations meet in Geneva, extend Multifiber Arrangement (due to expire 12/31) to 7/31/88.

Nov. 19. Bonn and Moscow sign final accord on Siberia pipeline.

Nov. 26–27. EEC meets in London, fails to agree on budget-sharing.

Dec. 1. Most US banks lower prime rate to 15¾%.

Dec. 2. US specialty steel concerns ask import protection; US steel companies meet with Reagan 12/4, agree to delay antidumping suits until after US-EEC talks.

Dec. 9–11. OPEC meets in Abu Dhabi, agrees to cut some prices by 20¢–$1 a barrel.

Dec. 14–15. EEC meets in London, again fails to agree on budget.

Dec. 16. Japan adopts import-expansion steps to counter world criticisms.

Dec. 17. Chicago bank becomes 2nd to raise prime to 15¾% after 11/30 low of 15½%.

Dec. 21. Libya cuts oil prices; top grade at $37/barrel.

Dec. 22. International Trade Commission rules steel imports harm US industry.

WESTERN EUROPE AND CANADA

Jan. 1. Greece joins European Economic Community (EEC).

Jan. 5. Portuguese Premier-designate Francisco Pinto Balsamão (named 12/22/80) names center-right Cabinet, sworn in 1/9; wins confidence vote 1/22, 133-97.

JAN. 10. Greece formally protests Greek-Turkish military aid provisions in US FY '82 aid bill; says it upsets power balance.

JAN. 14. Portuguese President Antônio Ramalho Eanes (reelected 12/7/80) sworn in for 5-year term.

JAN. 15. Turkish leader Gen. Kenan Evren promises constituent assembly plan by Oct.

—Social Democratic Mayor Dietrich Stobbe resigns in West Berlin loan scandal; former Bonn Justice Minister Hans-Jochen Vogel elected 1/23 to replace him.

JAN. 16. Former British MP Bernadette Devlin McAliskey and husband seriously wounded by gunmen at their home. Former Ulster Speaker, Sir Norman Stronge, and son slain 1/21.

JAN. 24. British Labor Party votes to let local organizations choose own leaders; former EEC head Roy Jenkins and former Foreign Secretary David Owen form new "Council for Social Democracy" 1/25.

JAN. 29. Spanish Premier Adolfo Suárez (named '76) resigns; Deputy Premier Leopoldo Calvo Sotelo succeeds him 1/30. King Juan Carlos postpones US visit.

JAN. 30. Norse Premier Odvar Nordli (elected '76) resigns over US arms stockpiling. Gro Harlem Brundtland named first woman Premier 2/3; sworn in 2/4.

FEB. 5–6. French President Valéry Giscard d'Estaing and West German Chancellor Helmut Schmidt meet in Paris (see East-West).

FEB. 10. Britain names Lord Moran Canadian High Commissioner to succeed Sir John Ford, accused by Canada 2/5 of interfering in Constitution issue.

FEB. 23. Civil guards led by Lt. Col. Antonio Tejero Molina seize lower house of Spanish Cortes, take some 345 deputies hostage. Coup ends in failure 2/24, with release of hostages and surrender of Tejero.

FEB. 25. Spanish Cortes endorses Calvo government, 186-158, in vote interrupted by coup; all-civilian cabinet sworn in 2/26.

— Army deputy chief Gen. Alfonso Armada Comyn removed and Lt. Gen. Jaime Milans del Bosch jailed for their role in Spain coup attempt.

FEB. 27. Millions in Spain march in support of King and democracy; Basque separatist political-military branch declares "unconditional ceasefire."

MAR. 6. President Ronald Reagan asks Senate ratification of Canada boundary treaty (signed 3/29/79); approved 4/29, 91-0. Fisheries treaty is withdrawn for now.

MAR. 10–11. Reagan visits Canada Prime Minister Pierre Elliott Trudeau.

MAR. 11–20. UN-sponsored intercommunal Cyprus talks held in Ankara.

MAR. 14. Turkish Premier Bulent Ulusu reports start of trials of 68 accused of torture by international human rights groups.

MAR. 16. British austerity budget approved, 325-270, despite opposition of 30 Conservatives.

MAR. 19. Canadian Conservatives easily win Ontario election.

MAR. 23–24. EEC summit held in Maastricht, Holland.

MAR. 26. Turks jail Kurdish-born former Minister Serafettin Elci. Anti-Kurd drive stepped up prior to 4/13 trial of 447 terrorists.

— British Social Democratic Party officially formed with Owen as leader.

MAR. 31. Newfoundland Appeals Court unanimously rules Trudeau constitutional revision plan illegal without consent of provinces.

— Belgium Premier Wilfried Martens resigns over economic policy. Finance Minister Marc Eyskens asked to form government 4/2. Eyskens Cabinet sworn in 4/6.

APR. 9. Maze Prison hunger striker Robert Sands defeats Protestant Harold West in Britain Parliament by-election.

APR. 12. Three successive nights of race riots in South London injure 200.

— Greece protests repeated Turkish violations of Aegean airspace.

APR. 13. Quebec Premier René Levesque (Parti Quebeçois) reelected as party wins 80 of 122 seats; Liberals win 42.

APR. 16. Bomb found at US Army base at Wiesbaden, West Germany.

APR. 19–23. Severe riots break out in major British cities.

APR. 24. National Salvation Party leader Necmettin Erbakan and 33 followers go on trial in Ankara for plotting Islamic state.

APR. 25. Government offers bill to end military supervision as Portugal marks 7th year of democratic rule.

APR. 26, MAY 10. In two-round French election Socialist François Mitterrand wins 51.76% of vote, President Valéry Giscard d'Estaing 48.24%; Left and Center-left in control first time since '58. Communists, led by Georges Marchais win 15.4% of vote, down from around 20%.

APR. 29–MAY 8. Sixth round of Cyprus intercommunal talks held in Athens.

MAY 5. Sands dies on 66th day of fast. Britain sends 600 extra troops to Ulster 5/6. Other Irish Republican Army (IRA) hunger strikers die 5/12, 5/20, 5/21.

MAY 8. Swedish Premier Thorbjorn Falldin (Center Party) resigns on income tax issue. Forms 2-party minority Cabinet 5/22.

MAY 7. Juan Carlos aide wounded, 3 officers slain, dozens injured in Madrid Basques attack. Calvo accuses unnamed foreign states 5/8 of fomenting terror.

— US and 16 other countries meet in Paris on aid to Turkey.

MAY 10. Vogel resigns after Bonn opposition Christian Democrats win West Berlin city election without majority. Christian Democrat Richard von Weizsächer elected 6/14 after 4 Free Democrats back him.

MAY 13. Pope John Paul II shot, seriously wounded in Vatican Square; 2 tourists also wounded. Police arrest escaped Turkish prisoner Mehmet Ali Agca, who is sentenced 7/22 to life imprisonment.

MAY 21. Irish Parliament dissolved; Prime Minister Patrick Haughey (elected 12/79) sets 6/11 election.

— Mitterrand sworn in, names Pierre Mauroy acting Prime Minister; names Cabinet 5/22 with Claude Cheysson as Foreign Minister, excludes Communists.

MAY 21–22. Schmidt visits Reagan (*see* East-West).

MAY 26. Italy Prime Minister Arnaldo Forlani quits after uncovering some 953 alleged members of secret Masonic group, including government aides.

— Results from 5/24 Cyprus election for 35-seat assembly show President Spiros Kyprianou's Democratic Party won 8 seats; Glafkos Clerides' Democratic Rally 12; Communists 12; others 3.

— Barcelona police uncover plot against Juan Carlos.

JUNE 3. Mitterrand in first interview backs stepped up world security efforts, Israel *and* Palestine recognition; will not "collectivize" economy.

JUNE 4. UN Security Council extends UN Force in Cyprus another 6 months.

JUNE 5. Bonn approves budget with 7.2% growth, and defense outlays below NATO goal of 3% a year.

JUNE 11. Giovanni Spadolini (Republican Party) asked to form Italian government after Forlani fails 6/10.

JUNE 14, 21. French Socialists win 285 out of 491 Assembly seats in two-round election; Communists win 44 seats, a loss of 42.

JUNE 17. Results of 6/11 Irish election for 166-seat Dail show Haughey's Fianna Fail won 78 seats; Garret Fitzgerald's Fine Gael 65; Labor 15. On 6/20 Haughey asks backing of 6 independents to end impasse.

JUNE 18. Greece breaks off talks with US on bases until after 10/18 elections.

JUNE 19. Canada Supreme Court decides not to rule on Constitution revisions, ending hope for accord by 7/1.

JUNE 22. Pierre Mauroy named French Prime Minister.

—Britain introduces bill to ban prisoners from running in elections as 7th IRA prisoner joins fast in Maze.

JUNE 22–23. Mitterrand meets with Communists on cooperation, names four Communists to Cabinet, including Charles Fiterman as Transport Minister.

JUNE 23. Spain arrests 3 officers and 5 civilians for plot against government; 4th officer arrested 6/25.

JUNE 28. Spadolini and 27-member coalition cabinet (first secular government in 36 years) sworn in; backed by Senate 7/9, 182-124, by Deputies 7/11, 369–247.

—Rauf Denktash reelected President of Turkish Federated State of Cyprus.

—Irish Labor Party backs Fitzgerald. On 6/30 he is chosen seventh Prime Minister, 81-78.

JUNE 30. Turkey announces plan to form constituent assembly made up of junta and 160-member consultative assembly.

JUNE 30–JULY 1. EEC summit meets in Luxembourg (*see* Middle East: Afghanistan).

JULY 1. British Labour Party in shift backs unified Ireland.

JULY 2. First Assembly of Seventh Legislature of Fifth French Republic opens; pledges support for El Salvador leftists.

JULY 3. Riots erupt in London, spread to 10 cities and Scotland in worst civil unrest since 1930s. Tough anti-riot steps announced 7/13, calm restored 7/14.

JULY 8. Irish Commission says Britain reneged on plan for liberalized rules. Hunger strikers die 7/8, 7/13.

— France plans to nationalize 11 industries, some banks and create over 200,000 jobs.

JULY 10. Trudeau visits Reagan on Ottawa economic summit, bilateral issues.

JULY 18. Some 15,000 persons attack British Embassy in Dublin as Britain again rejects 5 IRA prisoner demands.

JULY 19. Lisbon Military Council vetoes bill allowing private banking; on 7/20 Christian Democrats reject denationalization.

JULY 27. Thatcher announces $1-billion youth job program hours after renewed Liverpool violence that continues 7/28.

—Britain Prince Charles marries Lady Diana Spencer in St. Paul's Cathedral.

JULY 31. IRA hunger striker Pat Quinn's family orders medical care. Seventh, 8th, 9th hunger strikers die 8/1, 8/2, 8/8 respectively.

AUG. 10. Pinto resigns Portuguese premiership after failing to receive unanimous party backing; renamed 8/25 after Christian Democrat Diego Freitas do Amaral accepts vice-premiership 8/23.

AUG. 20. Tenth IRA prisoner dies since 3/1 start of hunger strike. "Prisoners' candidate" Owen Carron wins Sands seat in rural by-election.

AUG. 27. US-Spain talks open on renewal of '76 US bases pact due to expire 9/21.

AUG. 31. Explosion at US base in Ramstein, Germany injuries 20; Baader-Meinhof terrorist faction claims credit. At Weisbaden 7 US cars set afire 9/1.

SEPT. 3. Bonn votes compromise austerity budget with 1.8% cut in defense.

SEPT. 11. Finnish Prime Minister Mauno Koivisto assumes duties of ailing President Urho Kekkonen, who resigns 10/27; Jan. 17–18 vote set on permanent successor.

SEPT. 13–14. In Norway general election Conservative Party led by Kare Willoch defeats Bruntland's Labor Party.

SEPT. 15. US NATO Commander Gen. Frederick J. Kroesan unhurt in attack on his car; 2 bombs defused near US Frankfurt base on 9/16.

SEPT. 16. British Liberal Party convention backs alliance with Social Democrats.

SEPT. 19–21. Dutch police battle thousands of protestors at nuclear plant site.

SEPT. 21. Center-left Belgian cabinet resigns.

SEPT. 23. France approves $9-billion nationalization of 5 major industries, 36 domestic banks.

OCT. 3. IRA calls off 7-month hunger strike. On 10/6 Britain agrees to changes that stop short of prisoner demands.

OCT. 10. IRA bomb explosion in London kills 2, injures 50; 10/17 London explosion kills former military chief in Ulster Sir Stewart Pringle.

OCT. 18. In Greek election Andreas Papandreou (Panhellenic Socialist Movement) defeats Prime Minister George Rallis (New Democracy); wins 174 seats of 300-member assembly. New Cabinet sworn in 10/21.

OCT. 18–19. Mitterrand and Reagan confer in Williamsburg, Va.

OCT. 22. British Liberal-Social Democratic candidate wins by-election in Tory stronghold.

OCT. 23. Turkish assembly begins work on new charter; demands more power 11/21.

OCT. 29. Spanish Cortes lower house, 186-146, backs NATO entry; Senate on 11/6 backs entry 106-60-1.

NOV. 5. Nine province leaders agree to accept Canada charter amendments, Quebec remains opposed.

NOV. 8. Socialists gain at expense of Left and Right in Belgium general election. Flemish leader Herman Vanderpoorten asked 11/12 to form government.

NOV. 12. Danish Prime Minister Anker Jorgenson's government falls, election set for 12/8.

NOV. 18. Britain sends 600 more troops to Ulster, bringing total to 11,000.

NOV. 22. Papandreou announces timetable for removal of US bases and end of NATO role; backed by Parliament 11/24, 172–113.

NOV. 23. Democratic Unionist Party head Rev. Ian Paisley leads 4,000 Irish Protestants in military formation to protest British policy.

NOV. 26. Former British Labor Party official Shirley Williams, running as Social Democrat, wins by-election by 5,289 votes in Tory suburb of Crosby.

— Canada lower house backs charter changes, 246-24.

DEC. 1. Calvo in Portugal Cabinet shuffle names 2 deputy prime ministers, 6 new ministers.

DEC. 6. Over 100 officers sign letters defending 2/23 coup on 3rd anniversary of Spanish Constitution.

DEC. 14. Premier Dom Mintoff wins 3rd 5-year term in 12/12 Malta assembly elections.

— Martens forms center-right Social Christian cabinet; sworn in 12/17.

DEC. 17. Red Brigades kidnap US NATO officer Brig. Gen. James L. Dozier from his Verona apartment.

EAST-WEST POLITICAL/MILITARY ISSUES

JAN. 15. Defense Secretary-designate Caspar Weinberger in *New York Times* interview says renewal of 1972 Antiballistic Missile Treaty (ABM) beyond '82 "not automatic."

JAN. 16. US-Norway Memorandum of Understanding on stockpiling US weapons signed in Washington, and enters into force.

JAN. 27–APR. 10, MAY 5–DEC 18. Conference on Security and Cooperation in Europe (CSCE) meets in Madrid.

JAN. 28. US Secretary of State Alexander M. Haig in first news parley accuses USSR of promoting terrorism.

FEB. 2. President Ronald Reagan says he will meet with USSR whenever it wants to discuss "legitimate" nuclear arms cuts.

FEB. 3. Weinberger (confirmed 1/20) says he favors neutron bomb deployment.

FEB. 4. Holland's 2 main parties sign statement opposing neutron bomb.

— Haig in message to allies, says US has made no decision yet on neutron bomb.

FEB. 5–6. French President Valéry Giscard d'Estaing and West German Chancellor Helmut Schmidt meet in Paris, warn Soviet intervention in Poland would endanger détente, stress West seeks arms balance, not superiority.

FEB. 10. Pentagon notifies Congress it plans to sell $500 million-worth of F-16s to Austria—first such sale to a neutral.

— Weinberger says neutron bomb would offset USSR tank advantage. Bonn openly criticizes US 2/12 for not consulting with allies.

FEB. 16. US at CSCE says it now backs French plan to monitor NATO-Warsaw Pact military movements.

— Egypt becomes 114th nation to sign '68 nuclear nonproliferation treaty.

FEB. 18. Reagan in State of Union message proposes major peacetime military spending, citing $300 billion more spent by USSR since 1970; says US will still negotiate on arms reductions.

— US and UK sign Memorandum of Understanding on purchase of 28 British Rapier missile systems to protect US bases in Britain.

FEB. 23. Soviet President Leonid I. Brezhnev's address to opening session of 26th Communist Party Congress proposes *inter alia* US-USSR summit meeting, moratorium on medium-range missiles in Europe.

FEB. 27. USSR at UN Disarmament Conference (UNDC) in Geneva offers to resume 3-power nuclear test-ban talks adjourned 11/80.

MAR. 3. State Department says US will adhere to SALT I and II pending policy review if USSR does.

MAR 9. US and allies report Brezhnev letters repeating 2/23 missile freeze plan; Haig says talks cannot take place at expense of West's nuclear strength.

MAR. 9–10. West German Foreign Minister Hans Dietrich-Genscher visits Washington, says Bonn will meet its NATO commitments despite economic problems, agrees to link summit to Polish developments.

MAR 18. Pentagon reports successful Soviet test 3/14 of operational killer satellite —first in 3 years.

— Warsaw Pact maneuvers, "Soyuz 81" open around Poland.

MAR. 21. National Security Advisor Richard V. Allen in Washington address assails Europe's "outright pacifist sentiments."

MAR. 23. *The New York Times* reports Jan. and Mar. Scandilux (Belgium, Denmark, Luxembourg, Netherlands, Norway) meetings held to protest Pershing and cruise missile deployment.

MAR. 28. CIA draft report discounts direct Soviet terrorist role.

MAR. 31. NATO Special Consultative Group on long-range theater nuclear forces (LRTNF) holds 7th meeting in Brussels; rejects Brezhnev call for missile freeze.

APR. 4. Over 15,000 in Bonn stage protest march over LRTNF deployment.

APR. 7–8. NATO Nuclear Planning Group meets in Bonn; joint statement notes USSR SS-20s now number 220, backs twin goals of LRTNF modernization and verifiable arms accord.

APR. 8. State Department says Brezhnev call for missile freeze "not serious."

APR. 14. Weinberger tells press USSR must move troops from around Poland before arms talks resume.

APR. 17. Brezhnev hints USSR would like to resume '78–'79 talks on space weapons curbs.

APR. 24. Reagan ends 1/4/80 grain embargo, but warns he will stop USSR "aggression wherever it takes place" (*see also* World Economy).

APR. 25. Haig speech to newspaper editors calls USSR main source of insecurity, says it backs terrorism, "war by proxy."

MAY 4–5. NATO Council meets in Rome; rejects call for LRTNF freeze.

MAY 9. Haig in Syracuse University speech calls USSR spiritually exhausted and thus more dangerous enemy.

MAY 12–13. NATO Defense Planning Committee (DPC) meets in Brussels, backs US deployments outside Europe, reaffirms '77 decision on 3% defense outlay rise.

MAY 19. State Department says US not legally bound by expired '72 ABM treaty nor unratified SALT II pact.

MAY 20–22. Schmidt visits Reagan; joint statement confirms two-track policy of "deterrence and defense, arms control and disarmament."

MAY 27. Reagan speech at West Point pledges continuing military buildup, says treaties no substitute for arms, attacks USSR as "evil force" aimed at destroying US.

MAY 29. USSR harshly attacks Schmidt; invites former West German Chancellor Willy Brandt to Moscow.

JUNE 2. After nuclear review, France says Mururoa atom tests will resume.

— French Foreign Minister Claude Cheysson visits Bonn, calls for reduction of SS-20s; backs Pershing and cruise-missile deployment.

JUNE 4. Pentagon says US has authorized new long-range cruise missile to be deployed after mid-'82; sees no conflict with SALT protocol expiring at end of '81.

JUNE 14. East Berlin holds first election since '49 in defiance of 4-power accords.

— Genscher urges USSR to agree to gradual SS-20 withdrawal.

JUNE 16. Reagan at press conference says USSR shows signs of collapse and Polish events are opening "cracks" in communism.

JUNE 17. TASS in bitter attack condemns Reagan "militaristic ideology," calls China arms sales offer "provocative" (*see* East Asia: China and Taiwan).

JUNE 23. Brezhnev renews 2/23 call for missile talks, omits summit proposal.

JUNE 25. Britain announces development of new $10-billion Trident system; will cut conventional Navy force.

JUNE 26. TASS reports Brezhnev offer not to attack Nordic countries if they declare area nuclear-free zone.

JUNE 29–30. EEC summit proposes Afghan peace plan (*see* Middle East: Afghanistan).

JUNE 29–JULY 2. Brandt visits Moscow; urges early US-USSR summit.

JULY 2. Haig meets with Soviet Ambassador to the US, Anatoli Dobrynin, says test of future relations will be USSR response to Cambodia and Afghanistan.

JULY 12–13. Schmidt-Mitterrand Bonn meeting (*see* Western Europe) agrees SS-20 and Backfire bomber deployment changed military balance.

JULY 14. Haig in speech to Foreign Policy Association expresses US hope for intermediate-range missile talks with USSR by mid-Dec., says Soviet SS-20 force now totals 750 warheads.

JULY 16. Reagan policy statement commits US to curbing nuclear arms spread, says US will again be "reliable supplier" of nuclear technology.

JULY 19. Reagan letter to Schmidt confirms commitment to formal Nov. arms talks after Sept. preparatory talks.

JULY 28. Confidential Pentagon study on allied defense outlays says Canada, Denmark, Japan not doing fair share.

JULY 29. On eve of US-India talks (*see* Middle East: India), US says it will resume uranium shipments. India agrees to forego tests and convert spent fuel for arms.

JULY 31. Weinberger voices regret over 7/30 cuts in West German military outlays; White House and State Department issue formal regrets, rejected by Bonn 8/3.

AUG. 5. General Accounting Office report says US lacks military means to carry out '80 Presidential Directive 59 on countervailing nuclear strategy; says sustained Soviet buildup has changed nuclear balance.

AUG. 6. Reagan orders full neutron bomb production for stockpiling in US without actual European deployment. TASS 8/9 criticism stops short of saying USSR will follow suit.

AUG. 11. Haig in New Orleans speech to Bar Association outlines 4 "pillars" of US foreign policy—economic and military strength; reinvigorated alliances; peaceful progress in developing countries; and cooperation with USSR in exchange for "restraint and reciprocity."

AUG. 13. Reagan in California says US would consult with allies before deploying neutron bomb.

AUG. 18. USSR at UNDC revives 3/78 draft treaty to ban neutron weapons.

AUG. 24. Schmidt says Bonn would accept neutron bombs "under certain conditions" already agreed to in '78.

SEPT. 7. Brezhnev in first remark on neutron bomb says USSR has "proper counterbalance" to any new weapons.

SEPT. 12. In Rome, Schmidt and Prime Minister Giovanni Spadolini call for early US-USSR missile talks; demand US consultation on all defense-economy issues.

SEPT. 13. Haig in West Berlin says data now confirm USSR and allies used lethal chemicals in Asia and Afghanistan.

— Thousands in West Germany protest planned NATO missile deployment.

SEPT. 22. Gromyko at UN General Assembly attacks US policy from Salvador to Afghanistan, says it promotes arms race, warns West on Poland.

— Reagan letter to Brezhnev released in New York hopes 9/23 talks can set "framework of mutual respect."

SEPT. 23. Haig and Gromyko hold 4-hour "frank" meeting in New York; 9/24 statements issued in Moscow and Washington set 11/30 arms talks in Geneva.

SEPT. 28. Haig and Gromyko meet at Soviet Mission; to meet again 1/82.

SEPT. 29. Weinberger releases detailed Pentagon study on *Soviet Military Power.*

OCT. 1. Italy agrees to deploy missiles in Sicily if US-USSR talks fail.

OCT. 9. East and West German public figures issue joint call for US-USSR pullout from both Germanys.

OCT. 10. Over 250,000 at Bonn rally protest US missile plans.

OCT. 16. US Ambassador Arthur A. Hartman arrives in Moscow ending 9-month embassy vacancy.

— Reagan tells editors tactical nuclear exchange would not necessarily mean all-out US-USSR nuclear war. Brezhnev 10/20 asks US to reject idea as Weinberger in Europe tries to calm outraged European reaction.

OCT. 21. Reagan says any threat to Europe is threat to US.

— NATO defense ministers meet in Scotland, reaffirm 2-track approach to arms control.

OCT. 22. Weinberger London speech to Royal Institute of International Affairs warns against appeasement, lack of will.

OCT. 24. Over 150,000 stage anti-nuclear rally in London; 100,000 in Rome protest US missiles in Sicily; thousands march in Paris and Brussels.

OCT. 26. Romanian President Nicolae Ceauşescu calls on USSR to pull out SS-20s and US not to deploy new missiles in Europe.

OCT. 27. USSR submarine runs aground in shallow waters near Swedish naval base; rejoins USSR flotilla 11/6 after Soviet captain submits to Swedish interrogation. Swedish protest that submarine was carrying nuclear weapons, rejected by Moscow 11/11.

Nov. 1. Brezhnev in *Der Spiegel* interview says US sets unrealistic arms talks conditions.

Nov. 3. Brezhnev claims new SS-20s have less destructive power than earlier force of SS-4s and SS-5s; says USSR has kept existing parity since 6/18/79 Vienna treaty. Haig 11/6 disputes remarks.

— Weinberger calls US arms buildup essential prerequisite to 11/30 Euromissile talks.

Nov. 4. Haig says NATO has plan for low-level nuclear warning explosion in case of conventional war; Weinberger 11/5 says no such plan exists. USSR Defense Minister Dmitri F. Ustinov calls Haig statement "serious danger."

Nov. 9. Reagan at news conference repeats 10/16 views on limited nuclear war.

Nov. 11. Greece backs 10/20 Bulgaria plan for Balkan nuclear-free zone; says NATO membership and US bases separate issues.

Nov. 12. Over 100,000 Romanians in peace march call for East-West disarmament.

— France announces plan to modernize nuclear strike force.

Nov. 18. In televised address, Reagan endorses so-called "zero option" which would cancel planned NATO LRTNF missile deployments if Soviets scrap all SS-20, SS-4 and SS-5 missiles. Speech draws broad support in US, West Europe; TASS terms it "propaganda ploy."

Nov. 23-25. Brezhnev and Gromyko visit Bonn. Separate Bonn-Moscow talks set at ambassadors' level.

Nov. 24. Schmidt says Soviets genuinely want arms cuts but doubt US aims; calls both sides' proposals "starting positions," not real basis for accord.

Nov. 27. Over 200,000 stage anti-missile protest in Florence.

Nov. 30-DEC. 17. First round of missile talks held in Geneva with Paul H. Nitze and Yuli A. Kvitsinsky as US and USSR delegation heads, respectively.

DEC. 3-5. Weinberger visits Ankara; U.S.-Turkish joint defense group set up.

DEC. 5. Thousands in Romania stage anti-nuclear protest.

DEC. 8–9. NATO DPC meets in Brussels; Greece blocks communiqué, citing lack of security guarantees against Turks.

DEC. 10. Greek Prime Minister Andreas Papandreou announces curbs on NATO role.

DEC. 10–11. NATO Council meets in Brussels, formally asks Spain to join alliance; special statement backs missile deployment in 2 years if Geneva talks fail.

DEC. 11. Schmidt visits East German leader Erich Honecker for first talks since '70.

DEC. 18. Marked by sharp exchanges over Poland, deadlocked CSCE in Madrid adjourns until 2/9/82.

DEC. 22. Brezhnev, responding to 12/4 NBC-TV questions, says summit meeting with Reagan is best way to revive contacts.

SOVIET UNION AND EASTERN EUROPE

JAN. 1. Poland leaders' New Year's messages warn of economic problems; USSR says Solidarity could become political opposition.

JAN. 5. Solidarity leader Lech Walesa and Deputy Prime Minister Mieczyslaw Jagielski fail to agree on 5-day work week.

JAN. 7. Solidarity defies Party, votes 5-day work week; most factory workers take off Saturday 1/10.

JAN. 10. Party leader Stanislaw Kania warns private farmers on forming union.

JAN. 22. Workers in 10 Poland cities stage warning strikes after talks fail on 5-day work week.

JAN. 24. Millions in Poland heed 1/23 Walesa call for Saturday boycott.

JAN. 26. Polish student sit-ins over curriculum and passports spread; wildcat strikes erupt 1/27 around Poland.

JAN. 29. President Ronald Reagan warns USSR against invading Poland; Secretary of State Alexander M. Haig, Jr. warns of impact on ties in note to Soviet Foreign Minister Andrei A. Gromyko.

JAN. 31. Warsaw and union reach accord on added free Saturdays in '81 and 5-day, 40-hour work week in '82.

FEB. 2. Kania says "instigators" trying to make Solidarity into political opposition group.

FEB. 6. Ten-day Bielsko-Biala strike ends as Warsaw agrees *inter alia* to oust local officials; Church mediates for first time.

FEB. 9. Poland Prime Defense Minister Wojciech Jaruzelski replaces Jozef Pinkowski as Prime Minister; on 2/12 asks "90 days of peace," announces cabinet shakeup, economic program.

FEB. 10. Poland Supreme Court rules against farmers' union.

— US State Department now says USSR move into Poland not "imminent."

FEB. 12. USSR-East German joint military exercises held in East Germany.

FEB. 15. Kania flies to Czechoslovakia, meets with Communist Party leader Gustav Husak; meets with Party chief Erich Honecker 2/27 in East Germany.

FEB. 18. Poland students at Lodz University end 26-day strike; win right to form union and other concessions.

FEB. 20. Farmers in Rzeszow, Poland end government-building sit-ins after accord on farm prices, local administration.

FEB. 23. USSR President Leonid I. Brezhnev addresses opening session of 26th Soviet Communist Party Congress (*see* East-West).

FEB. 24. Kania at Soviet Congress says Poles can resolve their own problems.

FEB. 26. State Department says US will defer repayment of $88-million Polish loan for 4 months.

MAR. 3. Soviet Congress ends; Brezhnev reelected for 5-year term, Nikolai Podgorny and 3 other key Central Committee members out.

MAR. 4. Kania, Jaruzelski meet with Brezhnev, Gromyko; agree defense of Communism concerns entire Soviet bloc.

MAR. 5. US State Department warns of "gravest consequences" should USSR intervene in Poland.

MAR. 10. Lodz workers stage one-hour strike over dismissal of 4 workers; Walesa and Jaruzelski meet in Warsaw.

MAR. 11. Jaruzelski to name government-union commission to investigate physical attacks on union members.

MAR. 18. Warsaw Pact "Soyuz '81" maneuvers open around Poland, led by Pact chief Marshal Victor G. Kulikov instead of host-country defense minister; maneuvers extended 3/26.

MAR. 19. Poland riot police break up 3-day Bydgoszcz farmers' sit-in; 3 die after police beatings. Kania meets with Party chief Janos Kadar in Hungary.

MAR. 20. Strikes erupt in 4 cities over 3/19 police action, Solidarity calls 3/23 national strike alert.

MAR. 23. Poland Politburo emergency session in statement says union takes political actions, blames extremists for spreading unrest.

MAR. 24. European Economic Community (EEC) warns USSR, offers Poland economic aid.

— Union sets warning strike 3/27, general strike 3/31 if 3/25 union talks fail.

MAR. 27. Millions in Poland stage 4-hour protest strike over 3/19 violence after government delays second meeting with unions 3/26. Talks resume; Solidarity calls off strike 3/31 although accord reached 3/30 falls short of union demands.

— US Senate resolution, 96-0, says US cannot "be indifferent" to Soviet intervention.

APR. 1. First large meat rationing since World War II begins in Poland. Butter and grains added to list 4/14; (sugar rationed 3/1).

APR. 2. Jagielski meets with Haig, Vice President George Bush in Washington; Bush announces $70 million surplus-food gift to Poland.

— Pravda criticizes Kania's handling of Poland crisis; repeats attacks 4/3.

APR. 3. US State Department in new warning notes Soviet troop airlift into Legnica in southwest Poland.

APR. 3-6. Yugoslavia troops put down riots by Albanian separatists in Kosovo autonomous province, impose curfew. Official toll at 11 dead, 57 wounded, 22 arrested.

APR. 5. Brezhnev flies to Prague for 16th Czech Communist Party Congress 4/6 as Pravda for 4th day demands crackdown on Poland unions.

APR. 6. Czech party leader Husak in tough speech likens crisis to '68 Soviet intervention, restates Brezhnev Doctrine. Brezhnev speech 4/7 says Poles can solve own problems.

APR. 10. Poland Parliament calls for 2-month strike ban, recognizes importance of union movement.

APR. 11. East German Communist Party Congress opens 6-day meeting; voices qualified support for Poland Communist Party, reelects Honecker 4/16. Poland delegation makes indirect plea for patience 4/12.

APR. 17. Warsaw agrees to farmers' demands to form rural Solidarity as of 5/10.

APR. 23-24. USSR Politburo member Mikhail A. Suslov pays surprise visit to Poland. On 4/25 TASS calls unnamed Poland party members "revisionists."

APR. 24. Reagan ends 15-month USSR grain embargo. Haig says on 4/25 US could reimpose embargo, take other steps if USSR invades Poland.

APR. 29 30. Poland Communist Party Central Committee meets, ousts former Premier Jozef Pinkowski and alternate member Emil Wojaszek; Kania speech asks "socialist renewal," democratic reforms.

MAY 6. Czech ex-Foreign Minister Jiri Hajek, 7 activists arrested; 12 more arrested by 5/8 in ongoing crackdown.

MAY 12. Warsaw court grants legal recognition to Polish farm union, led by Jan Kulaj.

MAY 15. Sergej Krajger succeeds Cvijetin Mijatovic as new Yugoslav president.

MAY 19-20. Nineteen bankers from 11 countries meet in Frankfurt on rescheduling $2.37 billion long-term Poland debt.

MAY 25. Press agency reports former Poland leader Edward Gierek aides Jerzy Olszewski, Edward Barszcz committed suicide.

MAY 28. Stefan Cardinal Wyszynski dies in Warsaw. On 7/7 Pope John Paul II names Bishop Jozef Glemp to succeed him.

JUNE 5. Harsh Soviet letter criticizes Polish leaders for inability to handle crisis.

JUNE 7. Deputy Prime Minister Mieczyslaw Rakowski warns Poland in danger, with allies losing patience.

— Solidarity votes to go ahead with 6/9 warning strike in 4 cities over delay in punishment of aides responsible for 3/19 violence. On 6/9 union asks workers to delay strike.

JUNE 9. Bulgaria State Council President Todor Zhivkov reelected 6/9. Prime Minister Stanko Todorov replaced 6/16 by Central Committee Secretary Grisha Filipov, who is elected head of new Parliament.

JUNE 11. State Department charges USSR meddling in Poland; East German press refers to Kania without his title in letter published by USSR 6/5.

JUNE 12. Jaruzelski shuffles Cabinet, replaces 5 Ministers, orders crackdown on anti-Soviet and anti-Warsaw actions, stresses serious economic situation.

June 24–25. Bankers meeting in Paris reach compromise on deferring $2.37-billion Poland debt.

July 2. Harsh Czech letter to Poles says counterrevolutionaries taking over Party, advises 7/14 Congress be delayed.

July 2–4. Council for Mutual Economic Assistance meets in Sofia, Bulgaria; no aid offered to Poland.

July 3. Jaruzelski dismisses 8 Ministers, all but one involved in economy.

July 3–5. Gromyko visits Warsaw. Joint communiqué in effect restates Brezhnev Doctrine.

July 8. Some 40,000 Poland dock workers in 3 Baltic cities strike briefly for more pay, better conditions. On 7/9 6,000 LOT airline workers strike for 4 hours to keep manager they elected. Walesa condemns both strikes.

July 13. Middle-rank USSR delegation, led by Moscow city leader Viktor V. Grishin, to attend 7/14 Poland Party Congress.

July 14–20. Extraordinary Polish Communist Party Congress held in Warsaw; ousts former party leader Edward Gierek and 6 associates; elects 200 Central Committee members by secret ballot; reelects Kania in secret ballot; hears Jaruzelski announce wage freeze and 110% price rises; adopts 2-year term limit for party leaders.

July 24. Monthly 7.7-pound meat ration in Poland cut by 20%; thousands stage hunger protests 7/27 in Kutno and Lodz.

July 28. US announces new long-term $50-million loan to Poland for 350,000 tons of corn.

July 30. Solidarity leaders meet in Gdansk on growing food protests.

July 31. Jagielski replaced by Labor Minister Janusz Obodowski; 2 more generals named to Cabinet.

Aug. 1. In first statement since end of Party Congress, Poland Politburo warns Solidarity of explosion, says "no hunger in Poland." Jaruzelski meets with army chiefs 8/2.

Aug. 7. Harshest Warsaw attack yet calls union arrogant as thousands of Silesia miners/industry workers stage 4-hour strike.

Aug. 8. Kulikov said to meet with Jaruzelski without Kania.

Aug. 11. Krosno 8/9 protest eases as Poland Trade Union Minister Stanislaw Cjosek arrives in Gdansk for talks.

Aug. 11–12. New Poland Central Committee meets, hears Kania warn of national tragedy, asks union to end food protests.

— Solidarity asks end of food protests until its Oct. convention, urges workers to give up 8 free Saturdays

Aug. 12. Joint Poland-East Germany maneuvers in northwest Poland begun 8/10 are extended. TASS 8/13 announces Sept. maneuvers in Byelorussia.

Aug. 14. Kania, Jaruzelski hold one-day meeting with Brezhnev in Crimea; 8/15 conciliatory communiqué pledges more economic aid.

Aug. 18–20. Poland printers strike over access to media.

Aug. 23. USSR on front page of press warns East bloc to hold to Communist line faithfully and sharply cautions against "excessive debt" to West.

Aug. 28. US-Poland accord signed; defers $380.9-million Poland debt for 5–8 years.

— Yugoslav press reports first Albanian purge in 6 years under way.

Aug. 29–30. Warsaw-union talks held on access to media.

Sept. 5–10. Solidarity holds part 1 of first national convention in Gdansk, hears Walesa plead for unity (9/5); asks referendum on factory control, sends message of support to East bloc workers if they create union (9/8); calls for free parliament elections, eased passport rules (9/10).

Sept. 12. Haig visits President Krajger, backs Yugoslav independence.

Sept. 16. Tough Warsaw statement says Solidarity broke '80 accords.

Sept. 18. Warsaw releases harsh 9/17 Soviet letter calling for crackdown, warns of danger to Polish state; US State Department says letter constitutes meddling.

Sept. 21. Letter from Soviet workers to Polish workers invokes Warsaw Pact obligations to defend socialist system; *Pravda* prints reminder of '56 Hungary and '68 Czech crises.

Sept. 23. Belgrade backs Solidarity, says USSR interferes.

Sept. 24. Jaruzelski announces crackdown on anti-USSR actions in Poland.

Sept. 26–Oct. 7. Solidarity convention, part 2, held; reelects Walesa for 2-year term (10/2); adopts 2-year economic plan, threatens strike over price rises (10/7).

Oct. 13. Wildcat strikes erupt in 3 Poland cities over food shortages; some 12,000 textile workers occupy mill.

— Warsaw party calls Kania "submissive."

OCT. 16. Kania asks strike suspension through winter; proposes that National Unity Front include all sides.

OCT. 18. Kania (named 9/6/80) resigns, Jaruzelski assumes post; Central Committee resolution asks renegotiation of '80 accords.

OCT. 20. Poland police fight 5,000 Katowice protesters angry over arrest of 3 activists. By 10/22 strikes and strike threats spread to 28 provinces.

OCT. 23. Warsaw announces army deployment in small units to help resolve "local disputes" as of 10/26.

OCT. 28. Millions of Poles stage 1-hour strike; Jaruzelski backs USSR positions.

OCT. 30. Solidarity asks end to "uncontrolled" strikes; on 10/31 parliament asks immediate strike halt.

NOV. 1–7. Albania 8th Party Congress held, discusses Kosovo unrest, reelects Party leader Enver Hoxha (in power since World War II).

NOV. 4. Jaruzelski, Walesa, Glemp meet for first time; agree on forming body to end crisis.

NOV. 6. US-Czech accord signed in Prague on return to Czechs of 18.4 tons of gold seized by Nazis in return for settlement of $81.5 million in claims by Americans.

NOV. 12. Over 200,000 Poles end 22-day wildcat strikes; 190,000 students strike nationwide in sympathy with student protest in Radom over choice of dean.

NOV. 16. Brezhnev report says food output, distribution biggest Soviet problem. Supreme Soviet approves 11th USSR 5-year plan 11/17.

NOV. 17. Warsaw, Solidarity open first negotiations since 8/29; set agenda 11/18.

NOV. 19. Poland army announces 11/20 pullback of troops deployed 10/26.

NOV. 21. US scientists urge Brezhnev to avert hunger strike begun 11/22 by Nobel peace laureate Andrei Sakharov and wife over refusal to let stepson's fiancé join him in US. Exit visa granted, strike ended 12/8; stepson and fiancé reunited in US 12/20.

NOV. 24. Kulikov and Gribkov meet with Jaruzelski in Warsaw.

NOV. 27–28. Poland Central Committee meeting backs "extraordinary" steps to ban strikes, curbs press and other rights.

DEC. 2. Police backed by army break up sit-in, begun 11/25, at Warsaw fire cadets' academy. On 12/6 Solidarity votes day of protest 12/17 over assault.

DEC. 4. Poland and Western banks agree on $2.4 billion debt rescheduling.

DEC. 8. Catholic Church discloses Glemp appeal to both sides to resume dialogue.

DEC. 10. Walesa at start of union meeting in Gdansk says Solidarity cannot "retreat any longer." TASS says Poland crisis directly affects Soviet security, condemns Church role.

DEC. 12. Solidarity leadership, discussing new series of demands including free national elections, union access to media and joint party-union control of economy, calls for referendum on future of Poland's socialist government if demands are not met.

DEC. 13. Jaruzelski declares state of martial law in Poland, suspending civil rights, union operations, and announcing formation of new Military Council for National Salvation. Union extremists, Gierek, 26 other former leaders arrested; Walesa flown to Warsaw.

DEC. 14. Widespread strikes crushed in major Poland cities as US suspends all pending aid. TASS calls events an "internal matter."

— White House warns of "grave" results if repression continues.

— EEC ends 2-day London meeting, warns USSR not to interfere in Poland.

DEC. 16. Poland asks foreign banks for further $350 million loan to repay $500 million in overdue interest by 12/31; request refused after Zurich meeting 12/21–12/22.

— Reagan says Poland unions suppressed with full Soviet knowledge, warns against direct Soviet intervention.

— Warsaw sources report 12/11 Kulikov visit to Warsaw.

DEC. 18. Albania Prime Minister Mehmet Shehu (in office since '54) commits suicide.

DEC. 19. Rakowski, head of suspended Poland Trade Unions Committee, named head of new Socio-Political Committee.

— Poland Ambassador to US Romuald Spasowski requests US asylum.

DEC. 20. US says it will hold USSR responsible for any "excesses" in Poland. USSR denies role 12/21.

DEC. 21. Warsaw reports 2,800 coal miners on strike since 12/15, reject appeals to end protest.

DEC. 21–27. Papal delegate Archbishop Luigi Poggi visits Warsaw.

DEC. 22. Pope meets with Polish Msgr. Bronislaw Dabrowski, says he backs all workers.

DEC. 23. Reagan in television address outlines aviation, fishing and credit curbs against Poland; in letter to Jaruzelski he warns of high cost of "crime." Also announces he wrote

Brezhnev warning of concrete anti-Soviet steps if crackdown in Poland continues.

— EEC joint statement, delivered to Poles 12/22, condemns human, civil rights violations.

Dec. 24. Jaruzelski, in conciliatory speech, says martial law lesser of 2 evils and independent union still possible.

— Polish Ambassador to Japan Zdzislaw Rurarz defects 12/23, flies to US; in 12/28 testimony to Congress he says martial law planned since Mar. under Soviet pressure.

— Haig cites importance of joint allied pressure in easing Poland situation.

Dec. 25. Solidarity secretly urges continued protests to pressure reported Church-Party talks.

— Pope, in departure from Christmas message text, asks future liberty for Poles.

Dec. 30. Jaruzelski sets up 3 groups to plan Poland political, economic, social reforms; promises shorter work week, lifts curfew 12/31.

— Pope, in strongest statement yet, fears for fate of those arrested.

— US says USSR jamming Voice of America broadcasts.

— Rakowski visits Bonn; Schmidt in Florida says US sanctions against USSR "will not change the world."

MIDDLE EAST AND SOUTH ASIA

GENERAL

Jan. 19. Defense Department approves $2-billion Saudi arms deal.

Feb. 16. State Department announces North Yemen freed 2 Americans 2/8, held as Israeli spies for a year.

Feb. 18. Saudis in goodwill move release 21 jailed Americans.

Feb. 23. Conservatives defeat radical nationalists in Kuwait national elections; new Cabinet named 3/4.

Mar. 6. US says it will sell Saudis equipment to upgrade F-15 warplanes.

Mar. 19. Secretary of State Alexander M. Haig in Senate testimony says US seeks "consensus of strategic concerns" to counter USSR in the region.

Mar. 21. Jordan's King Hussein says Syria President Hafez al-Assad involving Middle East in East-West rivalries, attacks Syria role in Lebanon.

Apr. 21. White House announces it will sell Saudis 5 Airborne Warning and Control System (AWACS) aircraft (see Middle East: Arab-Israeli Conflict).

Apr. 24. Defense Secretary Caspar Weinberger announces new Persian Gulf command with unified Rapid Deployment Force (RDF) to protect oil fields.

May 9. Nepal holds first parliamentary elections in 20 years for 111-seat assembly.

May 25–26. Persian Gulf heads of state meet in Abu Dhabi, initial Gulf Cooperation Council charter on development and security.

May 30. Bangladesh President Ziaur Rahman, 2 aides, several bodyguards slain in Chittagong by rebel soldiers led by Maj. Gen. Mohammed Abdul Manzur; Vice President Abdus Sattar becomes Acting President.

May 31. Rebellion crushed; Manzur, 2 others killed; 20 army officers arrested 6/2.

June 6. United Arab Emirates (UAE) President Sheikh Zayed bin Sultan al-Nahiyan says RDF, not USSR, threatens Gulf.

June 7. US and Egypt sign $2-billion accord for 2 nuclear plants.

Aug. 17. Sri Lanka declares emergency in 10-day-old ethnic riots.

Aug. 17–19. Presidents Muammar al-Qaddafi (Libya), Mengistu Haile Mariam (Ethiopia), Ali Nasser Mohammed (South Yemen) meet in Aden, sign cooperation treaty.

Sept. 3–4. Over 1,000 Sadat critics, including journalist Mohammed Hassanein Heikel, arrested in crackdown on Cairo mosques.

Sept. 5. Sadat speech to Parliament says extremist Islamic groups to be dissolved and Coptic Pope Shenuda III deposed.

Sept. 7. Cairo to supervise 40,000 Mosques, appoint clerics. Referendum 9/10 backs Sadat 99.45%.

Sept. 15. Sadat expels Soviet ambassador, 6 aides and 1,000 other Russians for subversion. USSR retaliates in kind 9/17.

Oct. 6. Sadat assassinated during military parade marking '73 Israeli war; 11 other officials reported dead, 38 wounded including 3 US military officers. Four to 8 Moslem fanatics led by Maj. Ahmed Hassan el-Istanbuli arrested.

Oct. 7. Egyptian Vice President Hosni Mubarak named President and Prime Minister pending 10/13 referendum; Haig warns Libya, USSR not to interfere.

Oct. 10. Former US Presidents Nixon, Ford, Carter join US delegation to Sadat funeral.

Oct. 11. Haig meets with Mubarak, pledges US arms delivery speedup; meets with Begin.

Oct. 13. Mubarak confirmed in referendum, sworn in 10/14.

Oct. 14. US sends 2 AWACS planes to Egypt as precautionary measure; planes returned to U.S. 10/28.

Oct. 16. Mubarak orders nationwide roundup of Moslem extremists; 230 in "terrorist religious group" arrested 10/18; 350 more seized 10/24.

Oct. 19. Mubarak blames "limited net" of "fanatics" for Sadat murder.

Nov. 3. Cairo says all leaders in Sadat murder arrested.

Nov. 7. UAE unanimously reelects al-Nahiyan President for second 5-year term.

Nov. 8. Mubarak in first address backs improved living standards, nonalignment, and Camp David accords.

Nov. 9. Syria elects new 4-year People's Council; ruling Baath Socialists win 60% of seats, Communists lose all 8 previously held.

Nov. 10. Madagascar reports calm restored in Tananarive after 2-day civil riots.

Nov. 15. Bangladesh President Sattar defeats Awami League candidate Kamal Hossein with 66% of vote.

— RDF opens exercises in Egypt, Sudan, Somalia, Oman.

Nov. 21. Trial of 24 indicted for Sadat murder opens in Cairo.

Nov. 25. Mubarak frees Heikal and 30 others arrested in Sept.

— Arab League summit meets in Fez, Morocco (see Middle East: Arab-Israeli Conflict).

Dec. 2. North and South Yemen sign cooperation pact in Aden.

Dec. 12. Cairo frees former Premier Mohammed Abdel Salam el-Zayyat and 16 others held since August; arrests over 2,000 extremists in 12/20 crackdown.

Dec. 16. Saudi Arabia and Bahrain announce arrest of 60 Arabs in Iran-backed plot to bring down conservative Gulf governments.

Dec. 17. RDF chief Lt. Gen. Robert C. Kingston says US holding regional talks to set up forward headquarters.

Dec. 20. Saudi-Bahrain security pact signed; Iran accused of "exporting terrorism."

Arab-Israeli Conflict

Jan. 22. Arab League Council extends mandate of Arab Deterrent Force in Lebanon 6 months.

Jan. 26. Israel Knesset Foreign Affairs Committee approves 3 of 10 projected West Bank settlements.

Jan. 29. Israel attacks Palestine camps from Sidon-Tyre to Nabatiye after 1/28 rocket attacks on north Israeli towns.

Feb. 2. President Ronald Reagan says settlements "not illegal," Palestine Liberation Organization (PLO) must be part of peace process despite use of "terrorism."

Feb. 8. Egypt President Anwar el-Sadat in letter to Israel Prime Minister Menachem Begin backs Camp David accords, and opposes 6/80 West European initiative for comprehensive peace conference.

Feb. 10. Sadat at European Parliament in Luxembourg sees Europe's initiative as complement to US efforts.

Feb. 15. Jordan King Hussein in London rejects role in autonomy talks, backs European plan.

Feb. 20. Israel Foreign Minister Yitzhak Shamir visits Washington, urges autonomy talks before 6/30.

Feb. 23. Egypt Vice President Hosni Mubarak says US and Egypt agreed to delay autonomy talks.

Mar. 6. State Department says US will sell Saudis equipment to enhance combat capability of 62 F-15 warplanes.

Mar. 26. Lebanon Prime Minister Shafiq al-Wazzan announces 600 more Lebanese troops have joined UN Interim Force in Lebanon (UNIFIL).

— Muslim-Christian factions end 16-hour Beirut bombing after truce called by Syria.

Apr. 2. Worst Muslim-Christian violence since '76 cease-fire erupts in Beirut; Syrian-Christian violence in Zahle in Bekka Valley results in some 37 killed, 160 injured. Two brief truces in Zahle break down 4/4.

Apr. 4-8. US Secretary of State Alexander Haig in first Middle East trip visits Egypt (4/4-4/5), Israel (4/5-4/6), Jordan (4/6-4/7) and Saudi Arabia (4/7-4/8).

APR. 8. Lebanon President Elias Sarkis arranges 18th Zahle truce since 4/2, meets with UN official Brian Urquhart, US Under Secretary of State Morris Draper.

APR. 14. Israel for first time discloses aid to Christians in Lebanon.

APR. 15. Lebanon Christians offer talks on "equal basis" but insist on Syria departure.

APR. 16. Phalangist leader Bashir Gemayel criticizes 4/15 Reagan letter to Syria President Hafez al-Assad calling for peace, admits Israeli arms aid.

— Israeli jets strike Tyre, Sidon bases, shell PLO bases in south.

APR. 19. Palestine National Council ends 9-day Damascus meeting; decides to raise political pressure on US.

APR. 21. White House formally announces Saudi arms deal including 5 Airborne Warning and Control System (AWACS) planes. On 4/22 White House and State Department stress firm commitment to Israel as Begin officially voices opposition to sale.

APR. 25. Zahle 4/24 cease-fire broken as Syria resumes artillery and air attacks.

APR. 27. Israel jets bomb southern Lebanon second day; Syria reports capture of peaks around Bekka.

APR. 28–29. Syria Foreign Minister Abdel Halim Khaddam meets with Christian leaders in Beirut.

APR. 29. Syria moves SAM missiles into Bekka Valley; Israel reports 6 more missiles on 4/30.

APR. 29–30. West German Chancellor Helmut Schmidt visits Saudi Arabia, rules out arms sales for now.

MAY 3. Israel threatens military action unless Syria removes missiles by 5/5.

— Khaddam meets with rival factions in Syria; US and USSR urge Israel-Syria calm.

MAY 4. Reagan note to Begin asks Israeli restraint.

MAY 5. Reagan announces former Assistant Secretary of State Philip C. Habib will go to Middle East.

MAY 8. Syria formally rejects Israeli demands to remove missiles; US and Israeli aides in Washington report Begin 5/5 agreement to delay military action.

MAY 11. Begin reports more Syria missiles moved into Lebanon and on borders, some manned by Libyans.

MAY 13. Habib arrives Beirut with compromise plan. Haig 5/14 says Assad agreed to discuss pullout from peaks around Zahle.

MAY 16–18. Habib in Riyadh seeks Saudi aid on peace plan.

MAY 17. Israeli Cabinet votes to give more time to Habib effort.

MAY 18. State Department reports constructive Saudi role in Habib effort; Begin rejects Saudi role, calls Saudi regime "most corrupt" in world.

MAY 19. Two Beirut newspapers report "modified" Habib plan backed by Saudis.

MAY 20. Egyptian Foreign Minister Kamal Hassan Ali says Sinai troop accord reached in principle; force will be headed by US civilian.

MAY 21. Begin widens terms to include removal of missiles from Syrian territory bordering on Lebanon.

— UN Security Council (UNSC) Resolution 485 (1981) renews UN Disengagement Observer force mandate to 11/30, 14-0-0, with China not participating.

MAY 24. Begin office discloses 8/78 secret pledge (renewed 4/8/81) to defend Christians against Syria air attacks,

MAY 26. Arab League foreign ministers, meeting in Tunis, in 12-point resolution back Syria; form Arab follow-up committee on Lebanon (Kuwait, Lebanon, Saudi Arabia, Syria).

— King Hussein arrives in USSR on first visit in 5 years; backs Mideast conference.

MAY 26–28. Egypt, Israel, US meet in Cairo on Sinai force.

MAY 27. Habib recalled to US.

— Saudis send envoy to Beirut after 2-year absence.

MAY 28. Israeli jets destroy Libya SAM-9 missiles at Damur.

MAY 29. Habib tells Reagan negotiated peace is "achievable."

— PLO leader Yasir Arafat 5/28 remarks released; admit Libya troops fighting alongside PLO since '72.

JUNE 1–5. Islamic Conference Organization meets in Baghdad, calls for Lebanon cease-fire.

JUNE 2–3. Israeli jets strike PLO targets near Tyre and Tripoli. Israel confirms preemptive strikes resumed 5/28.

JUNE 4. Begin and Sadat meet for first time in 18 months at Sharm el-Sheikh in Sinai.

JUNE 6. Thirtieth Beirut cease-fire in 9 weeks broken.

JUNE 7–8. Follow-up committee meets in Beit Ed Din, Lebanon. Syria said to insist on public Christian disavowal of Israeli ties.

JUNE 8. Israel announces its F-15, F-16 jets in 6/7 raid destroyed French-made Iraq reactor,

Osirak; says attack necessary to prevent Iraq production of nuclear bomb. US State Department delays Habib mission.

JUNE 9. Habib opens second round of talks in Beirut.

JUNE 10. US postpones 11/12 delivery of 4 F-16's pending review of possible Israel violation of '52 Arms Export Control Act limiting use of US equipment for self-defense.

JUNE 11. Arab League and PLO meet in Damascus; ask UN sanctions against Israel.

JUNE 12–19. UNSC emergency session unanimously backs US-Iraq draft resolution condemning 6/7 Israel raid on Iraq reactor.

JUNE 18. Begin sees Habib, agrees to give mission more time.

JUNE 23. Iraq President Saddam Hussein cites 6/7 raid, asserts Arabs need nuclear arms.

JUNE 23–25. Special Arab follow-up committee on Lebanon meets in Jidda.

JUNE 24. Bipartisan group of 54 senators in letter to Reagan says AWACS sale not in US best interest; 224 in House sign resolution against sale.

JUNE 25. US announces tripartite preliminary accord on Sinai force.

— Habib ends 2nd round of talks, says immediate war danger receded.

JUNE 30. Syria ends 91-day Zahle siege under accord arranged by follow-up committee. Lebanese police replace Christian militias 7/2.

— France in policy shift backs Camp David accords.

— Israel holds election for 120-seat Knesset. Official returns 7/9 give Begin Likud coalition 48 seats, Labor Party 47, religious and right-wing parties 16.

JULY 4–5. Arab special follow-up committee meets in Beirut.

JULY 6. State Department says Habib goal still to keep Israel from attacking Syria missiles.

JULY 7. Gemayel says letter to Sarkis offers to swap Israeli aid for Arab Deterrent Force pullout.

JULY 9. Habib opens 3rd round of talks.

JULY 10. Israel F-15's strike southern Lebanon first time since 6/2 lull; PLO shells Israeli border towns.

JULY 12. Israel strikes southern Lebanon targets again as Habib meets with Begin in Jerusalem.

JULY 15. Syria rules out missile compromise as Habib arrives in Damascus.

JULY 16. Saudis announce they will pay full repair cost of Iraq reactor.

JULY 17. Israeli jets bomb PLO targets in Beirut; 300 die, 800 injured.

— UNSC emergency session voices concern over casualties.

JULY 19. Haig links F-16 delivery to Israeli help in reducing tensions.

JULY 20. Ottawa summit statement deplores escalation, calls for restraint by all sides.

— Reagan suspends delivery of 10 more F-16s indefinitely.

JULY 21. Begin rejects 7/20 Haig letter asking cease-fire; rejects talks with PLO except through Habib contact with Beirut.

— UNSC resolution unanimously calls for cease-fire.

JULY 22. PLO reports 2 major Israeli attacks near Beaufort Castle and Zahrani oil refinery; 4 Israeli raids on 2 bridges kill at least 50.

— Defense Secretary Caspar Weinberger criticizes Begin's military actions; White House and State Department on 7/23 stress even-handed US calls for restraint.

JULY 23. Secretary General Kurt Waldheim reports Arafat ordered "maximum" PLO restraint; UNIFIL tells Israeli defense aide Arafat agreed to cease-fire.

JULY 24. Habib announces Israel agreement to end raids if PLO ends Lebanon buildup. PLO in later statement accepts cease-fire.

JULY 25–26. Follow-up committee meets in Lebanon; confirms Gemayel agreed not to deal with Israel.

JULY 27. Weinberger links F-16 deliveries to continuing cease-fire and Mideast settlement.

JULY 29. Israel jets down Syria MiG that tried to intercept them. Israel resumes reconnaissance flights over Lebanon 8/2.

AUG. 3. In State Department ceremony Egypt and Israel sign accord on 2,500-member Sinai "Multinational Force and Observers" (MFO).

AUG. 5–6. Sadat visits Washington, asks US-PLO talks.

AUG. 7. Saudi Prince Fahd offers 8-point peace plan that recognizes Israeli right to exist. Israel rejects plan 8/9.

AUG. 16. Begin rejects Fahd plan; Arafat says it could lead to peace.

AUG. 17. Haig announces end of 10-week F-16 delivery ban.

AUG. 22. Follow-up committee meets with Saudis on 9/3.

— US aides say long-range Saudi need for US technical support allows control over AWACS.

AUG. 24. AWACS $8.5 billion arms deal formally sent to Congress; Under Secretary of State for Security Affairs James Buckley reaffirms US commitment to Israel security. *The New York Times* 8/30 says key systems to be excluded.

Aug. 25–26. Begin and Sadat meet in Alexandria, agree to resume autonomy talks 9/23.

Aug. 27. Begin regrets 7/17 Beirut civilian deaths, which he puts at 60-80, not 300.

Aug. 29. PLO denounces terrorist attack on Vienna synagogue.

Sept. 4. French Ambassador Louis Delamare slain in Beirut; Arafat and Gemayel deplore "crime."

Sept. 9–10. Begin meets with Reagan; agree on strategic cooperation through joint maneuvers, US medical stockpiling in Israel, joint security planning.

Sept. 12. Haig meets with Fahd in Spain. Unnamed Saudi aide strongly denies reports Fahd did not object to Israel-US deal.

— Follow-up committee negotiates open passage across Beirut "Green Line." PLO shifts 2 armored units to south Lebanon.

Sept. 15–18. Israel and Egypt hold technical talks in West Jerusalem.

Sept. 18–20. Arab Steadfastness and Confrontation Front (Algeria, Libya, South Yemen, Syria, PLO) meets in Libya on strategy to offset US-Israel 9/10 accord.

Sept. 23–24. Palestine autonomy talks held in Cairo.

Sept. 25. Saudis reject joint US-Saudi control of AWACS.

Sept. 28. Weinberger says AWACS sale will promote "strategic consensus" in Southwest Asia.

Oct. 1. Reagan at news parley says US would not allow Iran-type Saudi takeover, implicitly criticizes Israel.

Oct. 2. Haig meets Saud in New York. State Department later reaffirms Haig 10/1 view that lack of qualified personnel will require US presence on AWACS.

Oct. 3. Mubarak meets with Haig in New York.

Oct. 4. Israel approves replacement 11/1 of middle-rank military aides with civilians in West Bank, Gaza.

Oct. 5. Shamir speech to Foreign Policy Association dismisses Fahd peace plan.

Oct. 6. Sadat assassinated (*see* Middle East: General).

— Mubarak after Sadat murder says Cairo stands by its commitment, (*see* Middle East: General); Haig on 10/7 backs ongoing strong Cairo role in autonomy talks.

Oct. 9. Begin in Cairo for 10/10 Sadat funeral meets with Mubarak; meets with Haig 10/11.

Oct. 12–15. Arafat visits Japan at Japan's invitation.

Oct. 14. House, 301-111, rejects AWACS sale; Senate Foreign Relations Committee, 9-8, rejects it. Senate debate put off to 10/26.

Oct. 16. Former Israeli Defense and Foreign Minister Moshe Dayan dies.

Oct. 17. Reagan tells editors US backs Saudis to prevent Iran-type takeover; says AWACS deal vital to US "credibility."

Oct. 20. State Department announces European Economic Community (EEC) agreement in principle to join MFO.

— Brezhnev announces full diplomatic status for PLO mission.

Oct. 25–27. Egypt Foreign Minister Ali visits Israel.

Oct. 26. Joint State-Defense 10-part statement says US has commitments but no formal treaties with some Mideast states, calls AWACS deal a "commitment."

Oct. 27. Brezhnev revives '77 Mideast conference plan, widens it to include Europe and other nations.

Oct. 28. Reagan letter to Senate "certifies" Saudi accord not to use planes against Israel.

— Senate 52-48, approves AWACS sale.

Oct. 29. Begin says sale "serious danger," avoids condemning US; Cairo calls it "turning point" in US policy. Arafat says it allows for Arab-Israel "coexistence."

Nov. 1. Begin asks US to reject plan as "obstacle" to "Camp David process." Fahd on 11/2 calls Camp David a "dead end."

Nov. 2. Leftist-PLO disarmament accord reached in West Beirut.

— Over 2,000 West Bank students battle Israel troops in 6 towns to protest 11/1 civil rule and mark '64 Balfour Declaration; university closed 11/4.

Nov. 2–3. King Hussein visits Washington. On 11/4 confirms purchase of USSR air defense equipment.

Nov. 3–5. British Foreign Secretary Lord Carrington visits Riyadh, praises Saudi plan. Haig protests remarks to British Embassy.

Nov. 7–8. Follow-up committees meets in Beirut, sets multi-Arab patrol on arms flows, renews cease-fire call.

Nov. 8. Begin says any nation backing EEC '80 Venice Declaration cannot join MFO.

Nov. 9. Israeli Defense Minister Ariel Sharon threatens military action against Syrian missiles.

— Saudis report chasing Israeli jets out of their airspace; Sharon, 11/12, says air patrols will continue.

Nov. 10. Reagan at news conference renews praise for Fahd plan.

Nov. 11–12. Cabinet-level autonomy talks held in Cairo.

— Weinberger in New York says US insists on formal recognition of Israel's right to exist.

Nov. 22–24. Arab League foreign ministers meet in Morocco. Summit 11/29 deadlocks, breaks up in 4 hours over Saudi plan.

Nov. 23. Britain, France, Italy, Netherlands issue statements jointly, individually and with 6 EEC colleagues on decision to join MFO.

Nov. 28. Haig says Israeli Sinai pullout certain, only force makeup in doubt.

Nov. 29–Dec. 11. Habib undertakes 4th round of "shuttle diplomacy."

Nov. 30. Sharon and Weinberger sign strategic cooperation memorandum of understanding in Washington. US on 12/2 denies Sharon remarks that accord has secret annex giving Israel benefits.

Dec. 3. US-Israel joint statement reaffirms Camp David accords as only basis for peace and Sinai MFO.

Dec. 14. Knesset backs Begin bill, 63-21, to annex Golan Heights; Syria says move is "declaration of war."

Dec. 15. Haig summons Israel Ambassador Ephraim Evron as Weinberger calls Golan annexation "provocative."

Dec. 17. UNSC calls Golan move illegal, threatens sanctions (unanimous).

— UN General Assembly, 94-16 (US)-18, condemns move, asks end of all aid to Israel.

Dec. 18. US suspends 11/30 strategic pact, pending $200-million yearly Israel arms sales to US area forces.

Dec. 20. Begin tells US Ambassador Samuel Lewis that US treats Israel like a "vassal state"; calls suspension tantamount to cancellation.

Dec. 22–23. Assad visits King Faisal, gets full Saudi support.

Dec. 23. Fahd delays indefinitely 1/19 U.S. visit.

— Shamir defends Begin, hopes for restored trust as Knesset defeats no-confidence motion, 57-47.

Dec. 25. Sharon says 11/30 pact still in force; annexation prompted by U.S. plan to force return of all occupied lands.

IRAN AND IRAQ

Jan 3. Algerian intermediaries present latest US hostage proposal to Tehran.

Jan. 6. Iran Premier Mohammed Ali Rajai says Ayatollah Ruhollah Khomeini accepts Algerian offer to act as guarantor of hostage accord.

Jan. 7. US Deputy Secretary of State Warren M. Christopher flies to Algiers, meets with Foreign Minister Ben Yahia as US President-elect Ronald Reagan gives qualified support to accord.

Jan. 9. Christopher reports continuing problems over frozen assets, extends visit; extends it again on 1/10.

Jan. 14. Majlis (Iranian parliament) approves bill authorizing Tehran to conduct binding assets negotiations with US.

Jan. 14–17. UN mediator Olof Palme (Sweden) visits Iraq and Iran on second peace mission.

Jan. 15. Executive Affairs Minister Bahzad Nabavi accepts US terms as Iran informal reply outlines "substantive" response to US position.

Jan. 16. Iran says "no obstacles" remain to hostage release. British, US financial and legal experts meet with US-Algerian team in Algiers.

Jan. 17. Iraq President Saddam Hussein says Iran counteroffensive "crushed"; Rajai claims war created 1.5 million Iran refugees.

Jan. 18. US agrees to transfer $6 billion through Bank of England; Iran agrees to repay all US bank loans immediately.

Jan. 19. Christopher signs accords outlining US-Iran commitments and claims settlement procedures.

Jan. 20. Fifty-two hostages leave Iran for Algeria after 444 days of captivity, are transferred to US custody in Algiers and flown to US military hospital in Wiesbaden, Germany; greeted there 1/21 by former President Jimmy Carter, other top US officials.

Jan. 21. Iran President Abolhassan Bani-Sadr under new attack as Iran leaders clash over handling of hostage talks.

Jan. 22. Reagan says US will fully carry out terms of hostage accords.

Jan. 26. Iran Majlis endorses hostage accords.

Jan. 29. Taif Islam conference (see Middle East: General) calls for Iran-Iraq cease-fire, forms mediation committee. Khomeini rejects offer 1/28, urges fight until victory.

Feb. 2. Iran announces major offensive against Iraq and Kurdish rebels in Kurdistan and Azerbaijan.

Feb. 9. Pakistan Foreign Minister Agha Shahi says Iran and Iraq agree to accept Islamic peace mission.

Feb. 18–21. Palme visits Iraq and Iran on 3rd mission.

Feb. 24. Reagan signs order suspending lawsuits against Iran; Treasury Department issues rules for transfer of $2 billion in assets to Federal Reserve Bank.

Feb. 28–Mar. 5. Islamic peace mission led by Guinea President Sékou Touré visits Iran, Kuwait, Iraq; call for cease-fire rejected by Iran 3/6 and by Iraq 3/11.

Mar. 6. Bani-Sadr backers and opponents clash in Tehran; 45 injured. On 3/8 Majlis member Ayatollah Sadegh Khalkhali asks Bani-Sadr trial; protests banned.

Apr. 1. On 2nd anniversary of Islamic Republic Khomeini calls for purge of Revolutionary Guards and judiciary.

Apr. 8. Nonaligned peace group arrives in Iraq.

Apr. 21. Iraq-USSR technical-economic aid pact signed in Baghdad.

June 8. Khomeini attacks Bani-Sadr as backers stage protest over 6/7 ban on Bani-Sadr newspaper. On 6/10 Bani-Sadr loses army post; Central Bank Chief Ali Riza Nobali, his last ranking aide, also dismissed.

June 11. Tehran rallies ask Bani-Sadr trial, execution. Bani-Sadr says 6/12 coup under way to oust him; reported in hiding on 6/13.

— Over 3,000 Iranians die in Kerman earthquake.

June 20. Nationwide protests erupt; 19 killed, 200 injured, 30 arrested in Tehran as Majlis opens formal Bani-Sadr impeachment session. Arrest of Bani-Sadr ordered 6/21.

June 22. Bani-Sadr stripped of powers, 3-man Presidential Council (Rajai, Majlis Speaker Hashemi Rafsanjani, Chief Justice Mohammed Beheshti) named to rule until 7/24 election.

June 28. Bomb explosion at Islamic party headquarters kills Beheshti; 20 Majlis and 10 Cabinet members are among 72 dead, Rajai and Nabavi wounded.

July 2. US Supreme Court, 9–0, rules US-Iran assets accord legal.

July 16. Some 200 Iran leftists arrested in rising political violence; death toll since 6/20 reaches 200.

July 24. Iran presidential elections held; Rajai declared winner 7/27 with over 80% of 14 million votes cast.

July 29. Bani-Sadr and Mujahedeen leader Massoud Rajavi flee Iran in hijacked air force plane; arrive Paris 7/30, granted asylum.

July 30–31. Thousands protest Bani-Sadr asylum at French Embassy in Tehran. Paris on 8/5 urges French citizens to leave Iran, recalls Ambassador Guy Georgy; Iran bars, then allows, departure after 4-day delay.

Aug. 13. Three gunboats in delivery from France to Iran hijacked by pro-Shah group; hijackers surrender 8/19, granted French asylum 8/20.

Aug. 30. Rajai, 8 others killed, 15 wounded in bombing of Rajai office. Interior Minister Mohammed Riza Mahdavi-Kani named provisional Prime Minister.

Sept. 20. New leftist purge announced; 149 executed; Khomeini 9/23 asks purge of teachers and students.

Sept. 27. Iran says Abadan siege broken with 600 Iraqi casualties in surprise attack; Iraq concedes tactical defeat 9/28.

— Mujahedeen battle Islamic guards in 7-hour Tehran street fight; 57 more executed bringing execution total since June to 1,350.

Oct. 2. Mohammed Ali Khameini wins Iran presidency with 95% of 16.8 million votes cast; becomes first clergyman to hold post.

Oct. 15. Mahdavi-Khani resigns as Iran Premier.

Oct. 24. Pars press agency admits over 1,000 Iran government officials killed since June.

Oct. 27. Hussein Moussavi named Premier; confirmed 10/29; Cabinet approved 11/2.

Dec. 12. U.S. rejects Iran request to buy spare parts for F-14 warplanes.

AFGHANISTAN, INDIA, PAKISTAN

JAN. 5. Afghan and Pakistan statements made public in New Delhi back UN role in talks on Soviet pullout.

JAN. 27. Islamic summit meeting (*see* Middle East: General) calls for immediate Soviet pullout from Afghanistan.

FEB. 4. India announces it will reprocess spent uranium because of US delay in shipping nuclear fuel.

FEB. 11. UN Secretary-General Kurt Waldheim names UN Under Secretary Javier Pérez de Cuellar (Peru) as special representative in Afghanistan procedural talks.

FEB. 18. Afghan President Babrak Karmal arrives Moscow; 2/26 joint communiqué says Soviet troops will remain in Afghanistan until "outside aggression" stops.

MAR. 2. Pakistan dissidents hijack Pakistan airliner to Kabul, demand release of political prisoners. Plane forced to Syria where hijackers surrender 3/14 after Pakistan releases 55 prisoners 3/12.

MAR. 9. President Ronald Reagan in TV interview says US would consider arms for Afghan rebels if asked.

MAR. 25. Pakistan Chief Justice and 8 justices dismissed for rejecting 3/24 President Mohammed Zia ul-Haq order to amend Constitution.

MAR. 27. White House reports it will soon resume military training of Pakistanis; Zia says strong Pakistan and aid to Afghan rebels "complementary."

APR. 4. Pakistan police clash with 4,000 supporters of former President Zulfikar Ali Bhutto at his grave on first anniversary of his death.

APR. 9. Pakistan offers US $13.6 million to rebuild US Embassy ransacked 11/21/79.

APR. 17. India Foreign Ministry official Eric Gonsalves meets with US Secretary of State Alexander Haig on nuclear fuel shipments; voices concern over Pakistan aid. On 4/22 Gonsalves threatens to end adherence to safeguards treaty unless US ships nuclear fuel.

MAY 12. House Foreign Affairs Committee unanimously defers lifting 6/79 curbs on Pakistan military aid until Pakistan clarifies its nuclear policy. Senate Foreign Relations Committee on 5/13 votes to lift curbs, 10–7.

JUNE 8. India-Pakistan senior aides at Islamabad meeting agree to revitalize '72 Simla accord.

JUNE 11. In major cabinet shakeup Karmal gives up premiership to Council of Ministers Chairman Sultan Ali Kishtmand of dominant Parcham faction.

JUNE 14. In India elections for 6 lower house seats, Prime Minister Indira Gandhi's Congress Party keeps 4, wins 5th in first major test since her return to power. Rajiv Gandhi wins his late brother Sanjay's seat.

JUNE 15. State Department announces $3-billion 5-year military-economic aid to Pakistan, including sale of F-16 warplanes at end of 2-day Pakistan visit by Under Secretary of State for Security Affairs James L. Buckley. Buckley says 6/24 Zia "absolutely assured" him Pakistan has no plans to develop nuclear arms.

JUNE 28. China and India meet on Himalaya border dispute (*see* East Asia: China).

JUNE 29–30. European Economic Community foreign ministers propose 2-stage Afghan Conference, initially involving UN Security Council, Pakistan, Iran, with Afghan rebels joining 2nd stage.

JULY 6. British Foreign Secretary Lord Carrington in USSR presents EEC Afghan plan; Foreign Minister Andrei A. Gromyko calls it "unrealistic" and TASS rejects it 7/18; USSR gives detailed objections 8/5.

— Western sources report high Soviet casualties in Afghanistan, with only major cities "safe"; Kabul army defections said to be at crippling level with teenagers now being drafted.

JULY 10. Indira Gandhi voices concern over F-16s for Pakistan, confirms negotiations with France on Mirage jets.

JULY 22. Western sources report fierce 3-day battle in Kabul suburb of Paghman last week, costliest since Soviet invasion.

AUG. 6. State Department aides report USSR rejected US proposals in last 2 months for secret talks on Afghanistan; says no US arms going to rebels, even indirectly.

AUG. 17. India to buy 1.51 million tons of US wheat for $293 million—first such purchase since food sufficiency attained in '77.

AUG. 18. Pérez reports talks in Kabul and Islamabad Aug. 3–10 resulted in accord on 4-point agenda; both sides bypassed rebels.

AUG. 24. Kabul agrees to active UN role, drops call for separate talks with Iran and Pakistan.

SEPT. 15. State Department and Pakistan Embassy formally announce 6-year, $3.2-billion US aid package including speeded delivery of F-16s.

SEPT. 16. Pakistan proposes talks with India on border troop cuts, nonaggression pact.

SEPT. 25. Dacca says India attacked 4 border posts 9/24, killed 18.

SEPT. 28. UN aides say 10-day indirect Afghan-Pakistan talks deadlocked.

OCT. 20. Senate in voice vote asks Reagan annual report on Pakistan nuclear activities. On 10/12 it votes India-Pakistan aid cutoff, 51–46, if nuclear device is tested.

OCT. 24. International Monetary Fund approves $5.8-billion India loan over US objections.

Nov. 10. Four top Afghan defense aides reported training in USSR since Sept.

— Iran proposes 3-nation Islamic force to replace USSR while Afghans study future plans. Pakistan says 11/11 proposal has merit; Kabul rejects it 11/15.

Nov. 18. UN General Assembly renews demand "foreign troops" leave Afghanistan, 116-23-12.

DEC. 23. US defense analysts report USSR ready to bolster its 85,000-man force in Afghanistan.

EAST ASIA AND THE PACIFIC

GENERAL

JAN. 2. Palau Islands become independent as Republic of Belau.

JAN. 15. Republic of Korea (ROK) President Chun Doo Hwan chosen as presidential candidate at first meeting of new Democratic Justice Party (DJP).

JAN. 17. ROK opposition forms Democratic Korea Party (DKP) to replace outlawed New Democratic Party, with Yoo Chi Song as its candidate.

JAN. 19. North Korea President Kim Il Sung rejects 1/11 Chun proposal to exchange visits.

JAN. 23. Chun commutes dissident Kim Dae Jung's death sentence to life in prison; Reagan praises move. Martial law (in force since 5/17/80) lifted 1/24, but tight security measures remain.

JAN. 29. Japan announces it will double foreign economic aid in 1981–85.

FEB. 1–3. Chun visits Reagan; US pledges to keep 39,000 troops in ROK, normalize ties.

FEB. 25. ROK electoral college elects Chun for 7-year term; sworn in 3/3.

MAR. 25. In national elections DJP wins majority in 276-member ROK National Assembly.

MAR. 26. State Department confirms agreement in principle to send ROK 36 F-16 warplanes.

APR. 9. Japan freighter collides with US nuclear submarine and sinks in East China Sea; 2 of 15 Japan crewmen die. US accident report delayed 36 hours; Reagan sends personal regrets to Japan Prime Minister Zenko Suzuki 4/18.

APR. 28. Defense Secretary Caspar Weinberger in San Francisco urges Japan to strengthen its defense, stresses Soviet threat in Asia.

— Suzuki criticizes US for not consulting on grain embargo move of 4/26 (see World Economy).

MAY 7–8. Suzuki meets with Reagan; joint communiqué pledges increased Japan defense efforts.

MAY 16. Japan Foreign Minister Masayoshi Ito resigns after press reports say Suzuki bowed to US on defense; Health Minister Sunao Sonoda succeeds him.

MAY 18. Former US Ambassador Edwin O. Reischauer discloses '60 US-Japan oral accord allowed Navy to carry nuclear arms in and out of Japan.

MAY 20. US says Secretary of State Alexander M. Haig's June visit to Japan canceled, reportedly by mutual agreement; joint naval exercises suspended 5/21.

JUNE 9. North Korea rejects renewed 6/5 Chun proposal for meeting.

JUNE 19. Sonoda meets Haig in Manila, rejects larger defense outlays.

JUNE 29. Japanese defense chief Joji Omura meets with Weinberger in Washington; resists pressure to increase military strength.

AUG. 26. North Korea fires missile at US reconnaissance plane "above high seas." US protest rejected at 9/1 Panmunjom meeting.

SEPT. 19. Smuggled prisoner accounts say ROK holds 15,000 in camps without trial. ROK on 9/25 says it legally holds 3,228 common criminals.

OCT. 4. Japan-USSR agree to meet regarding disputed Kurile Islands, other issues.

OCT. 12–14. Palestine Liberation Organization leader Yasir Arafat visits Japan at latter's invitation.

Nov. 30. In major shakeup Suzuki replaces 15 of 20 Cabinet ministers.

CHINA AND TAIWAN

JAN. 7. People's Republic of China (PRC)-US scheduled air service resumes after 32 years.

JAN. 18. PRC blames US for Dutch decision to sell 2 submarines to Republic of China (ROC) on Taiwan; recalls envoy from Netherlands 2/27.

JAN. 24. Jiang Qing, wife of Mao Zedong, and former Shanghai Mayor Zhang Chunqiao receive suspended death sentences; Lin Biao posthumously indicted. On 1/25 8 other surviving Cultural Revolution leaders get 16 years to life imprisonment.

FEB. 11. Party Deputy Chairman Deng Xiaoping reports former Premier Hua Guofeng stripped of powers.

FEB. 12. US Nuclear Regulatory Commission approves export of 3 reactors to ROC.

MAR. 2. International Monetary Fund approves $550-million loan to PRC.

MAR. 6. PRC formally cancels steel mill accords with 3 Japanese firms.

MAR. 9. PRC-USSR 1951 accord on Amur River navigation rights renewed.

MAR. 18. *People's Daily* says Mao only one of many great PRC leaders.

MAR. 23. Former President Gerald Ford in Beijing assures PRC of continued US commitment to improving relations.

MAY 14. PRC press attacks statement by White House counselor Edwin Meese that US remains committed to '79 Taiwan Relations Act.

MAY 30. PRC offers to let ROC fly relatives to Beijing funeral of Soong Ching-ling, Sun Yat-sen widow, who died 5/29.

JUNE 2. US Embassy announces PRC accord, signed 2 weeks earlier, with Export-Import Bank.

JUNE 4. State Department lifts trade curbs against PRC.

JUNE 6. Vatican names Dominic Tang Yiming Archbishop—first since '55; move is condemned by PRC 6/11 as interference.

JUNE 9. Reagan asks ratification of PRC consular convention signed 9/17/80.

JUNE 13. Secretary of State Alexander M. Haig, Jr. in Hong Kong says closer US-PRC ties a "strategic imperative" in face of growing Soviet threat. In Beijing 6/14–6/16 Haig announces US decision in principle to sell arms to PRC.

JUNE 17. TASS calls arms sales decision "provocative."

— Senior US aides report joint PRC-US tracking station in operation near Soviet border since '79; PRC denies post exists 6/18.

JUNE 26–28. PRC Foreign Affairs Minister Huang Hua visits Prime Minister Indira Gandhi; agree on Sept. Himalaya border talks, deadlocked since '62. Talks held 12/10–12/14 in Beijing.

JUNE 27–29. Sixth plenum of PRC Central Committee names Hu Yaobang party head, Zhao Ziyang deputy head; Deng heads Military Commission, Xi Zhongxun named party secretary.

JUNE 30. Central Committee resolution to mark party's 7/1 60th anniversary portrays Mao as brilliant leader who nevertheless made "grave errors."

AUG. 24. Former President Jimmy Carter begins 10-day visit to PRC.

SEPT. 5. US-PRC cultural exchange pact signed in Beijing.

SEPT. 29. Chairman Hu assails "bourgeois liberalism"; sharp attack ends debate on extent of creative freedom.

SEPT. 9. PRC Standing Committee head Ye Jianying proposes 9-point PRC-ROC reunification plan, quickly rejected by ROC.

OCT. 3. PRC offers sea, air, mail links with ROC; ROC President Chiang Ching-kuo reaffirms 10/7 he will never negotiate.

NOV. 11. PRC warns US on ROC arms sales.

NOV. 15. Haig says ROC arms issue "worrisome specter"; calls PRC reunification offer meaningful.

DEC. 16. PRC, Japan sign $1.38-billion industrial aid accord in Tokyo.

SOUTHEAST ASIA

JAN. 3. Socialist Republic of Vietnam (SRV) troops cross Thai border in first reported incursion there since 6/80.

JAN. 17. Philippines President Ferdinand E. Marcos ends '72 martial law; limited powers returned to National Assembly 1/19.

JAN. 24. UN aides say Cambodia (Kampuchea) now has enough food. On 2/25 UN Food and Agriculture Organization says some $235-million worth still needed in '81.

JAN. 28. Cambodia, Laos, SRV foreign ministers meet in Ho Chi Minh City (Saigon), propose regional conference on Cambodia; SRV offers conditional Cambodia pullout.

JAN. 29. Marcos announces he will seek another term, sets up election reform committee; on 2/5 united opposition announces election boycott, demands charter revision.

JAN. 30. PRC Prime Minister Zhao Ziyang in Bangkok rejects Cambodia conference, pledges ties with area communist parties will not harm relations with Association of Southeast Asian Nations (ASEAN) member states.

FEB. 17. Pope John Paul II arrives in Manila for 6-day visit; delivers human rights homily.

FEB. 26. Former Cambodia leader Norodom Sihanouk in shift agrees to talk with Khmer Rouge and non-communist factions on common effort against SRV-backed regime of Heng Samrin.

FEB. 28. Thai Democratic Party quits coalition over oil dispute. Prime Minister Prem Tinsulanonda forms new cabinet 3/10.

MAR. 6. Thais reject Soviet President Leonid I. Brezhnev's plea for regional meeting on Cambodia.

MAR. 28. Islamic extremists hijack Indonesia jet to Thailand, demand release of 20 prisoners; Indonesia commandoes storm jet 3/31, kill 4 of 5 hijackers, free all 55 hostages.

APR. 1. Thailand deputy army chief Gen. Sant Chipatima fails in coup attempt. Prem remains in charge with backing of royal family; rebels flee 4/3, ending 6th coup attempt since '71.

APR. 7. Philippines plebiscite backs Marcos charter amendments by 4-1 margin, giving him 6-year term, unlimited reelection; over 6 million stage illegal boycott. Finance Minister Cesar Virata named Prime Minister 4/8; confirmed 7/28.

APR. 26. SRV holds first national election since '76 unification for 496-seat parliament from list selected by Vietnam Fatherland Front.

MAY 2. US says it will back efforts to unify anti-Heng Samrin groups in Cambodia; PRC reported sending military aid to Son Sann, leader of opposition forces.

MAY 8. PRC says it killed over 100 SRV troops in 5/7 attack on border town.

MAY 9. Sihanouk in Beijing says he accepted PRC offer to equip 3,000 troops to fight Heng Samrin.

MAY 21. US aides report at least 2 US-guided Laotian patrols went into Laos in response to reports US POWs still alive there.

MAY 29. Cambodia ruling People's Revolutionary Party elects Defense Minister and Vice President Pen Sovan Secretary-General.

MAY 30. US reportedly reverses policy limiting refugees; wants to stop forcible Thai repatriations of 140,000 Cambodians. (As of 4/30 Thai camps held 257,346 refugees.)

JUNE 1. UN aides report Secretary-General Kurt Waldheim has approved UN Conference on Cambodia 7/13–7/17. Cambodia, Laos, SRV announce 6/14 they will boycott conference.

JUNE 16. In first Philippines presidential elections since '69 Marcos wins 88% of votes; Marcos opponents boycott polls.

JUNE 17–20. ASEAN holds annual meeting in Manila, calls for SRV Cambodia pullout, UN peacekeeping force, disarming all factions.

JUNE 20. Haig at Manila news conference after separate meetings with ASEAN foreign ministers says US will stand by its regional military commitments to counter USSR and its "proxies"; will not normalize ties with SRV.

JULY 1. Marcos inaugurated; Vice President George Bush pledges US support.

JULY 4. SRV National Assembly elects Communist Party founder Truong Chinh to head 5-man State Council with wide power, reelects Prime Minister Pham Van Dong; party secretary Le Duan keeps post.

JULY 7. SRV turns over remains of 3 US servicemen killed during Vietnam War.

JULY 13–17. UN Conference on Cambodia held in New York; seven-nation committee formed to maintain contact with parties to conflict.

JULY 16. Mahathir bin Mohamad succeeds Hussein Onn as Malaysia Prime Minister.

SEPT. 2–4. Sihanouk, Son Sann and Khieu Samphan meet in Singapore and agree to form anti-Heng Samrin coalition. Khieu Samphan leaves 9/5 without naming representative to coalition.

SEPT. 18. UN General Assembly (UNGA) backs Pol Pot UN seat, 77-37-31.

OCT. 4. Two-week voting begins for 475-seat Burma Parliament; former General U San Yu succeeds President Ne Win 9/9.

OCT. 21. UNGA calls for pullout of all foreign forces from Cambodia, 100-25-19.

OCT. 28. Burma and US sign $30 million economic aid accord—first since '66.

Nov. 30. Pol Pot communiqué accuses Son Sann of takeover, but says coalition plan will be studied.

Dec. 3. Son Sann visits Washington; arms aid request rejected.

Dec. 5. Council of State President (as of 7/81) Heng Samrin succeeds Pen Sovan as party Secretary-General.

Dec. 18–24. Four Vietnam veterans visit Hanoi at SRV invitation, meet 12/22 with Foreign Minister Nguyen Co Thach, who says he will deal with veterans, not U.S., on 2,500 U.S. soldiers still missing there.

AFRICA

Jan. 6. Libya and Chad announce merger after Chad President Goukouni Oueddi visits Libya.

Jan. 7–13. UN conference on Namibia held in Geneva ends in failure. South Africa says Western proposal "premature."

Jan. 9. France reinforces troops in Africa; Organization of African Unity (OAU) calls emergency meeting on Chad.

Jan. 10. Zimbabwe Home Affairs Minister Joshua Nkomo and Manpower Secretary Edgar Z. Tekere removed. President Robert Mugabe names Nkomo Minister without Portfolio 1/27.

Jan. 13. Compulsory black schooling begins in South Africa.

Jan. 19. State Department says US has verified assurances Somalia is not fighting in Ogaden, clearing way for implementation of '79 $40-million arms aid pact.

Jan. 21. Angola downs 3 South African planes in defense against raids begun 10 days ago.

Jan. 22. Black students end 9-month school boycott in South Africa.

Jan. 29. South Africa raids African National Congress (ANC) headquarters in Maputo, Mozambique; 14 persons killed.

Jan. 30. UN aides report 250,000 Ugandans face famine as tribal strife and drought cut harvest by two-thirds.

Feb. 7. Blacks boycott opening session of mixed-race South African President's Council.

Feb. 13. Six-day-old mutiny by Nkomo supporters in Bulawayo, Zimbabwe crushed; some 300 killed.

Feb. 20. Zimbabwe announces start of diplomatic ties with USSR.

Mar. 2. UN General Assembly (UNGA) 112-22(US)-6, rejects South Africa credentials.

Mar. 4. Four US diplomats expelled from Mozambique for spying; another American detained 3/12. US stops food aid 3/20.

— Reagan in TV interview with Walter Cronkite says US should back Pretoria while it tries to solve its problems; Botha calls statement a realistic policy shift.

Mar. 6. UNGA resolution, 114-0-22(US) calls for trade embargo against South Africa.

Mar. 11. Official Uganda journal confirms Feb. massacre of thousands of civilians by berserk militiamen.

Mar. 12. Official Morocco sources report Libya contract with West German rocket firm Otrag for medium-range missiles.

Mar. 15. In Central African Republic (CAR) elections, President David Dacko wins 6-year term over Prime Minister Ange Patasse. Dacko declares emergency 3/30 after Patasse backers riot.

Mar. 16. Egypt confirms arms help for Chad rebels.

— Head of Namibia Democratic Turnhalle Alliance Dirk Mudge visits US despite State Department objections.

Mar. 19. State Department says South African officers asked to leave 3/14 because military status omitted on visas.

Mar. 24. White House says US UN Ambassador Jeane J. Kirkpatrick unaware of South African officers' identities at previously undisclosed 3/15 meeting.

Mar. 23–24. Zimbawe Aid Donors Conference held in Salisbury.

Mar. 25. Deputy Assistant Secretary of State Morris Draper tells House panels arms sales to Morocco will no longer be based on Western Sahara settlement.

Apr. 6–23. Chester A. Crocker, Assistant Secretary of State-designate for African Affairs, visits 10 African nations, presents modified Namibia plan based on "Zimbabwe formula," i.e. charter agreement before supervised elections.

Apr. 9–10. UN-sponsored Conference on African Refugees meets in Geneva. US pledges $285 million of $470-million program.

APR. 14–16. Crocker in Pretoria on 6th leg of tour is refused meeting with Prime Minister P. W. Botha.

APR. 16. Frontline states (Angola, Botswana, Mozambique, Tanzania, Zambia, Zimbabwe) meet in Luanda on eve of Crocker arrival, condemn moves to repeal Clark Amendment and Namibia policy.

APR. 17. Zaïre Prime Minister Nguza Karl-i-Bond resigns; former Interior Minister Joseph Nsigna succeeds him 4/23.

APR. 21–30. UN Security Council (UNSC) meets on Namibia. US, France, Britain veto 4 resolutions calling for sanctions against South Africa.

APR. 22–23. Western "contact group" (US, Canada, Great Britain, France, West Germany) meets in London, agrees to seek revised UN Namibia plan.

APR. 27–29. Libya President Muammar al-Qaddafi visits USSR for first time in 4 years.

APR. 28. Tanzania announces pullout begun of 10,000 troops in Uganda since 1/79. Withdrawal completed 6/30 except for 1,000 police officers.

APR. 29. In South Africa parliamentary elections ruling National Party wins 131 of 165 seats; small right-wing Herstigte National Party wins 13.8% of popular vote, up 4%.

APR. 30. Crocker in briefing says he told Angola that Cuba pullout is necessary for the resumption of international effort on Namibia.

MAY 6. US orders Libya mission to US closed, cites support for terrorism, African meddling.

MAY 12. House Foreign Affairs Committee (HFAC) 19-5, rejects repeal of Clark Amendment; on 5/13 Senate Foreign Relations Committee (SFRC), 10–2, links repeal to progress on Namibia.

MAY 14–15. South Africa Foreign Minister Roelof F. Botha meets with Haig and Reagan.

MAY 16. State Department says US asked Botha for "statement of commitment" toward Namibia solution.

MAY 21. Rockefeller Foundation study, *South Africa: Time Running Out*, calls for continued arms and investment embargos against South Africa until blacks get "effective share" of power.

MAY 25. Banned ANC calls boycott of 20th birthday celebration of South Africa Republic. Riot police storm Durban campus 5/27 after students burn flag.

MAY 29. Morocco holds first parliamentary elections in southern Spanish Sahara since '79 annexation.

MAY 31. Crocker memo 2/7/81, approved by Haig, says Namibia strategy linked to Cuban pullout from Angola, Angola power-sharing with anti-Marxist rebel head Jonas Savimbi.

JUNE 2. Crocker says US will aid any African country that resists Libya "interventionism," especially in Chad.

JUNE 3. Militant black union ends 2-week strike at Ford and General Motors plants in Port Elizabeth, South Africa.

JUNE 11–15. Deputy Secretary of State William P. Clark visits South Africa, Namibia, Zimbabwe.

JUNE 17. Crocker tells House panel US will "disengage" from Namibia effort if Pretoria continues to delay settlement.

JUNE 19. Liberia executes 13 in plot to oust Master Sergeant Samuel K. Doe.

JUNE 22. Zambia ousts 2 US Embassy employees, arrests Zambia aide in alleged CIA plot; denied by US 6/23.

— In South Africa's harshest crackdown since Botha took office, 30 black union leaders and students arrested in last 3 weeks; 4 arrested in 6/26 raids on black union office.

JUNE 24–27. OAU summit meets in Nairobi; unanimous resolution condemns US "collusion" with Pretoria, calls for Africa peacekeeping force in Chad.

JUNE 26. King Hassan II at OAU offers to accept cease-fire, supervised referendum on Morocco role in Western Sahara.

JULY 12. South Africa attack on South West Africa Peoples' Organization (SWAPO) base 90 miles inside Angola leaves 114 persons dead.

JULY 23. Contact group issues joint statement on Namibia after Ottawa summit (*see* World Economy), stresses need for urgent action.

JULY 24. Kenya, Tanzania, Uganda meet in Nairobi, agree to replace East African Community dissolved in '77.

JULY 30. Socialist party head Kukil Samba Sanyang leads coup attempt against Gambia President Dawda Kairaba Jawara, in London for Prince Charles' wedding. Rebellion crushed by 8/4 with help of Senegal troops; over 100 hostages freed 8/6, 10 rebels captured 8/9.

AUG. 1. ANC South African leader Joe Gqabi slain in Salisbury. ANC rockets hit military complex near Pretoria 8/13.

Aug. 7. Mugabe names Army Chief Gen. Andrew (Sandy) Maclean head of all Zimbabwe armed forces.

Aug. 19. Three South Africa ANC members receive death sentence for '80 refinery bombing and police station attacks.

— Two US Navy F-14 warplanes shoot down 2 Libya jets after being fired on during US naval exercises in Gulf of Sirte within territorial limit claimed by Libya. US note warns further attacks will also be met by force.

Aug. 20. Reagan says "impressive" encounter shows US rejection of Libyan waters claim; Qaddafi in Aden (see Middle East: General) denounces US. Haig, 8/21, says incident closed.

— Over 1,000 South Africans, mostly whites, protest 8/19 arrest of 2,000 Cape Town squatters.

Aug. 21. Gambia and Senegal announce merger plan with each keeping own sovereignty.

Aug. 23. Qaddafi in Abu Dhabi concedes Libya fired first during Gulf of Sirte incident.

Aug. 24. US affirms anti-apartheid stand; has no comment on refusal to join diplomatic protest over 8/19 squatters' arrest.

Aug. 25. Somalia orders Libya mission to Mogadishu closed.

— Angola reports South African invasion 60 miles inside its borders, appeals to UN; Pretoria says 8/26 its troops were pursuing SWAPO rebels. US State Department 8/26 says attack must be seen in light of Cuba troops in Angola.

Aug. 31. US casts solitary veto against UNSC resolution condemning South Africa raid into Angola.

Sept. 1. Gen. Andre Kolingba takes over from Dacko as head of state of CAR; forms military cabinet 9/2.

Sept. 3–14. UNGA holds special session on Namibia; 9/14 resolution condemns Pretoria, singles out US for 8/31 veto.

Sept. 3. Haig in interview reports progress in secret talks with Pretoria on Namibia.

Sept. 9. Angola at UN says 15,000 South Africa troops still inside its borders.

Sept. 19. USSR concedes 2 soldiers killed, one captured in Angola raids, asks immediate return of bodies and prisoners.

Sept. 21–22. Crocker meets with Pretoria aides in Zurich.

Sept. 24. Contact group meets in New York, announces timetable for "final negotiations."

Oct. 5. Sudan President Gaafer al-Nimeiry dissolves both parliaments to decentralize power. Egypt President Anwar el-Sadat reaffirms support if Libya attacks.

Oct. 6. Sadat assassinated (see Middle East: General).

Oct. 12. US sources report pledge to speed up arms to Sudan after State Department Counselor Robert C. MacFarlane visits Khartoum.

Oct. 13. Hassan says Soviet-made missiles shot down 2 Morocco jets in major Sahara battle.

Oct. 19. Morocco jets chase rebels into Mauritania; Polisario downs Morocco helicopter 10/23.

Oct. 21. Aide to ex-intelligence agent Edwin P. Wilson says Wilson recruited US pilots, mechanics for Libya air force.

Oct. 26. Contact group formally presents revised Namibia plan in Windhoek; Democratic Turnhalle Alliance accepts 10/30, asks enforcement guarantees.

Oct. 27. France confirms arms deliveries to Goukouni; latter on 10/30 demands Libya pullout to make way for inter-Africa force.

Nov. 1. Tunisia holds first multiparty elections in 25 years for new 136-seat assembly; all seats won by ruling Destourian Socialist Party.

Nov. 3–4. French African leaders meet in Paris; French President François Mitterrand pledges active military-economic role; resolution asks Africa peace force in Chad.

Nov. 4. Libya commander in Chad says troops will be out in week after sudden Qaddafi evacuation order 11/3.

— US military group led by Assistant Defense Secretary Francis J. West arrives Rabat.

Nov. 14. Senegal-Gambia confederation, Senegambia, formed under Senegal President Abdou Diouf; formally signed 12/17.

Nov. 22. Newsweek reports special Libya squads set up to assassinate Reagan, other top aides; Libya 11/23 asks UN inquiry.

Nov. 26. Seychelles reports 11/25–11/26 coup attempt by over 100 mercenaries foiled. South Africa arrests 44 mercenaries who escaped to Durban aboard hijacked Air India jet.

Nov. 27–28. Five African nations meet in Nairobi, agree to send troops to Chad by 12/17.

Nov. 28. Western defense sources confirm 11/27 Polisario claim it occupied 2 bases evacuated by Morocco 11/9.

DEC. 3. US law officials say 5 Libya terrorists in US with plan to assassinate Reagan and other top aides. Qaddafi denies charges, 12/6.

— Ciskei homeland declared independent by South Africa.

DEC. 7. South Africa reports series of invasions 11/1–11/20, 150 miles inside Angola.

DEC. 10. Reagan asks 1,500 Americans to leave Libya, bans U.S. travel to that country.

DEC. 21. Treaty on East and South African Preferential Trade Area signed in Lusaka.

DEC. 31. Former air force pilot Lt. Jerry J. Rawlings ousts Ghana President Hilla Liman (elected 12/79), sets up Provisional National Defense Council.

LATIN AMERICA

CARIBBEAN AND MEXICO

JAN. 3. US farm experts Michael P. Hammer and Mark D. Pearlman, El Salvador farm institute head slain. Junta President José Napoleón Duarte blames rightists.

JAN. 5. President-elect Ronald Reagan and Mexico President José López Portillo meet in Juarez.

JAN. 11. Duarte sets nationwide curfew after 1/10 start of rebel offensive; rebels seize San Salvador radio station, call for general strike. Over 9,000 slain in '80 violence.

JAN. 12. Puerto Rico pro-independence group (Macheteros) destroys 9 jets at Muniz air base; claims 12/3/79 ambush of US Navy bus.

JAN. 14. US resumes delivery of $5-million Salvador "non-lethal" military aid cut off 12/5; cites Cuba-Nicaragua arms flow.

— Salvador opposition Revolutionary Democratic Front (FDR) leader Guillermo Manuel Ungo announces readiness to discuss political settlement.

JAN. 16. Federal Bureau of Investigation (FBI) reports arrest of 7 anti-Castro exiles. Second round of talks with Cuba on 2,000 undesirable refugees ends in failure.

JAN. 17. US Ambassador Robert E. White tells State Department El Salvador is taking no "positive action" to solve 12/4 murder of 4 US nuns.

JAN. 18. US authorizes another $5 million for combat equipment to El Salvador.

JAN. 19. US-Jamaica $40-million economic aid pact signed in Washington.

JAN. 22. US suspends $75 million in economic aid to Nicaragua over aid to Salvador rebels; $9.6-million wheat sale suspended 2/10.

JAN. 30. US moves to expel 3,900 Haitians who entered US since 10/80/81.

FEB. 1. White relieved; career diplomat Frederic L. Chapin named acting US ambassador to El Salvador 2/3.

FEB. 5. *The New York Times* publishes captured leftist documents showing '80 USSR-Cuba pledge to supply arms to Salvador rebels; USSR denies charge 2/14 but says there are no transshipment curbs on its arms sales.

FEB. 16–20. Assistant Secretary for European Affairs Lawrence S. Eagleburger visits 5 European allies on backing for US policy toward El Salvador.

FEB. 19. State Department memorandum calls El Salvador "textbook case" of Communist aggression and a major Soviet political thrust into Central America.

— López Portillo affirms close Cuba ties on signing sugar accord.

FEB. 20. Secretary of State Alexander M. Haig, Jr. briefs allied ambassadors, says Cuba main source of trouble in El Salvador.

FEB. 22. White House adviser Edwin Meese warns Cuba US will take "necessary steps" to stop Salvador arms flow, including possible naval blockade.

FEB. 23. State Department issues report, "Communist Interference in El Salvador," with texts of 2/5 rebel documents.

FEB. 24. Cuba President Fidel Castro at USSR Communist Party Congress assails US blockade threat.

FEB. 28. State Department reports Managua gave "assurances" on arms shipments.

MAR. 2. State Department says $25 million in military equipment and 20 more military advisers (19 already there) to be sent to El Salvador.

MAR. 3. Salvador rightist Roberto D'Aubuisson says US backs military government, boasts of CIA link.

MAR. 4. Shots strafe US Embassy in San Salvador; Haig warns against rightist coup. Chapin implicates D'Aubuisson.

— Nicaragua State Council drops Arturo Cruz Porras and Moisés Hassán Morales; Sandinistas now in control.

MAR. 5. Duarte names electoral commission for '82 Salvador elections.

MAR. 6. Reagan defends Salvador arms aid, warns against rightist coup.
MAR. 11. Britain and Guatemala sign accord on Belize independence.
— White says he was dismissed over criticisms of US Salvador policy.
MAR. 17. US Salvador Embassy sprayed with rifle fire after visiting Rep. Clarence D. Long says he opposes presence of US military advisers.
— In San José, Costa Rica, 3 US Embassy guards wounded in bomb attack on US van.
MAR. 18. Under Secretary of State for Political Affairs Walter J. Stoessel, Jr. tells Senate Foreign Relations Committee (SFRC) US has not ruled out force to stop Cuba arms flow.
— Haig tells House Foreign Affairs Committee (HFAC) USSR has Central America "hit list."
MAR. 22. Final group of US military advisers arrives in Salvador; total at 56.
MAR. 25. Gunmen fire on US Salvador Embassy, causing wide damage.
MAR. 26. Bomb injures 3 as Honduras Constituent Assembly opens; 50 reported killed last week in Honduras-Salvador border crossfire.
MAR. 28. Trinidad and Tobago Prime Minister Eric Eustace Williams dies (in power since 1963); Agriculture Minister George Chambers succeeds him 3/30.
APR. 1. State Department suspends $15-million Nicaragua economic aid over arms to Salvador rebels.
APR. 6. Career diplomat Deane R. Hinton named US Ambassador to El Salvador; arrives 5/30.
APR. 19. Nicaragua leader Ortega Saavedra at Havana World Peace Council meeting reveals recent protest to US on exile training camp in Florida.
APR. 24. Castro reportedly tells visiting West German aide Cuba arms shipments now over, favors political solution.
— Nicaragua reports 20,000-ton USSR grain shipment, $100-million Libya loan and $64 million in Cuban technical aid since US ended aid.
APR. 26. CBS-TV reports FBI evidence links 6 soldiers to 12/4 murders; On 5/9 Salvador confirms arrests were made 4/29.
APR. 29. Under Secretary of State for Security Affairs James L. Buckley says Salvador arms now come from Cuba via Honduras. HFAC, 26-7, bans military aid until junta agrees to control killings.
MAY 6. Salvador rejects international mediation plan backed by FDR.
MAY 7. Mexico and Nicaragua sign 2-year, $200 million economic aid pact.
MAY 11. SFRC, 11-1, asks Reagan certify Salvador human rights, economic progress despite Haig 5/11 objections. HFAC passed similar measure 12 days ago.
MAY 12. US delegation meets with Guatemala President Fernando Lucas García on US aid, cut off in '77.
JUNE 8-9. López Portillo visits Reagan.
JUNE 17. Senate in voice vote backs funds for "Radio Free Cuba."
JUNE 18. US defends 2/23 report on Salvador arms flows in detailed reply to critical US press reports.
JUNE 23. US-Mexico pact signed, setting up joint trade board.
— Ronald Webster sworn in as Anguilla Chief Minister after his People's Party won 6/22 Assembly election.
JUNE 26. International Bank for Reconstruction and Development Consultative Group for Caribbean (set up in '77) ends 4-day Washington meeting, pledges $700 million development aid 7/1.
JUNE 29. Dominican Republic President Silvestre Antonio Guzmán Fernández (elected 5/78) announces he will not seek reelection in '82.
JUNE 30. In returns from 6/18 Barbados election, Labour Party defeats Democratic Labour Party of Prime Minister Errol Walton Barrow.
JULY 11. Haig and Venezuela, Mexico, Canada foreign ministers meet in Nassau on Caribbean aid.
JULY 12. Salvador Bishop Arturo Rivera y Damas accuses army in murder of 27 civilians; also deplores 7/7 murder of 28 peasants.
JULY 16. Assistant Secretary for Inter-American Affairs Thomas O. Enders in major address to World Affairs Council backs Salvador elections but insists on need for more US economic/military aid.
JULY 30. Haig written testimony to Senate panel says Soviet arms shipments to Cuba up steeply in last 7 months, with some weapons reshipped to Central America.
AUG. 1. Former Panama President Omar Torrijos Herrera killed in plane crash.
AUG. 7-8. Castro visits López Portillo in Cozumel, Mexico in hastily arranged meeting; ties reaffirmed despite Cuba exclusion from Cancún meeting.

Aug. 11–12. Enders visits Managua in first high-level US-Nicaragua meeting of Reagan presidency.

Aug. 18. Costa Rica rejects US UN Ambassador Jeane Kirkpatrick's remarks that it needs military help to fight Communist subversion; says it needs economic aid.

Aug. 27. Salvador Defense Minister José Guillermo Garcia says 6 arrested 4/29 for murder of US nuns to be freed for lack of evidence.

Aug. 28. Haig accuses Salvador rebels of "straight terrorism," says Cuba-USSR arms flows continue, repeats pledge to seek stability with "justice"; USSR on 8/29 calls remarks arrogant.

— Joint Mexico-French declaration recognizes rebels as "representative political force"; Duarte on 8/29 says statement constitutes "interference."

Sept. 2. Nine Latin nations criticize 8/28 Mexico-France statement as "interference."

Sept. 9. Enders in New York speech outlines Caribbean aid plan; calls for private enterprise role, military aid when needed.

Sept. 14. Salvador army opens search-destroy campaign in 8 provinces.

Sept. 20. British Honduras becomes independent as Belize with George C. Price as Prime Minister.

Sept. 20–21. Duarte visits Washington, stresses need for economic aid.

Sept. 23. Senate, 54–42, asks biannual Reagan certification of Salvador political-economic progress before receiving US aid.

— Two US military advisers shot and wounded in Honduras, Parliament bombed; leftist group says 9/24 anti-"Yankee imperialism" drive has begun.

Sept. 25. Planning and Budget Minister Miguel de la Madrid Hurtado named presidential candidate in '82 Mexico election.

Sept. 30. US-Haiti cooperation accord to stop migrant flow announced. President Jean-Claude Duvalier asks US economic aid.

Oct. 19. French President François Mitterrand arrives in Mexico from US; reportedly says US aid to Salvador prolongs "horrible war."

Oct. 25. Coast Guard intercepts first boatload of 57 Haitians under 9/30 Reagan order.

Oct. 29. Jamaica breaks ties with Cuba over refusal to extradite 3 murder suspects.

Nov. 1. Antigua becomes independent as Antigua and Barbuda under Prime Minister Vere Bird.

Nov. 4. Key US aides report Salvador war stalemated. Haig said to ask Pentagon on possible military actions against Cuba, Nicaragua.

Nov. 8. Duarte denies stalemate, rejects foreign troops, stresses Salvador economic needs. Reagan 11/10 rules out troops.

Nov. 10. UN estimates 9,250 slain in El Salvador in Jan.–June '81—more than in all of '79.

Nov. 17–19. Venezuela President Luis Herrera Campíns visits Washington, opposes Nicaragua intervention and 8/28 Mexico-France statement on El Salvador.

Nov. 22. Haig and White House Counselor Edwin Meese in separate interviews warn Nicaragua on radical drift.

Nov. 23. Secretary of Defense Caspar Weinberger announces upgrading of 2-year-old Caribbean command.

Nov. 23–24. Haig visits Mexico, warns against hasty Nicaragua moves, presents US ratification instruments of Protocol I (signed by US 5/26/77) to Tlatelolco Treaty (2/14/67).

Nov. 29. Roberto Suazo Córdova defeats Ricardo Zuñiga Augustinus in first Honduras vote since Gen. Policarpo Paz García seized power in '72.

Dec. 2. Haig meets with Nicaragua Foreign Minister, Rev. Miguel d'Escoto Brockman in Castries, St. Lucia.

Dec. 7. Organization of American States General Assembly backs 3/12/82 Salvador general election.

Dec. 10. Banks delay rescheduling of Costa Rica $2.66-billion debt, pending International Monetary Fund formula.

Dec. 15. State Department aide says US will train 1,500 Salvador soldiers in U.S., that military has action plan if Reagan orders intervention..

Dec. 16. Against US opposition, UN General Assembly resolution, 68-22-53 calls for Salvador junta negotiations with rebels.

Dec. 20. Two Salvador rebels report 12/15 meetings at State Department.

SOUTH AMERICA

Jan. 19. US adviser to Bogota language school Chester A. Bitterman 3rd, kidnapped by Apr. 19 Movement ("M-19"); slain 3/7.

JAN. 23. Ecuador formally protests border firing by Peru helicopter.

JAN. 28–FEB. 1. Peru-Ecuador border war erupts in Andes Cordillera del Condor area claimed by both sides. Argentina, Brazil, Chile and US, guarantors of 1942 Rio Protocol, meet in Brasilia, order cease-fire 2/1.

FEB. 2. Organization of American States (OAS) foreign ministers meet in emergency session in Washington. On 2/9 *The New York Times* reports resolution asks cease-fire but leaves solution up to Rio guarantors.

FEB. 20. President Ronald Reagan lifts 11/79 ban on exports to Chile imposed after refusal to extradite 3 suspects in 9/21/76 murder of former Chile diplomat Orlando Letelier.

FEB. 20–23. Sporadic fighting renewed along Ecuador-Peru border.

FEB. 25. Inter-American extradition convention signed in Caracas.

— US vetoes UN Human Rights Commission resolution asking continued attention on Chile.

FEB. 27. Argentina arrests 8 human rights activists, seizes files on 6,000 missing persons.

MAR. 11. Chile President Augusto Pinochet Ugarte (elected 9/11/80) sworn in for 8-year term under new Constitution.

MAR. 16–17. Argentina President-designate, Gen. Roberto Eduardo Viola visits Washington.

MAR. 18. Treaty of Montevideo establishing Latin America Integration Association (ALADI, signed 8/12/80) enters into force.

MAR. 19. Reagan asks Congress to lift ban on military aid to Argentina.

MAR. 20. Former Argentina President Isabel Martínez de Perón (arrested 3/24/76) given 8-year prison term; freed 7/6, flies to Spain 7/10.

MAR. 29. Viola sworn in as Argentina's 38th president; succeeds Jorge Rafael Videla (named 3/76); presents 13-man Cabinet, including 7 civilians.

MAY 4. Bolivia arrests rightist group that took over Occidental Petroleum branch 5/3 and demanded ouster of President Luis García Meza.

MAY 6. Chile announces it will no longer cooperate with Inter-American Human Rights Committee.

MAY 12. Bolivia says it crushed 5/11 rebellion led by Col. Emilio Lanza in Cochabamba.

MAY 24. Ecuador President Jaime Roldós Aguilera, Defense Minister Marco Subía Martínez killed in air crash. Vice-President Oswaldo Hurtado Larrea assumes presidency.

MAY 26. García says he will quit Bolivia presidency 8/6; asks armed forces to pick successor by 7/17.

MAY 30. US District Court overturns previous findings, acquits 2 found guilty in Letelier murder.

JUNE 12. Chile Foreign Minister René Rojas Galdames visits US, discusses arms sales ban repeal.

JULY 8. A 7/1 US letter to Congress says Reagan will back development loans to Argentina, Chile, Paraguay, Uruguay based on State Department determination of "significant" human rights improvement.

AUG. 1. Retired army head, Gen. Gregorio Alvarez named Uruguay President for 3 ½-year term as of 9/11; succeeds Aparacio Méndez (named '76).

AUG. 4. García quits Bolivia presidency; 3-man junta led by Gen. Waldo Bernal assumes power 8/5, rebels give up 8/8 after junta agrees to consult on "lasting solution" and crackdown on drug traffic.

AUG. 11. Chile expels 4 politicians who protested jailing of 2 union leaders.

AUG. 13. US vetoes $20-million Inter-American Development Bank (IADB) loan to Guyana on technical economic grounds.

AUG. 31. Bomb attacks in Lima strike US Embassy, home of Ambassador Edwin G. Corr and 4 US-connected firms.

SEPT. 4. Bolivia junta names Gen. Celso Torrelio Villa president; sworn in 9/5.

SEPT. 18. Brazil President João Baptista Figueiredo suffers heart attack; Vice President Aureliano Chaves becomes Acting President 9/20; Figueiredo resumes duties 11/12.

SEPT. 30. US Senate in voice vote repeals Argentina military sales ban.

OCT. 13–14. Vice President George Bush visits Colombia and Brazil (10/14–10/16) where he announces special exemption for nuclear fuel purchase.

NOV. 7. Over 100,000 in Buenos Aires protest military rule, lack of jobs.

NOV. 20. Viola temporarily steps down because of heart trouble.

DEC. 2-11. OAS General Assembly meets in Castries, St. Lucia; backs Salvador '82 election 12/7.

DEC. 11. Viola removed; Argentina army chief Gen. Leopoldo Galtieri names Social Minister Adm. Carlos Lacoste interim President; Galtieri sworn in as President 12/22.

OTHER GLOBAL DEVELOPMENTS

Jan. 15. UN General Assembly (UNGA) elects State Department Legal Adviser Stephen M. Schwebel to International Court of Justice.

Feb. 2–Mar. 13. UN Commission on Human Rights holds annual session in Geneva, approves Declaration on Religious Intolerance.

Feb. 8–13. Ninety-four nonaligned nations meet in New Delhi.

Mar. 3. US says it will not back Law of the Sea treaty, pending review.

Mar. 9–Apr. 30, Aug. 3–29. Third UN Law of the Sea Conference holds 10th session in New York and Geneva, elects Tommy Koh (Singapore) as President to succeed H.S. Amerasinghe (Sri Lanka), who died 12/80.

Apr. 12. Reusable US space shuttle *Columbia* blasts into orbit from Cape Canaveral, Fla., piloted by John W. Young and Navy Captain Robert L. Crippen; lands at Edwards Air Force Base, Calif., 4/14 after 36 orbits.

May 4–21. Against lone US opposition, World Health Organization adopts voluntary code of ethics discouraging baby-formula marketing and promotion, 118-1-3. House condemns US stand 6/16, 301-100; Senate follows suit 6/18, 89-2.

May 16–17. Major free-world news organizations meet in Talloires, France, adopt declaration to fight New International Information Order endorsed by United Nations Educational, Scientific and Cultural Organization (UNESCO).

June 6. UN refugee committee puts world refugee total at 12.6 million as of 1/1/81; focus shifts from Asia to Africa.

Sept. 15–Dec. 18. UNGA holds 36th Regular Session, Part I, in New York, selects Ismat Kittani (Iraq) by lot to succeed Rudiger von Wechmar (West Germany) as President. Belize elected 156th UN member on 9/25.

Sept. 17. House votes 372-19 to cut off UNESCO funds over controversial press control resolutions.

Oct. 6. US UN Ambassador Jeane J. Kirkpatrick sends private letter to 40 states asking for explanation of "malicious" anti-US stand in 9/28 non-aligned foreign ministers' communiqué.

Oct. 14. UN High Commission for Refugees receives Nobel Peace Prize.

Oct. 30. USSR launches unmanned Venus-13 spacecraft.

Nov. 11. Antigua and Barbuda becomes 157th UN member.

Nov. 12. Second *Columbia* flight launched; ends 11/14, 3 days early because of fuel cell failure.

Dec. 9. US completes review of Law of the Sea Treaty, asks revisions.

Dec. 11. UN Security Council ends deadlock begun 10/27, chooses Javier Pérez de Cuéllar (Peru) to succeed Kurt Waldheim (Austria; elected '71), as UN Secretary General for 5-year term as of 1/82; approved in UNGA by acclamation, 12/15.

ERRATA

Winter 1981/82

1. In Sylvia Ann Hewlett's article, "Coping with Illegal Immigrants," the third paragraph, on pp. 358-9, contains language and formulations similar to that used in an editorial in *The New York Times* on May 27, 1981. The author regrets that a footnote citing this editorial was inadvertently dropped when the manuscript was being revised for publication.

2. In Susan Kaufman Purcell's "Mexico-U.S. Relations"; on p. 379, line 9, for "nearly 3,000-mile shared border" read "nearly 2,000-mile shared border."